T0211793

Lecture Notes in Computer Science   12088

More information about this series at http://www.springer.com/series/7412

Karina Mariela Figueroa Mora ·
Juan Anzurez Marín · Jaime Cerda ·
Jesús Ariel Carrasco-Ochoa ·
José Francisco Martínez-Trinidad ·
José Arturo Olvera-López (Eds.)

Pattern Recognition

12th Mexican Conference, MCPR 2020
Morelia, Mexico, June 24–27, 2020
Proceedings

 Springer

Editors
Karina Mariela Figueroa Mora ⓘ
Facultad de Ciencias Físico Matemáticas
Universidad Michoacana
de San Nicolás de Hidalgo
Morelia, Mexico

Juan Anzurez Marín ⓘ
Facultad de Ingeniería Eléctrica
Universidad Michoacana
de San Nicolás de Hidalgo
Morelia, Mexico

Jaime Cerda ⓘ
Facultad de Ingeniería Eléctrica
Universidad Michoacana
de San Nicolás de Hidalgo
Morelia, Mexico

Jesús Ariel Carrasco-Ochoa ⓘ
Computer Science
Instituto Nacional de Astrofísica,
Óptica y Electrónica
Sta. Maria Tonantzintla, Mexico

José Francisco Martínez-Trinidad ⓘ
Computer Science
Instituto Nacional de Astrofísica,
Óptica y Electrónica
Sta. Maria Tonantzintla, Mexico

José Arturo Olvera-López ⓘ
Faculty of Computer Science
Autonomous University of Puebla
Puebla, Mexico

ISSN 0302-9743   ISSN 1611-3349 (electronic)
Lecture Notes in Computer Science
ISBN 978-3-030-49075-1   ISBN 978-3-030-49076-8 (eBook)
https://doi.org/10.1007/978-3-030-49076-8

LNCS Sublibrary: SL6 – Image Processing, Computer Vision, Pattern Recognition, and Graphics

This Springer imprint is published by the registered company Springer Nature Switzerland AG
The registered company address is: Gewerbestrasse 11, 6330 Cham, Switzerland

Preface

The Mexican Conference on Pattern Recognition 2020 (MCPR 2020) was the 12th event in the series organized by Facultad de Ingeniería Eléctrica and Facultad de Ciencias Físico Matemáticas of Universidad Michoacana de San Nicolás de Hidalgo and the Computer Science Department of the National Institute for Astrophysics Optics and Electronics (INAOE) of Mexico, under the auspices of the Mexican Association for Computer Vision, Neurocomputing and Robotics (MACVNR), which is a member society of the International Association for Pattern Recognition (IAPR). MCPR 2020 was due to be held in Morelia, Mexico, during 24–27, 2020.[1]

This conference aims to provide a forum for the exchange of scientific results, practice, and new knowledge, as well as promoting collaboration among research groups in Pattern Recognition and related areas in Mexico and around the world.

In this edition, as in previous years, MCPR 2020 attracted not only Mexican researchers but it also included worldwide participation. We received contributions from 17 countries. In total 67 manuscripts were submitted, out of which 31 were accepted for publication in these proceedings and for presentation at the conference. Each of these submissions was strictly peer-reviewed by at least two members of the Program Committee, all of them experts in their respective fields of Pattern Recognition, which resulted in these excellent conference proceedings.

Beside the presentation of the selected contributions, we were very honored to have three outstanding invited speakers:

- Prof. René Vidal, Mathematical Institute for Data Science, The Johns Hopkins University, USA
- Prof. Ricardo Baeza-Yates, Graduate Data Science Programs, Northeastern University at Silicon Valley, USA
- Prof. Salvador Elías Venegas-Andraca, School of Engineering and Sciences, Tecnológico de Monterrey, Mexico

These distinguished researchers gave keynote addresses on various Pattern Recognition topics during the conference. To all of them, we express our appreciation for these presentations.

We would like to thank all the people who devoted so much time and effort to the successful running of the conference. In particular, we extend our gratitude to all the authors who contributed to the conference. We are also very grateful for the efforts and the quality of their reviews of all Program Committee members and additional reviewers. Their work allowed us to maintain the high-quality standard of the conference and provided a conference program of high standard. Finally, but not less important, our thanks go to the Universidad Michoacana de San Nicolás de Hidalgo for providing key support to this event.

---

[1] The conference was held virtually due to the COVID-19 pandemic.

We are sure that MCPR 2020 provided a fruitful forum for the Mexican Pattern Recognition researchers and the broader international Pattern Recognition community.

June 2020

Karina Mariela Figueroa Mora
Juan Anzurez Marín
Jaime Cerda
Jesús Ariel Carrasco-Ochoa
José Francisco Martínez-Trinidad
José Arturo Olvera-López

Organization

MCPR 2020 was sponsored by Facultad de Ingeniería Eléctrica and Facultad de Ciencias Físico Matemáticas of Universidad Michoacana de San Nicolás de Hidalgo and the Computer Science Department of the National Institute of Astrophysics, Optics and Electronics (INAOE).

General Conference Co-chairs

Karina Mariela Figueroa Mora	Universidad Michoacana de San Nicolás de Hidalgo, Mexico
Juan Anzurez Marín	Universidad Michoacana de San Nicolás de Hidalgo, Mexico
Jaime Cerda	Universidad Michoacana de San Nicolás de Hidalgo, Mexico
Jesús Ariel Carrasco-Ochoa	National Institute of Astrophysics, Optics and Electronics (INAOE), Mexico
José Francisco Martínez-Trinidad	National Institute of Astrophysics, Optics and Electronics (INAOE), Mexico
José Arturo Olvera-López	Autonomous University of Puebla (BUAP), Mexico

Local Arrangement Committee

Casimiro Olivares Juan Ángel
Cervantes Cuahuey Brenda Alicia
García Velázquez Luis Miguel
Gutiérrez Altamirano Izamar
Olivares Rojas Juan Carlos
Rivera Loaiza Cuauhtémoc

Scientific Committee

Alexandre, L. A.	Universidade da Beira Interior, Portugal
Araujo, A.	Universidade da Beira Interior, Brazil
Benedi, J. M.	Universidad Politécnica de Valencia, Spain
Borges, D. L.	Universidade de Brasília, Brazil
Camargo, J.	Universidad Nacional de Colombia, Colombia
Castellanos, G.	Universidad Nacional de Colombia, Colombia
Castelan, M.	CINVESTAV, Mexico
Cerda-Jacobo, J.	UMSNH, Mexico
Das, A.	Inria Sophia Antipolis, France
Díaz, M.	Universidad del Atlántico Medio, Spain

Dos-Santos, J. A.	Universidade Federal de Minas Gerais, Brazil
Escalante-Balderas, H. J.	INAOE, Mexico
Facon, J.	Pontifícia Universidade Católica do Paraná, Brazil
Fierrez, J.	Universidad Autonoma de Madrid, Spain
Fiori, M.	Universidad de la República, Uruguay
Fumera, G.	University of Cagliari, Italy
Furnari, A.	Università degli Studi di Catania, Italy
Godoy, D.	UNICEN, Argentina
Godoy-Calderon, S.	CIC-IPN, Mexico
Goldfarb, L.	University of New Brunswick, Canada
Gomez-Barrero, M.	Darmstadt University of Applied Sciences, Germany
Grau, A.	Universitat Politécnica de Catalunya, Spain
Haindl, M.	Institute of Information Theory and Automation, Czech Republic
Heutte, L.	Université de Rouen, France
Hurtado-Ramos, J. B.	CICATA-IPN, Mexico
Jiang, X	University of Münster, Germany
Kampel, M.	Vienna University of Technology, Austria
Kim, S. W.	Myongji University, South Korea
Klette, R.	The University of Auckland, New Zealand
Kober, V.	CICESE, Mexico
Lazo-Cortés, M. S.	INAOE, Mexico
Levano, M. A.	Universidad Católica de Temuco, Chile
Malmberg, F.	Uppsala University, Sweden
Mendoza, M.	Universidad Técnica Federico Santa María, Chile
Montes-Y-Gomez, M.	INAOE, Mexico
Morales, A.	Universidad Autónoma de Madrid, Spain
Morales, E.	INAOE, Mexico
Nappi, M.	Università degli Studi di Salerno, Italy
Negri, P.	CONICET, Argentina
Oliveira, J. L.	Universidade de Aveiro, Portugal
Palagyi, K.	University of Szeged, Hungary
Pedrosa, G. V.	Universidade de Brasília, Brazil
Perez-Suay, A.	Universitat de València, Spain
Pina, P.	Instituto Superior Técnico, Portugal
Pistori, H.	Dom Bosco Catholic University, Brazil
Quiros-Ramirez, M. A.	University of Konstanz, Germany
Real, P.	University of Seville, Spain
Ruiz-Shulcloper, J.	UCI, Cuba
Salas, J.	CICATA-IPN, Mexico
Sánchez-Díaz, G.	Universidad Autónoma de San Luis Potosí, Mexico
Sánchez-Salmerón, A. J.	Universitat Politècnica de València, Spain
Sansone, C.	Università di Napoli, Italy
Sossa-Azuela, J. H.	CIC-IPN, Mexico
Sucar, L. E.	INAOE, Mexico

Tolosana, R.	Universidad Autónoma de Madrid, Spain
Turki, T.	King Abdulaziz University, Saudi Arabia
Valev, V.	University of North Florida, USA
Vitria, J.	University of Barcelona, Spain
Xia, G. S.	Wuhan University, China

Additional Referees

Caetano, C.
Ramirez-Alonso, G.
Lucas, G.
Solorio, S.
Nath-Chowdhury, P.
Sperl, G.
Ortega-Mendoza, R. M.

Sponsoring Institutions

Universidad Michoacana de San Nicolás de Hidalgo (UMSNH)
National Institute of Astrophysics, Optics and Electronics (INAOE)
Mexican Association for Computer Vision, Neurocomputing and Robotics (MACVNR)
National Council of Science and Technology of Mexico (CONACYT)

Contents

Pattern Recognition Techniques

Image Processing and Analysis

Computer Vision

Industrial and Medical Applications of Pattern Recognition

Natural Language Processing and Recognition

Artificial Intelligence Techniques and Recognition

Pattern Recognition Techniques

Fruit Classification for Retail Stores
Using Deep Learning

Jose Luis Rojas-Aranda$^{(\boxtimes)}$, Jose Ignacio Nunez-Varela, J. C. Cuevas-Tello,
and Gabriela Rangel-Ramirez

School of Engineering, Universidad Autonoma de San Luis Potosi,
San Luis Potosí, Mexico
joseluisrojasaranda@gmail.com, {jose.nunez,cuevas}@uaslp.mx,
gabriela.rangel@alumnos.uaslp.edu.mx
http://www.ingenieria.uaslp.mx/

Abstract. Payment of fruits or vegetables in retail stores normally require them to be manually identified. This paper presents an image classification method, based on lightweight Convolutional Neural Networks (CNN), with the goal of speeding up the checkout process in stores. A new dataset of images is introduced that considers three classes of fruits, inside or without plastic bags. In order to increase the classification accuracy, different input features are added into the CNN architecture. Such inputs are, a single RGB color, the RGB histogram, and the RGB centroid obtained from K-means clustering. The results show an overall 95% classification accuracy for fruits with no plastic bag, and 93% for fruits in a plastic bag.

Keywords: Deep learning · Convolutional Neural Networks · Fruit classification

1 Introduction

Retail stores rely on cashiers or self-service checkout systems to process the customers' purchases. Since most products have barcodes that can be scanned, the checkout time has already been minimized. However, fruits and vegetables are commonly processed differently. The cashier or the customer need to manually identify the class of product being bought and look for it in the system. With that application in mind, our purpose is to present an initial approach for fruit classification in order to check its feasibility for such application.

Fruit classification is a complex problem due to all the variations that can be encountered. In general, two classification problems can be identified: i) classification of fruits of different types (e.g., to differentiate between oranges and apples) [3], and ii) classification of varieties of the same fruit (e.g., to differentiate among apple varieties such as, red delicious, honeycrisp, golden delicious, gala, etc.) [7]. However, even focusing on the first type of problem, precise classification is still difficult to achieve due to differences in shape, color, ripening

© Springer Nature Switzerland AG 2020
K. M. Figueroa Mora et al. (Eds.): MCPR 2020, LNCS 12088, pp. 3–13, 2020.
https://doi.org/10.1007/978-3-030-49076-8_1

stages, etc. Another problem, directly related to the purchase of fruits in retail stores, is that fruits can be inside a plastic bag. This research work deals with the first type of classification (i.e., classification of fruits of different types), where fruits can be inside or without a plastic bag.

Recent advancements in Convolutional Neural Networks (CNN) [16] make them suitable for this problem. The ImageNet Large Scale Visual Recognition Challenge (ILSVRC)[12] was an annual competition that started in 2010 and ended in 2017[1]. Given an image, the goal was to recognize the different objects within such image. Since 2012, CNN have had an outstanding performance in the task of image classification, because the winner of ILSVRC used a model based on deep CNN trained on raw RGB pixel values, known as AlexNet [9]. Besides AlexNet, several CNN architectures have been defined throughout the years, such as LeNet, ZFNet, GoogleNet, VGG, ResNet, YOLO, MobileNetV2, among others [16]. In 2015, ResNet was the winner of ILSVRC exceeding for the first time the human-level accuracy (5% error) [5,12] with a 3% of testing error.

This paper proposes an improved CNN architecture based on MobileNetV2 [14] to classify fruits, where it proposes the addition of different input features (besides the input images), in order to improve its accuracy. Such additional inputs features are related to the color of the fruits. Thus, we present experiments using a single RGB color, the RGB histogram, and the RGB centroid obtained from K-means clustering. In addition, we created a new fruit dataset for three types of fruits: apples, oranges and bananas; also considering fruits in transparent plastic bags. The results show an overall 95% classification accuracy for fruits without plastic bag, and 93% for fruits inside a plastic bag.

The paper is is organized as follows. Section 2 summarizes related work on fruit classification. Section 3 describes the proposed classification method. Section 4 presents some experiments and analyzes the results of the classification performance. Finally, Sect. 5 discusses the conclusions and future work.

2   Related Work

There are several research works for fruit recognition and classification with different goals and applications [4]. One of this applications refers to agriculture and fruit harvesting. *DeepFruits* is a Faster Region-based CNN (known as R-CNN). Their model employs transfer learning using ImageNet, and two types of input images: color (RGB) and Near-Infrared (NIR). The images correspond to seven fruits still attached to their corresponding tree/plant, so this application is oriented to agricultural robots for harvesting fruit and vegetables. The images were taken by some of the authors and others obtained from Google Image searches [13]. *Deep Count* is another application for robotic agriculture using a Deep Neural Network (DNN), where the authors propose a modified Inception-ResNet architecture. Their research only focuses on tomato images from Google Images [11]. Another related application is *Deep Fruit Detection* for robotic harvesting in orchards. That research employs Faster R-CNN and

---

[1] http://image-net.org/.

compares the performance against other architectures such as VGG and ZFNet. They also explore the number of training images, transfer learning and data augmentation. They study three fruits: apple, mango and almond; with RGB images generated by themselves [2]. Finally, *MangoYOLO* is also a CNN model but for mango harvest forecast. *MangoYOLO* is compared with other CNN architectures including Faster R-CNN with VGG and ZFNet, SDD and YOLO. Their research explores the number of training images and transfer learning with PASCAL VOC, COCO and ImageNet. They obtained their own RGB images at night with a special LED system mounted on a farm vehicle to obtain consistent illumination conditions [8]. The above research works have to consider other factors such as working outdoors, variations in lighting conditions and the fact that fruits/vegetables are still attached to the trees.

Besides agriculture, retail applications can greatly benefit from the classification of fruits and vegetables. Hossain et al. [6], proposed two CNN architectures, a light model of six CNN layers, and a VGG-16 fine-tuned model. They also created their own dataset by collecting images from the Internet. Another research work proposed a double-track method using a two nine-layer CNN [7]. The input of the first network are images with background, then the second network works with a single fruit selected from a region of interest. Rather than classifying types of fruits, they classified six varieties of apples. Finally, Femling et al. [3], describes a hardware system for retail stores able to classify ten types of fruits. They make use of a dataset comprised of images from ImageNet and taken with their system's camera. As in our case, they made use of CNN architecture based on MobileNet. It is important to note that the works just reviewed do not consider the fruits to be inside plastic bags, as this paper does.

3   Application of the Proposed Method

This section presents our proposed method for solving the fruit classification problem. First, a new dataset is introduced, then we explain the chosen CNN architectures and training methods.

3.1   Dataset

Data is an essential part of Deep Learning. Therefore, it is important to select the correct input data according to our goals. For fruit classification, there exists a dataset called Fruits-360 [10], which consists of 28736 training images and 9673 testing images. It contains 60 different classes of fruits, where some classes refer to varieties of a fruit (e.g., for apples they have six varieties). A major drawback of this dataset is that the images are small (100×100 pixels), which makes it difficult to differentiate between some fruits. Also, the images have no background, thus it does not scale very well to real-world applications.

Therefore, we decided to create our own dataset. Since our main goal is to replicate a store environment, the fruits were placed over a stainless steel sheet and the photos were taken from the top. We chose to work with three types of fruit: apples, oranges and bananas. We introduce variation in the dataset, by taking images of the fruits at different positions and rotations (see Fig. 1). We also consider that in the checkout process the fruits are generally inside a transparent plastic bag, so photos of the fruits in a bag were also taken. The photos were taken using the front camera of an iPhone 6. The dataset contains: 443 images of apples (297 for training and 146 for testing); 363 images of oranges of (242 for training and 121 for testing); and, 231 images of bananas of (156 for training and 75 for testing). In total, 1067 images were collected, 725 for training and 342 for testing.

3.2   Selecting a CNN Architecture

The selection of a CNN architecture depends on the problem one is trying to solve. There is no unique architecture for all problems. Thus, selecting the right one becomes a problem on its own. Currently the top performing architecture, that won the ILSVRC competition in 2017, [12] is the *Ensamble C* developed by the *WMW team*, but it has the disadvantage of being computational expensive to train and for making predictions. On the other hand, MobileNets are CNN architectures that deal with the computational complexity problem by implementing a more efficient and lightweight architecture, and could run on mobile or embedded devices achieving high-level performance. Since our goal is to work in retail stores, we have chosen to use the MobileNetV2 [14] architecture for being lightweight and robust.

3.3   Transfer Learning

Transfer learning is a machine learning approach where a model developed for one task becomes the starting point for a model of a different task [15]. This technique works really well when the available dataset is not large enough, and also the model converges faster. Therefore, we trained MobileNetV2 with transfer learning using weights from a model trained with the ImageNet dataset.

There are several ways to train a model using transfer learning. For our work, we first loaded the pre-trained model and discarded the last layer. This is a dense layer with 1000 neurons that serves as a classifier of the previous feature map. Once discarded, we set the rest of the layers to *not trainable* (this prevents the weights in a given layer from being updated). Then, at the end of the network we added another dense layer, but now with the number of classes of fruits we want to predict. This allows to keep all the features extracted from the ImageNet model, and re-purpose it to the fruit classification problem. Then, we trained the model for 20 epochs using the base learning rate of $1e^{-4}$. After the first 20 epochs, we set the layers from the 100 layer up to the last layer (155) to *trainable*, and we trained the network for another 20 epochs. But this time, we set the learning to 1/10 of the base learning rate in order to *fine-tune* the model. This forces the weights to be tuned from generic feature maps to features associated specifically with our dataset.

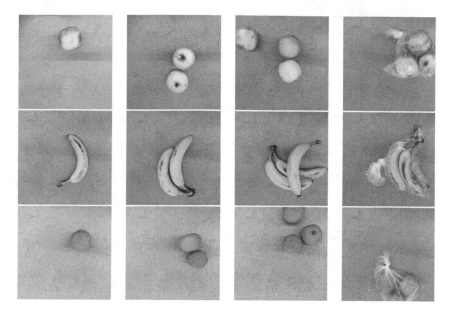

Fig. 1. Examples of training images of the dataset created.

In this work, the models are trained using TensorFlow [1], with the implementation of MobileNetV2 provided by Keras. The standard RMSPropOptimizer is used, with both, decay and momentum set to 0.9. We use batch normalization after every layer, where the standard weight decay is set to 0.00004 as described in [14]. The base learning rate is set to $1e^{-4}$ and a batch size set to 50. The models were trained using an iMac with a 3.5 GHz Intel Core i5, and 8 GB of RAM 1600 MHz DDR3. Figure 2 shows a preliminary comparison of the models performance when trained with transfer learning and with weights initialized randomly, using our dataset. It is clear that the results prove that with random weights the model is not able to learn, while the model trained with transfer learning reaches almost 0.80 accuracy.

3.4 Improving MobileNetV2

One way to visualize what a CNN model is learning is by looking at the convolutional layers activations, in order to see what information is being retained by the layers. Figure 3 shows the activations, of the first convolutional layer, of two different fruits. At the top row images show activations of an orange, while at the bottom row are activations of an apple. As can be noticed, for the model both fruits are similar. It mainly retains the shape of the fruit and its texture. This information might not be enough to differentiate between both fruits due to their similar shape. One missing feature that, in this case, would be important for such differentiation is the color of the fruits. Therefore, the accuracy of the model can be improved if additional input features (related to the fruit's color)

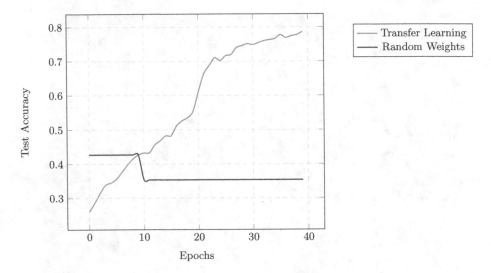

Fig. 2. Comparing the test accuracy using our dataset and transfer learning

are feed into the model. This work proposes three different input features and their corresponding modifications to the model.

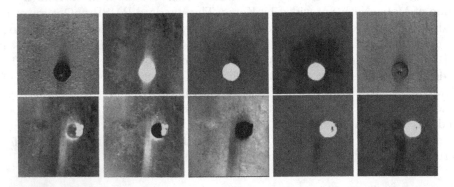

Fig. 3. Similar activations of the first convolutional layer of an orange (top image) compared to an apple (bottom image)

Single RGB Fruit Color. Besides the image, one additional input feature is to provide the model with a vector with RGB color values of the fruit to be classified. This color should be the one that represents, in general, the given fruit. For instance, bananas would be represented by the yellow color, thus the model receives the vector with RGB color values $[1.0, 1.0, 0.0]$; in the case of an orange the vector would be $[1.0, 0.64, 0.0]$. This vector with three RGB values is feed into the model.

RGB Histogram. An image histogram is a graph that summarizes how many pixels are at different scale levels of a given image [17]. For this work, the histogram of each RGB channel was obtained, resulting in a vector of 765 input values, which are then feed into the model. Figure 4 shows an example of an image RGB histogram. At this moment, one disadvantage is that most of the values would correspond to the background colors.

RGB Centroid Using K-Means. Finally, we make use of a hybrid machine learning (ML) approach. The idea is to combine different ML algorithms in order to complement each other. K-Means is a clustering algorithm that tries to partition the data into K clusters (subgroups). When applied to an image, it could find groups of colors that represent such image. For this work, we set the number of groups to three, as shown in the Fig. 5. The three RGB colors found (9 values) are fed into the model.

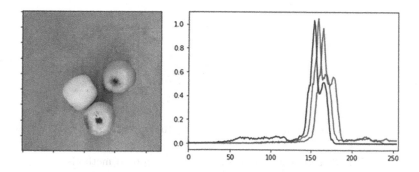

Fig. 4. Example of an image RGB histogram

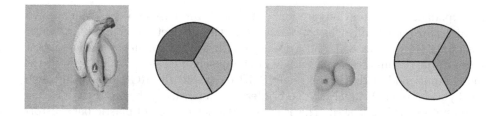

Fig. 5. Example of the RGB Centroid using K-Means

In the case of the RGB color and RGB histogram, a multi-input model is implemented. The model takes as input the image and a vector with the color data, as shown in Figs. 6b and 6c. The image is feed into the CNN (i.e., the MobileNetV2 architecture), while the color data is feed into a dense layer. The result of both networks is then concatenated and the final prediction is made using *softmax* activation. Using K-Means, the model is considered a hybrid model. We implemented the K-Means algorithm in TensorFlow as a Keras layer, this allows the model to internally produce the K colors, and then, these are concatenated at the end of the process (as shown in Fig. 6d). For our experiments, we chose to use three centroids ($k = 3$), resulting in 9 RGB values. In the following section, we compare how the models perform using the methods just explained.

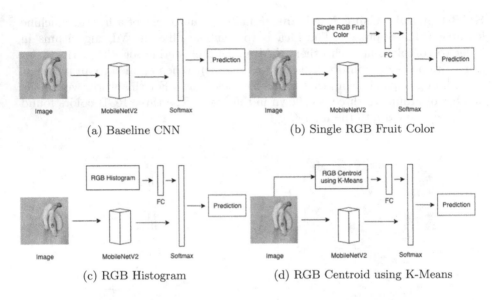

(a) Baseline CNN   (b) Single RGB Fruit Color

(c) RGB Histogram   (d) RGB Centroid using K-Means

Fig. 6. Different architectures of the proposed methods

4   Experiments and Results

As explained in the previous section, our models are based on the MobileNetV2 architecture and trained in two versions of the dataset we created: i) images with only fruits (no bags), and ii) images with fruits without and inside plastic bags. Table 1 compares the accuracy of the baseline model (MobileNetV2), the multi-input models (both, the single RGB color and the RGB histogram), and the hybrid model (MobileNetV2 + K-Means). In all cases, the accuracy is higher when no plastic bag is used. This is expected since the use of plastic bags distort the look of the fruits. The baseline model (MobileNetV2), with no additional color information, has high accuracy on the training set, but has the lowest on the testing set. Meanwhile, all three models that use additional color information achieved better accuracy in general. Particularly, the model using the single RGB color obtained the highest accuracy at 0.95 and 0.93, for both versions of the dataset, respectively. The relatively lower accuracy achieved by the hybrid model could be due to the fact that, out of three colors obtained, only one is related to the color of the fruit. The other two colors are related to the background, which should be not be taken into account. Therefore, one course of future work is to try to eliminate as much background information as possible. Figure 7 compares the testing data accuracy over time of the different proposed methods in this paper, using the complete dataset.

Table 1. Comparing the accuracy of the trained models.

Model	In plastic bag		No plastic bag	
	Train accuracy	Test accuracy	Train accuracy	Test accuracy
MobileNetV2	0.98	0.78	0.99	0.82
MobileNetV2 + Single color	0.98	**0.93**	0.99	**0.95**
MobileNetV2 + Histogram	0.99	0.82	0.99	0.92
MobileNetV2 + K-Means	0.98	0.86	0.99	0.90

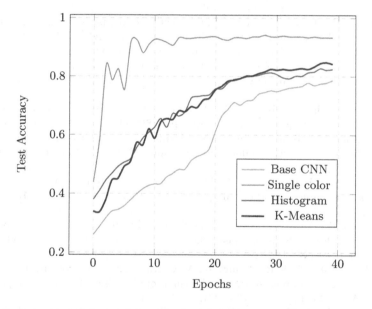

Fig. 7. Accuracy of the models trained with images containing fruits in bags.

5   Conclusions and Future Work

This paper proposed an improved CNN architecture, based on a lightweight CNN architecture called MobileNetV2, by considering additional input features, besides the input images. Such input features improved the accuracy of the model by adding information about the color of the fruits. These input features are: i) the single RGB fruit color, ii) the RGB histogram, and iii) the RGB centroid using K-Means. The single RGB color achieved the best overall accuracy: 95% classification accuracy for fruits with no plastic bag, and 93% for fruits in a plastic bag. Due to the lack of data, a new dataset was introduced consisting of 725 images for training and 342 for testing; and considers three classes of fruits (apples, oranges and bananas). The dataset also considers fruits inside plastic bags. As further research, we are exploring the minimum number of training images to achieve the highest accuracy. Along with this, data augmentation has been not explored using our proposed dataset. We also would like to measure the sensitivity to illumination. On the other hand, we plan to compare the accuracy of the proposed lightweight CNN architecture against other state-of-the-art CNN networks with GPU hardware and our dataset.

References

1. Abadi, M., Agarwal, A., Barham, P., Goodfellow, I., et. al.: TensorFlow: Large-scale machine learning on heterogeneous systems (2015). https://www.tensorflow.org/, software available from tensorflow.org
2. Bargoti, S., Underwood, J.: Deep fruit detection in orchards. In: 2017 IEEE International Conference on Robotics and Automation (ICRA), pp. 3626–3633 (2017)
3. Femling, F., Olsson, A., Alonso-Fernandez, F.: Fruit and vegetable identification using machine learning for retail applications. In: 14th International Conference on Signal-Image Technology & Internet-Based Systems (SITIS), pp. 9–15. IEEE (2018)
4. Hameed, K., Chai, D., Rassau, A.: A comprehensive review of fruit and vegetable classification techniques. Image Vis. Comput. **80**, 24–44 (2018)
5. He, K., Zhang, X., Ren, S., Sun, J.: Deep residual learning for image recognition. In: Proceedings of the IEEE Conference on Computer Vision and Pattern Recognition, pp. 770–778 (2016)
6. Hossain, M.S., Al-Hammadi, M., Muhammad, G.: Automatic fruit classification using deep learning for industrial applications. IEEE Trans. Ind. Inf. **15**(2), 1027–1034 (2018)
7. Katarzyna, R., Paweł, M.: A vision-based method utilizing deep convolutional neural networks for fruit variety classification in uncertainty conditions of retail sales. Appl. Sci. **9**(19), 3971 (2019)
8. Koirala, A., Walsh, K.B., Wang, Z., McCarthy, C.: Deep learning for real-time fruit detection and orchard fruit load estimation: benchmarking of 'MangoYOLO'. Precis. Agric. **20**(6), 1107–1135 (2019)
9. Krizhevsky, A., Sutskever, I., Hinton, G.E.: Imagenet classification with deep convolutional neural networks. In: Pereira, F., Burges, C., Bottou, L., Weinberger, K. (eds.) Advanced in Neural Information Processing Systems, vol. 25, pp. 1097–1105 (2012)
10. Mureşan, H., Oltean, M.: Fruit recognition from images using deep learning. Acta Universitatis Sapientiae Informatica **10**(1), 26–42 (2018)
11. Rahnemoonfar, M., Sheppard, C.: Deep count: fruit counting based on deep simulated learning. Sensors **17**(4), 905 (2017)
12. Russakovsky, O., Deng, J., et al.: Imagenet large scale visual recognition challenge. Int. J. Comput. Vis. **115**(3), 211–252 (2015)
13. Sa, I., Ge, Z., Dayoub, F., Upcroft, B., Perez, T., McCool, C.: A fruit detection system using deep neural networks. Sensors **16**(8), 1222 (2016)

14. Sandler, M., Howard, A., Zhu, M., Zhmoginov, A., Chen, L.C.: MobileNetV2: inverted residuals and linear bottlenecks. In: Proceedings of the IEEE Conference on Computer Vision and Pattern Recognition, pp. 4510–4520 (2018)
15. Shin, H.C., Roth, E.A.: Deep convolutional neural networks for computer-aided detection: CNN architectures, dataset characteristics and transfer learning. IEEE Trans. Med. Imaging **35**(5), 1285–1298 (2016)
16. Sze, V., Chen, Y.H., Yang, T.J., Emer, J.S.: Efficient processing of deep neural networks: a tutorial and survey. Proc. IEEE **105**(12), 2295–2329 (2017)
17. Tan, L., Jiang, J.: Fundamentals of analog and digital signal processing. Author-House (2007)

Towards Dendrite Spherical Neurons
for Pattern Classification

Wilfrido Gómez-Flores[1](✉) (iD) and Juan Humberto Sossa-Azuela[2,3] (iD)

[1] Centro de Investigación y de Estudios Avanzados del IPN, Unidad Tamaulipas,
87130 Ciudad Victoria, Tamaulipas, Mexico
wgomez@cinvestav.mx
[2] Instituto Politécnico Nacional, Centro de Investigación en Computación,
07738 Mexico City, Mexico
hsossa@cic.ipn.mx
[3] Tecnológico de Monterrey, Escuela de Ingeniería y Ciencias,
Av. General Ramón Corona 2514, Zapopan, Jalisco, Mexico

Abstract. This paper introduces the Dendrite Spherical Neuron (DSN) as an alternative to the Dendrite Ellipsoidal Neuron (DEN), in which hyperspheres group the patterns from different classes instead of hyperellipses. The reasoning behind DSN is simplifying the computation of DEN architecture, where a centroid and covariance matrix are two dendritic parameters, whereas, in DSN, the covariance matrix is replaced by a radius. This modification is useful to avoid singular covariance matrices since DEN requires measuring the Mahalanobis distance to classify patterns. The DSN training consists of determining the centroids of dendrites with the k-means algorithm, followed by calculating the radius of dendrites as the mean distance to the two nearest centroids, and finally determining the weights of a softmax function, with Stochastic Gradient Descent, at the output of the neuron. Besides, the Simulated Annealing automatically determines the number of dendrites that maximizes the classification accuracy. The DSN is applied to synthetic and real-world datasets. The experimental results reveal that DSN is competitive with Multilayer Perceptron (MLP) networks, with less complex architectures. Also, DSN tends to outperform the Dendrite Morphological Neuron (DMN), which uses hyperboxes. These findings suggest that the DSN is a potential alternative to MLP and DMN for pattern classification tasks.

Keywords: Dendrite Morphological Neuron · Spherical dendrite · Simulated Annealing · Pattern classification

1 Introduction

Artificial Neural Networks (ANN) are mathematical models inspired by the biological neurons in the nervous system of the animals, which can be described as mapping an input space to an output space [7]. Probably, the Multilayer Perceptron (MLP) is the most common ANN used in practice for pattern classification tasks. MLP training requires adjusting the synaptic weights of each

K. M. Figueroa Mora et al. (Eds.): MCPR 2020, LNCS 12088, pp. 14–24, 2020.
https://doi.org/10.1007/978-3-030-49076-8_2

neuron by minimizing a loss function (e.g., cross-entropy), where the backprop-agation algorithm is often used. The inner product between the neuron inputs and the synaptic weights produces a linear combination that is modified by a nonlinear activation function (e.g., the sigmoid function). Thus, the MLP divides the input space with a hypersurface, which is built by combining the responses of several neurons distributed in one or more hidden layers.

In nonlinear separability scenarios, the MLP could require a complex archi-tecture to separate the input space accurately. The Dendrite Morphological Neu-ron (DMN) is an alternative technique that reduces the complexity of the clas-sification models since nonlinear classification problems can be solved by using a single neuron. The morphological processing involves minimum and maximum operations, which can generate complex nonlinear decision boundaries [8].

A typical DMN has dendrites defined as hyperboxes in $\mathbb{R}^D$, where D is the dimensionality of the input space. A set of hyperboxes can model each class pattern, where the minimum and maximum operations determine if an input pattern is inside of a hyperbox; therefore, the input pattern is assigned to the class of the most active dendrite. The DMN training consists of distributing the hyperboxes over the input space such that every class pattern is covered accu-rately, where heuristic methods [8], evolutionary computation [3], and stochastic gradient descent (SGD) [9] have been used for this purpose.

Because DMN uses hyperboxes, the produced decision boundaries are com-plex piecewise linear functions. In order to obtain smoother decision boundaries, it is feasible to replace the hyperboxes with other geometrical shapes. In this context, Arce *et al.* [2] proposed a neuronal model called Dendrite Ellipsoidal Neuron (DEN), where an input pattern is assigned to the class of the dendrite (i.e., hyperellipse) with the minimum Mahalanobis distance. A hyperellipse is defined by two parameters: centroid and covariance matrix. In DEN, the cen-troid positions within the input space are defined by the k-means algorithm, in which k is the number of dendrites within a class. Next, for obtaining rotated hyperellipses, the covariance matrix of each cluster is calculated. Note that a class is modeled by k dendrites, where a dendrite clusters only a fraction of samples from the class. Therefore, as the value of k increases, the number of samples in the dendrite decreases, so that there could be variables with zero variance, generating a singular covariance matrix. Consequently, the calculation of the Mahalanobis distance cannot be performed for that dendrite since it is required to invert its covariance matrix.

To overcome this inconvenience, we propose a simplification of the DEN model by using spheres instead of ellipses to get a new neuronal model called Dendrite Spherical Neuron (DSN), in which the full covariance matrix of a den-drite is replaced by a radius that depends on the closeness among centroids. Moreover, the computation of the DNS response is more straightforward than DEN because covariances and matrix inversions are no longer necessary.

2   DSN Architecture

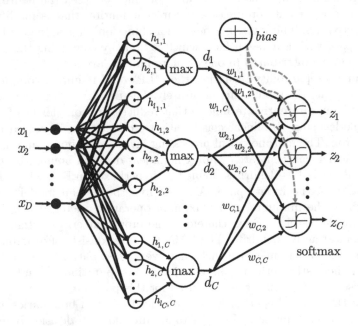

Fig. 1. Neural architecture for a DSN with softmax function at the output. The jth class is modeled by the dendrite cluster with response d_j, for $j = 1, \ldots, C$ classes.

Fig. 1 shows the neural architecture for a DSN, in which each class is represented by a cluster of dendrites, that is, a set of hyperspheres in $\mathbb{R}^D$. The DSN output is performed the linear combination of dendrite responses d_j, for $j = 1, \ldots, C$ classes, and the softmax function gives the probability of the input pattern $\mathbf{x} = [x_1, \ldots, x_D]^T$ belongs to the jth class. Thus, the assigned class is given by the maximum probability rule [6]:

$$\hat{t}_j = \arg\max_{j=1,\ldots,C} \left(z_j(\mathbf{x}) \right), \tag{1}$$

where z_j is the response of the jth output node defined as

$$z_j(\mathbf{x}) = \sigma \left(w_{0j} + \sum_{k=1}^{C} w_{k,j} d_j(\mathbf{x}) \right), \quad j = 1, \ldots, C, \tag{2}$$

where $\sigma(\cdot)$ is the softmax function, $w_{k,j}$ is a weight value to connect the kth cluster to the jth output node, w_{0j} is the bias, and d_j is the output of the jth dendrite cluster:

$$d_j(\mathbf{x}) = \max_{i=1,\ldots,l_j} \left(h_{i,j}(\mathbf{x}) \right), \tag{3}$$

where $h_{i,j}$ is the output of the ith dendrite for the jth class:

$$h_{i,j}(\mathbf{x}) = r_{i,j} - \| \mathbf{x} - \mathbf{c}_{i,j} \|^2, \tag{4}$$

where $\|\cdot\|$ is the Euclidean norm, $\mathbf{c}_{i,j} \in \mathbb{R}^D$ is the centroid of the dendrite, and $r_{i,j} > 0$ is its corresponding radius.

Figure 2 illustrates the three possible responses of a dendrite given in Eq. 4. A dendrite obtains its maximum response when $\mathbf{x} = \mathbf{c}$, that is, $h(\mathbf{x}) = r$. As $\mathbf{x}$ moves away from the centroid, the dendrite response decreases to zero on its boundary, and becomes negative outside of the dendrite region. Thus, the most active dendrite cluster can be identified with Eq. 3.

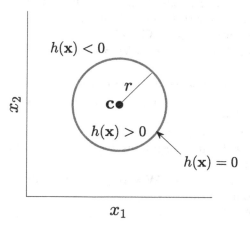

Fig. 2. A hypersphere in 2D generated by its dendrite parameters $\mathbf{c}$ and r. The response is positive when the pattern $\mathbf{x}$ is inside of the hypersphere, it is zero when $\mathbf{x}$ is on the hypershpere boundary, and it is negative when $\mathbf{x}$ is outside of the hypersphere.

3 DSN Training

Let $\mathbf{X} = \{\mathbf{x}_1, \ldots, \mathbf{x}_N\}$ be a training set with N observations, where the ith sample is a D-dimensional vector $\mathbf{x}_i = [x_{i,1}, \ldots, x_{i,D}]^T$, which is associated to a class label $t_i \in \{1, \ldots, C\}$.

Algorithm 1 shows the pseudocode for training a DSN based on the k-means algorithm and SDG. First, the centroids of dendrites are calculated with the k-means algorithm (lines 3–8), where the parameter $k = l_j$ is the number of hyperspheres in a class. Next, to reduce the overlap between dendrite regions, the mean distance to the two nearest centroids determines the radius of a dendrite (lines 9–10). Finally, the cluster dendrite responses are calculated from the entire training set (Eqs. 3 and 4), which are used to obtain the weights of the softmax function by minimizing the cross-entropy loss function with SDG (lines 12–13).

Notice that Algorithm 1 requires the number of dendrites per class, which is problem-dependent and is typically not known *a priori*. It is desirable a DSN configuration with a reduced number of dendrites and a high classification rate. This goal can be achieved by using an optimization procedure to maximize the

---

Algorithm 1: DSN training based on k-means and SDG.

Input: Training patterns $\mathbf{X} = \{\mathbf{x}_1, \ldots, \mathbf{x}_N\}$; targets $\mathbf{t} = [t_1, \ldots, t_N]$; number of classes C; number of dendrites per class $[l_1, \ldots, l_C]$
Output: A structure DSN

1 DSN $\leftarrow \emptyset$ // initialize dendrite structure
2 $\mathbf{C} \leftarrow \emptyset$ // initialize temporal array of centroids
3 **for** $j = 1, \ldots, C$ **do**
4   Get patterns of the jth class from $\mathbf{X}$ to obtain the subset $\mathbf{X}_j$
5   Obtain l_j centroids with k-means from $\mathbf{X}_j$ to get $C_j = [\mathbf{c}_{1,j}, \ldots, \mathbf{c}_{l_j,j}]$
6   Concatenate centroids $\mathbf{C} \leftarrow [\mathbf{C} + C_j]$
7   Save centroids: DSN.$\mathbf{c}_{i,j} \leftarrow \mathbf{c}_{i,j}, \forall i = 1, \ldots, l_j$
8 **end for**
9 Measure the pairwise distance between centroids in $\mathbf{C}$
10 Calculate the mean distance of $\mathbf{c}_{i,j}$ to the 2-nearest centroids to get its corresponding radius $r_{i,j}, \forall i, j$
11 Save radii: DSN.$r_{i,j} \leftarrow r_{i,j}, \forall i, j$
12 Obtain the cluster dendrite responses $d_j(\mathbf{x}), j = 1, \ldots, C$, for all samples in $\mathbf{X}$ to obtain $\mathbf{Y} = \{\mathbf{y}_1, \ldots, \mathbf{y}_N\}$
13 Calculate the softmax weights $\mathbf{W} = [\mathbf{w}_1, \ldots, \mathbf{w}_C]$ with SDG and cross-entropy from the tuple $(\mathbf{Y}, \mathbf{t})$
14 Save weights: DSN.$\mathbf{W} \leftarrow \mathbf{W}$
15 **return** DSN

---

classification accuracy with few dendrites. Herein, the Simulated Annealing (SA) algorithm is employed to tune the DSN configuration automatically.

SA is a stochastic local search method for global combinatorial optimization, which allows gradual convergence to a near-optimal solution. SA performs a sequence of moves from a current solution to a better one according to specific transition rules while occasionally accepting some uphill solutions in order to guarantee diversity in the domain exploration and to avoid getting caught at local optima. The optimization process is managed by a cooling schedule that controls the number of iterations [1]. Thus, SA is useful to find the combination of the number of dendrites per class that results in the best classification rate in a finite number of iterations.

Algorithm 2 shows the pseudocode for DSN tuning with the SA algorithm. In line 3, the number of dendrites per class is randomly initialized in the range $[1, \sqrt{N_j}]$, where N_j is the number of patterns in the jth class. In line 10, the neighborhood structure generates a new solution by randomly moving (or not) backward or forward the number of dendrites per class. In lines 13–16, a DSN solution is accepted if its accuracy is higher than the previous solution; otherwise, a probability of acceptance criterion is applied, which depends on the current temperature. With this scheme, the current solution may be accepted even if it is worse than the previous solution, which is useful to avoid local optima.

Algorithm 2: DSN tuning based on simulated annealing.

Input: Training set $(\mathbf{X}, \mathbf{t})$; validation set $(\tilde{\mathbf{X}}, \tilde{\mathbf{t}})$; number of classes C
Output: Best solution $\mathbf{z}^*$

1 Set initial temperature, T_0
2 $t \leftarrow 0$
3 Create randomly an initial solution, $\mathbf{z}_0 = [l_1, \ldots, l_C]$
4 Train DSN with $\mathbf{z}_0$ and training set $(\mathbf{X}, \mathbf{t})$ // Algorithm 1
5 Evaluate the accuracy $f(\mathbf{z}_0)$ with validation set $(\tilde{\mathbf{X}}, \tilde{\mathbf{t}})$
6 Best solution, $\mathbf{z}^* \leftarrow \mathbf{z}_0$
7 **do**
8      $t \leftarrow t + 1$
9      $T_t \leftarrow 0.9 \cdot T_{t-1}$
10   Generate random solution $\mathbf{z}$ from the neighborhood
        $\mathcal{N}(\mathbf{z}_{t-1}) = \mathbf{z}_{t-1} + \mathbf{r}_t$, where $r_l \in \{-1, 0, 1\}$
11   Train DSN with $\mathbf{z}$ and training set $(\mathbf{X}, \mathbf{t})$ // Algorithm 1
12   Evaluate the accuracy $f(\mathbf{z})$ with validation set $(\tilde{\mathbf{X}}, \tilde{\mathbf{t}})$
13   **if** $f(\mathbf{z}) > f(\mathbf{z}_{t-1})$ **then**
14        $\mathbf{z}_t \leftarrow \mathbf{z}$
15   **else if** $\mathcal{U}(0, 1) \leq \exp\left(\frac{f(\mathbf{z}) - f(\mathbf{z}_{t-1})}{kT_t}\right)$ **then**
16        $\mathbf{z}_t \leftarrow \mathbf{z}$
17   **if** $(f(\mathbf{z}_t) > f(\mathbf{z}^*)) \vee ((f(\mathbf{z}_t) = f(\mathbf{z}^*)) \wedge (\sum_c \mathbf{z}_t < \sum_c \mathbf{z}^*))$ **then**
18        $\mathbf{z}^* \leftarrow \mathbf{z}_t$
19 **until** *cooling condition is reached*
20 **return** $\mathbf{z}^*$

Finally, in lines 16–17, the best solution is updated if its accuracy is lower than the current solution, or if both solutions have the same accuracy and the current solution has less number of dendrites than the current best solution.

4 Experiments

For evaluating the classification performance of the DSN approach, synthetic and real-world datasets are considered. The former comprises three didactic 2D datasets for illustrating the nonlinear boundaries generated by a DSN trained with Algorithm 2. On the other hand, ten real-world datasets were obtained from the UCI Machine Learning Repository [5], whose characteristics are summarized in Table 1. These datasets were also previously used to evaluate DMN, and DSN approaches [2,9].

For comparison purposes, the real-world datasets are also classified by MLP with one hidden layer, DMN initialized with the dHpC method and trained with SGD [9], and DEN trained with a hill-climbing algorithm for determining the number of dendrites per class [2]. In order to find statistical differences between

Table 1. Real-world datasets and their characteristics: identifier (ID), number of instances (N), number of classes (C), and dimensionality (D).

ID	Dataset	N	C	D
D_1	Breast cancer wisconsin	569	2	30
D_2	Glass identification	214	6	10
D_3	Heart dIsease cleveland	297	2	13
D_4	Hepatitis	112	2	18
D_5	Iris data	150	3	4
D_6	Page blocks	5409	5	10
D_7	Pima Indians diabetes	768	2	8
D_8	Seeds	199	3	7
D_9	Thyroid gland data	215	3	5
D_{10}	Wine recognition data	178	3	13

methods, the Kruskal–Wallis test ($\alpha = 0.05$) is used to evaluate whether the medians of the approaches compared differ under the assumption that the shapes of the underlying distributions are the same. Also, the correction for multiple testing on the basis of the same data is made by the Bonferroni method.

The k-fold cross-validation method (with $k = 10$) is used to built training and test sets to measure the classification accuracy (i.e., the hit rate) of neural models. Moreover, in Algorithm 2, the training set is partitioned again into two parts to create the training (80%) and validation (20%) sets.

It is worth mentioning that a procedure of grid search and k-fold cross-validation (with $k = 5$) determines the number of hidden neurons that maximizes the accuracy of the MLP network, where the number of hidden neurons is increased from 5 to 100 neurons, in steps of 5 [4].

5   Results

Figure 3 shows the distribution of hyperspheres per class (i.e., dendrites) for each synthetic dataset. The SA algorithm determined the number of dendrites that maximized accuracy. For instance, it is notable that only three dendrites (one per class) are required for correctly classifying all the patterns of the Ring dataset (Fig. 3(b)). The corresponding decision regions obtained by the DSN approach are also illustrated in Fig. 3. Notice that nonlinear decision boundaries are built, which are capable of modeling complex class distributions.

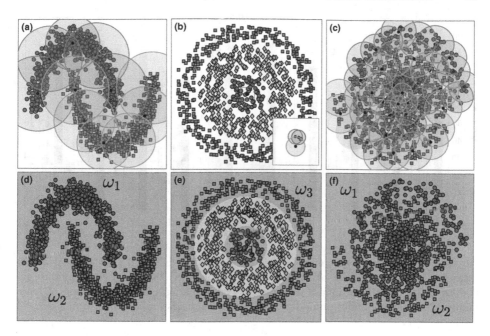

Fig. 3. Top row, the distribution of hyperspheres for the 2D synthetic datasets. The number of dendrites is: (a) Horseshoes: 11, (b) Rings: 3 (with zoom to view hyperspheres), and (c) Two-spirals: 46. Bottom row, the decision regions generated by the DSN approach. The classes are represented by ω_1 (class 1), ω_2 (class 2), and ω_3 (class 3). The accuracy measured on the validation set is: (d) Horseshoes: 100%, (e) Rings: 100%, and (f) Two-spirals: 93%.

In the case of real-world datasets, Fig. 4 shows the accuracy results obtained by MLP, DMN, DEN, and DSN neural models. It is remarkable that DSN outperformed the DEN approach in eight of ten datasets, and obtained competitive results in relation to DMN and MLP methods. Moreover, the multiple comparisons with the Kruskal–Wallis test and Bonferroni correction determined that DSN did not present statistically significant differences with MLP ($p = 0.7035$) and DMN ($p = 0.3037$), whereas DSN and DEN were statistically significantly different ($p < 0.0001$).

In addition, for all the datasets, the DSN presented a simpler structure than MLP and DEN. For instance, for the Thyroid Gland dataset (D_9), MLP obtained an accuracy of 97.2% with 41 hidden neurons, whereas DSN reached an accuracy of 96.8% with four dendrites. Also, for the Page Blocks dataset (D_6), the accuracy of DEN is 91.1% with 71 dendrites, whereas DSN used 59 dendrites to attain an accuracy of 93.8%.

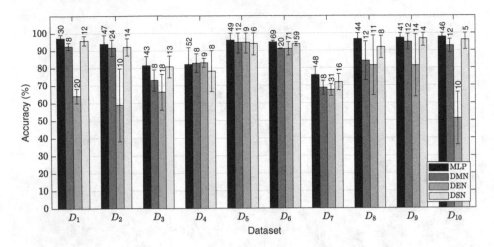

Fig. 4. Accuracy results of neural models MLP, DMN, DEN, and DSN for real-world datasets. The height of the bars represents the mean of 10-folds of cross-validation. The error bars are the standard deviations. The numerical values in the top of bars denote the average number of hidden neurons or dendrites for each neural model.

6   Discussion and Conclusions

In this paper, it was presented the theoretical basis of the Dendrite Spherical Neurons (DSN) for pattern classification. The DSN can be categorized in the family of neuronal models with dendritic processing, like Dendrite Morphological Neurons (DMN) and Dendrite Ellipsoidal Neurons (DEN). These neural models are an alternative to the Multilayer Perceptron (MLP) to solve classification problems with a simple architecture. Moreover, the DSN model can be viewed as a simplification of the DEN model, whose covariance matrix is diagonal with all its elements equal. DSN can overcome potential issues found in DEN, such as singular covariance matrices when a dendrite clusters a small number of patterns, while maintaining the smoothness of decision boundaries.

The number of dendrites in DSN is a free parameter that should be tuned adequately. Thus, we proposed an optimization procedure based on the Simulated Annealing (SA) algorithm, in which the classification accuracy is maximized, while the number of dendrites is used as a constraint. Notice that this scheme does not guarantee the minimum number of dendrites, which represents a limitation of the proposed method. Hence, the problem of DSN tuning can be further extended to multiobjective optimization, in which the accuracy is maximized, and the number of dendrites is minimized.

The experiments with real-world datasets revealed that DSN tended to reach better accuracy results than DMN. This behavior is because the DMN strongly depends on its initial solution (here was used the dHpC method) that is refined by Stochastic Gradient Descent (SGD); therefore, the error obtained in the initial solution will be carried to the final solution. Unlike to DMN, DSN does not refine an initial solution but uses the k-means algorithm to distribute the dendrites over the input space, while the SGD is used to train the weights of the softmax function at the output of the neuron.

On the other hand, DEN obtained the lowest classification performance. This behavior is because dendrites are created independently for each class without considering the interaction between dendrites of different classes, causing overlaps in transition regions between classes. This drawback is addressed in the DSN model by considering the closeness between dendrites for calculating the radius of the hyperspheres.

DSN obtained competitive results concerning MLP for classifying real-world datasets. However, MLP obtained more complex structures than DSN; that is, MLP usually requires more hidden neurons than dendrites in DSN to model the same classification problem. Therefore, DSN can be potentially used for classification problems where computational resources are limited.

Future work involves a study of the effect of the number of dendrites on the DSN classification performance. Also, an extensive study with larger datasets and other kinds of classifiers is pending. Besides, the accuracy of DNS can be improved by using other distance metrics to measure the closeness between patterns as well as applying to SDG mechanisms of momentum and adaptive learning rate.

Acknowledgements. We want to express our sincere appreciation to CINVESTAV-IPN and the Instituto Politécnico Nacional for the support provided to carry out this research. This research was supported by a Fondo SEP-Cinvestav 2018 grant (No. 145), and SI-IPN 20190007 and SIP-IPN 20200630.

References

1. Amine, K.: Multiobjective simulated annealing: principles and algorithm variants. J. Multivar. Anal. **143**, 1–13 (2019)
2. Arce, F., Zamora, E., Fócil-Arias, C., Sossa, H.: Dendrite ellipsoidal neurons based on k-means optimization. Evol. Syst. **10**(3), 381–396 (2018). https://doi.org/10.1007/s12530-018-9248-6
3. Arce, F., Zamora, E., Sossa, H., Barrón, R.: Differential evolution training algorithm for dendrite morphological neural networks. Appl. Soft Comput. **68**, 303–313 (2018)
4. Barbero-Jimenez, A., Lopez-Lazaro, J., Dorronsoro, J.R.: Finding optimal model parameters by deterministic and annealed focused grid search. Neurocomputing **72**(13), 2824–2832 (2009)
5. Dua, D., Graff, C.: UCI machine learning repository (2017). http://archive.ics.uci.edu/ml
6. Duda, R., Hart, P., Stork, D.: Pattern Classification, 2nd edn. Wiley, New York (2012)
7. Priddy, K.L., Keller, P.E.: Artificial Neural Networks: An Introduction (SPIE Tutorial Texts in Optical Engineering), vol. TT68. SPIE- International Society for Optical Engineering, Bellingham (2005)

8. Sossa, H., Arce, F., Zamora, E., Guevara, E.: Morphological neural networks with dendritic processing for pattern classification. In: Vergara Villegas, O.O., Nandayapa, M., Soto, I. (eds.) Advanced Topics on Computer Vision, Control and Robotics in Mechatronics, pp. 27–47. Springer, Cham (2018). https://doi.org/10.1007/978-3-319-77770-2_2

9. Zamora, E., Sossa, H.: Dendrite morphological neurons trained by stochastic gradient descent. Neurocomputing **260**, 420–431 (2017)

Comparison of Recurrent Neural Networks for Wind Power Forecasting

Erick López[1(✉)], Carlos Valle[2], Héctor Allende-Cid[3], and Héctor Allende[1]

[1] Departamento de Informática, Universidad Técnica Federico Santa María,
Valparaíso, Chile
{elopez,hallende}@inf.utfsm.cl

[2] Departamento de Computación e Informática, Universidad de Playa Ancha,
Valparaíso, Chile
carlos.valle@upla.cl

[3] Escuela de Ingeniería Informática, Pontificia Universidad Católica de Valparaíso,
Valparaíso, Chile
hector.allende@pucv.cl

Abstract. Integrating wind power to the electrical grid is complicated
due to the stochastic nature of the wind, which makes its prediction a
challenging task. Then, it is important to devise forecasting tools to support this task. For example, a network that integrates an Echo State Network architecture and Long Short-Term Memory blocks as hidden units
(ESN+LSTM) has been proposed, showing good performance against
a physical model. This paper proposes to compare this network versus Echo State Network (ESN) and Long Short-Term Memory (LSTM),
to forecast wind power from 1 to 24 h ahead. Results show than the
ESN+LSTM model outperforms the performance reached for ESN and
LSTM, in terms of MSE, MAE, and the metrics used in the Taylor
diagram. In addition, we observe that the advantage of this network is
statistically significant during the first moments of the forecast horizon,
in terms of T-test and Wilcoxon-test.

Keywords: Wind power forecasting · Recurrent Neural Networks ·
Echo State Network · Long Short-Term Memory · Multivariate time
series

1 Introduction

One of the current challenges in the world is the integration of Non-Conventional
Renewable Energy (NCRE) sources into the global energy matrix. Among these
sources, wind energy presents great challenges for its integration, where one of
its critical factors is its stochastic nature. In this context, it is necessary to
have different forecasting tools that allow us to make better schedule of the
different sources that make up an electrical matrix, such that it allows us to
support the operational and economic tasks of the system [9]. Among the models

© Springer Nature Switzerland AG 2020
K. M. Figueroa Mora et al. (Eds.): MCPR 2020, LNCS 12088, pp. 25–34, 2020.
https://doi.org/10.1007/978-3-030-49076-8_3

proposed in the literature, Recurrent Neural Networks (RNNs) have reported good performance in wind energy forecasting.

In particular, the ESN+LSTM recurrent neural network proposed in [12] has showed good performance in this task. Therefore, in this paper, we compare the ESN+LSTM model against its base models: LSTM and ESN.

To evaluate these models, we use a dataset from a wind farm in NorthEast Denmark. The time series to model is formed by wind speed, wind direction, temperature, month, day, hour, and wind power. Standardized metrics will be used, measuring cumulative performance, because we will address the multi-ahead step forecasting problem. In addition, the Taylor diagram is used to draw some conclusions about the performance of the models, as well as a parametric and non-parametric test to validate some results.

The rest of the paper is organized as follows. In Sect. 2 we describe the context of wind power problem. Section 3 we describe briefly the recurrent networks that will be compared. Next, we describe the experimental setting on which we tested the models and we review the results. Finally, the last section is devoted to conclusions and future work.

2   Wind Power Generation

The wind power generation is the result of transforming the kinetic energy of the wind into electrical energy, traditionally by rotating turbine blades. The power output from a wind turbine can be calculated by the following equation:

$$P = \left(\frac{1}{2} \rho \pi R^2 v_1^3 \right) \cdot C_p, \tag{1}$$

where ρ is the density of the air, R is the length of blades plus the rotor radius, v_1 is wind speed that enters the turbine, and C_p is a coefficient of power provided by the manufacturer, with a theoretical upper limit of 16/27, known as Betz limit. Note that the power output is proportional to the wind speed, which it has a stochastic nature, depending on different meteorological factors, hindering its integration into the existing electricity supply system [9].

In the literature, there are different proposals to address wind power forecasting, being possible group by in four categories [3,9]: (i) persistence method, that simply replicates the last recorded value to make the forecast; (ii) physical methods that takes a detailed description of the physical conditions of the wind farm (including turbines, terrain geography, and meteorological conditions) to model the wind power by means of differential equations and downscaling techniques [10,13]; (iii) statistical methods that try to exploit the possible underlying dependency structure of data, under certain assumptions, by time series modeling techniques [2,11]; (iv) machine learning methods that attempt to discover underlying relationships of dataset, without an a priori structural hypothesis [5,14].

The last category has been received special interest nowadays, achieving great performance in different tasks. Particularly in wind power forecasting, the recurrent neural network models stand out from other machine learning methods since it would allow modeling time series in a natural way.

3   Forecasting Models

In this section, we present three approaches of recurrent neural networks, which aim to solve the vanishing gradient problem, and have been reported good performances in time series modeling. Further, we use these models for experimental comparisons.

Long Short-Term Memory (LSTM)

In [6] is proposed a class of recurrent network replacing the basic unit (neuron) of a traditional network by a *block of memory*. This block contains one or more *memory cells*. Each memory cell is associated with "gates" (activation functions) for controlling the information flow moving through the cells. Each auto-connected memory cell is so-called "Constant Error Carousel" (CEC) linear unit, whose activation is the state of the cell as shown in Fig. 1. The CEC solves the problem of vanishing (or explosion) gradient [1]. Since the local error back flow remains constant within the CEC, without growing or decreasing, while not a new entry or external signal error appears. However, its training process can be computationally expensive, due to the complexity of its architecture. Besides, it might overfit depending on the values of its hyperparameters such as the number of blocks, the learning rate or the maximum number of epochs.

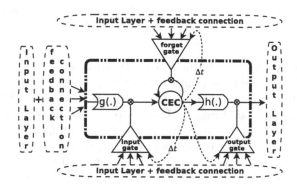

Fig. 1. LSTM architecture with 1 block and 1 cell.

Echo State Network (ESN)
Another RNN that has performed well in time series forecasting is the model proposed by Jaeger [8]. This model is very simple and easy to implement, consists of three layers (input, hidden and output), where the hidden layer is formed by a

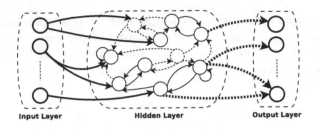

Fig. 2. ESN topology.

large number of perceptron kind neurons, with a low rate of connectivity among them (allowing self-connections), and they are randomly connected as depicted in Fig. 2. An interesting property is all weights are initialized randomly (usually using a normal o uniform centred on zero). Next, it rescales the recurrent weight matrix to get a spectral radius close to one. Finally, only the output layer weights are fixed using a ridge-regression. The output hidden neurons is computed by the following expression,

$$s(t) = (1 - a) \cdot s(t - 1) + a \cdot f(\text{net}(t)), \tag{2}$$

where $s(t)$ is the output of a hidden neuron in the instant t, $a \in [0, 1]$ is a leaking rate that regulates the speed update of the internal dynamics, i.e., it is adjusted to match the speed of the dynamics of $x(t)$ and $\hat{y}(t)$. Here, $x(t)$ is the input to the network and $\hat{y}(t)$ is the output of the network at time t. Moreover, $f(\cdot)$ is a hyperbolic tangent activation function and $\text{net}(t)$ is the input signal to the neuron. Furthermore, as the hidden states are initialized to zero $s(0) = 0$, it is necessary to define the number of steps θ that the recurrent states are updated without being considered in the process of adjusting the output layer. The above is because the states are initialized to zero, $s(0) = 0$.

Echo State Network with Long Short-Term Memory (ESN+LSTM)
Given the advantages and some limitations identified on LSTM and ESN models, ESN+LSTM [12] is proposed to integrate the architecture of an ESN with LSTM units as hidden neurons (see Fig. 3). This proposal permits to train all network weights through the following strategy: i) The input and hidden layer is trained by an online gradient descent (OGD) algorithm with one epoch, using as target the input signal; ii) Next, the output layer is adjusted with a regularized quantile regression, using as target the desired output; iii) Finally, the whole network is trained with an OGD algorithm with one epoch and the desired target.

The first step aims to extract characteristics automatically as the autoencoder approach. The second step aims to use a quantile regression in order to obtain a robust estimate of the expected target. It should be noted that the hidden layer is sparsely connected, and its weights matrix keep a spectral radius close to one. In this model, the main hyperparameters to be tune are the hidden units number, the spectral radius, and the regularization parameter.

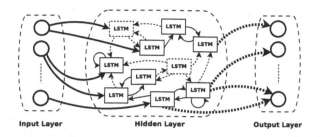

Fig. 3. ESN+LSTM topology.

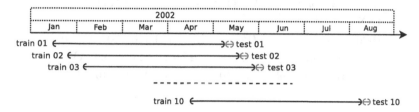

Fig. 4. Time series split scheme for cross-validation approach

4   Experiments and Results

For assessing the presented models, we use a dataset from the Klim Fjordholme wind farm (57.06°N, 9.15°E) [7], that consists of generated power measurements and predictions of some meteorological variables (wind speed, wind direction and ambient temperature).

We work with hourly time series, no missing values. The dataset is composed of 5376 observations, starting at 00:00 on 14 January 2002 to 23:00 on 25 August 2002. The attributes considered to model are: wind speed, wind direction, temperature, month, day, hour and wind power. All features are normalized to the $[-1, 1]$ range using the min-max function and predictions are denormalized before computing the performance metrics.

A cross-validation approach is used to train and select the best hyperparameters configuration. The time series is divided into $R = 10$ subseries, and the performance of each model is evaluated in each of them (see Fig. 4).

To evaluate the performance of the models, we use some standardized metrics: Mean Squared Error (MSE) and the Mean Absolute Error (MAE). Additionally, we show a Taylor diagram to compare graphically the Pearson correlation coefficient (ρ), the root-mean-square error (RMSE), and the standard deviation (SD). In this work, the performance will be checked over multi-step ahead forecasting, which is generated using the multi-stage approach [4].

For a single subseries r, the different metrics are based on the error $e_r(\cdot)$ at h hours ahead, defined for equation (3),

$$e_r(T + h|T) = y_r(T + h) - \hat{y}_r(T + h|T),\qquad(3)$$

Table 1. Parameters for tuning.

LSTM	
Hidden layer size	$: J \in \{10, 20, \ldots, 100, 110, 120, \ldots, 500\}$
Number of epochs	$:$ **epoch** $\in \{1, 10, 50, 100, 150, 200\}$
ESN	
Hidden layer size	$: J \in \{10, 20, \ldots, 100, 110, 120, \ldots, 500\}$
Leaking rate	$: a \in \{0.1, 0.2, 0.3, \ldots, 0.8, 0.9, 1\}$
Spectral radius	$: \alpha \in \{0.1, 0.2, 0.3, \ldots, 0.8, 0.9, 1\}$
Regularization coeff	$: \lambda \in \{10^{-5}, 10^{-4}, 10^{-3}, 10^{-2}, 10^{-1}\}$
ESN+LSTM	
Hidden layer size	$: J \in \{10, 20, \ldots, 100, 110, 120, \ldots, 500\}$
Spectral radius	$: \alpha \in \{0.1, 0.2, 0.3, \ldots, 0.8, 0.9, 1\}$
Regularization coeff	$: \lambda \in \{10^{-5}, 10^{-4}, 10^{-3}, 10^{-2}, 10^{-1}\}$

where $y_r(T + h)$ is the desired output at instant $T + h$ of subseries r, T is the index of the last point of the series used during training, h is the number of steps ahead, and $\hat{y}_r(T + h|T)$ is the estimated output at time $T + h$ generated by the model for subserie r. Then, the metrics are calculated by the following equations,

$$\mathrm{MSE}_{(r)} = \frac{1}{H} \sum_{h=1}^{H} (e_r(T + h|T))^2, \qquad \mathrm{MSE} = \frac{1}{R} \sum_{r=1}^{R} \mathrm{MSE}_{(r)}, \qquad (4)$$

$$\mathrm{MAE}_{(r)} = \frac{1}{H} \sum_{h=1}^{H} |e_r(T + h|T)|, \qquad \mathrm{MAE} = \frac{1}{R} \sum_{r=1}^{R} \mathrm{MAE}_{(r)}, \qquad (5)$$

where R is the total number subseries, and H is the ahead step limit used.

The parameters that will be tuning for the different networks are shown in Table 1. For the ESN and ESN+LSTM, first we tune the number of hidden units, keeping fixed $\alpha = 0.5$ and $\lambda = 0.001$. Next, α and λ are tuned. In three networks, the output layer uses the identity function as the activation function. In addition, the ESN and ESN+LSTM use direct connections from the input layer to the output layer. The weights of each matrix are generated from a uniform distribution $(-0.1; 0.1)$, independently of each other. Sparse arrays were also used when connecting the input layer with the hidden layer. Thus, configurations with the lowest error over the test set obtained for each model are: LSTM ($J = 30$, **epoch** $= 100$), ESN ($J = 470$, $a = 0.4$, $\alpha = 0.6$, $\lambda = 10^{-5}$), and ESN+LSTM ($J = 190$, $\alpha = 0.5$, $\lambda = 10^{-3}$).

Figure 5 shows the MSE for different values of H used. It can be seen that ESN+LSTM achieves a lower error, extending this advantage from $H = 1$ to $H = 12$, later its performance is similar to the one of obtained from the LSTM. We also view that ESN is the network that presents the greatest error to different

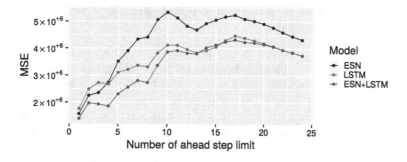

Fig. 5. MSE by each ahead step limit, H, used.

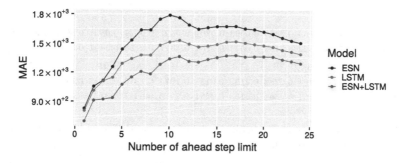

Fig. 6. MAE by each ahead step limit, H, used.

steps ahead. A similar scenario can be seen by observing the behavior of MAE (see Fig. 6). In this case, ESN+LSTM presents better performance for all H values. While ESN again presents the highest error, reaching a performance similar to LSTM during the first moments $H \in \{1, 2, 3\}$.

Although ESN+LSTM achieves the lowest error in terms of MSE and MAE for different H, this advantage may be due to the randomness of the system. Then, a hypothesis test for paired samples will be evaluated, since each model was tested with the same sub-series, to later build the global indicators.

Test 1 $\quad H_0 : \mu_{esn} \leq \mu_{esn+lstm} \quad$ vs $\quad H_1 : \mu_{esn} > \mu_{esn+lstm}$

Test 2 $\quad H_0 : \mu_{lstm} \leq \mu_{esn+lstm} \quad$ vs $\quad H_1 : \mu_{lstm} > \mu_{esn+lstm}$

For both cases, a parametric and nonparametric test will be used: t-test and wilcoxon-test. Table 2 and 3 show the p-values to validate the statistical significance if MSE of ESN+LSTM is lower than other models.

Using the t-test, it is observed that in the case of Test 1, ESN+LSTM is significantly lower than ESN from $H = 4$ to $H = 9$, for a significance level of 10%. Next, the advantage observed in Fig. 5 would not be significant. On another hand, in the Test 2, the advantage presented by ESN+LSTM over LSTM is significative from $H = 3$ to $H = 5$, using the same significance level. If we use the wilcoxon-test, the advantage shown by ESN+LSTM over ESN is significant from

Table 2. T-test's p-values by each ahead step limit used, for MSE. Best results at highlighted in gray background.

H	1	2	3	4	5	6	7	8	9	10	11	12
Test 1	0.2202	0.2455	0.1973	0.0563	0.0560	0.0642	0.0660	0.0659	0.0922	0.1249	0.1464	0.1634
Test 2	0.1645	0.1417	0.0722	0.0366	0.0636	0.1342	0.2103	0.2188	0.2906	0.3812	0.3966	0.4150

H	13	14	15	16	17	18	19	20	21	22	23	24
Test 1	0.1770	0.1748	0.1722	0.1701	0.1695	0.1824	0.1936	0.2031	0.2104	0.2192	0.2308	0.2256
Test 2	0.4794	0.5675	0.5483	0.4688	0.4111	0.4093	0.4504	0.4766	0.4882	0.4969	0.4945	0.4944

Table 3. Wilcoxon-test's p-values by each ahead step limit used, for MSE. Best results at highlighted in gray background.

H	1	2	3	4	5	6	7	8	9	10	11	12
Test 1	0.2768	0.3178	0.2768	0.0486	0.0963	0.0801	0.0527	0.0527	0.0801	0.0967	0.1611	0.1611
Test 2	0.0654	0.2158	0.0322	0.0137	0.0527	0.0801	0.1377	0.2158	0.2461	0.3125	0.2783	0.2461

H	13	14	15	16	17	18	19	20	21	22	23	24
Test 1	0.1875	0.1611	0.2461	0.2783	0.2158	0.2158	0.1875	0.1875	0.2783	0.3125	0.3125	0.2783
Test 2	0.3477	0.3477	0.2461	0.2461	0.2158	0.2461	0.2783	0.3477	0.3125	0.3477	0.3477	0.3477

Table 4. T-test's p-values by each ahead step limit used, for MAE. Best results at highlighted in gray background.

H	1	2	3	4	5	6	7	8	9	10	11	12
Test 1	0.1037	0.1748	0.1129	0.0399	0.0397	0.0469	0.0350	0.0343	0.0393	0.0454	0.0605	0.0649
Test 2	0.0684	0.0650	0.0077	0.0057	0.0235	0.0675	0.1223	0.1037	0.1085	0.1275	0.1260	0.0865

H	13	14	15	16	17	18	19	20	21	22	23	24
Test 1	0.0790	0.0822	0.0861	0.0960	0.0932	0.0939	0.0955	0.1107	0.1218	0.1223	0.1282	0.1216
Test 2	0.1153	0.1442	0.1540	0.1468	0.1536	0.1570	0.1825	0.2055	0.2268	0.2241	0.2197	0.2144

Table 5. Wilcoxon-test's p-values by each ahead step limit used, for MAE. Best results at highlighted in gray background.

H	1	2	3	4	5	6	7	8	9	10	11	12
Test 1	0.1181	0.2386	0.1432	0.0486	0.0776	0.0654	0.0322	0.0322	0.0322	0.0527	0.0801	0.0801
Test 2	0.0527	0.0801	0.0029	0.0098	0.0244	0.0801	0.0967	0.1377	0.1611	0.1611	0.1611	0.0801

H	13	14	15	16	17	18	19	20	21	22	23	24
Test 1	0.1377	0.0967	0.1377	0.1377	0.1377	0.1377	0.1377	0.1611	0.2158	0.1875	0.1611	0.1611
Test 2	0.1162	0.1162	0.1162	0.1377	0.1611	0.1875	0.1611	0.1875	0.1875	0.1875	0.2158	0.1875

$H = 4$ to $H = 10$. While comparing ESN+LSTM and LSTM, it is appreciated that better performance is achieved when $H = 1$ and from $H = 3$ to $H = 6$.

When using the MAE metric, the Table 4 shows the results of applying the t-test. We observe that ESN+LSTM is significatively lower than ESN from $H = 4$ to $H = 14$ for a significance level of 10%. While in Test 2, ESN+LSTM model presents a better performance from $H = 1$ to $H = 6$ to a significance level of

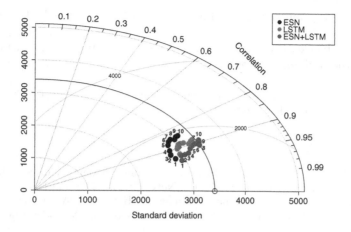

Fig. 7. Taylor Diagram. Each number close to point represents the ahead step limit used H.

10%. Finally, Table 5 shows the results using the wilcoxon-test for MAE. The ESN error improvement is presented when $H \in \{4, \ldots, 12\}$ and $H = 14$. And when $H \in \{1, \ldots, 7\}$, ESN+LSTM improves to LSTM with a 10% of significance.

Additionally, Fig. 7 shows the Taylor Diagram using only from $H = 1$ to $H = 10$. It is observed that ESN+LSTM achieves better performance based on correlation, RMSE, and SD, compared ESN and LSTM model for the same ahead step limit H. It is also appreciated that, as the forecast horizon increases, the correlation decreases, as does the RMSE increases, but the SD generated by the model is close to the real one.

5   Conclusions and Future Work

This work compares the performance of three recurrent neuronal networks for wind power forecasting task. The experimental results show that the ESN+LSTM model is able to capture the underlying dynamics and to predict several steps ahead better than ESN and LSTM models. Since the metrics used were defined cumulatively, it is expected that all three models will exhibit an increase in error as the forecast horizon increases. As our results show, the performance of the chosen networks begins to deteriorate as H grows. However, at least up to $H = 10$, ESN+LSTM performes better based on the Taylor diagram. Besides, according to t-test over MAE results, ESN+LSTM outperformed ESN during the first 19 steps ahead (except for $H = 1, 2, 3$) and outperformed LSTM during the first 6 steps ahead. Similar behavior is observed in the other cases. The above suggests that ESN+LSTM model is a good alternative to consider for short-term forecasting, especially considering that this model uses just 2 epochs, while the LSTM needs more epochs to learn the time series. As a future work, we would like to test these models using more data from other locations around the world. Also, given that ESN+LSTM uses as hidden units LSTM blocks, it would be interesting to evaluate the performance of this model by changing those units to GRU blocks. Finally, one can explore the capabilities of these networks to address the problem of prediction intervals.

Acknowledgments. This work was supported in part by Fondecyt 1170123 and in part by Basal Project AFB 1800082.

References

1. Bengio, Y., Simard, P., Frasconi, P.: Learning long-term dependencies with gradient descent is difficult. IEEE Trans. Neural Netw. **5**(2), 157–166 (1994)
2. Cadenas, E., Rivera, W., Campos-Amezcua, R., Heard, C.: Wind speed prediction using a univariate ARIMA model and a multivariate NARX model. Energies **9**(2), 109 (2016)
3. Chang, W.Y.: A literature review of wind forecasting methods. J. Power Energy Eng. **2**, 161–168 (2014)
4. Cheng, H., Tan, P.-N., Gao, J., Scripps, J.: Multistep-ahead time series prediction. In: Ng, W.-K., Kitsuregawa, M., Li, J., Chang, K. (eds.) PAKDD 2006. LNCS (LNAI), vol. 3918, pp. 765–774. Springer, Heidelberg (2006). https://doi.org/10.1007/11731139_89
5. De Aquino, R.R.B., Souza, R.B., Neto, O.N., Lira, M.M.S., Carvalho, M.A., Ferreira, A.A.: Echo state networks, artificial neural networks and fuzzy systems models for improve short-term wind speed forecasting. In: IJCNN, pp. 1–8. IEEE (2015)
6. Hochreiter, S., Schmidhuber, J.: Long short-term memory. Neural Comput. **9**(8), 1735–1780 (1997)
7. Iversen, E.B., Morales, J.M., Møller, J.K., Trombe, P.J., Madsen, H.: Leveraging stochastic differential equations for probabilistic forecasting of wind power using a dynamic power curve. Wind Energy **20**(1), 33–44 (2017)
8. Jaeger, H.: The "echo state" approach to analysing and training recurrent neural networks. GMD Report 148, GMD - German National Research Institute for Computer Science (2001)
9. Jung, J., Broadwater, R.P.: Current status and future advances for wind speed and power forecasting. Renew. Sustain. Energy Rev. **31**, 762–777 (2014)
10. Li, L., Liu, Y.Q., Yang, Y.P., Han, S., Wang, Y.M.: A physical approach of the short-term wind power prediction based on CFD pre-calculated flow fields. J. Hydrodyn. Ser. B **25**(1), 56–61 (2013)
11. Liu, Y., Roberts, M.C., Sioshansi, R.: A vector autoregression weather model for electricity supply and demand modeling. J. Mod. Power Syst. Clean Energy **6**(4), 763–776 (2018). https://doi.org/10.1007/s40565-017-0365-1
12. López, E., Valle, C., Allende, H., Gil, E., Madsen, H.: Wind power forecasting based on echo state networks and long short-term memory. Energies **11**(3), 526 (2018)
13. Madsen, H., Nielsen, H.A., Nielsen, T.S.: A tool for predicting the wind power production of off-shore wind plants. In: Proceedings of the Copenhagen Offshore Wind Conference & Exhibition, Copenhagen (2005)
14. Perera, K.S., Aung, Z., Woon, W.L.: Machine learning techniques for supporting renewable energy generation and integration: a survey. In: Woon, W.L., Aung, Z., Madnick, S. (eds.) DARE 2014. LNCS (LNAI), vol. 8817, pp. 81–96. Springer, Cham (2014). https://doi.org/10.1007/978-3-319-13290-7_7

Classification of *Cattleya Trianae* and Its Varieties by Using Colorimetry

Manuel G. Forero[1]([✉]) [iD], Carlos E. Beltrán[2], Armando Troncoso[1], and Christian González-Santos[1]

[1] Semillero Lún, Facultad de Ingeniería, Universidad de Ibagué, Ibagué, Colombia
{manuel.forero,christian.gonzalez}@unibague.edu.co,
armandotroncosolugo@gmail.com
[2] Semillero Lún, Facultad de Ciencias Naturales y Matemáticas, Universidad de Ibagué, Ibagué, Colombia
carlos.beltran@unibague.edu.co

Abstract. Orchids in general, like *Cattleya trianae*, have been characterized mostly by taxonomic and visual studies. However, colour is not used for classification. Here, a new method for identifying and classifying orchids of different varieties of *Cattleya trianae* is introduced. This method is not subjective and uses the colour information obtained from the central axis of the *Cattleya trianae* lip. To this end, a new acquisition protocol was established, which uses a new device for image acquisition of the labellum's central axis from the hippocampus to the epicentre. The colour patterns found between samples of the same variety were adjusted and it was verified by using correlation they can be employed to identify each variety. Finally, a support vector machine was used to classify and identify four *Cattleya trianae* varieties, finding that a linear kernel was enough to classify them with an accuracy of 100% .

Keywords: Orchids · *Cattleya trianae* · Plant classification · Orchid varieties

1 Introduction

The family of orchids, to which the *Cattleya trianae* belongs, shown in Fig. 1 (a), is the most abundant in the world. The number of species is close to 30,000 [1, 2]. In fact, it is the family of plants that exhibits the most advanced characteristics from an evolutionary point of view, which is why it is in the process of diversification, a circumstance that is reflected in the abundance and diversity of species. Orchids are more numerous in the tropics than in other regions of the world [3]. In general terms, the orchid flora of tropical America outnumbers species in other continents [4]. Northwest of South America has the highest number of orchid species. In Colombia, orchids are found in practically all natural ecosystems and occupy the first place as the family of plants with the highest number of species threatened with extinction [5]. There is a great risk to orchids, due to the high levels of endemism in Colombia and the high conversion rates of their ecosystems, to uses such as agriculture and livestock [6].

© Springer Nature Switzerland AG 2020
K. M. Figueroa Mora et al. (Eds.): MCPR 2020, LNCS 12088, pp. 35–44, 2020.
https://doi.org/10.1007/978-3-030-49076-8_4

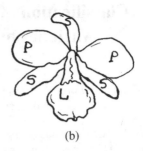

(a)   (b)

Fig. 1. (a) *Cattleya trianae* orchid. (b) Parts: sepal (S), petal (P) and labellum (L).

Cattleya trianae is endemic of Colombia and its distribution is restricted to the upper basin of the Magdalena River, especially in the departments of Tolima, Huila, part of Caqueta and to a lesser extent in Cundinamarca, at altitudes between 600 and 1940 m. In the visual characterisation, *Cattleya trianae* is usually described by its flower, composed of lavender colour petals, twice as large as the sepals as shown in Fig. 1 (b). There are several colour variations among the species. Varieties include the standard or type, semi-alba, alba, concolor variety 1, concolor variety 2, amesiana, coerulea, bull blood or rubra and splash; being different between them by the colour distribution and intensity on petals and, in particular, on the lip.

In the last years, many species of orchids have entered into critical levels due to the difficulty in designing conservation strategies [4]. This is because of their complex life cycles and that they cannot take place without appropriate population studies [5, 8]. Most orchids studies have been limited to population analysis or to visual characterisation of terrestrial species or epiphytic habit and litofic. These studies are difficult and complex, on one hand, due to the variability of the different properties of the flower within the same variety, like shape, texture, pattern and colour and, on the other hand, flowers of different species and varieties are very similar. The characterisation and taxonomic classification of orchids is often done visually by their pattern and morphology, but also based on other types of characteristics such as colour. Therefore, identification requires good experience and it is done mainly by employing subjective methods based on visual and taxonomic properties [3, 7]. Accordingly, it is necessary to develop an objective and reproducible method, i.e., one that will produce the same result independent of the user.

The first classifications of the orchid date back to the 18th century when the Swedish botanist Carlo Linnaeus wrote about it in his compendium "Species plantarum" [7]. The popularity of the flower continued to grow, being even the object of studies of specialists like Charles Darwin, who was interested by its process of reproduction. From the nineteenth century, the work of the experts focused on finding and cataloging orchid species, emphasizing their characteristics and differences. At the beginning, these studies were visually done and nowadays, genetic analysis is also employed for the differentiation of genotypes.

The automatic classification of plants based on the shape, texture and colour of leaves and flowers is an active field in computer vision. These methods usually compare a new specimen against a catalog to identify the plant. Several methods have been developed to identify plants of different species based on flower images. Nilsback and Zisserman worked in the HSV colour space and employed gradient orientation histograms and the SIFT shape descriptors to get colour, texture and shape characteristics of flowers. A multikernel framework with a SVM was employed for classification [9]. Guru employed cooccurrence matrices and Gabor filters to characterise texture, and classification was done using a k-nearest neighbours method [10]. Mabrook et al. employed SURF and Lab to get shape and colour descriptors to identify flowers of different species and also a SVM for classification [11]. Kumar et al. used RGB colour indexes, as well as leaf shape characteristics to identify plants [12]. Qi et al. employed colour SIFT descriptors and linear SVM for classification [13]. Zawbaa et al. used SIFT and SFTA to describe the characteristics of the flower and SVM and random forest to classify different kinds of flowers [14]. Khan et al. developed new colour descriptors and used them to classify flowers of the Flower-102 base, employing a non-linear SVM [15]. Guo et al. developed a deep sparse coding framework for the visual characterization of flowers of different species in the Oxford-102 flowers database [16]. They employ local contracted sparse coding to extract intermediate local features and local orientation histograms. Hong et al. classifies flowers based on colour and shape descriptors, and employs k-means and history matching to classify [17]. Among the works of identification in orchids, we can mention the works of Arwatchananukul et al. in *paphiopedillum*, who use texture and colour [18]. Sani et al. compared different classification methods Naive Bayes, k-nearest binary tree and sequential minimal optimisation employing colour and texture characteristics through the use of HSV moments, HSV histograms and segmentation based fractal textures SFTA features. They classified two species of *dendrobium* flowers using directly the images of orchids through neural networks [19]. Puttemans et al. classified *phalaenopsis* transforming the images into space Lab and using linear SVM [20].

The above methods do not take into account the colour distribution of the flower, which can be used to recognise Cattleya trianae varieties and do not enable the colour of the labellum of one variety to be related to the colour of another. Until now the studies of characterisation of the varieties of *Cattleya trianae* are made only of visual form. In the literature review, no reference was found where these techniques were used for *Cattleya trianae* characterisation, i.e., a study that uses objective techniques, independent of the user and therefore reproducible, since the previous studies depend on the visual concept of each specialist. Therefore, the proposed study, specifically developed for biologists, based on colorimetric analysis from photographs of the lip under controlled lighting conditions is a necessary and novel step for the characterization of the *Cattleya trianae* lip that can be extended in the future to the study of other varieties of flowers. We proposed a new method to study the flowering of *Cattleya trianae* s.p and its varieties, using techniques of image processing and pattern recognition for the characterization of their labellum, from images acquired with a digital camera. The middle axis of each lip is proposed as a kind of fingerprint to identify the flowers, see Fig. 2.

Fig. 2. Orchid's labellum or lip.

2 Materials

To develop the method, pictures from 99 flowers of four *Cattleya trianae* varieties were taken in situ. Flowers were dissected without damaging their original colour, following the method of classical taxonomic and phylogenetic identification based on visual traits. Images were acquired in RAW format, since it does not introduce losses by compression and stores all the information collected by the camera sensor. Images were taken with an 18 megapixel Canon 7D camera and employing a Canon EF 100 mm f/2.8 USM macro lens, used in biological research to document studies in plant species allowing to appreciate details that often go unnoticed and allowing images to be acquired at close range with low colour distortion and focus on the entire image Fig. 3. To establish an acquisition protocol, 99 flowers of orchids of the *Cattleya trianae* type, concolor var. 1, concolor var. 2 and alba varieties were photographed. Photographs were acquired using the minimum available sensitivity (ISO 100) to minimize noise amplification. The aperture was adjusted so that the entire region of interest was focused, being generally f/11 or less and the shutter speed was set so that the orchid appeared well lit avoiding saturation of the histogram and using the maximum dynamic range available. The speed was generally set to 1/8 s, whereby a trigger cable was used to avoid movement of the camera during acquisition. Various aperture and velocity values were tested, in addition to controlled ambient lighting techniques, until good quality images were obtained. It was found that the best lighting was given with natural light, without direct exposure of the sun, using a parasol. 58 flowers were necessary to adjust the protocol and ensure that in all cases they acquire good quality images that could be used for the study.

Fig. 3. Image acquisition method.

3 Methods

To assure that colours in the different images were the same and coincided with the real colour, they were calibrated by using the colour chart presented in Fig. 4 and following the protocol established by the chart manufacturer [7].

Fig. 4. Chart used to adjust the colour.

Images were obtained during bloom and most of them served to develop the acquisition protocol. To fix the labellum, the device shown in Fig. 5 was created, consisting of three brass sheets, a square one used as a base where the labellum is placed and two smaller rectangular sheets to fix the labellum. They were fastened to the square base by using two magnets located under the base. The central axis of the labellum, from the epichile to hipochilo, was chosen as fingerprint because this section of the flower contains all the range of colour and change of intensity present in *Cattleya trianae*, given that the labellum is used by the plant to attract pollinators.

(a)　　　　　　　　　　　　　　　(b)

Fig. 5. Base developed to fix the labellum. (a) Top and bottom view. (b) Side view.

The colour profiles of the central area of each labellum were obtained, as shown in Fig. 6. To reduce noise, a fringe of the central axis was used and the average of the colour values in each column of the profile was calculated.

Given that flower size is variable and the distance from the *Cattleya trianae* to the camera also changes from one acquisition to another, profiles were normalised by using a method similar to the one employed in electroencephalography (EEG), used to adjust EEG signals to obtain evoked potential responses, as shown in Fig. 7.a. To this aim, the colour channel profile that presented maximum amplitude variation was chosen. Then, all signals were aligned in such a way that the first and last local minimum or maximum local of the profile coincide. The profiles of the other two channels were also aligned by using the same calibration.

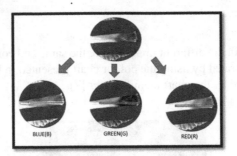

Fig. 6. Acquisition of RGB profiles

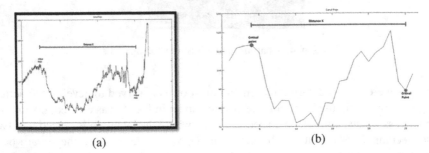

| (a) | (b) |

Fig. 7. Normalization and sampling of channel profiles. (a) Channel chosen. (b) Channel sampled.

Although the images of the central axis were taken by using the same protocol, some profiles were longer; thereby, to assure that profiles corresponded to the same equivalent part of the central axis, the distance between the first and the minima or maxima, used as reference points, was calculated and 20 equally spaced samples were taken. Three additional samples were taken before the first reference point and three others after the last one, making a total of 26 equally space samples per channel profile, and a total of 78 samples used as descriptors for each flower, significantly reducing data processing and noise, as shown in Fig. 7.b.

4 Results

From the 99 images acquired, only 41 were usable, given that most were used to establish the acquisition protocol. Figure 8 shows the orchids varieties used in this study. To verify if the profiles could be used as a kind of fingerprint to identify *Cattleya trianae* varieties, the correlation between the samples of each variety were calculated. The correlation between the profiles of the different varieties of *Cattleya trianae* are displayed in Table 1. As it can be seen, a high correlation appears between several profiles from the different varieties and the highest correlation between samples of the same variety.

To classify and identify each variety of *Cattleya trianae*, some popular classification algorithms were studied. Among them, it was decided to use support vector machines (SVM) for this work, which has important advantages over neural networks (ANN), another very popular method. The advantages of SVM are that the solution converges towards a global minimum instead of local minima and models depend on a few parameters, so modelling is easier.

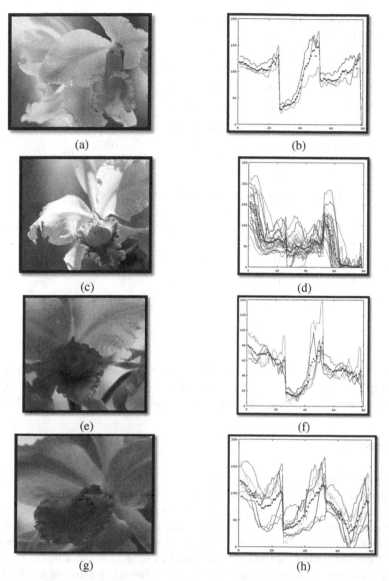

Fig. 8. Orchid varieties. (a) Alba. (c) Standard or type. (e) Concolor var. 1. (g) Concolor var. 2. (b), (d), (f) and (h) show the profiles and the average of the three channels altogether, one behind the other for the four varieties. It can be observed that there is a characteristic pattern for each variety, where the pattern dotted with black asterisks represents the average value for that variety. This average pattern was employed to find the correlations.

To train the SVM, the 26 samples obtained by each channel were used as characteristic descriptors. In this way, a descriptive vector of 78 characteristics was formed, to which a label was added according to the variety to which the sample belongs (groups 1, 2, 3 and 4). The SVM was implemented using a linear kernel, given the low number

Table 1. Average correlation of the three colour profiles, between samples of the same variety and against the other varieties.

Orchid	Type	Alba	Concolor var. 1	Concolor var. 2
Type	0.901	0.1224	0.606	0.5757
Alba	0.1261	0.9515	0.7006	0.6824
Concolor v. 1	0.5414	0.6426	0.8342	0.7643
Concolor v. 2	0.586	0.602	0.82	0.871

Table 2. Vector classification results of the vector machine.

Orchid	Number of samples	True positives	True negatives	False positives	False negatives
Type	24	100%	0%	0%	0%
Alba	3	100%	0%	0%	0%
Concolor 1	8	100%	0%	0%	0%
Concolor 2	6	100%	0%	0%	0%

of samples and the data set was subdivided into three randomly distributed groups, 60% for training, another 20% for model fit and the remaining 20% for validation, using cross-correlation with which a 100% successful classification result was obtained.

5   Discussion

Table 1 presents the averaged values of the correlations between varieties of *Cattleya trianae* and the average profile of each of them. It is observed that the highest correlation is always between the average profile and the profiles of their respective varieties. Therefore, it is possible to use the profile of the lip central axis to perform the *Cattleya trianae* classification and identification. As it can be seen in Table 2, there is a very high correlation between two similar varieties (concolor var. 1 and concolor var. 2), being coincident with the colour profile of both flowers. It also can be observed in Fig. 8 (b), (d), (f) and (h), the profiles of the green channels of the alba, concolor var. 1 and concolor var. 2 are very similar. Therefore, by analysing the correlation between channels can provide information about the similarity between colour components of the varieties, making it also possible to be used to get information about the common origin of different varieties of *Cattleya trianae*.

6 Conclusions

A new method to identify and classify orchids of the different varieties of the *Cattleya trianae* was presented. This method is objective and reproducible, allowing to automate this procedure. It was shown the central axis of the label (from hipochilo to epichilo), can be employed as a fingerprint to identify varieties of *Cattleya trianae*. A protocol was set up to images of the labellum central axis of the *Cattleya trianae* (from the epichile to hipochilo) and its varieties. The results show the profile of this zone can be used as a fingerprint to classify and identify its varieties. The highest correlation was between similar varieties (concolor var. 1 and concolor var. 2), being coincident with the colour profile of the flowers, suggesting this new tool could be employed to study the common origin of different varieties.

Acknowledgements. This work was supported by project #14-314-INT Universidad de Ibagué.

References

1. Dressler, R.: How many orchid species? In: Proceedings Second International Orchid Conservation Congress, pp. 155–158 (2005)
2. van Raveschot, V.G.: Aclimatación de plántulas de *Chloraea virescens* (Willd.) Lindl cultivadas in vitro. Universidad Austral de Chile (2009)
3. Dressler, R.: Phylogeny and Classification of Orchid Family. Dioscorides Press, Portland (1993)
4. Gentry, A.H., Dodson, C.H.: Diversity and biogeography of neotropical vascular epiphytes. Ann. Missouri Bot. Gard. **74**(2), 205–233 (1987)
5. Calderón Sáenz, E.: Libro rojo de plantas de Colombia. Orquídeas, primera parte. Instituto Alexander von Humboldt, vol. 6 (2007)
6. Dixon, K., Phillips, R.D.: The orchid conservation challenge. Lankesteriana Int. J. Orchid. **7**(1–2), 11–12 (2007)
7. Linnaeus, C.: Species Plantarum, 1753rd edn. Ray Society, London (1957)
8. Meisel, J.E., Kaufmann, R.S., Pupulin, F.: Orchids of Tropical America. Cornell University Press, Ithaca (2014)
9. Philbin, J., et al.: Lost in quantization: improving particular object retrieval in large scale image databases. In: IEEE Conference on Computer Vision and Pattern Recognition, pp. 1–8 (2008)
10. Guru, D., et al.: Texture features and KNN in classification of flower images. In: Fifth Indian International Conference on Artificial Intelligence, vol. 1 (2010)
11. Mabrouk, A.B., et al.: Image flower recognition based on a new method for color feature extraction. In: 2014 International Conference on Computer Vision Theory and Applications, vol. 2, pp. 201–206 (2014)
12. Mishra, P.K., et al.: A semi automatic plant identification based on digital leaf and flower images. In: IEEE International Conference on Advances in Engineering, Science and Management (ICAESM-2012), pp. 68–73 (2012)
13. Qi, L.S., et al.: Repurposing CRISPR as an RNA-guided platform for sequence-specific control of gene expression. Cell **152**(5), 1173–1183 (2013)
14. Zawbaa, H., et al.: An automatic flower classification approach using machine learning algorithms (2014)

15. Khan, N., et al.: Discriminative color descriptors. In: IEEE Conference on Computer Vision and Pattern Recognition, pp. 2866–2873 (2013)
16. Guo, L., Guo, C.: A deep sparse coding method for fine-grained visual categorization. In: International Joint Conference on Neural Networks, pp. 632–639 (2016)
17. Hong, S.W., Cho, L.: Automatic recognition of flowers through color and edge based contour detection. In: International Conference on Image Processing Theory, Tools and Applications (2012)
18. Arwatchananukul, S., et al.: POC: *paphiopedilum* orchid classifier. In: IEEE 14th International Conference on Cognitive Informatics & Cognitive Computing, pp. 206–212 (2015)
19. Sani, M.M., et al.: Classification of orchid species using neural network. In: IEEE International Conference on Control System, Computing and Engineering, pp. 586–589 (2013)
20. Puttemans, S., Goedemé, T.: Visual detection and species classification of orchid flowers. In: International Conference on Machine Vision Applications, pp. 505–509 (2015)

Analysis of Repair Costs of Scholar Buildings Affected by Earthquakes Using Data Mining. Case Study: Earthquakes of 2017 in Mexico

Graciela García-Rueda[1], Rosa M. Valdovinos[1], Jesús Valdés-González[1], Roberto Alejo[2], J. Leonardo González-Ruiz[1(✉)], and José R. Marcial-Romero[1]

[1] Facultad de Ingeniería, UAEM, CU, Cerro de Coatepec, Toluca, Mexico
leon.g.ruiz@gmail.com
[2] Instituto Tecnológico de Toluca, Av. Tecnológico s/n, 52140 Metepec, Mexico

Abstract. Earthquakes are events that cannot be predicted. However, when they occur, devastating consequences are shown in economic, social and structural areas, among others. In this paper, the mining of association rules is carried out in order to estimate the repair cost required by schools affected during the earthquakes of September 7th and 19th, of 2017 in Mexico. For that, we use the public data collected by the Mexican FONDEN.

Keywords: Data Mining · Association Rules · Analysis of the seismic risk

1 Introduction

Throughout history, the structures collapse is a factor that generates the most material and human losses when earthquakes occur. This is mainly due to the use of low quality materials, deficiencies in construction processes and non-compliance with standards, among some other causes [1].

Data Mining (DM) support the diagnosis and analysis of the structures performance. According to the data characteristics collected after an earthquake, the DM techniques most used is the Association Rules (AR) [2]. An example of its application in earthquake is presented by Martínez-Álvarez et al. [3] who apply descriptive techniques for obtaining Quantitative AR (QAR), and uses a regression method (M5P Algorithm) for predict the earthquakes occurrence based on the relationship between Frequency and magnitude in order to observe the earthquakes variation. The QAR obtained showed that for earthquakes of moderate magnitude (between 3.5–4.4) earthquakes occur after short time intervals, while for high magnitudes (earthquakes of magnitude 4.4 to 6.2) the time intervals in relation to the Frequency and Magnitude had a significant decrease.

In similar way Galán Montaño F. [4] uses DM techniques to describe the behavior of earthquakes according to their magnitude too. In their study,

© Springer Nature Switzerland AG 2020
K. M. Figueroa Mora et al. (Eds.): MCPR 2020, LNCS 12088, pp. 45–56, 2020.
https://doi.org/10.1007/978-3-030-49076-8_5

Montaño uses a genetic algorithm capable of finding frequent patterns and obtain behavior models of the time series according to the occurrence of earthquakes. The result shown that before an earthquake of magnitude greater than 4.5 occurs, it is high probability that an earthquake of magnitude 4.4 occur.

On September 7th 2017, an earthquake of magnitude 8.2 was registered in Oaxaca, Mexico, which caused damage to 57,621 homes, 1,988 schools, 102 cultural buildings and 104 public buildings [5]. Few days after, on September 19th 2017 occurs another earthquake of magnitude 7.1 with epicenter in Puebla, which damaged more than 150 thousand homes in Oaxaca, Chiapas, Guerrero, Puebla, Morelos and State of Mexico, with an estimated repair cost up to 38,150 million of Mexican pesos [6].

After these two earthquakes, in the education sector were registered 12,931 schools with damages: 577 will require a total reconstruction, 1,847 a partial reconstruction and the remains with minor damages. The repair costs was estimated around to the 13,650 million of Mexican pesos [7]. Other structures with affectation were historical and culturally valuable buildings, such as the archaeological zone of Chiapa de Corzo, Zocalo of Mexico City, the National Museum of Art, among others, whose repair has an estimated cost of 8000 million of Mexican pesos [8]. In this paper we apply association rule mining for estimate the repair cost required for reconstructing school buildings damaged by the earthquakes of September 7th and 19th, using the data provided by the Fund of Budget Transparency (the Mexican FONDEN).

It is important regarding that the data bases obtained during the earthquakes of September 7th and 19th are the first of that type that have been obtained in Mexico. For structural engineering purposes the data bases are not full completed, but the data contained is valuable to do by first time a study of earthquake engineering based on DM. One of the main contribution of the work is to explore the use of DM in earthquake engineering. The rules obtained are valuable because they describe the distribution of earthquake damage costs as a function of some basic structural characteristics of the buildings. These rules are exclusive for the earthquakes of September 7th and 19th in México and for the studied structures. Currently, there are not any parallel study of structural engineering that allows to validate the rules.

2   Association Rules

The AR is a technique for discovering interesting associations or correlations from a transactional data set, where the rows represent the transactions and the column the *items* [9]. Let $I = \{i_1, i_2, ..., i_n\}$ be a set of n attributes or *items* and $D = \{t_1, t_2, ..., t_n\}$ a set of transactions in a data set. $\forall t_i \in D$, $\exists\, Tid$ as an unique identifier where $Tid \subset I$ [10].

An association rule can be defined as an implication of the form $X \Rightarrow Y$, where X is the antecedent and Y is the consequent of the rule. For example the rule $\{Bread, Cheese\} \Rightarrow \{Ham\}$, means that, when $Bread$ and $Cheese$ occur, Ham also occurs. For validate the quality of the rules and the probability that they reflect real relationships, two of the most used metrics for this purpose are [11]: **Support:** Probability P that a set of *items* appears in several transaction, $support(X \Rightarrow Y) = P(X \cup Y)$, and **Confidence:** Fraction of transactions in which X and Y appears, $confidence(X \Rightarrow Y) = \frac{support(X \cup Y)}{support(X)}$.

There are different algorithms for obtaining AR, however in this paper we use the Apriori algorithm and the PSO-GES metaheuristic.

2.1 Apriori Algorithm

The Apriori algorithm is one of the first methods developed for association rules mining and is currently one of the most used. Apriori consider two stages [11]: firstly the algorithm identifies all the frequent *itemsets* and then convert them to an AR (see Algorithm 1).

Algorithm 1. *Apriori*

Require: Data set D

   MinSupport \\minimum expected value of an item in transactions

   $i = 0$ $Full\_Item(C_i)$ \\Includes all size 1 items in C

1: **while** $C_i \neq \oslash$ **do**
2:   **for** $X =$ element of C_i **do**
3:     **if** $MinimumSupport(X) \geq MinimumSupport$ **then**
4:       $L_i = L_i \cup X$
5:     **end if**
6:     $C_{i+1} = SelectCandidates(L_i)$ \\ Candidates with the MinSupport established
7:     $i = i + 1$
8:   **end for**
9: **end while**
10: **return** C

2.2 PSO-GES

PSO-GES (see Algorithm 2) is a metaheuristic that generates quality AR with relatively low execution times. The algorithm consists of two stages: in the first stage, the dataset is transformed into a binary matrix and non-frequent items are eliminated. In the second stage, rule mining is carried out through a Guided Exploration Strategy. In which only those items that positively influence the fitness of a rule are added during the particle evolution process. This is done by computing fast estimating, using the summary matrix, values for the support and confidence of the rule represented by a new particle [9].

3   Experimental Set-Up

3.1   Database Description

Dataset used in this work corresponds to infrastructure affected of schools during earthquakes of September 2017 in Mexico (ES17M dataset)[1]. ES17M consists of 19,194 records and 76 features, which was designed by Structuralist Experts in seismic risk analysis [1]. Starting from the total features in ES17M, only the most relevant to seismic risk analysis were chosen, leading 36 of the 76 available features (Table 1). The last four rows (funding source) have six values: cost, total amount of attention, amount exercised and description, which gives a total of 36 items.

Algorithm 2. PSO-GES

Require: Number of particles N
   Number of iterations T
   Number of AR that they want to find M
   Dataset D
   Number of partitions K
   Minimum Support $MinSup$
   Minimum Confidence $MinConf$
   Inertia Factor w
   Acceleration constants c_1 and c_2
Ensure: Returns the M best association rules found $GBests$
1: $Table \leftarrow CreateTable(D, K)$
2: $POP \leftarrow CreatePopulation(N)$
3: **while** t<T **do**
4:   **for** $i \leftarrow 0$ a $size(POP)$ **do**
5:     **for** $j \leftarrow 0$ a $size(P_i^t)$ **do**
6:       $v_i^{(t+1)} \leftarrow w * v_{ij}^t + c_i * rand_1 * (PBest_{ij}^t - P_{ij}^t) + c_2 * rand_2 * (GBest_{ij}^t - P_{ij}^t)$
7:       $P_{ij}^{t+1} \leftarrow UpdatePosition(P_{ij}^{t+1}, j, v_{ij}^{t+1}, Table, MinSup, MinCof)$
8:     **end for**
9:     **if** $Fitness(P_i^{t+1}) > Fitness(PBest_i)$ **then**
10:       $PBest_i \leftarrow P_i^{t+1}$
11:     **end if**
12:     **if** $Fitness(P_i^{t+1}) > Fitness(GBest_i)$ **then**
13:       $GBest_i \leftarrow P_i^{t+1}$
14:     **end if**
15:   **end for**
16: **end while**
17: **return** GBests

3.2   Preprocessing Data

The following procedure was performed in order to properly format the ES17M dataset as an input for the Apriori and PSO-GES algorithms:

1. Standardized data. All data were transformed into categorical data, which are represented for integer numbers from 0–9. For example, cost was categorized in amounts like 1 of (0 to 1000), 2 of (1001 to 10,000), among others.

---

[1] Budget Transparency Fund, Fuerza México, available from https://www.transparen ciapresupuestaria.gob.mx/es/PTP/fuerzamexico.

Strings like "no aplica" were replaced for categorical numbers as 0. Similar string meaning were clustered, for example, "piso", "pisos", "superficie", were included in the same category represented for an integer number.

2. Structural features generation. These were obtained from pdf documents, jpg or png images from official documents. Distance to the epicenter was computed and its relationship with the closeness to geologic faults lines.

3. Discretized and transactional dataset. The dataset was transformed in a binary matrix where 1 value represents the presence of an *item* and 0 value determines the absence of such a *item*; where *items* were obtained on step 1.

Table 1. Summary of the main database characteristics

Attribute	Description
Event Date	Date on which the natural disaster occurred
Workplace	Identification Key in the SEP Catalog
Enrollment	Number of students enrolled in the Educational Center
Entity	Name of the federative entity, according to the INEGI catalog of federative entities
Municipality	Name of the municipality, according to the INEGI catalog of municipalities
Location	Name of the location, according to the INEGI catalog of locations
Latitude	Geo-referenced coordinate of the point where the affected infrastructure is located
Longitude	
Type of damage	Classification, according to its severity of the type of damage suffered by the infrastructure
Damage detail	Description of the damages/affectations that the Infrastructure has
URL dictum	Electronic address of the Structural Verification dictum
Costs	Sum of the value reported by source of financing, which are: • Educational Reform Program • Schools at the 100% • Natural Disaster Fund-Immediate Partial Supports • Natural Disaster Fund-Reconstruction • Private insurance • Other budgetary programs and own resources of the Federal Entity

(continued)

Table 1. (*continued*)

Attribute	Description
Total amount of attention, Amount exercised	Sum of the reported value and sum of the exerted value of the total amount by funding source after updates to the original cost, which are: • Educational Reform Program • Schools at the 100% • Natural Disaster Fund-Immediate Partial Supports • Natural Disaster Fund-Reconstruction • Private insurance • Other budgetary programs and own resources of the Federal Entity
Description	General description of the works to be carried out by financing, which are: • Educational Reform Program • Schools at the 100% • Natural Disaster Fund-Immediate Partial Supports • Natural Disaster Fund-Reconstruction • Private insurance • Other budgetary programs and own resources of the Federal Entity
Structural description	Type of structure established in the INIFED structure catalog

Final ES17M dataset (transactional dataset) was generated by keeping only the column number where the presence of an *item* to be 1.

3.3   Algorithms Configuration

Python library[2] was used to run the Apriori algorithm, and PSO-GES was executed with the author's proprietary code[3]. The minimum support threshold was 0.00002 for both algorithms and the confidence threshold= 0.75. Additional PSO-GES parameters used in this work were set as it was presented in Ref. [9]: Population of 20 particles, constants c_1 and $c_2 = 2$, inertia $w = 1$, 10 epoch and one transaction per partition ($K = 1$).

---

[2] efficient-apriori 1.1.0, https://pypi.org/project/efficient-apriori/.

[3] Bernal Baró G. [9].

4   Results

Due to the databases used do not provide enough information to formally conduct a comprehensive and detailed study of the risk and seismic behavior, the analysis was focused on analyze the relationship between the repair costs and type of construction with variables as: epicentral distance, construction type, damage and seismic zone. For the experiments, the algorithms were adapted in their execution, that is to say, the resulting RA should consider: the epicentral distance and type of construction in the antecedent and type of damage, detail of the damage, total repair cost and seismic zone in the consequent. Derived from the execution of the aforementioned algorithms, the rules generated by the PSO-GES algorithm are presented, since the obtained results provided better RA for the seismic analysis.

4.1   Earthquake of September 7th, 2017

From the AR obtained (Table 2) is possible to determine that most of the schools affected by the earthquake are located in the seismic zone C (intermediate zone, where not so frequent earthquakes) and present moderate damage, mainly in the structure and finishes stand out. Bar graph of Figure 1 shows the relation between the repair costs, the epicentral distance and type of construction. In this graph we can seen that the greatest damage occurred in those schools with masonry walls and concrete slab. Similarly, it is generally appreciated that repair costs decrease as schools move away from the epicenter of the earthquake. Thus, at a lower epicentral distance, repair costs are greater than the repair costs of schools that are located at a greater epicental distance.

4.2   Earthquake of September 19th, 2017

Table 3 shows the most important AR obtained with earthquake data from September 19th. The AR obtained show that most of the affected schools are located in seismic zones C and B (intermediate zones, where earthquakes are not so frequently recorded), which presented moderate and severe damage, mainly were structural, in finishes and outdoors. Figure 2 shows a bar graph that relates the distance from the earthquake epicenter to damaged schools with the repair cost and the type of structure. In this case we can see that the greatest damages occurred in schools that are at an epicentral distance of 101 to 150 km. As for the type of construction, the schools most affected were those built based on masonry walls and light technology.

Table 2. Earthquake association rules of September 7th 2017

Distance	Antecedent	Consequent	Distance	Antecedent	Consequent
101-150 KM	Masonry walls and concrete slab	Moderate damage, Zone C / Structural damage, finishes, electrical installations / Total repair cost of $32,643,208-$36,723,608	**201-250 KM**	Masonry walls and concrete slab	Minor damage, Zone C / Structural damage / Total repair cost of $28,562,807-$32,643,207
	Steel and concrete slab	Moderate damage, Zone C / Structural damage / Total repair cost of $816,0802-$12,241,202		Steel and concrete slab	Moderate damage, Zone C / Equipment damage, outdoors / Total repair cost of $20,402,005-$24,482,405
	Steel and light roof	Minor damage, Zone C / Damage finishes / Total repair cost of $12,241,203-$16,321,603		Steel and light roof	Moderate damage, Zone C / Structural damage / Total repair cost of $20,402,005-$24,482,405
	Masonry walls and light roof	Moderate damage, Zone C / Structural damage / Total repair cost of $24,482,406-$28,562,806		Masonry walls and light roof	Moderate damage, Zone C / Structural damage, outdoors, finishes / Total repair cost of $24,482,406-$28,562,806
151-200 KM	Masonry walls and concrete slab	Moderate damage, Zone C / Structural damage, finishes / Total repair cost of $40,804,010-$44,884,410	**251-300 KM**	Masonry walls and concrete slab	Minor damage, Zone C / Outdoors damage, structural / Total repair cost of $16,321,604-$20,402,004
	Steel and concrete slab	Moderate damage, Zone C / Structural damage and damage to hydraulic and sanitary installations / Total repair cost of $32,643,208-$36,723,608		Steel and concrete slab	Moderate damage, Zone C / Structural damage and damage to hydraulic and sanitary installations / Total repair cost of $20,402,005-$24,482,405
	Steel and light roof	Moderate damage, Zone C / Structural damage / Total repair cost of $32,643,208-$36,723,608		Steel and light roof	Moderate damage, Zone C / Structural damage / Total repair cost of $20,402,005-$24,482,405
	Masonry walls and light roof	Moderate damage, Zone C / Structural damage, finishes / Total repair cost of $816,0802-$12,241,202		Masonry walls and light roof	Moderate damage, Zone C / Structural damage, outdoors, finishes / Total repair cost of $20,402,005-$24,482,405

It is important to note that, in contrast with the AR obtained form the earthquake of September 7th, the highest repair costs are not found for the shortest epicentral distances. In this case, the highest costs were presented by intermediate epicentral distances. This is explained because the Mexico City is located just at this epicentral distance (100 to 150 km), so having a large number of schools, the repair costs were higher. From the seismic point of view, this is explained due to the soil characteristics in certain areas of Mexico City, were the seismic waves could be amplified. From a practical point of view, this effect was because the accelerations produced in these areas of Mexico City are comparable to those that occur at sites closer to the earthquake epicenter.

5   Discussion

Historically, the provision of public data related to the damage caused by the earthquakes in Mexico was almost null until 2017. The difficulty of field surveys, data truthfulness, capture and processing times are some of the causes that in the past decades they prevented obtain this information. However, given the advances in technology and the wide use of ICTs, the recording of the damages caused by the earthquakes of September 7th and 19th, 2017 constitutes an invaluable source of information for study the behavior, impact and seismic risk. It is still pending to homologate these databases and rethink the type of data that is collected, in order to being able to make more formal studies about the behavior and seismic risk of the constructions. However, having the databases used in this

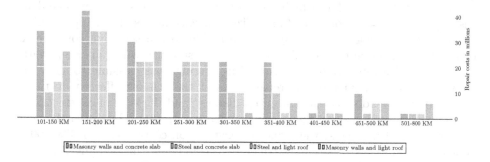

Fig. 1. Values included in the range of estimated costs of damage caused by the earthquake of September 7, 2017, depending on the epicentral distance and the type of construction.

Table 3. Earthquake Association Rules of September 19th 2017

	Antecedent	Consequent		Antecedent	Consequent
Distance 1-50 KM	Steel and Concrete Slab	Moderate damage, Zone C		Masonry Walls and Light Roofing	Severe damage, Zone B
		Structural damage			Structural damage
		Total repair cost of $28,562,807-$32,643,207			Total repair cost of $48,964,812-$53,045,212
	Masonry Walls and Light Roofing	Moderate damage, Zone C		Masonry Walls and concrete slab	Minor damage, Zone B
		Structural damage			Structural damage
		Total repair cost of $32,643,208-$36,723,608	**Distance 151-200 KM**		Total repair cost of $32,643,208-$36,723,608
Distance 51-100 KM	Masonry Walls and concrete slab	Moderate damage, Zone C		Steel and Concrete Slab	Minor damage, Zone B
		Structural damage			Structural damage, finishes
		Total repair cost of $32,643,208-$36,723,608			Total repair cost of $24,482,406-$28,562,806
	Steel and Concrete Slab	Moderate damage, Zone C		Steel and Light Roof	Minor damage, Zone B
		Structural damage			Structural damage, electrical installations
		Total repair cost of $36,723,609-$40,804,009			Total repair cost of $24,482,406-$28,562,806
	Steel and Light Roof	Moderate damage, Zone C		Masonry Walls and Light Roofing	Moderate damage, Zone B
		Structural damage			Structural damage
		Total repair cost of $32,643,208-$36,723,608			Total repair cost of $28,562,807-$32,643,207
	Masonry Walls and Light Roofing	Moderate damage, Zone C		Masonry Walls and concrete slab	Minor damage, Zone C
		Structural damage, finishes			Structural damage
		Total repair cost of $32,643,208-$36,723,608	**Distance 201-250 KM**		Total repair cost of $24,482,406-$28,562,806
Distance 101-150 KM	Masonry Walls and concrete slab	Severe damage, Zone D		Steel and Concrete Slab	Minor damage, Zone C
		Structural damage, finishes, outdoor			Daño estructural, equipo
		Total repair cost of $40,804,010-$44,884,410			Total repair cost of $24,482,406-$28,562,806
	Steel and Concrete Slab	Moderate damage, Zone B		Steel and Light Roof	Minor damage, Zone C
		Structural damage, finishes, outdoor			Structural damage, outdoor
		Total repair cost of $36,723,609-$40,804,009			Total repair cost of $24,482,406-$28,562,806
	Steel and Light Roof	Severe damage, Zone D			
		Structural damage, finishes, electrical, hydraulic and sanitary installations			
		Total repair cost of $44,884,411-$48,964,811			

work is already a great advance, because commonly other researchers are based on simulations or using only data as: latitude and longitude of the earthquake, magnitude, depth and location. However, this study can be used for different sectors such as health, housing, cultural heritage, among others, provided that the structure of the data is the same as that used in the case of studies.

In this sense, one of the main contributions of the research presented in this paper is the provision of a standardized knowledge base for using machine learning and DM algorithms, making it available to the scientific community for its exploitation and study. The initial results shown in this paper and with the support of an expert in Structural Engineering, was possible to show an overview of the behavior of the repair costs of the schools affected by these earthquakes, depending on the epicentral distance and the type of construction. It this way, it was found that the largest damage was produced by the earthquake of September 19th because the higher reconstruction costs exceed \$43'000,000, while the earthquake of September 7th needed costs below this amount. Also was possible to identify that for the earthquake of September 7th (with an epicenter on the Oaxaca coast), at greater epicentral distances the damages were lower compared with the costs recorded for schools located at an epicentral distances closest to the earthquake.

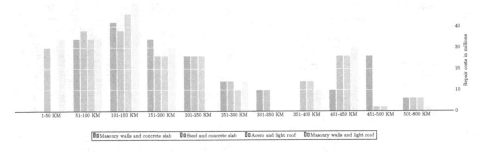

Fig. 2. Values in the range of estimated costs of damage caused by the earthquake of September 19, 2017, depending on the epicentral distance and the type of construction.

On the other hand, in the September 19th earthquake data, was observed how the repair costs increased for distances between 100 Km and 150 km. This behavior was congruent with the existing seismological models, that recognize an amplification of the accelerations in certain areas of Mexico City, which is located in this range of epicentral distances. This explains the increase in repair costs. Regarding the type of construction, it was possible to establish that the structures with masonry walls and light roof were the ones that presented the greatest damage in both earthquakes. With respect to the type of damage that occurred most, it correspond to the damage to the structure and finishes of the schools.

6   Conclusions and Future Works

With the results obtained, it is possible to conclude that the MD can be a useful tool to perform a seismic risk analysis, since it was capable to find relations among different variables related with studied earthquakes and structures. These variables were the distance from the earthquake epicenter to the schools, the type of structure (materials), the type of damage and the reparation costs. It is important to emphasize that the quality of the RA was stablished a confidence degree equal or greater than 75%. The study performed here was focused on obtain a description of the damages caused by the earthquakes of September 7th and 9th to the affected schools.

The open lines of study are initially oriented to study a priori the seismic risk of the constructions, that is, before an earthquake occurs, so the prediction is being worked on to determine the cost of a school if an earthquake of a certain magnitude occurs, having certain characteristics, located at a defined epicentral distance. In same way, is our interest to mining Association Rules for different scenarios of seismic risk analysis, taking specific values, either by the type of damage, seismic zone, federative entity, among other parameters of interest. In the same way, it is contemplated to replicate the preprocessing strategy to other types of buildings, such as hospitals and factories where the main challenge is to include the human losses that unfortunately occurred.

Acknowledgments. This work has been partially supported by the 5046/2020CIC UAEM project and the Mexican CONACYT under scholarship [930395].

References

1. Mondragón, F.P.: Estrategias para el modelado y el análisis sísmico de estructuras históricas. Ingeniería sísmica **1**(83), 1–7 (2010)
2. Gupta, S., Mamtora, R.: A survey on association rule mining in market basket analysis. Int. J. Inf. Comput. Technol. **4**(4), 409–414 (2014). ISSN:0974–2239
3. Álvaro, P.M.: Una metaheurística para la extracción de reglas de asociación. Aplicación a Terremotos. Master's thesis, Escuela Técnica Superior de Ingeniería Informática (2012)
4. Galán Montaño, F.J.: Metodología para el análisis de terremotos de gran magnitud. Master's thesis, Universidad de Sevilla (2013)
5. Ortiz, G.: Sismo de 8.2, el más intenso en casi un siglo en méxico, excelsior. https://www.excelsior.com.mx/nacional/2017/09/08/1187054. Accessed 16 Jan 2020
6. Milenio: Los daños por el sismo: reporte del gobierno federal. http://www.milenio.com/negocios/los-danos-por-el-sismo-reporte-del-gobierno-federal. Accessed 16 Jan 2020
7. EFE. Sep: reparar 12 mil 931 escuelas tras sismos costará 13 mil 650 mdp. http://www.eluniversal.com.mx/nacion/sociedad/reparar-12-mil-931-escuelas-tras-sismos-en-mexico-costara-760-millones-de-dolares. Accessed 16 Jan 2020
8. El Universal: Los monumentos dañados por el sismo del 19 de septiembre de 2017. http://www.eluniversal.com.mx/destinos/los-monumentos-danados-por-el-sismo-del-19-de-septiembre-de-2017. Accessed 16 Jan 2020

9. Gretel, B.B.: Diseño de una Metaheurística para el minado de reglas de asociación en bases de datos transaccionales. Master's thesis, Universidad Autónoma del Estado de México, Facultad de Ingeniería (2018)
10. Zyt, J., Klosgen, W., Zytkow, J.: Handbook of Data Mining and Knowledge Discovery. Oxford University Press, New York (2002)
11. Maria, R.Q., Orallo José, J.H., Cesar, F.R.: Introducción a la Minería de Datos. Pearson Prentice Hall (2004)

Basic Pattern Graphs for the Efficient Computation of Its Number of Independent Sets

Guillermo De Ita[ID], Miguel Rodríguez[✉][ID], Pedro Bello[ID], and Meliza Contreras[ID]

Faculty of Computer Science,
Benemérita Universidad Autónoma de Puebla, Puebla, Mexico
{deita,mrodriguez,pbello,mcontreras}@cs.buap.mx

Abstract. The problem of counting the number of independent sets of a graph G (denoted as $i(G)$) is a classic #P-complete problem. We present some patterns on graphs that allows us the polynomial computation of $i(G)$.

For example, we show that for a graph G where its set of cycles can be arranged as embedded cycles, $i(G)$ can be computed in polynomial time. Particularly, our proposal counts independent sets on outerplanar graphs.

Keywords: Recognition of graph patterns · Counting the number of independent sets · Exact counting

1 Introduction

Counting problems are not only mathematically interesting, but they arise in many applications. For example, if we want to know the probability that a formula in propositional calculus is true, or the probability that a graph remains connected given a probability of failure of an edge, we have to count to approximate such probabilities.

Regarding hard counting problems, the computation of the number of independent sets of a graph has been a key for determining the frontier between efficient counting and intractable counting procedures. Vadhan [8] showed that counting the number of independent sets in graphs of maximum degree 4 is #P-complete. Greenhill [3] refined the previous result showing that counting the number of independent sets on graphs of degree 3 is also #P-complete.

Following the line of exact algorithms, Dahllöf [1] has designed a method for counting independent sets and whose exact algorithm has a worst-case upper bound of $O(1.3247^n)$, n being the number of vertices of the input graph. While Okamoto [5] has shown a linear-time algorithm for counting the number of independent sets for chordal graphs. Efficient algorithms for counting independent

© Springer Nature Switzerland AG 2020
K. M. Figueroa Mora et al. (Eds.): MCPR 2020, LNCS 12088, pp. 57–66, 2020.
https://doi.org/10.1007/978-3-030-49076-8_6

sets have been achieved after to capture structure relations lying in the topology of the graphs, allowing to design special mathematical patterns for counting independent set only on those topologies.

On the other hand, many combinatorial problems ask about embeddings of graphs into other objects [4]. For instance, the polynomial time solvable *graph planarity* problem ask whether a given graph G can be embedded in the plane in such a way that no two edges intersect (except at a common endpoint). In our case, we are interested in a particular subclass of planar graphs, those graphs whose set of vertices can be arranged as incident with the outerface, this class of graphs are called outerplanar graphs. We present here, a novel algorithm for counting the number of independent sets on outerplanar graphs.

2   Notation

Let $G = (V, E)$ be an undirected graph with vertex set V and set of edges E. Two vertices v and w are called *adjacent* if there is an edge $\{v, w\} \in E$, connecting them. Sometimes, the shorthand notation of $u\ v$ is used for denoting the edge $\{u, v\} \in E$.

The *neighborhood* for $x \in V$ is $N(x) = \{y \in V : \{x, y\} \in E\}$ and its *closed neighborhood* is $N(x) \cup \{x\}$ which is denoted by $N[x]$. We denote the cardinality of a set A, by $|A|$. The degree of a vertex x, denoted by $\delta(x)$, is $|N(x)|$, and the degree of G is $\Delta(G) = max\{\delta(x) : x \in V\}$. The size of the neighborhood of x, $\delta(N(x))$, is $\delta(N(x)) = \sum_{y \in N(x)} \delta(y)$. A vertex v is *pendant* if $\delta(x) = 1$; and edge $e = \{x, y\}$ is *pendant* if x or y is a pendant vertex.

A path from v to w is a sequence of edges: $v_0 v_1, v_1 v_2, \ldots, v_{n-1} v_n$ such that $v = v_0$ and $v_n = w$ and v_k is adjacent to v_{k+1}, for $0 \le k < n$. The length of the path is n. A simple path is a path where $v_0, v_1, \ldots, v_{n-1}, v_n$ are all distinct. A cycle is a nonempty path such that the first and last vertices are identical, and a simple cycle is a cycle in which no vertex is repeated, except that the first and last vertices are identical. A graph G is acyclic if it has no cycles. P_n, C_n, R_n, K_n, N_n denote respectively, a path graph, a simple cycle, a start with one center node, the complete graph and the set of n nodes without any edge, all of those graphs have n vertices.

Given a graph $G = (V, E)$, let $G' = (V', E')$ be a subgraph of G if $V' \subseteq V$ and E' contains edges $v, w \in E$ such that $v \in V'$ and $w \in V'$. If E' contains every edge $v, w \in E$ where $v \in V'$ and $w \in V'$ then G' is called the *induced graph* of G. A *connected component* of G is a maximal induced subgraph of G, that is, a connected component is not a proper subgraph of any other connected subgraph of G. Note that, in a connected component, for every pair of its vertices x, y, there is a path from x to y. If an acyclic graph is also connected, then it is called a *free tree*.

Given a graph $G = (V, E)$, $S \subseteq V$ is an independent set in G if for every two vertices v_1, v_2 in S, $\{v_1, v_2\} \notin E$. Let $I(G)$ denote the set of all independent sets of G. An independent set $S \in I(G)$ is *maximal* if it is not a subset of any larger independent set and, it is *maximum* if it has the largest size among all independent sets in $I(G)$. The determination of the maximum independent set has received much attention since it is a NP-complete problem.

The corresponding counting problem on independent sets, denoted by $i(G)$, consists of counting the number of independent sets of a graph G. $i(G)$ is a #P-complete problem for graphs G where $\Delta(G) \geq 3$. $i(G)$ remains #P-complete when it is restricted to 3-regular graphs [3]. There are different polynomial procedures for computing $i(G)$ when $\Delta(G) \leq 2$ [1,6,7]. In fact, all of them have linear-time complexity. In the following sections, we present exact combinatorial procedures for computing $i(G)$ according to special patterns existing on the graphs.

3   Basic Graph Patterns for the Efficient Counting of Independent Sets

Since $i(G) = \prod_{i=1}^{k} i(G_i)$ where $G_i, i = 1, \ldots, k$ are the connected components of G [6], then the total time complexity for computing $i(G)$, denoted as $T(i(G))$, is given by the maximum rule as $T(i(G)) = max\{T(i(G_i)): G_i$ is a connected component of $G\}$. Thus, a first helpful decomposition of the graph is done via its connected components and from here on, we consider as an input graph only one connected component. We start analyzing the most simple cases for one connected component.

Case A:
Let $P_n = G = (V, E)$ be a graph consisting of a single sequence of nodes (path), i.e. $V = \{1, 2, ..., n\}$ and there exists an edge $e_i = \{i, i+1\}, i = 1, \ldots, n-1$, for each pair of sequential vertices.

We build the family $f_i = \{G_i\}, i = 1, \ldots, n$ where each $G_i = (V_i, E_i)$ is the induced graph of G formed by just the first i vertices of V.

We associate to each vertex $v_i \in V$ a pair (α_i, β_i) where α_i expresses the number of sets in $I(G_i)$ where the vertex v_i does not appear, while β_i conveys the number of sets in $I(G_i)$ where the vertex v_i appears, thus $i(G_i) = \alpha_i + \beta_i$.

The first pair (α_1, β_1) is $(1, 1)$ since for the induced subgraph $G_1 = \{v_1\}$, $I(G_1) = \{\emptyset, \{v_1\}\}$. If we know the value for (α_i, β_i) for any $i < n$, and as the next induced subgraph G_{i+1} is built from G_i adding the vertex v_{i+1} and the edge $\{v_i, v_{i+1}\}$, it is not hard to see that the pair $(\alpha_{i+1}, \beta_{i+1})$ is built from (α_i, β_i) applying the recurrence equation:

$$\alpha_{i+1} = \alpha_i + \beta_i \quad ; \quad \beta_{i+1} = \alpha_i \tag{1}$$

The series (α_i, β_i), $i=1,...,n$, built from recurrence (1), lead to $i(G_i) = \alpha_i + \beta_i$ for $i = 1, ..., n$. Thus, the computation of $i(G)$ is based on the incremental calculation of $i(G_i), i = 1, \ldots, n$. If we perform a linear search on the sequential graph G starting at an extreme, e.g. beginning at v_1 and moving to its incident vertex while the recurrence (1) is applied, then in linear time on the number of vertices, the formula $i(P_n) = i(G_n) = \alpha_n + \beta_n = F_{n+2}$ is obtained, and where F_n is the $nth-$Fibonacci number.

In order to process the number of independent sets on a path we will use *computing threads* or just *threads*. A computing thread is a sequence of pairs $(\alpha_i, \beta_i), i = 1, \ldots, n$ used for computing the number of independent sets on a path of n vertices.

Case B:
Let $G = (V, E)$ be a tree. Traversing G in depth first build a rooted tree, whose root node is any vertex $v \in V$, where v was the initial node for beginning the depth first search. We denote with (α_v, β_v) the pair associated with the node v ($v \in G$). We compute $i(G)$ while we are traversing by G in post-order.
Algorithm Count_Ind_Sets_trees(G
Input: G - a tree graph.
Output: The number of independent sets of G
Procedure:
Traversing G in post-order, and when a node $v \in G$ is left, assign:

1. $(\alpha_v, \beta_v) = (1, 1)$ if v is a leaf node in G.
2. If v is a parent node with a list of child nodes associated, i.e., $u_1, u_2, \ldots, u_k$ are the child nodes of v, as we have already visited all child nodes, then each pair $(\alpha_{u_j}, \beta_{u_j})$ $j = 1, \ldots, k$ has been determined based on recurrence (1). Then, let $\alpha_v = \prod_{j=1}^{k} \alpha_{v_j}$ and $\beta_v = \prod_{j=1}^{k} \beta_{v_j}$. Notice that this step includes the case when v has just one child node.
3. If v is the root node of G then return($\alpha_v + \beta_v$).

This procedure returns the number of independent sets of G in time $O(n + m)$ which is the necessary time for traversing G in post-order.

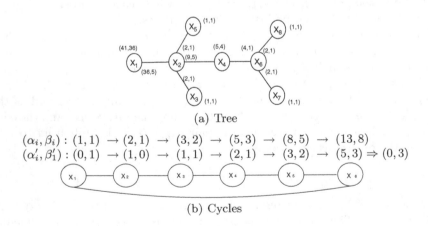

(a) Tree

$(\alpha_i, \beta_i) : (1, 1) \rightarrow (2, 1) \rightarrow (3, 2) \rightarrow (5, 3) \rightarrow (8, 5) \rightarrow (13, 8)$
$(\alpha_i', \beta_i') : (0, 1) \rightarrow (1, 0) \rightarrow (1, 1) \rightarrow (2, 1) \rightarrow (3, 2) \rightarrow (5, 3) \Rightarrow (0, 3)$

(b) Cycles

Fig. 1. Counting independent sets over trees and cycles

Example 1. *If $G = \{(x_1, x_2), (x_2, x_3), (x_2, x_4), (x_2, x_5), (x_4, x_6), (x_6, x_7), (x_6, x_8)\}$ is a tree, we consider the post-order search and let x_1 be the root node of the tree. The number of independent sets at each level of the tree is shown in Fig. 1(a). The procedure Count_Ind_Sets_trees returns for $\alpha_{x_1} = 41$, $\beta_{x_1} = 36$ and the total number of independent sets is: $i(G) = 41 + 36 = 77$.*

Case C:

Other basic case is when $G = (V, E)$, $n = m = |V| = |E|$ is a simple cycle, i.e. every vertex in V has degree two. In this case, the cycle can be decomposed as: $G = G' \cup \{c_m\}$, where $G' = (V, E')$, $E' = \{c_1, ..., c_{m-1}\}$. G' is a path of n vertices, and $c_m = \{v_m, v_1\}$ is called as back edge of the simple cycle G.

Observe that every independent set of G is an independent set of G', that is, $I(G) \subseteq I(G')$ since G has one edge more than G'. Thus, if $S \in I(G')$ and $v_1 \in S$ and $v_m \in S$ then S is not an independent set of G. Then, $I(G)$ can be built from $I(G')$ by eliminating those independent sets containing the vertices: v_1 and v_m, that is expressed in the following equation:

$$i(G) = i(G') - |\{S \in I(G') : v_1 \in S \wedge v_m \in S\}| \qquad (2)$$

For counting independent sets on a simple cycle, we can use two threads, one of those for computing $i(G')$ and the other thread for computing $|\{S \in I(G') : v_1 \in S \wedge v_m \in S\}|$. This last value can be computed fixing on $I(G')$ the independent sets where v_1 is involved, which is done by computing a thread $(\alpha'_i, \beta'_i), i = 1, ..., m$ where the pair $(\alpha'_1, \beta'_1) = (0, 1)$, considering in this way only the independent sets of $I(G')$ where v_1 appears. We apply (1) for computing the new series: (α'_i, β'_i), $i = 2, ..., m$ and also, in order to consider only the independent sets where v_m appears, the final pair (α'_m, β'_m) is taken only as $(0, \beta'_m)$.

In the following examples, we denote with $\rightarrow$ the application of recurrence (1) on (α_i, β_i) in order to obtain $(\alpha_{i+1}, \beta_{i+1})$. And, if we express the new series in terms of Fibonacci numbers, we have that $(\alpha'_1, \beta'_1) = (0, 1) = (F_0, F_1) \rightarrow (\alpha'_2, \beta'_2) = (1, 0) = (F_1, F_0) \rightarrow (\alpha'_3, \beta'_3) = (1, 1) = (F_2, F_1), ..., (\alpha'_m, \beta'_m) = (F_{m-1}, F_{m-2})$, and the value for the final pair $(\alpha'_m, \beta'_m) = (0, \beta'_m)$ is $(0, F_{m-2})$, then $|\{S \in I(G') : v_1 \in S \wedge v_m \in S\}| = 0 + \beta_m = F_{m-2}$.

Then, $i(G) = i(G') - |\{S \in I(G') : v_1 \in S \wedge v_m \in S\}| = \alpha_m + \beta_m - \beta'_m = F_{m+2} - F_{m-2}$. Thus, the following theorem is inferred.

Theorem 1. *If G is a simple cycle with n vertices then the number of independent sets of G, expressed in terms of the Fibonacci numbers, is: $i(G) = F_{n+2} - F_{n-2}$.*

Example 2. *Let $E = \{c_i\}_{i=1}^6 = \{\{x_1, x_2\}, \{x_2, x_3\}, \{x_3, x_4\}, \{x_4, x_5\}, \{x_5, x_6\}, \{x_6, x_1\}\}$ be the set of edges of a simple cycle $G = (V, E)$. Let $G' = (V, E')$ where $E = E' \cup \{c_6\}$, so G' is G without edge c_6. As G' is a sequence of 6 vertices then $i(G') = F_{6+2} = 21$. While the value for $|\{S \in I(G') : x_1 \in S \wedge x_6 \in S\}|$ is $F_{6-2} = 3$. Then, $i(G) = 21 - 3 = 18$ the computing is shown in Fig. 1(b).*

All the above graph topologies (case A, B and C) represent basic graph patterns that can be recognized and processed to compute its number of independent sets in linear-time. We call *Linear_NI* to the linear procedure that consists of the above three cases (A, B and C). *Linear_NI* will be applied to process any acyclic graph or simple cycles that we find as part of a more complex graph. In fact, in [2] a polynomial-time algorithm has been shown to compute $i(G)$ when G has linear compositions of the above patterns. We can now ask if there exists a family of cyclic connected graphs whose number of independent sets can be computed efficiently, in the next section, we show some families that fulfill this requirement.

4   Recognition of Embedded Cycles

Let $G = (V, E)$ be a connected graph with $n = |V|$, $m = |E|$ and such that $\Delta(G) \geq 2$.

In order to recognize more graph patterns for the efficient computation of $i(G)$, we present the case of the computation of $i(G)$ for outerplanar graphs. For this case, we introduce concepts about the decomposition of a graph by its set of embedded cycles.

If a depth-first search (abbreviated as dfs) is applied over G, starting the search, for example, with the vertex $v_r \in V$ of minimum degree, and selecting among different potential vertices to visit the vertex with minimum degree first and with minimum value in its label as a second criterion, we obtain an unique depth-first graph G' (into the set of all possible depth-first graphs), which we will denote as $G' = dfs(G)$. This dfs also builds an unique spanning tree T_G with v_r as the root node. In time $O(m+n)$, the dfs allows us to detect if G has cycles or not, and the edges forming each cycle. The edges in T_G are called *tree edges*, whereas the edges in $E(G) \backslash E(T_G)$ are called *back edges*. Let $e \in E(G) \backslash E(T_G)$ be a back edge, the union of the path in T_G between the endpoints of e with the edge e itself forms a simple cycle, such cycle is called a basic (or fundamental) cycle of G with respect to T_G. Each back edge $e = \{x, y\}$ holds the maximum path contained in the basic cycle that it is part of. We will call to such maximum path, the *internal path* of a fundamental cycle. Assuming that x is visited first than y during the dfs, we say that x is the start-vertex and y is the end-vertex of the back edge.

According to our particular depth-first search $G' = dfs(G)$ on G, we denote $\mathcal{C} = \{C_1, C_2, ..., C_t\}$ as the set of fundamental cycles found during such depth-first search. Notice that the combination of the procedure for trees and the processing of cycles (Eq. 2) can be applied for computing $i(G)$ if G is a graph where the depth-first search generates a tree and a set of independent fundamental cycles.

If two distinct base cycles C_i and C_j from $\mathcal{C}$ have common edges then we say that both cycles are *intersected*, that is, $C_i \triangle C_j$ form a new cycle, where $\triangle$ denotes the symmetric difference operation between the set of edges in both cycles. In fact, $C_i \triangle C_j = (E(C_i) \cup E(C_j)) - (E(C_i) \cap E(C_j))$ forms a composed cycle. If two cycles are non-intersected we say that they are *independent*. I.e. two independent cycles (C_i, C_j) hold $(E(C_i) \cap E(C_j)) = \emptyset$. Notice that $t = m - n + 1$ is the dimension of the $\mathbb{Z}_2$-vector space with the symmetric difference on the edge sets as addition, and $\mathcal{C}$ is a base in that $\mathbb{Z}_2$-vector space.

For an outerplanar graph G_o, the cycles in G_o can be considered as embedded cycles, see e.g. Fig. 2. In order to recognize when two cycles C_i and C_j can be expressed as embedded cycles, we use the or-exclusive operation. Given two intersected cycles C_i, C_j, we say that C_i is embedded into C_j, if:

a) $V(C_i) \subset V(C_j)$: the set of vertices of C_i is a subset of the vertices of C_j.

b) $|E(C_i) - E(C_j)| = 1$: there is only one edge from C_i which is not edge of C_j.

c) $C_i \oplus C_j = C_k$: being C_k a new cycle distinct to C_i and C_j and $\oplus$ is the or-exclusive operation between the edges of the cycles.

If the cycles C_i and C_j hold the previous three conditions, we say that C_i is embedded into C_j. Meanwhile, C_j is a cycle that semi-encloses C_i.

4.1   Processing Outerplanar Graphs

An outerplanar graph G_o could be redrawn in a planar way, where any pair of basic cycles is independent, or one of them is embedded into the other. Thus, G_o is planar, and all its vertices are not enclosed by any edge. Generating a planar drawing is often viewed as a separate problem, in part because drawing algorithms tend to create a planar embedding as a first step, and in part because drawing can be application dependent. In particular, a graph G_o is outerplanar if K_4 and $K_{2,3}$ are forbidden as a minus of G_o. Outerplanar graphs can be recognized in linear-time [9].

The embedding is a transitive characteristic among embedded cycles. If C_i is embedded into C_j, and C_j is embedded into C_k, then C_i is embedded into C_k. On the other hand, if C_i and C_j are two independent cycles, e.g. $(E(C_i) \cap E(C_j)) = \emptyset$, but there exists a cycle C_k such that C_i and C_j are embedded into C_k, e.g. $(V(C_i) \subset V(C_k))$ and $(V(C_j) \subset V(C_k))$, then we say that (C_k, C_j, C_i) is a tuple of embedded cycles.

A maximal list of embedded cycles $D = (C_1, C_2, \ldots, C_k)$ is a tuple of cycles such that for $i < k$, C_{i+1} is embedded into C_i, $i = 1, \ldots, k-1$, or there exists C_j in the tuple with $j < i \leq k$ such that C_i is embedded into C_j. In a maximal list of embedded cycles $D = (C_1, C_2, \ldots, C_k)$, the cycles are ordered by setting first the most external cycle followed by its internal cycle until arriving to C_k, which is the most internal cycle of the set of embedded cycles. Notice that a maximal list of embedded cycles D is also a graph that we denote by D.

Given a maximal list $D = (C_1, C_2, \ldots, C_k)$ of embedded cycles, the spanning tree of D is called the path of D and it is denoted by P_D. We consider an orientation on P_D; from left to right, or from down to up, according to the drawing of D. The first vertex v_0 of P_D is called the initial vertex of D. Meanwhile, the last vertex v_f of P_D is called the final vertex of D. We will denote as (α_i, β_i) to the pair associated to the vertex $v_i \in V(P_D)$. Given a maximal list of embedded cycles D, we present in this section how to compute $i(D)$.

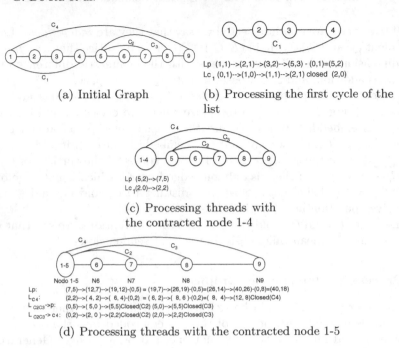

(a) Initial Graph

(b) Processing the first cycle of the list

(c) Processing threads with the contracted node 1-4

(d) Processing threads with the contracted node 1-5

Fig. 2. Computing $i(D)$ with D a maximal list of embedded cycles

Theorem 2. *Given a maximal list of embedded cycles D, $i(D)$ is computed in linear-time on the size of D.*

Proof. We present as proof a linear-time algorithm for the computation of $i(D)$. A main thread, denoted by Lp, is associated to P_D. This thread is always active during all the counting process.

The computation of $i(D)$ is done by traversing in depth-first order the path P_D from its initial node v_0 to its final node v_f. The cycles in D are visited from the most external to the internal cycles according to the depth-first search. Each cycle $C_i, i = 1, 2, \ldots, k$ has a corresponding computing thread L_{C_i}. The computation of $i(C_i)$ follows the case (C) for a simple cycle, described in the previous section. Recurrence (1) is applied on the current pairs $(\alpha_i, \beta_i)_{LC} \rightarrow (\alpha_i + \beta_i, \alpha_i)_{LC}$ when a new vertex v_{i+1} of P_D is visited. Each time that an initial vertex of a cycle C_i is visited, the pair $(0, \beta_l)$ is associated to the thread L_{C_i}, where β_l is the value of the second component of the pair (α_l, β_l) associated to Lp, see e.g. Figs. 2(b) and 2(d). When the computation arrives to the end-vertex v of a cycle C_j with corresponding pairs $(\alpha_v, \beta_v)_{C_j}$, then the pair $(0, \beta_v)$ is subtracted to all current computing thread. Afterwards, the computing thread L_{C_j} is closed and stops from being in the computation of $i(D)$. When a cycle C_j has been computed, C_j may be contracted in only one vertex v_{C_j}, and the pair $(\alpha_{C_j}, \beta_{C_j})$, which resulted from the processing of the cycle C_j, is associated to v_{C_j}.

This process continues processing all cycle in D until the depth-first search arrives to the final vertex v_f of D. If (α_f, β_f) is the pair associated to v_f, then $i(D) = \alpha_f + \beta_f$.

We illustrate in the following example, the computation of $i(D)$ when D is a maximal list of embedded cycles.

Example 3. *In Fig. 2(a), we show the input list of embedded cycles D. In Fig. 2(b), as the first cycle of the list is computed, then two computing threads are formed. The path of D is visited in linear way, and at the same time, the recurrence (1) is applied on the current pairs of the computing threads, see Fig. 2(c). Finally, Fig. 2(d) shows the final process of computing on all active threads giving as a result that $i(D) = 40 + 18 = 58$.*

All outerplanar graph can be decomposed in a set of maximal list embedded cycles. For this, let us consider as input to $G_o = (V, E)$ an outerplanar graph. We associate a tree T, called the embedding tree of G_o. Given an embedding tree T of a maximal list of embedded cycles, the final vertex v_f of the list is selected as the root node of T, which make to T a rooted embedding tree. The construction of T satisfies the following properties.

1. The nodes of T are maximal list of embedded cycles.
2. Two nodes v_a, v_b of T are adjacent only if the root vertex of v_a is an internal vertex of the maximal embedding of v_b.
3. For every vertex $v \in V(G_o)$, the subgraph $T_v \subset T$ induced by the maximal embedded cycles containing v is a tree.

Each node v_t of an embedding tree T is formed by a maximal list of embedded cycles, where the final vertex v_f of the list of embedded cycles will be the root node for the subtree $T_{v_t} \subset T$. We show in Fig. 3 a decomposition of an outerplanar graph G_o in its set of maximal embedded cycles, and the formation of the embedding tree T of G_o.

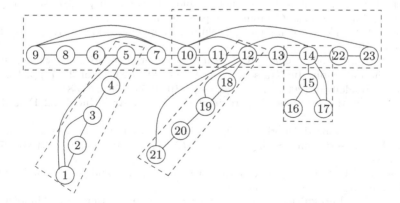

Fig. 3. A decomposition of an outerplanar graph G_o in its set of maximal embedded cycles

Theorem 3. *Let G_o be an outerplanar graph and let T be the embedding tree of G_o, then $i(G_o)$ is computed in polynomial time on the size of G_o.*

Proof. We present as proof a polynomial time algorithm for the computation of $i(G_o)$. A pre-order search on the embedding tree T follows the linear-time procedure developed in the case (B) of the previous section for computing the number of independent sets on tree topologies. Meanwhile, the algorithm presented in Theorem (3) is applied for computing $i(v_t)$ when a node $v_t \in V(T)$ is visited. The combination of both procedures builds a method for the computation of $i(T)$ in polynomial time on the size of the input graph G_o.

5   Conclusions

Computing the number of independent sets of a graph G, denoted as $i(G)$, is a classic #P-complete problem for graphs of degree 3 or higher. We establish that if the depth-first graph of a given graph G has no intersected cycles, then the computation of $i(G)$ is a tractable problem. We have presented a novel algorithm for computing $i(G)$ for any outerplanar graph G.

Our proposal for computing $i(G)$ do not impose restrictions on the degree of the graph, but rather, it depends on its topological structure. Those previous cases allows to establish a finer border between the classes FP and #P for the problem of counting independent sets. Furthermore, our proposal can be adapted to consider other counting problems.

References

1. Dahllöf, V., Jonsson, P.: An algorithm for counting maximum weighted independent sets and its applications. In: Proceedings of Thirteenth Annual ACM-SIAM Symposium on Discrete Algorithms, pp. 292–298. ACM, San Francisco (2002)
2. De Ita, G., López-López, A.: A worst-case time upper bound for counting the number of independent sets. In: Janssen, J., Pralat, P. (eds.) CAAN 2007. LNCS, vol. 4852, pp. 85–98. Springer, Heidelberg (2007). https://doi.org/10.1007/978-3-540-77294-1_9
3. Greenhill, C.: The complexity of counting colourings and independent sets in sparse graphs and hypergraphs. Comput. Complex. **9**(1), 52–72 (2000)
4. Johnson, D.S.: The NP-completeness column: an ongoing guide. J. Algorithms **6**(3), 434–451 (1985)
5. Okamoto, Y., Uno, T., Uehara, R.: Linear-time counting algorithms for independent sets in chordal graphs. In: Kratsch, D. (ed.) WG 2005. LNCS, vol. 3787, pp. 433–444. Springer, Heidelberg (2005). https://doi.org/10.1007/11604686_38
6. Roth, D.: On the hardness of approximate reasoning. Artif. Intell. **82**(1), 273–302 (1996)
7. Russ, B.: Randomized Algorithms: Approximation. Generation, and Counting. Distinguished Dissertations. Springer, London (2001). https://doi.org/10.1007/978-1-4471-0695-1
8. Vadhan, P.: The complexity of counting in sparse, regular, and planar graphs. SIAM J. Comput. **31**(2), 398–427 (2001)
9. Wiegers, M.: Recognizing outerplanar graphs in linear time. In: Tinhofer, G., Schmidt, G. (eds.) WG 1986. LNCS, vol. 246, pp. 165–176. Springer, Heidelberg (1987). https://doi.org/10.1007/3-540-17218-1_57

Towards Selecting Reducts for Building Decision Rules for Rule-Based Classifiers

Manuel S. Lazo-Cortés[1]([✉]), José Fco. Martínez-Trinidad[2],
Jesús A. Carrasco-Ochoa[2], and Nelva N. Almanza-Ortega[1]

[1] TecNM/Instituto Tecnológico de Tlalnepantla, Tlalnepantla de Baz, Mexico
{manuel.lc,nelva.ao}@tlalnepantla.tecnm.mx
[2] Instituto Nacional de Astrofísica, Óptica y Electrónica,
Sta. Ma. Tonantzintla, Mexico
{fmartine,ariel}@inaoep.mx

Abstract. In rule-based classifiers, calculating all possible rules of a learning sample consumes many resources due to its exponential complexity. Therefore, finding ways to reduce the number and length of the rules without affecting the efficacy of a classifier remains an interesting problem. Reducts from rough set theory have been used to build rule-based classifiers by their conciseness and understanding. However, the accuracy of the classifiers based on these rules depends on the selected rule subset. In this work, we focus on analyzing three different options for using reducts for building decision rules for rule-based classifiers.

1 Introduction

Rule-base classification is a Data Mining technique that consists in, given a set of training instances, identifying certain characteristics of the instances to construct rules that are later used for classifying new instances. Rule-based classifiers are easy to interpret, easy to generate and can correctly classify new instances. The advantages of rule-based classifiers are that they are extremely expressive since they are symbolic and operate with data attributes without any transformation.

The calculation of all possible rules of a training sample is a task that requires many computational resources due to its exponential complexity. So, finding ways to reduce the number of rules without affecting the accuracy of a classifier is still an open research problem, see for example [7].

On the other hand, feature selection is a significant task in supervised classification and other problems of pattern recognition focused on eliminating irrelevant and/or redundant attributes [10]. It consists in selecting subsets of the whole set of attributes to reduce the space dimension according to certain criteria.

The objective of reducing the dimensions is to find a minimum (or almost minimum) set of attributes that retains all the essential information of the training sample for further tasks of classification or description. Reducing the dimension can help to reduce the number of generated rules, as well as their length. These rules would be simpler and easier to interpret. Then, in practical applications, minimum length descriptions are preferred (see for example [1,5,6,16]).

© Springer Nature Switzerland AG 2020
K. M. Figueroa Mora et al. (Eds.): MCPR 2020, LNCS 12088, pp. 67–75, 2020.
https://doi.org/10.1007/978-3-030-49076-8_7

Reducts have been used to build classifiers based on rules [8,9]. A reduct is a minimum subset of attributes that retains the same discernibility capacity as the whole set of attributes when considering objects belonging to different classes [12]. Decision rules derived from reducts are useful in practice because of their conciseness and understandability. Nevertheless, usually the number of reducts is too high and consequently the number of rules is too high too.

In this work, we focus our effort on analyzing the following three questions at using reducts for building rules in rule-based classifiers: should we use all the reducts? Is it enough to use a single reduct? Is it enough using only the shortest reducts?

Here, we present a controlled experimentation as an approach to discuss the above questions. The rest of the document is organized as follows. Section 2 provides some preliminary concepts. In Sect. 3, we present the experiments and discuss the results. Our conclusions are summarized in Sect. 4.

2 Preliminaries

In this section, we present some definitions and notations to make the paper more understandable.

2.1 Reducts

In Rough Set Theory [12], the main data representation is a decision table, which is a special case of an information table. Formally, a decision table is defined as

Definition 1 *(decision table). A decision table is a pair* $S_d = (\mathcal{U}, A_t)$ *where* $\mathcal{U}$ *denotes the set of objects under study,* A_t *is the set of attributes used to describe the objects.*

It is important to introduce the definition of the indiscernibility relation.

Definition 2 *(indiscernibility relation). Given a subset of conditional attributes* $A \subseteq A_t$, *the indiscernibility relation is defined as* $IND(A|\mathbf{d}) = \{(u,v) \in \mathcal{U} \times \mathcal{U} :$ $\forall \mathbf{a} \in A, [\mathbf{a}(u) = \mathbf{a}(v)] \vee [\mathbf{d}(u) = \mathbf{d}(v)]\}$, *where* $\mathbf{a}(u)$ *denotes the value of the attribute* $\mathbf{a}$ *for the object* u.

We can find several definitions of reduct (see for example, [11]), nevertheless, according to the aim of this paper, we refer to reducts assuming the classical definition of discerning decision reduct [13] as follows.

Definition 3 *(reduct). Given a decision table* S_d, *an attribute set* $R \subseteq A_t$ *is called a reduct, if* R *satisfies the following two conditions:*

(i) $IND(R|\mathbf{d}) = IND(A_t|\mathbf{d})$;
(ii) *For any* $\mathbf{a} \in R, IND((R - \{\mathbf{a}\})|\mathbf{d}) \neq IND(A_t|\mathbf{d})$.

All attribute subsets satisfying condition (i) are called super-reducts.

This definition ensures that a reduct has no lower ability to distinguish objects belonging to different classes than the whole set of attributes, being minimal with regard to inclusion, i.e. a reduct does not contain redundant attributes or, equivalently, a reduct does not include other super-reducts. The original idea of reduct is based on inter-class comparisons.

Example 1. Given the following decision table, where $A_t = \{a_1, a_2, a_3, a_4, a_5\}$ is the set of attributes, $\mathcal{U} = \{u_1, u_2, u_3, u_4, u_5, u_6, u_7, u_8\}$ is the set of objects and **d** is the decision attribute.

$$M = \begin{array}{c|cccccc} & a_1 & a_2 & a_3 & a_4 & a_5 & \mathbf{d} \\ \hline u_1 & 4 & high & 0 & GR & 0 & 1 \\ u_2 & 3 & high & 1 & MX & 1 & 1 \\ u_3 & 3 & low & 0 & MX & 2 & 1 \\ u_4 & 2 & low & 1 & GR & 0 & 1 \\ u_5 & 5 & high & 1 & BC & 3 & 2 \\ u_6 & 7 & veryhigh & 1 & HG & 4 & 2 \\ u_7 & 7 & medium & 1 & TM & 3 & 3 \\ u_8 & 8 & medium & 0 & BC & 1 & 3 \end{array}$$

We have that $\{a_1, a_2\}$, $\{a_2, a_4\}$, $\{a_3, a_4\}$ and $\{a_1, a_3, a_5\}$ are reducts. Notice that for example $\{a_2, a_3\}$ does not fulfill the definition of reduct, since $\mathbf{a_2}(u_2) = \mathbf{a_2}(u_5) = high$ and $\mathbf{a_3}(u_2) = \mathbf{a_3}(u_5) = 1$ being $1 = \mathbf{d}(u_2) \neq \mathbf{d}(u_5) = 2$.

If in M we just keep the columns belonging to a reduct, you can easily see that the classes remain distinguishable, and each column is essential for that purpose.

M_1, M_2, M_3 and M_4 are the resulting decision tables when the representation space is reduced respectively to each one of the reducts.

$$M_1 = \begin{array}{c|ccc} & a_1 & a_2 & \mathbf{d} \\ \hline u_1 & 4 & high & 1 \\ u_2 & 3 & high & 1 \\ u_3 & 3 & low & 1 \\ u_4 & 2 & low & 1 \\ u_5 & 5 & high & 2 \\ u_6 & 7 & veryhigh & 2 \\ u_7 & 7 & medium & 3 \\ u_8 & 8 & medium & 3 \end{array}$$

$$M_2 = \begin{array}{c|ccc} & a_2 & a_4 & \mathbf{d} \\ \hline u_1 & high & GR & 1 \\ u_2 & high & MX & 1 \\ u_3 & low & MX & 1 \\ u_4 & low & GR & 1 \\ u_5 & high & BC & 2 \\ u_6 & veryhigh & HG & 2 \\ u_7 & medium & TM & 3 \\ u_8 & medium & BC & 3 \end{array}$$

$$M_3 = \begin{array}{c} \\ u_1 \\ u_2 \\ u_3 \\ u_4 \\ u_5 \\ u_6 \\ u_7 \\ u_8 \end{array} \begin{pmatrix} a_3 & a_4 & \mathbf{d} \\ 0 & GR & 1 \\ 1 & MX & 1 \\ 0 & MX & 1 \\ 1 & GR & 1 \\ 1 & BC & 2 \\ 1 & HG & 2 \\ 1 & TM & 3 \\ 0 & BC & 3 \end{pmatrix} \qquad M_4 = \begin{array}{c} \\ u_1 \\ u_2 \\ u_3 \\ u_4 \\ u_5 \\ u_6 \\ u_7 \\ u_8 \end{array} \begin{pmatrix} a_1 & a_3 & a_5 & \mathbf{d} \\ 4 & 0 & 0 & 1 \\ 3 & 1 & 1 & 1 \\ 3 & 0 & 2 & 1 \\ 2 & 1 & 0 & 1 \\ 5 & 1 & 3 & 2 \\ 7 & 1 & 4 & 2 \\ 7 & 1 & 3 & 3 \\ 8 & 0 & 1 & 3 \end{pmatrix}$$

2.2   Rule-Based Classifier

The generation of effective rules is essential for the development of any classifier that is easily understandable by the user. Any mechanism used for rule generation must maintain the underlying semantics of the feature set.

Typically, rule-based classifiers are sensitive to the dimensionality of the dataset since a large number of superfluous or redundant rules may appear. This makes it advisable to try to reduce the dimensionality of the data, and/or the length or complexity of the rules so that the resulting set of learned rules becomes manageable and can overcome the classification results obtained by using rules containing too many attributes.

To build the set of decision rules to be used in our rule-based classifiers, we used the tools included in the software RSES ver. 2.2.2 [4], which has been widely used in the literature, see for example [3,14,15].

In RSES, once the reducts of a decision table have been computed, each object in the training sample is matched against each reduct. This matching gives as result a rule having in its conditional part, the attributes of the reduct, each one associated with the values of the currently considered object, and in its decision part it has the class of this training object.

At classifying an unseen object through the generated rule set, it may happen that several rules suggest different decision values. In such conflict situations a strategy to reach a final result (decision) is needed. RSES provides a conflict resolution strategy based on voting. In this method, when the antecedent of a rule matches the unseen object, a vote in favor of the decision value of its consequent is cast. Votes are counted and the decision value reaching the majority of the votes is chosen as the class for the unseen object.

This simple method may be extended by assigning weights to rules. In RSES, this method (known as Standard Voting) assigns as weight for a rule the number of training objects matching the antecedent of this rule. Then, each rule votes with its weight and the decision value reaching the highest weight sum is considered as the class for the object.

Example 2. If we consider the table M_1 from Example 1, applying RSES, we obtain the following rules:

$(a1 = 4) => (d = 1[1])$
$(a1 = 3) => (d = 1[2])$

$(a2 = low) => (d = 1[2])$
$(a1 = 5) => (d = 2[1])$
$(a2 = veryhigh) => (d = 2[1])$
$(a2 = medium) => (d = 3[2])$
.....

the number in square brackets at the end means the support of the rule, i.e., the number of objects in the training sample having in their respective features the same values of the features in the antecedent of the rule.

Obviously, we can generate a set of rules from any subset of attributes or a set of subsets of attributes. For our study, we use all the reducts, each one of them individually, and all the shortest reducts as a set of attribute subsets..

3   Experiments

In this section, we show our experimentation in controlled conditions, as a first approach to study three different options to use reducts for building decision rules in rule-based classifiers.

For having controlled conditions in our experiments, we used four datasets (see Table 1) taken from the UCI Machine Learning Repository [2]. We select these datasets because they are small and have a small amount of reducts, and not all of them have the same length and the minimum length is reached in more than one reduct. The datasets *Glass* and *Heart(Statlog)* were previously discretized. All datasets were split into two folds, one for generating rules and the other for testing. For this, we used a ratio of 0.5.

For each dataset, the whole set of reducts for the training fold was computed by using RSES [18]. Table 1 shows the characteristics of the reducts: the third column contains the amount of reducts, the next three columns contain the maximum, minimum and average length respectively; and the last column contain the number of shortest reducts.

Table 1. Characteristics of reducts for the four datasets used in our experiments

Dataset	Attributes	Reducts	Max length	Min length	Avg length	Shortest
Glass	9	4	6	5	5.5	2
Heart-(Statlog)	13	62	8	5	6.8	2
Pima Indians Diabetes	8	12	6	4	4.5	8
Zoo	16	34	5	4	4.9	2

Figure 1 shows a screenshot of RSES for one of the projects executed in the study of the selected databases.

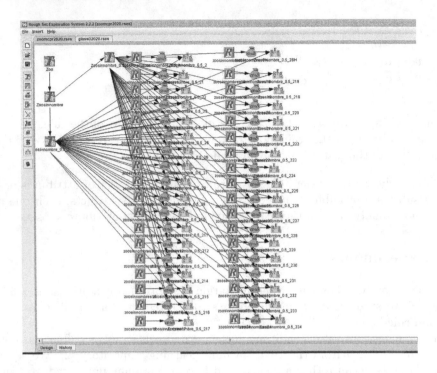

Fig. 1. Screenshot of the project Zoo in RSES

After computing the reducts, using again RSES, the before mentioned sets of rules were generated, first using all the reducts, then using each reduct separately, in addition the rule set considering only the shortest reducts was generated . To use an external selection criterion, the CAMARDF [19] algorithm was used, which generates a minimum length reduct, and the set of rules obtained from that shortest reduct was separately considered.

Each testing fold was classified using the rule-based algorithm standard voting, taking into account the four different cases:

1. the rules generated by all the reducts
2. the rules generated by each reduct individually
3. the rules generated by all the shortest reducts and
4. the rules generated by one shortest reduct obtained by the CAMARDF algorithm.

Table 2 shows the obtained results. The columns headed as *all*, *shortest* and *CAMARDF* contain the accuracies obtained for variants 1, 3 and 4, respectively. The remaining columns contain the maximum and minimum accuracy values obtained when applying variant 2.

As we can see from Table 2, for the second and third databases, the best result is achieved when considering the rules obtained from all reducts. In the case of Pima-diabetes, this result is also obtained if the rules generated by the

Table 2. Accuracies of the different rule-based classifiers for the four datasets

Dataset	All	Min	Max	Shortest	CAMARDF
Glass	0.60	0.46	0.55	**0.63**	0.53
Heart-(Statlog)	**0.89**	0.58	0.85	0.66	0.58
Pima Indians Diabetes	**0.69**	0.54	0.62	**0.69**	0.54
Zoo	0.94	0.84	**0.96**	0.88	0.88

shortest reducts are considered. For the Glass dataset, the best accuracy was achieved for the classifier built with the shortest reducts.

However, in the case of the Zoo dataset, neither the rule-based classifier built with all the reducts, nor the classifier built with the shortest ones, obtained the highest result. For this dataset, the best result was obtained twice, for a classifier based on an individual reduct, but in none of the cases it was obtained by using one of the shortest reducts. Taking into account that for this dataset there are 34 reducts, it means that if we randomly choose a reduct to generate the rules for a classifier, the probability of constructing one of maximum accuracy classifiers is approximately 0.06. If we decide to choose one of minimum length reducts, then the probability is 0.

Apparently, Sil and Das [17] report a different result for the Zoo dataset using the 10-fold cross-validation technique, although the authors' use of the term minimum length reducts is confusing. As they say, they achieve the minimum length reducts by eliminating the redundant attributes of each of the reducts, which is unclear.

Finally, if we decide to select just one shortest reduct to build the classifier using the CAMARDF algorithm, it never would achieve the best result, for any of the four datasets.

4   Conclusions

The problem of how to choose the best rules when building a rule-based classifier remains a problem to solve. Although some authors underestimate the task of computing all reducts of a dataset (perhaps covered by its requirement of excessive resources, given its exponential complexity), our preliminary experiments allow us to conclude that in certain cases, computing a single reduct, or only considering those with a minimum length can provide insufficient results compared to those obtained from all reducts.

These results do not lead us to suggest that all reducts should be computed in every problem. More than anything else, our purpose is to establish that it is an unclosed matter and to emphasize that it is justified to continue investigating effective strategies for the selection of rules, especially if for their construction we rely on reducts, given their properties with respect to the ability to discern between objects of different classes.

References

1. Arora, S., Anand, P.: Binary butterfly optimization approaches for feature selection. Expert Syst. Appl. **116**, 147–160 (2019)
2. Bache, K., Lichman, M.: UCI Machine Learning Repository. University of California, School of Information and Computer Science, Irvine (2013). http://archive.ics.uci.edu/ml
3. Barman, T., Rajesh, G., Archana, R.: Rough set based segmentation and classification model for ECG. In: Conference on Advances in Signal Processing (CASP), pp. 18–23. IEEE (2016)
4. Bazan, J.G., Szczuka, M.: The rough set exploration system. In: Peters, J.F., Skowron, A. (eds.) Transactions on Rough Sets III. LNCS, vol. 3400, pp. 37–56. Springer, Heidelberg (2005). https://doi.org/10.1007/11427834_2
5. El-Islem-Karabadji, N., Khelf, I., Seridi, H., Aridhi, S., Remond, D., Dhifli, W.: A data sampling and attribute selection strategy for improving decision tree construction. Expert Syst. Appl. **129**, 84–96 (2019)
6. Hansen, M., Yu, B.: Model selection and the principle of minimum description length. J. Am. Stat. Assoc. **96**, 746–774 (2001)
7. Herrera-Semenets, V., Pérez-García, O.A., Hernández-León, R., van den Berg, J., Doerr, C.: A data reduction strategy and its application on scan and backscatter detection using rule-based classifiers. Expert Syst. Appl. **95**, 272–279 (2018)
8. Lazo-Cortés, M.S., Martínez-Trinidad, J.F., Carrasco-Ochoa, J.A.: Class-specific reducts vs. classic reducts in a rule-based classifier: a case study. In: Martínez-Trinidad, J.F., Carrasco-Ochoa, J.A., Olvera-López, J.A., Sarkar, S. (eds.) MCPR 2018. LNCS, vol. 10880, pp. 23–30. Springer, Cham (2018). https://doi.org/10.1007/978-3-319-92198-3_3
9. Lazo-Cortés, M.S., Martínez-Trinidad, J.F., Carrasco-Ochoa, J.A.: On the use of constructs for rule-based classification: a case study. In: Carrasco-Ochoa, J.A., Martínez-Trinidad, J.F., Olvera-López, J.A., Salas, J. (eds.) MCPR 2019. LNCS, vol. 11524, pp. 327–335. Springer, Cham (2019). https://doi.org/10.1007/978-3-030-21077-9_30
10. Liu, H., Motoda, H.: Computational Methods of Feature Selection. Chapman & Hall/CRC, Boca Raton (2007)
11. Miao, D.Q., Zhao, Y., Yao, Y.Y., Li, H.X., Xu, F.F.: Reducts in consistent and inconsistent decision tables of the Pawlak rough set model. Inf. Sci. **179**(24), 4140–4150 (2009)
12. Pawlak, Z.: Rough sets. Int. J. Comput. Inf. Sci. **11**, 341–356 (1982)
13. Pawlak, Z.: Rough sets, Theoretical Aspects of Reasoning About Data, pp. 315–330. Kluwer Academic Publishers, Dordrecht (1992)
14. Rana, H., Lal, M.: A rough set theory approach for rule generation and validation using RSES. Int. J. Rough Sets Data Anal. **3**(1), 55–70 (2016)
15. Rana, H., Lal, M.: A comparative study based on rough set and classification via clustering approaches to handle incomplete data to predict learning styles. Int. J. Decis. Support Syst. Technol. **9**(2), 1–20 (2017)
16. Si, H., Zhou, J., Chen, Z., Wan, J., Xiong, N., Zhang, W., Vasilakos, A.: Association rules mining among interests and applications for users on social networks. IEEE Access **7**, 116014–116026 (2019)
17. Sil, J., Das, A.K.: Variable length reduct vs. minimum length reduct-a comparative study. Procedia Technol. **4**, 58–68 (2012)

18. Skowron, A., Bazan, J., Szczuka, M., Wroblewski, J.: Rough Set Exploration System (version 2.2.2). http://logic.mimuw.edu.pl/~rses/
19. Zhou, J., Miao, D., Feng, Q., Sun, L.: Research on complete algorithms for minimal attribute reduction. In: Wen, P., Li, Y., Polkowski, L., Yao, Y., Tsumoto, S., Wang, G. (eds.) RSKT 2009. LNCS (LNAI), vol. 5589, pp. 152–159. Springer, Heidelberg (2009). https://doi.org/10.1007/978-3-642-02962-2_19

Towards Inpainting and Denoising Latent Fingerprints: A Study on the Impact in Latent Fingerprint Identification

Ernesto Ramírez-Sáyago[1], Octavio Loyola-González[1(✉)] [iD],
and Miguel Angel Medina-Pérez[2] [iD]

[1] Tecnologico de Monterrey, Vía Atlixcáyotl No. 2301, Reserva Territorial
Atlixcáyotl, 72453 Puebla, Mexico
A00513925@itesm.mx, octavioloyola@tec.mx
[2] Tecnologico de Monterrey, Carr. al Lago de Guadalupe Km. 3.5, 52926 Atizapán,
Estado de México, Mexico
migue@tec.mx

Abstract. In this paper, we provide a study about the impact of the most prominent inpainting and denoising solutions on the latent fingerprint identification. From an in-depth analysis, we show how some of the analyzed inpainting and denoising solutions can improve up 63% for Rank-1 and 26% for Rank-20 the fingerprint identification rates when state-of-the-art minutiae extractors are used. Nevertheless, it is necessary to create new denoising and inpainting solutions that are specifically built to deal with latent fingerprints and their associated issues.

Keywords: Latent fingerprint · Inpainting · Denoising · Deep learning

1 Introduction

Fingerprints are invaluable biometric features that have widely been adopted among law enforcement for verifying and identification of an individual. There exist two categories for clustering fingerprints: (i) impressions, which are acquired under controlled conditions; and (ii) latent fingerprints, which are unintentionally left by someone when manipulating objects and are thus particularly useful at crime scenes. However, due to the nature of the problem, latent fingerprints are usually incomplete and distorted images, presenting broken ridges and containing noisy background, which hinders their analysis during investigations due to their low-quality [14].

Figure 1 shows three examples of latent-rolled pairs of identified fingerprints from database NIST-SD27 [3]. Notice that latent fingerprints present incomplete and distorted images, containing noisy backgrounds. Consequently, as was recently reported in [14], the fingerprint identification rates are lower than 10%, 13 %, and 24% for Rank-1, weighted Rank-20, and Rank-100, respectively.

An idea to get better fingerprint identification rates is to improve the quality of latent fingerprints. Some authors [1,6,9,10,12] have been studying how

K. M. Figueroa Mora et al. (Eds.): MCPR 2020, LNCS 12088, pp. 76–86, 2020.
https://doi.org/10.1007/978-3-030-49076-8_8

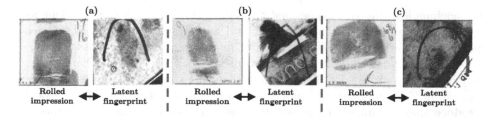

Fig. 1. Three examples of latent-rolled pairs of identified fingerprints from database NIST-SD27 [3]. Each latent fingerprints in NIST-SD27 is labeled according to its quality (a) good, (b) bad, and (c) ugly. Notice that, unlike the rolled impressions, the latent fingerprints contain partial information and higher levels of noise.

improving fingerprint impressions by using denoising and inpainting solutions. These solutions have positively impacted on the obtained accuracy for fingerprint verification. However, the literature has focused on studying denoising and inpainting solutions by using fingerprints obtained in controlled situations (impressions), which present higher quality than latent fingerprints.

As far as we know, there is no study on the impact of inpainting and denoising solutions for latent fingerprints. Hence, in this paper, we introduce the first study testing inpainting and denoising solutions on latent fingerprint databases.

Our study shows that fingerprint identification can be improved by using inpainting and denoising solutions, which were trained by using impressions. From our experiment result, we can conclude that the fingerprint identification rates can be improved up 63% for Rank-1 and 26% for Rank-20 when inpainting and denoising solutions are used. However, the fingerprint identification rates were not always improved by using inpainting and denoising solutions; or using some combination of them. Hence, we provide a set of recommendations for improving these solutions; and, consequently, the fingerprint identification rates.

This paper is organized as follows: Sect. 2 provides related work about inpainting and denoising solutions proposed for fingerprints. After, Sect. 3 presents our study related to the impact of the proposed inpainting and denoising solutions on latent fingerprints. Next, Sect. 3 provides our experimental setup as well as experimental results obtained from our study. Also, this section (Sect. 3) provides an in-depth analysis of the obtained results. Finally, Sect. 4 presents our conclusions and future work.

2   Related Work

Latent fingerprints are acquired from uncontrolled conditions (usually at crime scenes), hence containing noise, incomplete information, and perturbations produced by their forming mechanism. Besides, latent fingerprints suffer distortions due to their acquisition procedure. Unlike controlled fingerprint acquisitions, all these hostile conditions produce low-quality latent fingerprint images, which are vital for capturing criminals [14]. The acquired low-quality images motive to machine learning researchers and fingerprint experts to create solutions for improving the quality of these images, and as a result, increasing the finger-print identification rates [6]. Notice that fingerprint images are usually composed of thin ridges, and it is critical to preserve and keep them sharp during any restoration process for their reliable use during the fingerprint identification procedure. Any unintentional procedure that brakes or distorts the ridges can produce spurious minutiae, impacting negatively on the identification rate (a minutia is a minute detail on the ridges of a fingerprint, often ridge ending or bifurcation, which, together with other ones, are essential for the identification of people [14]).

One of the most prominent approaches for improving the quality of finger-print images is to use denoising and inpainting solutions [1,6,9–12]. One of the pioneer solutions was proposed in [10], using the approach of *curvelet transforms*; which is a type of multiscale geometric transforms based on Fourier transformations for improving the quality of fingerprint images. Another solution was proposed in [12], where the authors use ridge orientation-based clustered dictionaries for creating a sparse denoising framework.

An essential advance on Machine Learning was the beginning of the Neural Artificial Network-based approach. However, the most significant progress was made when the CNN-based approach arrived, which has gained an enormous attraction in recent years. Consequently, several denoising and inpainting solutions based on CNNs were proposed for improving the quality of fingerprint images [1,6,9,11].

One of the pioneers and most prominent CNN-based solutions is U-Net, which was published in [11]. Figure 2 shows that U-Net's architecture contains two 3×3 convolutions, each followed by a rectified linear unit (ReLU) and a 2×2 max pooling operation with stride 2 for down-sampling. At the final layer, a 1×1 convolution is used to map each 64-component feature vector to the desired number of classes. In total, the network has 23 convolutional layers. Although this CNN was initially proposed for biomedical image segmentation, specifically for cell tracking challenge, its architecture has been a template for creating new CNNs by using its encoding and decoding procedure. It is essential to highlight that U-Net allows obtaining good fingerprint identification by improving the quality of fingerprint images.

The following three solution for improving the fingerprint images are based on the U-Net's architecture:

CVxTz was proposed in [6], which is similar to the U-net's architecture, excepting that CVxTz pad the input with zeros instead of mirroring the edges. CVxTz's architecture is suitable for improving the quality of fingerprint images because it takes into account a more broad context when predicting a pixel [6], and also it uses additional data augmentation. CVxTz was trained and tested by using a synthetic dataset[1] containing 84,000 fingerprint images (275×400 pixels), which were generated using a synthetic fingerprint generator

---

[1] This dataset can be downloaded from http://chalearnlap.cvc.uab.es/dataset/32/description/.

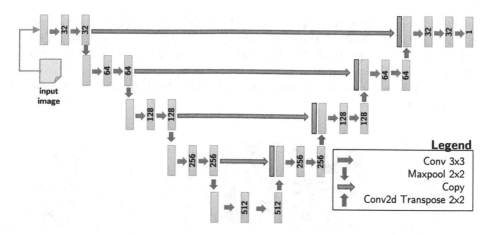

Fig. 2. U-net's architecture [11]. Its encoding and decoding procedure has widely been used to create other CNNs for improving the quality of fingerprint images.

(Anguli) [4]. All generated images were artificially transformed by adding background and random filters (blur, brightness, contrast, elastic transformation, occlusion, scratch, resolution, and rotation). The generated dataset contains 168,000 fingerprint images (84,000 fingerprint images - one ground-truth and one degraded image - per fingerprint). The results were assessed by using the mean absolute error (MAE) measure, where CVxTz allows obtaining the lowest MAE value (0.0189). The main drawback of CVxTz is that the used fingerprints were generated artificially, which means that the performance could significantly be degraded if the trained model is applied to real latent fingerprints.

U-Finger (a.k.a rgsl888) [9] was recently proposed as an alternative for denoising and inpainting on fingerprint images. U-Finger's architecture contains an encoding module where each convolutional layer is followed by spatial batch normalization and a ReLU neuron. From top to down, the four convolutional layers have 128, 32, 32, and 128 kernels of size 3×3, 1×1, 3×3, and 1×1, respectively. U-Finger's architecture's decode module provides a similar architecture as the encoding module excepting that the number of kernels in the four convolutional layers: 256, 64, 64, and 256. U-Finger was trained and tested by using the same dataset above mentioned for training the CVxTz solution. From experimental results, U-Finger obtains a worse MSE value (0.023579) than CVxTz (0.0189).

FDPMnet [1] was recently proposed for improving the quality of fingerprint images by using denoising and inpainting solutions. The encoding module consists of repeated two blocks of 3×3 convolutional layers, batch normalization layer, and ReLU activation. The decoding module is similar to encoding module, excepting that max-pooling is replaced by an upsampling layer which helps to reconstruct an output image. The final layer is a 1×1 convolution layer with a sigmoid activation function which gives the reconstructed output image. FDPMnet was trained and tested by using the same dataset above mentioned for training and testing the CVxTz and U-Finger solutions. From experimental results, FDPMnet obtained the worst MSE value (0.0268) compared to CVxTz (0.0189) and U-Finger (0.23579). The main reason why CVxTz reached better results against the two other ones could be that it presents almost double the network depth as compared to other proposals, and also it uses additional data augmentation.

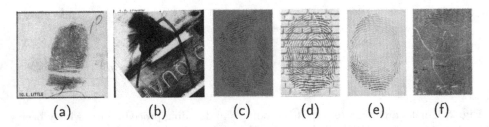

Fig. 3. Examples of fingerprints taken from the NIST-SD27 database [3] and the artificial dataset generated using Anguli [4]. An example of impression (a) and latent fingerprint (b), taken from a real scenario. From (c) to (f) contain fingerprints generated artificially.

Although the solutions above mentioned have managed impressive results, they have only been trained on fingerprints obtained in very controlled conditions, or on fingerprints generated synthetically by pieces of software. In Fig. 3, we show a set of fingerprints taken from a real database and other ones generated artificially. Notice that the quality of fingerprints generated artificially (c–f), which were transformed by using some filters, look like more the quality of an impression image (a) than the quality of a real latent fingerprint (b). Notice that the real latent fingerprint (b) contains some spots without visible ridges, different background textures, and different shades of gray.

From the reviewed papers and the analysis of Fig. 3, an novel avenue of study is open since there has been little research of fingerprint denoising and inpainting using latent fingerprints encountered in real-life situations instead of those taken from controlled situations or generated artificially. Hence, we proposed to analyze the performance of the most prominent denoising and inpainting solutions by using real latent fingerprints.

3 Studying the Impact of Inpainting and Denoising Solutions on the Latent Fingerprint Identification

This study aims to analyze the impact of the most prominent inpainting and denoising solutions on the latent fingerprint identification. To do so, we will analyze each solution separately as well as combinations of them by using two real latent fingerprint databases.

For a better understanding of our study, we have structured this section as follows: Sect. 3.1 presents our experimental setup, where databases, tested algorithms, and the methodological framework are described. Section 3.2 provides our experimental results and an in-depth analysis of these results.

3.1 Experimental Setup

For our experimentation, we have selected two latent fingerprint databases. On the one hand, NIST-SD27, which is a public database widely used in latent fingerprint studies [5,14]. On the other hand, we have a non-public database taken from a crime laboratory (from here on, *Proprietary*), which contains 568 rolled fingerprints (284 latent fingerprints and 284 impressions).

We selected three of the most prominent and popular minutiae extraction extractors, which have reported reasonable identification rates. Fingernet [13] and MinutiaeNet [8], which are based on convolutional networks; and Verifinger [7], a proprietary minutiae extractor developed by Neurotechnology.

We selected three of the most popular inpainting and denoising solutions for analysing their impact on the latent fingerprint identification: FDPMNet[2] [1], CVxTz[3] [6], and U-Finger[4] [9] (see Sect. 2 for more details).

We selected Minutia Cylinder-Code (MCC) [2] as a representation and matching technique for latent fingerprint identification. MCC has proven to obtain better identification rates than other several solutions. The authors of MCC provide a free and public SDK (SDKMCC[5]) for research purposes.

In our experiments, we use the identification rates plotted in the cumulative match characteristic (CMC) curve computed according to ISO/IEC 19795-1, which is the most used measure for assessing the fingerprint identification [14].

As the goal of this study is to analyze the impact of the most prominent inpainting and denoising solutions on the latent fingerprint identification, we will test every selected denoising and inpainting solution by themselves. After that, we will test all possible combinations of them (i.e., first run the solution A, then use the outputs as the inputs for solution B, and so on). Consequently, we will execute 15 combinations for each database (30 in total).

As representation and matching technique is the same, and we will only change the selected minutiae extractors as well as the combinations of the selected inpainting and denoising solutions, we will be able to see the following: (i) if the inpainting and denoising solution that were previously tried only on fingerprint impressions also work well with latent fingerprints; (ii) what is the combination of inpainting and denoising solutions improving the latent fingerprint identification rate; and (iii) what is the best combination among minutiae extractor and inpainting and denoising solutions for latent fingerprint identification.

---

[2] http://github.com/adigasu/FDPMNet.
[3] http://github.com/CVxTz/fingerprint_denoising.
[4] http://github.com/rgsl888/U-Finger-A-Fingerprint-Denosing-Network.
[5] http://biolab.csr.unibo.it.

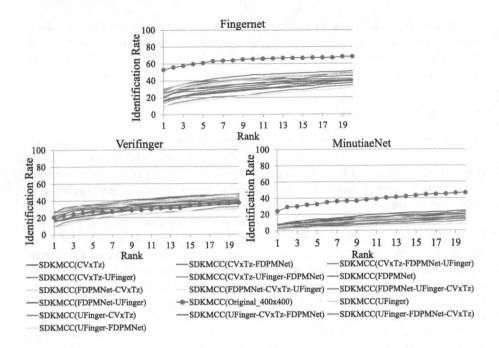

Fig. 4. CMC results for the NIST-SD27 database.

3.2 Experimental Results

Figure 4 shows the identification rates by using CMC curves (from Rank-1 to Rank-20) for each tested minutiae extractor on the NIST-SD27 database. This figure quantifies the ratio of correct identifications in the first place and among the 20 first ranks, respectively. From Fig. 4, we can notice that using Fingernet as a minutiae extractor, it allows obtaining the best results without using any inpainting and denoising solutions. The second-best result was obtained by only using FDPMNet, which presents an identification rate decrease of 48.91% (from 53.10% to 27.13%) for Rank-1 and an average identification rate decrease of 30.59% (from 63.91% to 44.36%) throughout the first-20 ranks.

From Fig. 4, we can notice a similar result to the one obtained by Fingernet but when MinutiaeNet is used. For MinutiaeNet, the best results come from not using any inpainting and denoising solutions. The second-best result was obtained by only using CVxTz, which presents an identification rate decrease of 67.74% (from 24.03% to 7.75%) for Rank-1 and an average accuracy decrease of 52.85% (from 38.02% to 17.93%) throughout the first-20 ranks.

Regarding the findings mentioned above, in Fig. 4, different results can be seen when Verifinger is used for extracting minutiae. The best result is coming from using CVxTz firstly and after, FDPMNet. This combination allows for obtaining an accuracy increase of 28.30% (from 20.54% to 26.36%) at Rank-1 and an average accuracy increase of 35.05% (from 30.08% to 40.62%) throughout the first-20 ranks. Also, notice that only the combinations FDPMNet-CVxTZ-UFinger and FDPMNet-UFinger-CVxTZ do not improve the results obtained by Verifinger without using any inpainting and denoising solutions.

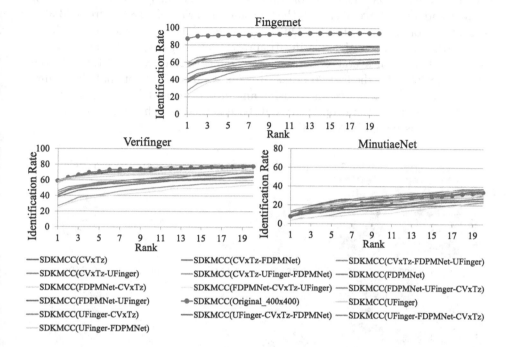

Fig. 5. CMC results for the Proprietary database.

Figure 5 shows from Rank-1 to Rank-20 identification rates by using CMC curves for each tested minutiae extractor on the Proprietary database. This figure quantifies the ratio of correct identifications in the first place and among the first-20 ranks, respectively. From Fig. 5, we can notice that using Fingernet as a minutiae extractor, it allows obtaining the best results without using any inpainting and denoising solutions. The second-best result was obtained by only using FDPMNet, which presents an identification rate decrease of 31.45% (from 87.32% to 59.86%) for Rank-1 and an identification rate decrease of 20.78% (from 92.45% to 73.24%) throughout the first-20 ranks.

From Fig. 5, we can notice that Verifinger obtains the best results from Rank-1 to Rank-8 without using any inpainting and denoising solutions. However, from Rank-9 to Rank-20, the best result is coming from using FDPMNet firstly and after, CVxTz. This combination decreases the identification rate in 5.95% (from 59.15% to 55.63%) for Rank-1, increases the identification rate in 1.06% (from 73.24% to 74.01%) throughout the first-20 ranks, and an identification rate increase of 3.29% (from 76.20% to 78.71%) from Rank-9 to Rank-20.

Other findings that we can notice from Fig. 5 is that, when using MinutiaeNet to extract minutiae from the proprietary database, the best results are coming from using CVxTz. Nevertheless, it is very close to the results obtained by the combination of using U-Finger firstly and after FDPMNet. When compared MinutiaeNet with and without using any inpainting and denoising solutions, CVxTz increases the identification rate of 63.67% (from 7.75% to 12.68%) for Rank-1 and, on average, increases the identification rate of 22.83% (from 23.36% to 28.70%) for the first 20 ranks. On the other hand, the combinations U-Finger and FDPMNet increase the identification rate of 59.09% (from 7.75% to 12.32%) for Rank-1 and, on average, increases the identification rate of 21.02% (from 23.36 to 28.27%) for the first 20 ranks. It is essential to highlight that the results obtained by MinutiaeNet (without using any inpainting and denoising solutions) fall drastically when the Proprietary database is used, which could indicate that MinutiaeNet is biased in NIST-SD27.

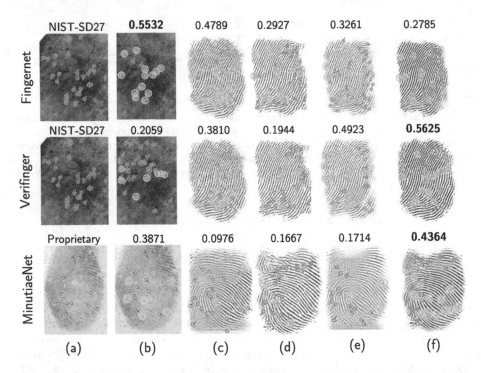

Fig. 6. Ground-truth minutiae and their matches (yellow circles) using different minutiae extractors, inpainting and denoising solutions, and two latent fingerprints. (a) latent fingerprint having minutiae extracted by a fingerprint expert. (b) the same latent fingerprint of (a) but having minutiae extracted by some of the three tested minutiae extractor (Fingernet, Verifinger, and MinutiaeNet). (c) it is the latent fingerprint (a) but filtered by CVxTZ. (d) it is the latent fingerprint (a) but filtered by FDPMNet. (e) it is the latent fingerprint (a) but filtered by U-Finger. (f) it is the latent fingerprint (a) but using the best combination of the tested inpainting and denoising solutions. Each latent fingerprint image having matched minutiae contains its associated F1 score value on top. (Color figure online)

For an in-depth analysis, Fig. 6 shows a comparison of the obtained results by using the ground-truth minutiae and their matches (yellow circles), the three tested minutiae extractors, the three tested inpainting and denoising solutions, and two latent fingerprints taking from the tested databases. From this figure, we can notice that FingertNet obtains the best F1 value for the NIST-SD27 database when inpainting and denoising solutions are not used. Also, we can see that Verifinger obtains the best F1 value for the NIST-SD27 database when the combination CVxTz and FDPMNet is used. Also, notice that Minutiae obtain the best F1 value for the Proprietary database when the combination FDPM-Net and U-Finger is used. All these findings can be corroborated by Figs. 4–5. Also, from Fig. 6, notice that the image quality for combination column (f) is better than using inpainting and denoising solutions alone. Furthermore, we can see that CVxTz (c) and U-Finger (e) provide blur on images, which makes it difficult to extract matched minutiae. Finally, from this figure, we can observe that Fingernet obtains the lowest number of spurious minutiae when inpainting and denoising solutions are not used. Nevertheless, for both Verifinger and MinutiaeNet, some inpainting and denoising combinations allow obtaining the best ratio between matched and spurious minutiae.

4   Conclusions

Denoising and inpainting solutions for fingerprint are of utmost importance since the fingerprint identification serves a crucial role in aiding police investigations for verifying and identifying people. However, most research on fingerprint denoising and inpainting focus on using fingerprint impressions, which contain less distortion than latent fingerprints, and they are obtained in controlled situations.

In this paper, we analyzed the impact of the most prominent inpainting and denoising solutions on latent fingerprint identification by using two latent fingerprint databases and three of the most popular minutiae extractors. From our results, we have found that using fingerprint denoising and inpainting solutions improve, in most cases, the identification rate of latent fingerprints even when dealing with images containing a noisy background and undefined ridges. On the one hand, the best denoising and inpainting solutions for NIST-SD27 are FDPM-Net when Fingernet is used, CVxTz when MinutiaeNet is used, and CVxTz firstly and after FDPMNet when Verifinger is used. On the other hand, the best denoising and inpainting solutions for Proprietary are FDPMNet when Fingernet is used, CVxTz, and the combination U-Finger firstly and after FDPMNet when MinuatiaeNet is used, and the combination FDPMNet firstly and after CVxTz when Verifinger is used.

From the analyzed solutions, we can conclude that they can improve up 63% for Rank-1 and 26% for Rank-20 the fingerprint identification rates when Verifinger or MinutiaeNet are used. Nevertheless, fingerprint identification was not always improved when these solutions were used jointly with Fingernet.

Our results and analysis open the door to future research aimed at studying and creating of denoising and inpainting solutions that are specifically built to deal with latent fingerprints and their associated issues. Another avenue of future research is to inspect further how existing techniques can be improved by data augmentation and deblurring using generative adversarial networks.

Acknowledgment. Authors want to thank the Computer Science department at Tecnologico de Monterrey, Campus Puebla, for paying the registration fee.

References

1. Adiga V, S., Sivaswamy, J.: FPD-M-net: fingerprint image denoising and inpainting using m-net based convolutional neural networks. In: Escalera, S., Ayache, S., Wan, J., Madadi, M., Güçlü, U., Baró, X. (eds.) Inpainting and Denoising Challenges. TSSCML, pp. 51–61. Springer, Cham (2019). https://doi.org/10.1007/978-3-030-25614-2_4
2. Cappelli, R., Ferrara, M., Maltoni, D.: Minutia cylinder-code: a new representation and matching technique for fingerprint recognition. IEEE Trans. Pattern Anal. Mach. Intell. **32**(12), 2128–2141 (2010)
3. Garris, M.D., Mccabe, R.M.: NIST Special Database 27: Fingerprint minutiae from latent and matching tenprint images. Technical report, National Institute of Standards and Technology, Gaithersburg, MD, USA (2000)
4. Haritsa, J., Ansari, A.H., Wadhwani, K., Jadhav, S.: Anguli: Synthetic Fingerprint Generator. https://dsl.cds.iisc.ac.in/projects/Anguli/. Accessed 15 Jan 2019
5. Lee, J., Jain, A., Tong, W., et al.: Image retrieval in forensics: tattoo image database application. IEEE MultiMedia **19**(1), 40–49 (2011)
6. Mansar, Y.: Deep end-to-end fingerprint denoising and inpainting. ArXiv abs/1807.11888 (2018)
7. Neurotechnology: Verifinger. https://www.neurotechnology.com/verifinger.html
8. Nguyen, D.L., Cao, K., Jain, A.K.: Robust minutiae extractor: Integrating deep networks and fingerprint domain knowledge. In: The 11th International Conference on Biometrics, 2018 (2018)
9. Prabhu, R., Yu, X., Wang, Z., Liu, D., Jiang, A.A.: U-Finger: multi-scale dilated convolutional network for fingerprint image denoising and inpainting. In: Escalera, S., Ayache, S., Wan, J., Madadi, M., Güçlü, U., Baró, X. (eds.) Inpainting and Denoising Challenges. TSSCML, pp. 45–50. Springer, Cham (2019). https://doi.org/10.1007/978-3-030-25614-2_3
10. Reddy, G.J., Prasad, T.J.C., Prasad, M.G.: Fingerprint image denoising using curvelet transform. Proc. Asian Res. Publ. Netw. J. Eng. Appl. Sci. **3**(3), 31–35 (2008)
11. Ronneberger, O., Fischer, P., Brox, T.: U-Net: convolutional networks for biomedical image segmentation. In: Navab, N., Hornegger, J., Wells, W.M., Frangi, A.F. (eds.) MICCAI 2015, Part III. LNCS, vol. 9351, pp. 234–241. Springer, Cham (2015). https://doi.org/10.1007/978-3-319-24574-4_28
12. Singh, K., Kapoor, R., Nayar, R.: Fingerprint denoising using ridge orientation based clustered dictionaries. Neurocomputing **167**, 418–423 (2015)
13. Tang, Y., Gao, F., Feng, J., Liu, Y.: Fingernet: an unified deep network for fingerprint minutiae extraction. In: 2017 IEEE International Joint Conference on Biometrics (IJCB), pp. 108–116. IEEE (2017)
14. Valdes-Ramirez, D., et al.: A review of fingerprint feature representations and their applications for latent fingerprint identification: trends and evaluation. IEEE Access **7**(1), 48484–48499 (2019)

Image Processing and Analysis

New Method for Extreme Color Detection in Images

Manuel G. Forero[1]([✉]) [iD], Julián Ávila-Navarro[2] [iD], and Sergio Herrera-Rivera[2] [iD]

[1] Semillero Lún, Grupo de Investigación D+TEC, Facultad de Ingeniería,
Universidad de Ibagué, Ibagué, Colombia
`manuel.forero@unibague.edu.co`
[2] Semillero Lún, Grupo de Investigación GMAE, Facultad de Ingeniería,
Universidad de Ibagué, Ibagué, Colombia
`{julian.avila,sergio.herrera}@unibague.edu.co`

Abstract. In image processing and computer vision, it is common to find applications, in which it is necessary to detect reference points characterized by extreme color, i.e., a primary color RGB or complementary CMY with very high saturation. Thus, there are cases in which a certain class of objects can be distinguished according to their characteristic extreme color, which can be used as landmarks or to identify objects. Therefore, there is an interest in identifying landmarks characterized by extreme colors. In this paper, a new method for detecting objects with an extreme color is introduced and compared with other approaches found in the literature. The methods are analyzed and compared using a color palette in which a transition between R, G, B, C, M and Y colors is generated. The results obtained show that the methods studied allow the specific colors to be adequately discriminated, while the proposed method is the only one that allows the full range of extreme colors R, G, B, C, M and Y to be detected, being more selective than the others, by taking practically the areas corresponding to each color separately .

Keywords: Extreme color · Robotics · Space color · Landmarks · Computer vision · Precision agriculture · Image analysis

1 Introduction

Color is a feature that has been exploited to a great extent in digital image processing, since it is a powerful tool that often facilitates the classification and identification of objects, which can be discriminated based on the large number of appreciable color tones [1]. In the area of computer vision it is common to find problems in which it is required to use the color information to carry out the detection of reference points that allow the tracking and definition of the behavior of objects that present particular characteristics and that are observed through sequences of images, obtained in a controlled environment [2–5]. On the other hand, in other areas such as agriculture and biology, the need has arisen to use color-based image processing techniques in order to apply them to problems such as the detection of weeds in crops [6, 7], the classification and study of different types of fruits that present significant changes in their color during the different stages

© Springer Nature Switzerland AG 2020
K. M. Figueroa Mora et al. (Eds.): MCPR 2020, LNCS 12088, pp. 89–97, 2020.
https://doi.org/10.1007/978-3-030-49076-8_9

of ripening, or due to the presence of defects or associated pests [8–10], counting of organisms [11], among others.

One of the problems that has become relevant in image studies is associated with the detection and segmentation of landmarks with high color intensity, mainly related to primary colors and their complements, which are used in the definition of color spaces, since there are specific applications, in which the objects of interest are easily distinguishable due to their high saturation in one of the RGB color components (Red-Green-Blue) [2, 6, 7]. Therefore, in the literature there are several techniques used for the detection of landmarks with a high saturation in one of the primary or complementary colors CMY (Cyan-Magenta-Yellow), which are defined as extreme colors [2, 6, 7].

After an extensive literature review it was found that there is no study on the techniques of detection of RGB extreme colors and their complements. Therefore, in this study we analyze the techniques found in the literature for the detection of the extreme colors that constitute the components of the RGB color space. In addition we introduce a new method for detecting the R, G, B, C, M, Y extreme colors. The exposed techniques are compared using a color table and a photograph, to study the quality of the approached methods and to define the cases in which their use is more appropriate, taking into account the detection ranges of the analyzed extreme colors.

2 Materials

In this work, forty images were employed to evaluate the methods studied. Two of them are shown in Fig. 1. The first one, shown in Fig. 1(a), consists of a synthetic colour palette, created with a transition between 0 and 255, which allows the visualization of each of the primary colors and their complements. The second, illustrated in Fig. 1(b), consists of a 2736 × 1824 pixel photograph, taken in a controlled environment, of several extreme color objects. In addition, three frames from a video, shown in Fig. 4, were used to demonstrate the properties of the method proposed in this work for object tracking. The photographs were acquired with a Canon 6D camera.

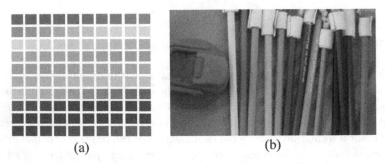

(a)   (b)

Fig. 1. Images used for method testing. (a) Synthetic color palette. (b) Photography of extreme colored objects. (Color figure online)

In the development of the research, a computer HP-2840, with 15.6GiB memory, Intel Xeon(R) CPU E5-2650v4 @ 2.20 GHz × 24, NVIDIA Quadro P600 graphics card and

Linux-Ubuntu 16.04LTS operating system was used. The image processing algorithms were written in Java as plugins of the free access software Imagej.

3 Methods

The proposed method starts with the analysis of the selected color channel with respect to the remaining channels in the RGB color space. To detect an extreme color, the channel of interest must be compared against the other two. Thus, if a basic color is extreme its value must be very high compared to the other two channels. For example, if an extreme red colored object is to be detected, the value of the red component must be compared to the values of the green and blue channels, as shown in Eqs. (1) and (2). If the value of the red channel is close to or equal to 255 and much higher than the values of the green and blue components, it is an extreme color. If the value of red is greater than the other two, but not much greater, it means that red is not extreme. If the value of red is lower than either of the other two components, the pixel hue is not red and at least one of the terms C_1 or C_2 will be negative.

$$C_1 = R - G \tag{1}$$

$$C_2 = R - B \tag{2}$$

From the above, it is possible to define an equation that combines the terms C_1 and C_2 into one and that allows determining if a color is extreme. Since C_1 and C_2 must be high values, a conjunction is made between these terms, using the fuzzy AND operation, since they are not binary values. This operation is equal to obtaining the minimum value between C_1 and C_2. In this way, the expression presented in Eq. (3) is found, which allows to determine if the color red is extreme.

$$ExtR = C_1 \& C_2 = min(C_1, C_2) \tag{3}$$

Based on the procedure described above, this idea can be extended to the complement colors CYM. In contrast to the previous procedure, the opposite operation is performed. The comparisons seen in Eqs. (1) and (2) are reversed as seen in Eq. (4), obtaining as a result that the green and blue colors of a point are highlighted and that mixing them with the operation And the opposite color cyan is obtained.

$$ExtC = min((G - R), (B - R)) \tag{4}$$

Three other methods found in the literature were compared with the proposed technique to evaluate their results. The first method studied, proposed by Arnal [11], a subtraction is made between the green and blue channels of an image (see Eq. (5)) in an attempt to detect the yellow color characteristic of the *Trialeurodes vaporariorum*. This method is a simple approximation that is not extended to the other basic colors or their opposites.

$$ExtY = G - B \tag{5}$$

In the work of García-Santillán et al. [7], a method is introduced for the detection of perennial weeds, characterized by their extreme green color, for which the chromatic components of the RGB space are initially normalized, dividing the value of each component by the maximum value of the spectral channel, as shown in Eqs. (6)–(8).

$$R_n = \frac{R}{R_{max}} \tag{6}$$

$$G_n = \frac{G}{G_{max}} \tag{7}$$

$$B_n = \frac{B}{B_{max}} \tag{8}$$

The value of each pixel is then normalized using Eqs. (9)–(10) so that the sum of the components of the normalized channels is equal to 1, as shown in Eq. (12).

$$RN = \frac{R_n}{R_n + G_n + B_n} \tag{9}$$

$$GN = \frac{G_n}{R_n + G_n + B_n} \tag{10}$$

$$BN = \frac{B_n}{R_n + G_n + B_n} \tag{11}$$

$$RN + GN + BN = 1 \tag{12}$$

Once the color components of each pixel have been normalized, objects characterized by an extreme green color can be segmented using the Eq. (13). This method requires empirically finding a threshold in the resulting image above which a color is considered extreme. This method can be used for the other colors in the RGB color space by replacing the first term of Eq. (9) with the color to be highlighted.

$$ExG = 2GN - RN - BN \tag{13}$$

In the work described by Forero et al. [6] a method is presented which, like the previous one, seeks to find the extreme green color of perennial weeds in cereal crops. For this purpose, the monochromatic image obtained with the BT.601 standard is subtracted from the green channel, as shown in Eq. (14). This method, unlike the previous ones, does not require the search for a threshold value for the detection of extreme color since a fixed value can be used. It can also be used to detect the other two colors in the RGB color space, as was used in the work of García-Vanegas et al. [2] for the detection of extreme red colored landmarks.

$$ExtG = G - (0.299R + 0.5876G + 0.114B) \tag{14}$$

4   Results

The color palette shown in Fig. 1. (a) was used to compare the results obtained with each method, which are presented in Fig. 2. As seen in Sect. 3, only the method proposed here can be used to detect the R, G, B, C, Y, M extreme colors.

Figure 3 presents the results obtained with the photograph covering several of the extreme colors presented in this work, which is studied to show the performance of the methods studied.

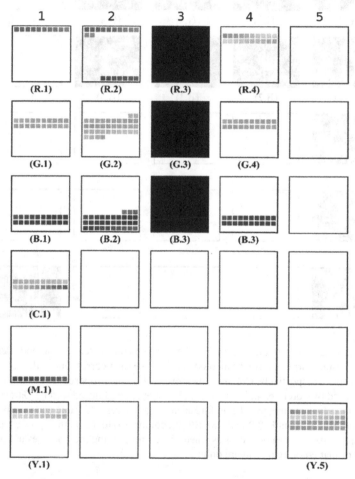

Fig. 2. Images obtained with the extreme color detection methods. The columns correspond to the methods studied, the rows correspond to the color channels R, G, B, C, M, Y respectively. Column (1) corresponds to the proposed method, column (2) to the technique used by Forero et al. [6], Column (3) to the method introduced by García-Santillán et al. [7] using the IsoData method [12] to find an automatic threshold value and Column (4) with manual threshold adjustment R(2;5), G(2;8), B(2;8), column (5) to the method presented by Arnal [11]. The empty boxes correspond to cases where the corresponding method does not provide for the detection of that color. (Color figure online)

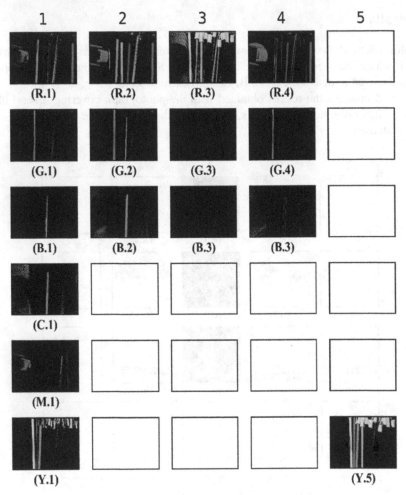

Fig. 3. Images obtained from the photo using the extreme color detection methods described in the text. The columns correspond to the methods studied; the rows correspond to the color channels R, G, B, C, M and Y respectively. Column (1) corresponds to the proposed method, column (2) to the technique used by Forero et al. [6], Column (3) to the method introduced by García-Santillán et al. [7] using the IsoData method [12] to find an automatic threshold value and Column (4) with manual threshold adjustment R(0;0), G(2;8), B(0;0), column (5) to the method presented by Arnal [11]. The empty boxes correspond to cases where the corresponding method does not provide for the detection of that color. (Color figure online)

Table 1 shows the average execution times obtained with each method over a total of 20 tests.

Table 1. Execution time of the evaluated methods.

Method	Execution time [s]
Proposed method	1.393
Forero et al. method [6]	1.093
García-Santillán et al. method [7] using the IsoData threshold adjustment	1.696
García-Santillán et al. method [7] with manual threshold adjustment	1.696
Arnal method [11]	1.462

Figure 4 presents the results obtained in the detection of an extreme yellow object using the method proposed in a video in which the object of study changes its position, lighting and surrounding objects.

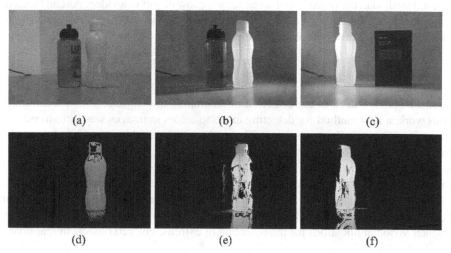

Fig. 4. Results obtained during the monitoring of frames (a), (b) and (c) of a video taken at different times. (d), (e) and (f) results obtained with the proposed method. As can be seen, the method allows the extreme yellow object to be detected properly. (Color figure online)

5 Discussion

As shown in Fig. 2, the only method that allows detecting extreme colored objects is the one proposed here, which, in addition, is more effective in detecting pure extreme colors and does not require the selection of a threshold. The method worked out by Forero et al. [6] detected blue shades in the green color and the same is true for the other colors, so this method is less selective. Concerning the method proposed by García-Santillán et al. [7] it can be seen that without the selection of the appropriate threshold the method fails as seen in Column 3, and even if a threshold is empirically selected, the method is not selective with red shades (column 4). With respect to Arnal's method [11], can be seen in column 5 which is the method that only considers an extreme color and that is not selective for the detection of extreme yellow color leaving tolerant green shades.

In Fig. 3 it can be seen that the proposed method detects the extreme colors for each shade being the most selective of the methods studied here. The method worked out by Forero et al. [6] was less selective with the shades as seen in Column 2, where it detects the extreme green color and lets blue shades through. In the method proposed by García-Santillán et al. [7] it is required to manually find an appropriate threshold to determine the extreme colors, which makes it impractical. As can be seen in Column 5 of Fig. 3, the method developed by Arnal [11] allows for the detection of extreme yellow color, but also erroneously detects green and red tones as yellow.

Table 1 shows that the proposed method is the fastest, taking less than half the time to perform than the other methods studied here. It is evident that the Forero et al. [6] method is the next fastest method and that the García-Santillán et al. [7] and Arnal [11] methods have similar execution times. Figure 4 shows the result obtained with the proposed method in the detection of an extreme yellow object in a video. As can be seen, the proposed method allows the object of interest to be detected under different light conditions and with different objects in the scene.

6 Conclusions

Extreme colors are used in the detection of landmarks in computer vision techniques. In this work, a new method for detecting extreme colors in images was introduced and compared with three other techniques. The method introduced here is the only one that allows the detection of extreme colors in the 6 channels R, G, B, C, Y, M, and it is also the most selective method in the detection of extreme colors compared to the other methods analyzed. It should be noted that the method does not require the adjustment of a threshold for each channel. The proposed method is a very fast one, with similar or even higher speeds than other techniques proposed previously, and can be used in computer vision applications for the detection of extreme colored objects in real time.

Acknowledgements. This work was supported by project #19-488-INT Universidad de Ibagué

References

1. Gonzalez, R.C., Woods, R.E.: Digital Image Processing. Pearson (2018)
2. García-Vanegas, A., Liberato-Tafur, B., Forero, M.G., Gonzalez-Rodríguez, A., Castillo-García, F.: Automatic vision based calibration system for planar cable-driven parallel robots. In: Morales, A., Fierrez, J., Sánchez, J.S., Ribeiro, B. (eds.) IbPRIA 2019, Part I. LNCS, vol. 11867, pp. 600–609. Springer, Cham (2019). https://doi.org/10.1007/978-3-030-31332-6_52
3. Leichter, I., Lindenbaum, M., Rivlin, E.: Mean shift tracking with multiple reference color histograms. Comput. Vis. Image Underst. **114**, 400–408 (2010). https://doi.org/10.1016/j.cviu.2009.12.006
4. Monroy Cruz, E., Garcia Barrientos, A., Espinoza Quesada, E.S., Garcia Carrillo, L.R., Tapia Olvera, R.: An unmanned ground vehicles experimental setup for image-based object tracking. IEEE Lat. Am. Trans. **13**, 2845–2850 (2015). https://doi.org/10.1109/TLA.2015.7350029

5. Sarrabezolles, L., Manzanera, A., Hueber, N.: Bio-inspired perception sensor (BIPS) concept analysis for embedded applications. In: Vera-Rodriguez, R., Fierrez, J., Morales, A. (eds.) CIARP 2018. LNCS, vol. 11401, pp. 428–435. Springer, Cham (2019). https://doi.org/10.1007/978-3-030-13469-3_50

6. Forero, Manuel G., Herrera-Rivera, S., Ávila-Navarro, J., Franco, C.A., Rasmussen, J., Nielsen, J.: Color classification methods for perennial weed detection in cereal crops. In: Vera-Rodriguez, R., Fierrez, J., Morales, A. (eds.) CIARP 2018. LNCS, vol. 11401, pp. 117–123. Springer, Cham (2019). https://doi.org/10.1007/978-3-030-13469-3_14

7. García-Santillán, I.D., Pajares, G.: On-line crop/weed discrimination through the Mahalanobis distance from images in maize fields. Biosyst. Eng. **166**, 28–43 (2018). https://doi.org/10.1016/j.biosystemseng.2017.11.003

8. Gan, H., Lee, W.S., Alchanatis, V., Ehsani, R., Schueller, J.K.: Immature green citrus fruit detection using color and thermal images. Comput. Electron. Agric. **152**, 117–125 (2018). https://doi.org/10.1016/j.compag.2018.07.011

9. Li, F., Song, X., Wu, L., Chen, H., Liang, Y., Zhang, Y.: Heredities on fruit color and pigment content between green and purple fruits in tomato. Sci. Hortic. (Amsterdam) **235**, 391–396 (2018). https://doi.org/10.1016/j.scienta.2018.03.030

10. Fu, L., et al.: Banana detection based on color and texture features in the natural environment. Comput. Electron. Agric. **167**, 105057 (2019). https://doi.org/10.1016/j.compag.2019.105057

11. Barbedo, J.G.A.: Using digital image processing for counting whiteflies on soybean leaves. J. Asia. Pac. Entomol. **17**, 685–694 (2014). https://doi.org/10.1016/j.aspen.2014.06.014

12. Ridler, T.W., Calvard, S.: Picture thresholding using an iterative selection method. IEEE Trans. Syst. Man. Cybern. **8**, 630–632 (1978). https://doi.org/10.1109/TSMC.1978.4310039

A Simple Methodology for 2D Reconstruction Using a CNN Model

Armando Levid Rodríguez-Santiago⑩, José Anibal Arias-Aguilar⑩,
Alberto Elías Petrilli-Barceló(✉)⑩, and Rosebet Miranda-Luna⑩

Graduate Studies Division, Universidad Tecnológica de la Mixteca,
Km. 2.5 Carretera a Acatlima, 69000 Huajuapan de León, Oaxaca, Mexico
`levid.rodriguez@gmail.com`, {`anibal,petrilli,rmiranda`}`@mixteco.utm.mx`
`http://www.utm.mx`

Abstract. In recent years, Deep Learning research have demonstrated their effectiveness in digital image processing, mainly in areas with heavy computational load. Such is the case of aerial photogrammetry, where the principal objective is to generate a 2D map or a 3D model from a specific terrain. In these topics, high-efficiency in visual information processing is demanded. In this work we present a simple methodology to build an orthomosaic, our proposal is focused in replacing traditional digital imagen processing using instead a Convolutional Neuronal Network (CNN) model. The dataset of aerial images is generated from drone photographs of our university campus. The method described in this article uses a CNN model to detect matching points and RANSAC algorithm to correct feature's correlation. Experimental results show that feature maps and matching points obtained between pair of images through a CNN are comparable with those obtained in traditional artificial vision algorithms.

Keywords: Deep Learning · CNN · 2D reconstruction · Aerial images

1 Introduction

Image stitching produces a mosaic that corresponds to a set of images taken from one or several cameras which overlap and are joined in a single image [6]. In the generation of this mosaic several computer vision techniques are used. We worked with aerial images and computer vision strategies combined with photogrammetry techniques.

The stitching process is usually made with traditional computer vision methods as shown in Fig. 1a. It begins with a drone flight plan to image acquisition of a selected area. Then placeholders with georeferenced points are added over a map as well as flight height and overlapping percentage between each pair of acquired images. Usually a mobile application is configured with these specifications to acquire the information autonomously. Some popular free apps to help in this stage are Pix4D and DroneDeploy.

© Springer Nature Switzerland AG 2020
K. M. Figueroa Mora et al. (Eds.): MCPR 2020, LNCS 12088, pp. 98–107, 2020.
https://doi.org/10.1007/978-3-030-49076-8_10

Then, an image processing stage is performed. It begins with feature extraction and continues with the identification and relationship of similar features between images in overlapping areas [8,17]. Key points operators [18] are mainly used as feature extraction algorithm. They use radiometric features such as points, edges, corners, etc. that can be detected in adjacent images under normal capture conditions. They are not robust to inclination, rotation, scale or lighting changes, however, in aerial images these conditions does not occur very often. To deal with these conditions, computer vision techniques are a good option, being one the most popular Scale Invariant Feature Transform (SIFT) algorithm. SIFT [19,20] processing has four steps:

1. Scale Space Extrema Detection: identify a location and scales key points using scale space extrema in the DoG (Difference-of-Gaussian) functions with different values of standard deviation.
2. Key point Localization: key point candidates are localized and refined by eliminating low contrast points.
3. Orientation Assignment: orientation of key point is obtained based on local image gradient.
4. Description Generation: compute the local image descriptor for each key point based on image gradient magnitude and orientation at each image sample point in a region centered at key point.

These steps generate a 128-dimension key point descriptor.

Once an interesting group of features have been extracted, the next step to do is features correlation or features correspondence. It consists of vector descriptor comparison. Several methods can be used: quadratic search, kd-tree data structure, etc. Erroneous correspondences (outliers) presented in the correlation are eliminated from estimation through fundamental matrix or essential matrix (if the internal parameters of the camera are known) [2,4]. This is difficult because internal parameters of the camera very often are unknow. Therefore, other strategies are found in the literature such as LMS (Least-Median-Square) and MAPSAC, however, one the most used strategy is RANSAC (Random Sample Consensus) [9,16], which is an iterative algorithm to determine a fundamental matrix. RANSAC is essentially composed of two steps that are iteratively repeated [27]:

- Hypothesize. First minimal sample sets (MSSs) are randomly selected from the input dataset and model parameters are computed using only elements of the MSS. Cardinality of MSS is the smallest sufficient to determine the model parameters (as opposed to other approaches, such as least squares, where parameters are estimated using all data available, possibly with appropriate weights).

- Test. In the second step, RANSAC checks which elements of the entire dataset are consistent with the model instantiated using parameters estimated in the first step. The set of such elements is called consensus set (CS).

RANSAC terminates when the probability of finding a better ranked CS drops below a certain threshold. In their original formulation the ranking of CS was its cardinality (i.e. CSs that contain more elements are ranked better than CSs that contain fewer elements).

This is the best option to adjust the correspondences and eliminate features that do not meet a reference value. The final stage is to build an orthomosaic with all previously performed procedures. In this step, computer vision techniques are used to join all photographs into one.

It should be noted that the most complex task is orthomosaic generation. It is extremely complex, however, recent research has demonstrated great efficiency of convolutional neural networks (CNN) in digital image processing [1,11,22], that is why this investigation uses a CNN to built an orthomosaic from Technological University of the Mixteca (UTM) campus with aerial images obtained from an Unmanned Aerial Vehicle (UAV).

2   Related Work

Aerial photogrammetry is a procedure to obtain plans for large land areas by means of aerial photographs [3]. The result is a 2D map or a 3D terrain model. To do this we need to apply computer vision techniques and algorithms.

Research has been carried out with the purpose of perform improvements such as the work of [13] where SIFT algorithm is used to feature extraction and digital surface models (DSM) were generated from UAV images in high resolution. Similarly, in [15], the author proposes to use new algorithms for surface reconstruction. These approaches demand still high computational complexity.

Nevertheless, recent research has included studies in Deep Learning approaches such as presented in [5,10,24,26] where they perform image pairing and 3D reconstructions using deep neuronal network techniques. Obtained results are quite acceptable, however, proposed models are very complex and often require additional information from external sensors [14].

3   Methodology

Our approach for orthomosaic reconstruction consists in replacing traditional digital image processing techniques with a Convolutional Neuronal Network. We propose two stages: feature extraction with a neuronal convolutional network and correspondences correction. Methodology is shown in Fig. 1. We can see the main change between both approaches for obtaining an orthomosaic: procedure shown in (Fig. 1a) involves the use of classical computer vision techniques for digital image processing, and we propose to change almost all of these complex processes with a single convolutional neural network as shown in (Fig. 1b).

The process mentioned above for obtaining and correlating features between images is a complex stage, with the extraction of features being one of the most difficult. However, Noh et al., and Teichmann et al. presents a proposal for feature extraction, DEep Local Feature (DELF). This model is particularly useful for

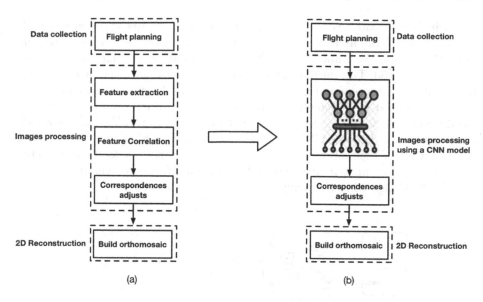

Fig. 1. Traditional methodology is shown on the left (a). We can see that it consists of five stages to obtain an orthomosaic. The most complex steps are those of digital image processing. On the right (b), our proposed methodology replaces the most complex stages of digital image processing with a CNN model

large-scale instance-level image recognition and to index image regions. This model detects and describes semantic local features which can be geometrically verified between images showing the same object instance [21, 25]. DELF use a ResNet50 [12] model trained on ImageNet Dataset [23] as a baseline to feature extracting layers trained with a classification loss. Features are localized based on their receptive fields, which are computed by means of convolutional and pooling layers of a Fully Convolutional Network (FCN). Code is provide in Tensorflow for building a model which could be used to train models for other applications.

Then, based on the DELF model and Noh's work, we used our new dataset including 880 aerial images rescaled to 250 × 250 pixels (Table 1). This dataset was created by capturing multiple aerial images of the entire university campus. Due to the terrain conditions of the campus, a minimum safe flight-height of 100 m and a maximum of 150 m were selected. Overlapping percentages among captured images were considered with two configurations, the first set with 30% both longitudinally and transversely, and the second 50% in both directions.

Table 1. UTM campus image dataset. This is the way images have been organized, so that they can be used to adjust the CNN model.

Height\Overlaping	30% × 30%	50% × 50%
100 mts.	200	400
150 mts.	100	180
Total	300	580

As in Noh's work, we used the original pre-trained ResNet50 model with ImageNet as a base, and we performed a fine-tuning procedure to improve our local descriptors. We employed a FCN at the output of *conv4_x* convolutional block of ResNet50. This output was adjusted in a way that it can be considered like a feature extraction and key points matching machine on aerial images and also this adjusted model could be a replacement for other key point detectors and descriptors. Neural model is shown with detail in Fig. 2. We can see a pair of images supplied to the CNN Pipeline. Internally, DEFL model is truncated at the output of the feature map to be connected to a FCN for finding vector descriptors of the input images and with it a geometric correction applied with the RANSAC algorithm for finally create the orthomosaic.

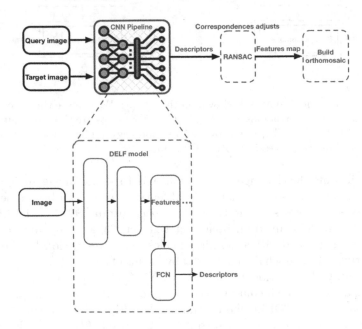

Fig. 2. CNN Pipeline. It uses the DELF model with ResNet50 trained on ImageNet.

After finding correspondences, outliers must be eliminated from estimation through the fundamental matrix since internal parameters of the camera are unknown. However, many of correspondences are faulty and estimating the parameter set with all coordinates is not enough. Therefore, RANSAC algorithm is used on top of the normal model to robustly estimate the parameter set by detecting outliers. The main objective is to determine geometric transformation between both images, that is, to define the fundamental matrix that relates two views of planar target. RANSAC algorithm can help computing the homography matrix [7,16] starting with acquired correspondences. Then, we use RANSAC with the feature vectors extracted from images as a set of observed data points. Moreover, as the model that can be fitted to data points we used an affine transform model. We end up having a set of source and destination coordinates which can be used to estimate the geometric transformation between both images and building an orthomosaic with all previously performed procedures.

4   Experimental Results

In order to evaluate our proposal we analyze qualitative results in two stages. In the first one, we determine the efficiency of our process for feature extraction and matching features in the dataset. In the second experiment, we check results for orthomosaic generation.

Our methodology achieves the goals to obtain a feature map by training a CNN model that encodes learning to select features for the matching task. Figure 3 shows feature correspondences between a pair of images from our database. It successfully matches them in a challenging environment as the UTM campus. It could include changes in contrast, sharpness, brightness and rotations in the images. Moreover, results shown that RANSAC algorithm improves correction of correspondences obtained in (Fig. 3a and 3b). Furthermore, matching points are acceptable and can be compared to those of SIFT algorithm, showing equivalent results Fig. 3c. It is a good benchmark by the SIFT algorithm robustness.

The described process permit to obtain acceptable feature maps to pair aerial images. In Fig. 4, it is shown an example of 2D reconstruction with high-resolution aerial images. In this experiment we used 100 images to perform an orthomosaic reconstruction. This images cover approximately an area of $100\,km^2$ from UTM campus (the campus has around 104 hectares). Some areas do not have constructions (Fig. 4a) and other have buildings (Fig. 4b). Resulting orthomosaics present high-definition details that are acceptable and suitable to be employed for several purposes.

On the other hand, we analyze the similarity of the resulting orthomosaics versus a manual reconstruction, an aerial image that covers the same area and an orthomosaic obtained from Pix4DMapper. We use Euclidean distance to determine the similarity between each one (smaller distance, greater similarity). The results are shown in Table 2. It shows that the resulting orthomosaics with our methodology are similar to those obtained by a traditional or manual process, but with high-definition details and less processing time.

(a)

(b)

(c)

Fig. 3. Figures show feature maps obtained with real images. (a) Matching points without geometric correction. (b) Geometric correction with RANSAC and (c) Results obtained with SIFT.

(a)   (b)

Fig. 4. 2D reconstructions of UTM campus. We present two examples of an orthomosaic reconstruction using 100 high definition images at an altitude of 150 m and 50% of overlapping (a) without buildings and (b) with buildings.

Table 2. Comparison between our resulting orthomosaics and other reconstructions. This table shows the Euclidean distance as a measure of similarity between orthomosaics. Manual reconstruction was performed with images at 50% of their original resolution. Aerial image was taken at twice the reference height. Pix4DMapper's orthomosaic only shows 75% of total established area.

Resulting orthomosaic vs	Euclidean distance
Manual reconstruction	11.564167
Image at twice of the reference height	16.99647
Orthomosaic from Pix4DMapper	20.794645

5 Conclusions

In this work a simple methodology to built orthomosaics using aerial images is presented. This study focuses on verify the methodology that uses a deep neuronal network model. Preliminary results generating orthomosaics have been verified qualitatively obtaining feature maps and matching points between images pairs.

Resulting orthomosaics were evaluated using Euclidean distance as a similarity measure. Orthomosaic obtained was compared with: a manual reconstruction, an image captured at a higher height and a reconstruction obtained with commercial software. It is showed that our methodology provides similar results to those obtained as described before but with a high-definition details. Our results are as well comparable with those obtained with traditional computer vision algorithms.

On the other hand, reconstruction of larger areas such as the entire campus of the university with a high-resolution orthomosaic map is being considered for future work.

References

1. Arandjelovic, R., Gronat, P., Torii, A., Pajdla, T., Sivic, J.: Netvlad: CNN architecture for weakly supervised place recognition. In: Proceedings of the IEEE Conference on Computer Vision and Pattern Recognition, pp. 5297–5307 (2016)
2. Arya, S., Mount, D.M., Netanyahu, N.S., Silverman, R., Wu, A.Y.: An optimal algorithm for approximate nearest neighbor searching fixed dimensions. J. ACM (JACM) **45**(6), 891–923 (1998)
3. Asale, R., Rae: fotogrametría: Diccionario de la lengua española, November 2019. https://dle.rae.es/fotogrametria
4. Barazzetti, L., Remondino, F., Scaioni, M.: Extraction of accurate tie points for automated pose estimation of close-range blocks. In: ISPRS Technical Commission III Symposium on Photogrammetric Computer Vision and Image Analysis (2010)
5. Chen, Y., Liu, L., Gong, Z., Zhong, P.: Learning CNN to pair UAV video image patches. IEEE J. Sel. Top. Appl. Earth Obs. Remote Sens. **10**(12), 5752–5768 (2017)
6. Cheng, Y., Xue, D., Li, Y.: A fast mosaic approach for remote sensing images. In: 2007 International Conference on Mechatronics and Automation, pp. 2009–2013. IEEE (2007)
7. Dung, L.R., Huang, C.M., Wu, Y.Y., et al.: Implementation of RANSAC algorithm for feature-based image registration. J. Comput. Commun. **1**(6), 46–50 (2013)
8. Escalante Torrado, J.O., Porras Díaz, H., et al.: Ortomosaicos y modelos digitales de elevación generados a partir de imágenes tomadas con sistemas uav. Tecnura **20**(50), 119–140 (2016)
9. Fischler, M.A., Bolles, R.C.: Random sample consensus: a paradigm for model fitting with applications to image analysis and automated cartography. Commun. ACM **24**(6), 381–395 (1981)
10. Ghamisi, P., Yokoya, N.: Img2dsm: height simulation from single imagery using conditional generative adversarial net. IEEE Geosci. Remote Sens. Lett. **15**(5), 794–798 (2018)
11. Gordo, A., Almazán, J., Revaud, J., Larlus, D.: Deep image retrieval: learning global representations for image search. In: Leibe, B., Matas, J., Sebe, N., Welling, M. (eds.) ECCV 2016, Part VI. LNCS, vol. 9910, pp. 241–257. Springer, Cham (2016). https://doi.org/10.1007/978-3-319-46466-4_15
12. He, K., Zhang, X., Ren, S., Sun, J.: Deep residual learning for image recognition. In: Proceedings of the IEEE Conference on Computer Vision and Pattern Recognition, pp. 770–778 (2016)
13. Li, J., Ai, M., Hu, Q., Fu, D.: A novel approach to generating DSM from high-resolution UAV images. In: 2014 22nd International Conference on Geoinformatics (GeoInformatics), pp. 1–5. IEEE (2014)
14. Li, S., Zhu, Z., Wang, H., Xu, F.: 3D virtual urban scene reconstruction from a single optical remote sensing image. IEEE Access **7**, 68305–68315 (2019)
15. Li, T., Hailes, S., Julier, S., Liu, M.: UAV-based SLAM and 3D reconstruction system. In: 2017 IEEE International Conference on Robotics and Biomimetics (ROBIO), pp. 2496–2501. IEEE (2017)

16. Li, X., Liu, Y., Wang, Y., Yan, D.: Computing homography with RANSAC algorithm: a novel method of registration. In: Electronic Imaging and Multimedia Technology IV, vol. 5637, pp. 109–112. International Society for Optics and Photonics (2005)
17. Lingua, A., Marenchino, D., Nex, F.: Automatic digital surface model (DSM) generation procedure from images acquired by unmanned aerial systems (UASS). RevCAD J. Geodesy Cadastre **9**, 53–64 (2009)
18. Lingua, A., Marenchino, D., Nex, F.: A comparison between "old and new" feature extraction and matching techniques in photogrammetry. RevCAD J. Geodesy Cadastre **9**, 43–52 (2009)
19. Lowe, D.G.: Object recognition from local scale-invariant features. In: Proceedings of the Seventh IEEE International Conference on Computer Vision, vol. 2, pp. 1150–1157. IEEE (1999)
20. Lowe, D.G.: Distinctive image features from scale-invariant keypoints. Int. J. Comput. Vis. **60**(2), 91–110 (2004)
21. Noh, H., Araujo, A., Sim, J., Weyand, T., Han, B.: Large-scale image retrieval with attentive deep local features. In: Proceedings of the IEEE International Conference on Computer Vision, pp. 3456–3465 (2017)
22. Radenović, F., Tolias, G., Chum, O.: CNN image retrieval learns from BoW: unsupervised fine-tuning with hard examples. In: Leibe, B., Matas, J., Sebe, N., Welling, M. (eds.) ECCV 2016. LNCS, vol. 9905, pp. 3–20. Springer, Cham (2016). https://doi.org/10.1007/978-3-319-46448-0_1
23. Russakovsky, O., et al.: Imagenet large scale visual recognition challenge. Int. J. Comput. Vis. **115**(3), 211–252 (2015)
24. Tang, J., Folkesson, J., Jensfelt, P.: Geometric correspondence network for camera motion estimation. IEEE Robot. Autom. Lett. **3**(2), 1010–1017 (2018)
25. Teichmann, M., Araujo, A., Zhu, M., Sim, J.: Detect-to-retrieve: efficient regional aggregation for image search. In: Proceedings of the IEEE Conference on Computer Vision and Pattern Recognition, pp. 5109–5118 (2019)
26. Weerasekera, C.S., Latif, Y., Garg, R., Reid, I.: Dense monocular reconstruction using surface normals. In: 2017 IEEE International Conference on Robotics and Automation (ICRA), pp. 2524–2531. IEEE (2017)
27. Zuliani, M.: Ransac for dummies. Vision Research Lab, University of California, Santa Barbara (2009)

Improvement of the Turajlić Method
for the Estimation of Gaussian Noise in Images

Manuel G. Forero[1]($\boxtimes$) (iD), Sergio L. Miranda[1] (iD), and Carlos Jacanamejoy-Jamioy[2] (iD)

[1] Semillero Lún, Facultad de Ingeniería, Universidad de Ibagué, Ibagué, Colombia
{manuel.forero,sergio.miranda}@unibague.edu.co
[2] Semillero Lún, Facultad de Ciencias Naturales y Matemáticas,
Universidad de Ibagué, Ibagué, Colombia
carlos.jacanamejoy@unibague.edu.co

Abstract. Gaussian noise estimation is an important step in some of the more recently developed noise removal methods. This is a difficult task and although several estimation techniques have been proposed recently, they generally do not produce good results. In a previous comparative study, among several noise estimation techniques, a method proposed in 2017 by Turajlić was found to give the best results. Although acceptable, they are still far from ideal. Therefore, several changes to this method are introduced in this paper to improve the estimation. Tests on monochromatic images contaminated with different levels of Gaussian noise showed that the modified method produces a significant improvement in the estimation of Gaussian noise, over 35%, at a slightly higher computational cost.

Keywords: Noise estimation · Gaussian noise · Image filtering · Smoothing filters · Noise reduction

1 Introduction

A common problem in image processing is noise, which affects the further analysis of the information contained in the images. For this reason, different methods of noise removal have been developed and several of the latest image filtering and edge detection techniques require an estimation of the noise level to obtain better results, since in this way their parameters can be automatically adjusted to make the filtering more or less aggressive, or in the case of edge detectors, to consider as borders only those abrupt changes that are greater than those produced by the noise. These techniques include: phase congruency to detect edges [1], smoothing filters such as the anisotropic operator [2], and some considered state-of-the-art, based on sparse modelling such as K-SVD [3].

The most studied type of noise in the literature is Gaussian, since it is the most frequently found in digital images. In general, noise estimation techniques can be classified in two groups, depending on whether they are performed in the spatial or the frequency domain. Spatial techniques can be grouped into three, those that subdivide the image in blocks, those that employ filtering and the hybrids [4, 5] that have emerged in recent

© Springer Nature Switzerland AG 2020
K. M. Figueroa Mora et al. (Eds.): MCPR 2020, LNCS 12088, pp. 108–117, 2020.
https://doi.org/10.1007/978-3-030-49076-8_11

years. In general, block-based techniques [6] try to identify uniform areas where intensity variations are ideally due to noise alone, and then statistical tools are used to estimate noise. Those based on filters obtain a high pass or bandpass image from the original to separate the noise from the signal and then estimate the remaining noise level in the obtained image. Techniques where the estimation is done in the frequency domain [7] perform an analysis of the image spectrum using a decorrelation transformation, such as the discrete wave transformation.

In a recent study [8] it was found that estimation methods do not provide a good approximation in the vast majority of cases and, in general, hybrid methods provide a better estimate. Among these methods is a two-stage method developed by Turajlić [9]. In the first one, the image is filtered with a bandpass filter and the resulting image is divided into non-overlapping blocks of 64×64 pixels. The approximate dispersion of each block is then calculated using an equation that greatly reduces the cost of the computation compared to the standard deviation calculation. The second stage, in which these blocks are subdivided according to the minimum standard deviation obtained, is continued for 15% of the blocks. Finally, 85% of the sub-blocks with lower dispersion are used to obtain the noise level estimate.

This document is organized as follows. Section 2 describes the materials and experimental framework used to assess the performance of the proposed improvement. Section 3 describes the original Gaussian noise estimation algorithm from Turajlić. Section 4 introduces the proposed improvements to the original algorithm. Section 5 shows and discusses the results obtained. Finally, Sect. 6 presents our conclusions.

2 Material

Twenty 512×512 pixels monochrome images, two synthetic and eighteen taken from [10–12], were used to calculate the correction factor of the proposed method, shown in the Appendix. Forty 512×512 pixels monochrome images, two synthetics and thirty images taken from [10–12] were used for method validation and to compare the results against the original method. The images were contaminated with different levels of Gaussian noise from $\sigma = 5$ to $\sigma = 40$ in increments of 5. The algorithms were written in Java as plugins of the freely available program ImageJ [13].

3 Turajlić Method

In the best case the noise estimate can be made easily, obtaining the standard deviation of a completely uniform region, ideally constituted by a single grey level, since it is assumed that the variations in intensity are due only to noise. Therefore, the most homogeneous blocks within the image are searched to make the estimation. However, in practice, it is not common to find completely uniform areas and signal variations affect noise estimation. To separate noise from signal, in some cases, band-pass or high-pass filters are used, as shown in Eq. 1, and the noise estimate is made on the obtained image. Following this trend, in 2017 Turajlić proposed a hybrid method for noise estimation [9], which consists of two parts. In the first one, the 15% of the most homogeneous areas of the image are found. To this end, the image is convoluted with the band-pass filter h given in Eq. 1 and the resulting image is divided into non-overlapping blocks of 64×64 pixels. The dispersion of each block is obtained by Eq. 2, which greatly reduces the calculation time compared to the standard deviation method. Then, the minimum standard deviation σ_{min} of all blocks is found.

$$h = \begin{matrix} 1 & -2 & 1 \\ -2 & 4 & -2 \\ 1 & -2 & 1 \end{matrix} \tag{1}$$

$$\hat{\sigma} = \sqrt{\frac{\pi}{2}} \frac{1}{6(W-2)(H-2)} \sum_{Image} |I(x, y) * h| \tag{2}$$

where W and H are the width and height of the block respectively.

In the second part, the homogeneous blocks found in the previous step, are subdivided into blocks of side equal to $\sigma_{min} \times k$, where k is a constant equal to 1.9, found empirically. Then the dispersion of each sub-block is estimated using Eq. 2 and the 85% of the sub-blocks with less dispersion are defined as homogeneous regions. Finally, the noise level estimate is calculated as the average of the final homogeneous blocks.

4 Enhanced Method

As mentioned above, in the original method proposed by Turajlić as part of the first step, the 64×64 pixel block, which has the minimum dispersion σ_{min}, is found. However, the dispersion of a block can be low, even if the noise in the image is high when the block is located in a very light or very dark region of the image, as the intensity cannot fall out of the available dynamic range $[0, L-1]$, where L is usually 255, which can lead to an erroneous estimation of the noise level, as can be observed in Fig. 1. To overcome this problem, it is verified that the gray level of all pixels within the block with the minimum dispersion σ_{min}, is in the range given by the block mean $\mu \pm 3\,\sigma_{min}$, as shown in Eq. 3. The block is discarded if the pixel intensities are not within the range. In this case, the next block with the lowest dispersion that meets the criteria given by Eq. 3 is searched for. Once found, its dispersion is taken as σ_{min}.

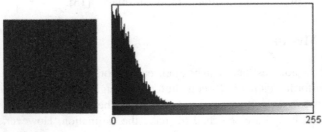

Fig. 1. Homogeneous dark area with an added noise of $\sigma = 25$ and its histogram. As can be seen in the image histogram, the probability density function of the noise is incomplete, thus affecting the estimation. The estimate found for this case is $\sigma = 15$.

$$0 \leq \mu_{i,j} - 3\sigma_{min} \wedge \mu_{i,j} + 3\sigma_{min} \leq 255 \tag{3}$$

where $\mu_{i,j}$ the mean of pixel intensity of block.

$$\hat{\sigma} = \sqrt{\frac{\pi}{2}} \frac{1}{A_F(W-2)(H-2)} \sum_{Image} |I(x,y) * h| \tag{4}$$

Although Eq. 2, proposed by Turajlić, allows an acceptable approximation of noise in 64×64 pixel blocks, it was found experimentally not to work well for calculating noise in the smaller sub-blocks [8]. To correct this problem, the number 6 in the denominator of Eq. 2 is replaced in the second stage of the method by an A_F fitting factor as shown in Eq. 4.

To find a suitable fitting factor A_F a study was performed on 20 images, 2 synthetic and 18 natural ones taken from [10–12], which are shown in Fig. 2. These were contaminated with different levels of Gaussian noise from 5 to 40 in increments of 5. Two tests were performed per image for the same noise level where the value of A_F varies from 4 to 10 in increments of 0.25. Then, the setting value that gave the best noise estimation for each image was taken, taking into account that the final noise of each image is given by the natural noise plus the added noise. Therefore, the standard deviation of the noise in the final image, obtained from adding noise to each study image, was found by Eq. 5 [6], where σ, σ_0 [14] y σ_{ADD} are the final, natural and added noise standard deviations. Finally, the function of the curve which best fits the data is calculated.

$$\sigma = \sqrt{\sigma_0^2 + \sigma_{ADD}^2} \tag{5}$$

Figure 3 shows the set of fitting values obtained by each image, for each level of aggregated noise. To find the fitting value A_F, the function that best approximates the set of points was searched for. Two approaches were taken for this purpose. In the first approach, a third degree polynomial function was used and, in the second one, an exponential function was used, both shown in Fig. 3. The results obtained with

Fig. 2. Images employed to find A_F.

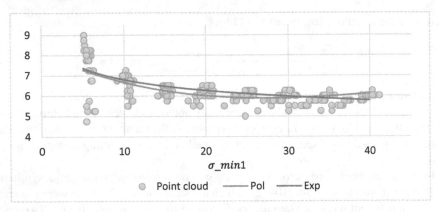

Fig. 3. F_A point cloud and approximation functions.

both functions are denoted as Exp and Pol. In both approaches, the minimum standard deviation of the first stage σ_{min1} was taken as the independent variable. The functions obtained are presented in Eqs. 6 and 7.

$$A_f = -0.00003779\sigma_{min1}^3 + 0.005\sigma_{min1}^2 - 0.189\sigma_{min1} + 8.09 \tag{6}$$

$$A_F = 8.8912(\sigma_{min1})^{-0.117} \tag{7}$$

5   Results

Forty images contaminated with different levels of Gaussian noise were used to evaluate the behavior of the Turajlić method and the modified ones titled EXP and POL. It should be noted that these were evaluated on two percentages of area. 15% of the image, equivalent to 10 blocks, and with 11%, equivalent to 7 blocks of 64×64 pixels. The execution time, mean square error (MSE) and the percentage of acceptable estimates were evaluated. This last measure is included, since in a previous work it was found that the published methods produce, in general, an estimate far from the real value. For a noise level estimate to be considered acceptable in this study, it must not exceed a 7% error. This error is calculated through Eq. 8, relative percentage error. On the other hand, MSE is calculated from Eq. 9.

$$ERP = \frac{|y - \hat{y}|}{y} * 100 \tag{8}$$

$$MSE = \frac{1}{n}\sum_{i=1}^{n} (y_i - \hat{y_i}) \tag{9}$$

Where y is the expected or ideal value and $\hat{y}$ is the estimated value.

As shown in Table 1, the percentage of the average relative error ERP Eq. 8 decreases when using the first proposed modification introduced in Sect. 4, which consists of verifying that the block with the minimum standard deviation (σ_{min1}) is adequate.

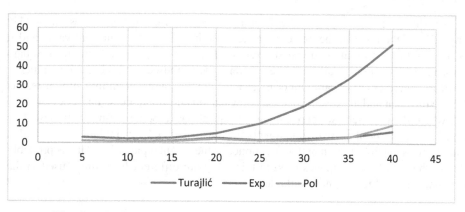

Fig. 4. MSE for each added noise level (σ_{ADD}), using 11% of the image.

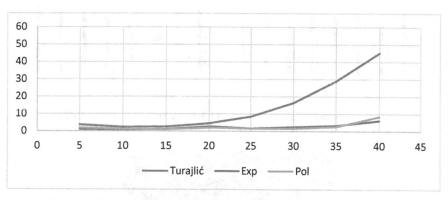

Fig. 5. MSE for each added noise level (σ_{ADD}), using 15% of the image.

Table 1. Average ERP with the 40 test images between σ_{min1} and the total noise standard deviation Eq. 5 of each image.

Mode	5	10	15	20	25	30	35	40
Turajlić	19%	11%	10%	11%	13%	15%	17%	18%
Proposed	18%	8%	6%	6%	5%	5%	5%	6%

Figure 6 shows the average method execution time for each added noise level. As expected, the proposed method run time is higher compared to the original due to the higher number of steps added. As can also be observed, the working area of the image does not significantly affect the execution time.

As shown in Fig. 4 y 5, if the Turajlić method is used in both cases (with 11% and 15% of the image), the noise estimate is further away from the real value and it is observed that from an aggregated noise level of 15 ($\sigma_{ADD} = 15$), the mean square error increases exponentially. On the contrary, the proposed methods achieve a better estimate regardless of the amount of noise added to the image, obtaining similar results for the different added noise levels, except when the additional noise has a deviation of 40, where the exponential approximation (Exp) allows a better estimate. It should be noted that the error of noise estimation obtained with Turajlić, original method, found in this study, is much higher than that mentioned in the original paper [9]. This is probably due to the fact that the images used in this study are different from those used in the original paper, which are not available.

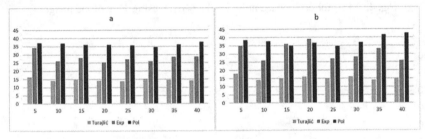

Fig. 6. Execution times in milliseconds. a) Using 11% of the image. b) Using 15% of the image.

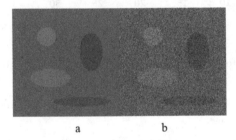

Fig. 7. a) Original image. b) Images degraded by noise $\sigma_{ADD} = 40$.

Table 2. Percentage of acceptable estimates using 11% and 15% of the image.

Mode	11%	15%
Turajlić	37.81%	37.19%
Exp	73.13%	72.81%
Pol	71.88%	69.69%

The modifications produced an increase of slightly less than twice the percentage of acceptable estimates from the original method (Table 2). It should be noted that during the process it was found that the improved method had a drawback since for images with a large amount of black or white background (with minimum or maximum pixel intensity) presented an appreciable estimation error greater than 30%.

As can be seen in Figs. 4 and 5 the estimation error increases significantly when the degradation is greater than 35, which is caused by the fact that the magnitude of changes due to noise are similar to those produced by the edges of the images, as illustrated in Fig. 7 and, therefore, the sub-block with minimum standard deviation may erroneously include edges of the image.

6 Conclusions

In this document an improvement was made on the original noise estimation method of Turajlić. The changes introduced allowed more accurate results to be obtained, improving the Gaussian noise level estimate by more than 30%, regardless of the percentage of blocks, 11 and 15%, taken in the first stage to estimate the noise in the second. In both cases the mean square error and the computation time is similar.

The first improvement, which consists of discarding the blocks whose Gaussian noise function is truncated, allows to decrease the noise estimation error. Furthermore, two proposed approaches, polynomial and exponential, for the calculation of an adjustment factor allowed to improve even more the accuracy of the estimation, being the error similar in both cases. However, when the noise level is higher than $\sigma = 35$ the exponential approach gives better results. The estimation method fails when the noise level is very close to the amplitude of the borders of the objects in the image, since abrupt changes produced by noise are confused with those of the signal.

Acknowledgements. This work was supported by project # 19-488-INT Universidad de Ibagué.

Appendix

Forty images, some of them shown in Fig. 8, were used in this study, Twenty-seven taken from [10], seven from [12] and four from [11]. The remaining two are synthetic images created by the image processing research laboratory Lún of the Universidad de Ibagué.

Fig. 8. Images of size 512 × 512 pixels used in this study. a) Obtained from [10], b) from [12] and c) from [11].

References

1. Kovesi, P.: Image features from phase congruency. Videre J. Comput. Vis. Res. **1**(3), 1–26 (1999)
2. Perona, P., Jitendra, M.: Scale-Space and Edge Detection Using Anisotropic Diffusion. IEEE, Berkeley (1990)
3. Aharon, M., Elad, M., Bruckstein, A.: K-SVD: an algorithm for designing overcomplete dictionaries for sparse representation. IEEE Trans. Signal Process. **54**(11), 4311–4322 (2006)
4. Park, R.-H., Yang, S., Jung, J.-H., Shin, D.-H.: Block-based noise estimation using adaptive Gaussian filtering. IEEE Trans. Consum. Electron. **51**(1), 218–226 (2005)
5. Begović, A., Turajlić, E.: Noise estimation using adaptive gaussian filtering and variable block size image segmentation. In: IEEE EUROCON 2017 - 17th International Conference on Smart Technologies, pp. 250–254 (2017)
6. Liu, W.: Additive white Gaussian noise level estimation based on block SVD. In: IEEE Workshop on Electronics, Computer and Applications, pp. 960–963 (2014)
7. Tang, C., Yang, X., Zhai, G.: Dual-transform based noise estimation. In: Proceedings of the IEEE International Conference on Multimedia Expo (ICME), pp. 991–996, July 2012
8. Forero, M.G., Miranda, S.L.: Gaussian noise estimation methods. In: Proceedings of the SPIE 11137, Applications of Digital Image Processing XLII, San Diego (2019)
9. Turajlić, E.: A fast noise level estimation algorithm based on adaptive image segmentation and Laplacian convolution. In: MIPRO, pp. 486–491 (2017)
10. Universidad de Granada: Test Images. http://decsai.ugr.es/cvg/dbimagenes/
11. ImageProcessing.com. http://www.imageprocessingplace.com/root_files_V3/image_databa ses.htm

12. University of Southern California: The USC-SIPI Image Database. http://sipi.usc.edu/databa se/database.php
13. Rasband, W.S.: ImageJ, U. S. National Institutes of Health, Bethesda, Maryland, USA 1997–2018. https://imagej.nih.gov/ij/
14. Immerkær, J.: Fast noise variance estimation. Comput. Vis. Image Underst. **64**, 300–301 (1996)

Spatial α-Trimmed Fuzzy C-Means Algorithm to Image Segmentation

Virna V. Vela-Rincón[✉], Dante Mújica-Vargas, Manuel Mejía Lavalle, and Andrea Magadán Salazar

Tecnlógico Nacional de México/CENIDET, Cuernavaca, Morelos, Mexico
{viryvela,dantemv,mlavalle,magadan}@cenidet.edu.mx

Abstract. An important aspect should be taken into account, when an image is segmented, the presence of atypical information. In this investigation an algorithm is proposed that is noise tolerant in the segmentation process. A method to image segmentation that combines Fuzzy C-Means (FCM) algorithm and Trimmed Means filter, called Spatial α Trimmed Fuzzy C-means, using local information to achieve better segmentation. The FCM is very sensitive to noise, and the Trimmed Means filter is used to eliminate outliers with a lower computational cost. Compared to some state-of-the-art algorithms, the proposed is faster and noise tolerant, demonstrating better performance in the metrics considered.

Keywords: Image segmentation · Fuzzy C-Means · α-Trimmed means filter · Spatial information

1 Introduction

Image segmentation is defined as a process by which an image is divided into homogeneous areas, each belonging to different objects with similar features (i.e. color, contrast, brightness, texture and so on) [16]. Segmentation has a many applications medical image analysis, autonomous vehicles, video surveillance, and augmented reality to count a few [8]. Generally, the image segmentation method are divided into histogram-based approaches [11], edge detection approaches [19], region-based approaches [15], clustering approaches [12].

One of the most popular image segmentation fuzzy algorithms is Fuzzy C-means (FCM), which gives each data a degree of membership through a distance measure to assign to the nearest group [6,17]. FCM is a noise sensitive algorithm, some investigations try to improve this algorithm, some guarantee noise immunity and preserve image details by incorporating local spatial and gray information together to enhances the clustering performance [5]; other try to reduce the high computational complexity that surge an iterative calculation of the distance between pixels within local spatial neighbors and clustering centers, based on morphological reconstruction and membership filtering [10]. There algorithms used to determinate the parameters by introducing density for each sample,

© Springer Nature Switzerland AG 2020
K. M. Figueroa Mora et al. (Eds.): MCPR 2020, LNCS 12088, pp. 118–128, 2020.
https://doi.org/10.1007/978-3-030-49076-8_12

where the density peaks are use to determinate the number of clusters and the initial membership matrix [13].

In this context, this paper considers the use of α-Trimmed Means filter to add robustness to FCM and to ensure better performance spatial relationship is added using a median and a mean filter. An important contribution is that α is not a simple parameter, it depends on the standard deviation of the data to be processed. Another important feature is the use of spatial information, since nearby pixels are more likely to belong to the same group. So, the objective of this paper is to segmented images that was corrupted with atypical information, specifically additive, multiplicative and fixed impulsive noise. The experimental results in different databases demonstrate that the proposed algorithm have a better performance compared to some algorithms of the state of the art being more tolerant to noise.

2   Background

2.1   Fuzzy C-Means

The Fuzzy C-means algorithm assigns each pixel to the nearest cluster, it allows a gradual membership in a closed interval of data $\mu \in [0, 1]$, with respect to the groups or regions of interest. This flexibility allows to express the membership of a data to all the groups or regions simultaneously. The problem of dividing a set of data into different groups is a the task of minimizing the square distances between the data and the centers of the groups. The objective function J_f is based on the sum of minimum square distances. Formally, a fuzzy clustering model of a given data set X in c groups is defined to be optimal when it minimizes the following objective function [4]:

$$J_f\left(X; U_f, C\right) = \sum_{i=1}^{n} \sum_{j=1}^{c} \mu_{ij}^m d_{ij}^2 , \tag{1}$$

where U_f represents the membership matrix and C a vector with the centers of the cluster, μ_{ij} is the membership of pixel x_i in the jth cluster, d_{ij}^2 is a norm metric, and the parameter m controls the fuzziness of the resulting partition, and $m = 2$ is regularly used. The objective function J_f is minimized by two steps. First the degrees of membership are optimized by setting the parameters of the groups, then the prototypes of the groups are optimized by setting the degrees of membership. The equations resulting from the two iterative steps form the Fuzzy C-Means clustering algorithm [4].

$$u_{ij} = \frac{1}{\sum_{k=1}^{c} \left(\frac{d_{ij}^2}{d_{ik}^2}\right)^{\frac{2}{m-1}}} = \frac{d_{ij}^{-\frac{2}{m-1}}}{\sum_{k=1}^{c} d_{ik}^{-\frac{2}{m-1}}} , \tag{2}$$

$$c_j = \frac{\sum_{i=1}^{n} \mu_{ij}^m x_i}{\sum_{i=1}^{n} \mu_{ij}^m} , \tag{3}$$

2.2 α-Trimmed Means Filter

It has been observed that the mean filter is more efficient in deleting Gaussian noise than the median filter, but it is less efficient in eliminating impulsive noise; while the median filter completely eliminates impulse noise. However, when there is Gaussian and impulsive noise, the trimmed means filter becomes an alternative between the mean and median filters.

The proposed algorithm is based on α-Trimmed Means filter [2], which does an ascending sorting of data, removing (trimming) a fixed fraction α ($0 \leq \alpha \leq 0.5$), called trimmed number, from high and low ends of sorted set, and calculate the average of the remaining values. This filter is given by:

$$\alpha\text{-trimmed mean filter}\{x_{(1)}, \dots, x_{(N)}; \alpha\} = \sum_{i=\alpha N+1}^{N-\alpha N} x_{(i)} \frac{1}{N - 2\alpha N} \qquad (4)$$

where N are the total number of samples and αN the number of samples trimmed at each side. The subscript with parentheses $x_{(i)}, i = 1, \dots, N$ indicates the order statistics for example, $x_{(1)} \leq x_{(2)} \leq, \dots, \leq x_{(N)}$.

3   Method

In this section, we present the proposed method to segment images with atypical information, this method combines the theory of the Fuzzy C-means algorithm and the α-Trimmed Means filter, It also incorporates the spatial relationship of the pixels.

3.1   Mathematical Formulation of α-Trimmed Fuzzy C-Means Algorithm with Spatial Information

To detect outliers grouped in a small group, we define the Spatial α-Trimmed Fuzzy C-means (STrFCM) algorithm, which trim a fraction of the data, reducing processing time. In addition, the spatial relationship between the pixels and their neighbors was used through filtered images using the mean and the median. A clustering algorithm is defined as optimal when it minimizes its objective function, in this case can be formulated as follows:

$$J_{Tr}(X, \bar{X}, \tilde{X}; U, C) = \sum_{i=1}^{H(\alpha)} \sum_{c=1}^{C} u_{ic}^m \|x_i - h_c\|^2 + \alpha_1 \sum_{i=1}^{H(\alpha)} \sum_{c=1}^{C} u_{ic}^m \|\bar{x}_i - h_c\|^2$$

$$+\alpha_2 \sum_{i=1}^{H(\alpha)} \sum_{c=1}^{C} u_{ic}^m \|\tilde{x}_i - h_c\|^2, \qquad \sum_{c=1}^{C} u_{ic} = 1, \quad u_{ic} \geq 0 \quad (5)$$

where u_{ic} is the membership degree of element x_i to each of the groups, $m > 1$ is the fuzziness parameter. I ranges on all the subsets of the objects, containing $H(\alpha) = \lfloor I \cdot (1 - \alpha) \rfloor$ objects ($\lfloor \cdot \rfloor$ is the integer part of a given value). In order to enhance robustness of clustering, it is considered to take a window of 3x3 around the pixel as vectors with the mean and median $\bar{X}, \tilde{X}$, respectively. α_1 and α_2 controls the compensation between the original image and the corresponding mean or median filtered image. To find the equations to update the membership matrix and the centers of the clusters, an optimization process must be carried out using Lagrange multipliers [14]. So, a new function $\mathcal{L}$ is defined:

$$\mathcal{L} = \sum_{i=1}^{H(\alpha)} \sum_{c=1}^{C} u_{ic}^m \|x_i - h_c\|^2 + \alpha_1 \sum_{i=1}^{H(\alpha)} \sum_{c=1}^{C} u_{ic}^m \|\bar{x}_i - h_c\|^2$$

$$+ \alpha_2 \sum_{i=1}^{H(\alpha)} \sum_{c=1}^{C} u_{ic}^m \|\tilde{x}_i - h_c\|^2 - \sum_{i=1}^{H(\alpha)} \lambda \left(\sum_{c=1}^{C} u_{ij} - 1 \right) \quad (6)$$

The necessary condition to minimize is that the partial derivatives of the Lagrange function become zero, that is

$$\begin{cases} \frac{\partial L}{\partial u_{ij}} = 0, & \Leftrightarrow \quad m u_{ij}^{m-1} \|x_i - h_j\|^2 + \alpha_1 m u_{ij}^{m-1} \|\bar{x}_i - h_j\|^2 \\ & \quad + \alpha_2 m u_{ij}^{m-1} \|\tilde{x}_i - h_j\|^2 = \lambda \qquad (a) \\ \frac{\partial L}{\partial \lambda} = 0, & \Leftrightarrow \quad \sum_{c=1}^{C} u_{ic} = 1 \qquad\qquad\qquad\qquad (b) \end{cases} \quad (7)$$

Solve for u_{ij} from Eq. 7.a, and get:

$$u_{ij} = \left[\frac{\lambda}{m(\|x_i - h_j\|^2 + \alpha_1 \|\bar{x}_i - h_j\|^2 + \alpha_2 \|\tilde{x}_i - h_j\|^2)} \right]^{\frac{1}{m-1}} \quad (8)$$

Summing these equations over clusters,

$$\sum_{c=1}^{C} u_{ic} = \sum_{c=1}^{C} \left[\frac{\lambda}{m(\|x_i - h_c\|^2 + \alpha_1 \|\bar{x}_i - h_c\|^2 + \alpha_2 \|\tilde{x}_i - h_c\|^2)} \right]^{\frac{1}{m-1}}$$

$$= \left(\frac{\lambda}{m} \right)^{\frac{1}{(m-1)}} \left\{ \sum_{c=1}^{C} \left[\frac{1}{\|x_i - h_c\|^2 + \alpha_1 \|\bar{x}_i - h_c\|^2 + \alpha_2 \|\tilde{x}_i - h_c\|^2} \right]^{\frac{1}{(m-1)}} \right\} = 1 \quad (9)$$

So,

$$\left(\frac{\lambda}{m} \right)^{\frac{1}{(m-1)}} = \frac{1}{\sum_{c=1}^{C} \left(\frac{1}{\|x_i - h_c\|^2 + \alpha_1 \|\bar{x}_i - h_c\|^2 + \alpha_2 \|\tilde{x}_i - h_c\|^2} \right)^{\frac{1}{m-1}}} \quad (10)$$

Replace in the Eq. 8 to get the update equation for membership degrees,

$$u_{ij} = \frac{\left(\|x_i - h_j\|^2 + \alpha_1 \|\bar{x}_i - h_j\|^2 + \alpha_2 \|\tilde{x}_i - h_j\|^2 \right)^{-\frac{1}{m-1}}}{\sum_{c=1}^{C} \left(\|x_i - h_c\|^2 + \alpha_1 \|\bar{x}_i - h_c\|^2 + \alpha_2 \|\tilde{x}_i - h_c\|^2 \right)^{-\frac{1}{m-1}}} \quad (11)$$

In a process similar to the previous one, the update equations for cluster centers can be obtained:

$$h_c = \frac{\sum_{i=1}^{I} u_{ic}^m [x_i + \alpha_1 \bar{x}_i + \alpha_2 \tilde{x}_i]}{(1 + \alpha_1 + \alpha_2) \sum_{i=1}^{I} u_{ic}^m} \tag{12}$$

It is important to mention that the trimmed data only applies to the adjustment of the centers of the clusters, where i extends only in the subset of the non-trimmed objects I. To avoid defining different parameters in the proposed method, it was decided to use the standard deviation, as a way to establish a reference value based on the dispersion that exists in the data. This mainly applies to the α parameter, and then extends over α_1 and α_2. α and α_2 in most experiments remain at 0.2, while α_1 ranges from 0.5 to 0.6.

4   Experimental Results

In this section, we first describe the considered metrics to measure the quality of Image Segmentation, second, the databases where the algorithm proposed was tested, and finally the comparatives results with others algorithms.

4.1   Metrics

The metrics used were:

– Accuracy, to measure the quality of the clustering.

$$Accuracy = \frac{TP + TN}{TP + TN + FP + FN} \tag{13}$$

– Recall, measure the positive data that were clustered correctly.

$$Recall = \frac{TP}{TP + FN} \tag{14}$$

– DICE similarity coefficient (DSC), quantify the overlap between segmentation results with the ground truth.

$$DSC = 2 \bullet \frac{\text{Area}(X \cap Y)}{\text{Area}(X) + \text{Area}(Y)} \tag{15}$$

– Jaccard similarity coefficient (JSC), was used to measure the quality of segmentation.

$$JSC = \frac{\text{Area}(X \cap Y)}{\text{Area}(X) + \text{Area}(Y) - \text{Area}(X \cap Y)} \tag{16}$$

Where TP are the true positives, TN the true negatives, FP the false positives and FN the false negatives. X and Y represent the ground truth and segmented images, respectively.

4.2   Databases

This algorithm was tested in the following databases: ISIC 2019 database, contains over 13,000 dermoscopic images, for this paper only tested on 50 images since the images are very similar [7], Sky database, a collection of 60 images with ground truth for sky segmentation [1], Weizmann Segmentation Evaluation Database with 200 gray level images along with ground truth segmentations [18], in Fig. 1 only three images are depicted (one for each database).

(a) ISIC 2019 database   (b) Sky database   (c) Weizmann database

Fig. 1. Sample image of each database.

4.3   Experimental Results

The algorithm was tested with Fuzzy C-means [3]; with a version FCM that incorporate spacial information (FCM_S2), the comparison is only against FCM_S2 and not against FCM_S1, because the first one has a better performance, the parameter α from this algorithm was 3.8 [6]; with the SOM artificial neural network [9]; and with an improved FCM algorithm based on morphological reconstruction and membership filtering (FRFCM). All of them were implemented in the MATLAB R2018b environment. The parameters used in each execution are $c = 2$, $m = 2$ and $\varepsilon = 0.00001$. To evaluate the segmentation performance two experiments were implemented, one for medical image (ISIC 2019 Database) and other to real images (Sky and Weizmann databases).

Medical Image Database. In Fig. 2 we can observe the quantitative results of the experiments with the three types of noise considered (Gaussian, Salt and Pepper and Speckle noise) on ISIC 2019 Database, the means value is zero to Gaussian and Speckle noise and the variance is defining by densities between 0.03 to 0.40 and 0.10 to 0.40, respectively; Salt and pepper noise images with densities between 3% to 40%. We can observe that the higher the density of the noise that corrupts the images, the algorithm of the proposal in most of the metrics considered shows a higher performance compared to the other algorithms, with an accuracy of approximately 95%. The qualitative results of the experiment are presented in Fig. 3, just to depict the results of the proposal algorithm, the segmentation result is shown by selecting the highest noise density with which the experiments were performed. Each row shows a result of the segmentation

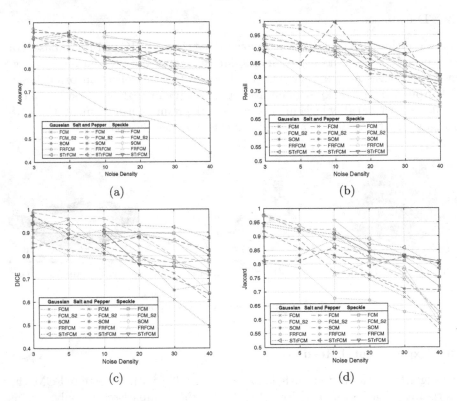

(a)   (b)

(c)   (d)

Fig. 2. Quantitative result of the experiments with four metrics considered in medical image with the proposed algorithm and image corrupted by the noises considered.

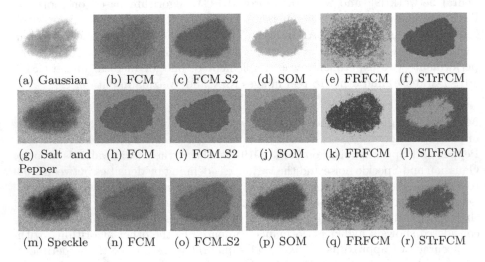

(a) Gaussian   (b) FCM   (c) FCM_S2   (d) SOM   (e) FRFCM   (f) STrFCM

(g) Salt and Pepper   (h) FCM   (i) FCM_S2   (j) SOM   (k) FRFCM   (l) STrFCM

(m) Speckle   (n) FCM   (o) FCM_S2   (p) SOM   (q) FRFCM   (r) STrFCM

Fig. 3. Qualitative result of the experiments in medical image with the proposed algorithm and image corrupted by the noises considered.

of each algorithm corrupted with the three types of noise considered. In all the type noises, the proposal algorithm shows a segmentation superior to the other methods, reinforcing the quantitative results.

Real Image Database. The second experiment performed on real image databases, Weizmann and Sky database, on Fig. 4 summarizes the quantitative results of the experiments performed in these databases, these demonstrate that the proposed method has an advantage over the other techniques with which it was compared, showing that the higher the noise the performance is better.

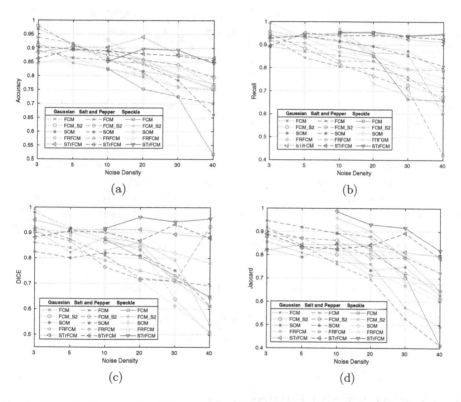

Fig. 4. Quantitative result of the experiments with four metrics considered in real images with the proposed algorithm and image corrupted by the noises considered.

The result of the previous segmentation shows that the algorithm of the proposal is tolerant to different types of noise. So, the qualitative result are presented on Fig. 5, just to depict the experiments, an image is shown, where each row is the result of segmentation with the three different types of noise, and the columns are the algorithms with which the comparison was made, here it is shown that the proposed algorithm has a higher performance than the other techniques.

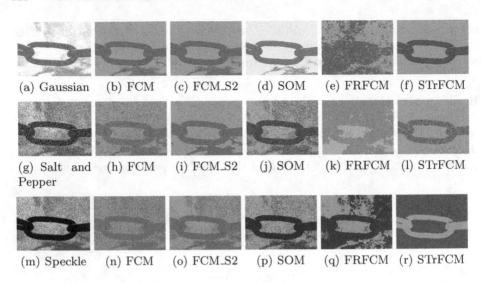

(a) Gaussian   (b) FCM   (c) FCM_S2   (d) SOM   (e) FRFCM   (f) STrFCM

(g) Salt and   (h) FCM   (i) FCM_S2   (j) SOM   (k) FRFCM   (l) STrFCM
Pepper

(m) Speckle   (n) FCM   (o) FCM_S2   (p) SOM   (q) FRFCM   (r) STrFCM

Fig. 5. Qualitative result of the experiments in real images with the proposed algorithm and image corrupted by the noises considered.

The execution time, as shown in Table 1 in which the proposed algorithm exceeds others, except the FCM. Despite the fact that FCM is faster than the proposed method, it has lower performance and this research seeks to achieve better segmentation precision. The proposed algorithm is faster because when trim is applied to the data it removes approximately 40% when $\alpha = 0.2$ or 60% when $\alpha = 0.3$, therefore the execution time is reduced.

Table 1. Execution time (seconds) of tested algorithms

	FCM	FCM_S2	SOM	FRFCM	STrFCM
Time	0.05	0.853	1.58	0.73	0.61

5   Conclusions and Future Work

This article focuses on the segmentation of images with atypical information, mainly adding to the images tested additive, multiplicative and impulsive fixed noise, with different densities. A technique was proposed that combines the Fuzzy C-Means algorithm and Trimmed Means filter, improving the segmentation performance since it also considers the spatial relationship between the pixels. We try to demonstrate that if spatial information is added to an algorithm, this will have a better performance. In the experiments we were able to verify this hypothesis, since our proposal algorithm had a better result than the rest of the selected algorithms. In addition it was experimented in different types of databases, medical and real images, obtaining high performance and demonstrating an average accuracy of 92%. Furthermore to the precision obtained, the algorithm proved to be faster than the other techniques. In many cases, our algorithm shows inferior performance in noise-free images, this happens because it was designed to be tolerant to image noise, which means that the algorithm result when there is no noise will not always be better than the methods for comparison. As future work, we plan to add texture or other characteristics to the images.

Acknowledgments. The authors of this work express their gratitude to CONACYT, as well as to the Tecnologico Nacional de Mexico/CENIDET for financing through the project "Diffuse Controller for adjusting stiffness coefficients of a deformable model for real-time simulation of the tissues of the human liver.

References

1. Alexandre, E.B.: IFT-SLIC: geração de superpixels com base em agrupamento iterativo linear simples e transformada imagem-floresta. Ph.D. thesis, Universidade de São Paulo (2017)
2. Bednar, J., Watt, T.: Alpha-trimmed means and their relationship to median filters. IEEE Trans. Acoustics, Speech, Signal Process. **32**(1), 145–153 (1984)
3. Bezdek, J.C., Ehrlich, R., Full, W.: FCM: the fuzzy c-means clustering algorithm. Comput. Geosci. **10**(2–3), 191–203 (1984)
4. Bezdek, J.C., Keller, J., Krisnapuram, R., Pal, N.: Fuzzy models and algorithms for pattern recognition and image processing, vol. 4. Springer, New York (1999). https://doi.org/10.1007/b106267
5. Cai, W., Chen, S., Zhang, D.: Fast and robust fuzzy c-means clustering algorithms incorporating local information for image segmentation. Pattern Recogn. **40**(3), 825–838 (2007)
6. Chen, S., Zhang, D.: Robust image segmentation using FCM with spatial constraints based on new kernel-induced distance measure. IEEE Trans. Syst. Man Cybern. Part B (Cybernetics) **34**(4), 1907–1916 (2004)
7. Combalia, M., et al.: BCN20000: dermoscopic lesions in the wild. arXiv preprint arXiv:1908.02288 (2019)
8. Forsyth, D.A., Ponce, J.: Computer Vision: A Modern Approach. Prentice Hall Professional Technical Reference, New Jersey (2002)
9. Kohonen, T.: The self-organizing map. Proc. IEEE **78**(9), 1464–1480 (1990). https://doi.org/10.1109/5.58325
10. Lei, T., Jia, X., Zhang, Y., He, L., Meng, H., Nandi, A.K.: Significantly fast and robust fuzzy c-means clustering algorithm based on morphological reconstruction and membership filtering. IEEE Trans. Fuzzy Syst. **26**(5), 3027–3041 (2018)
11. Li, M., Wang, L., Deng, S., Zhou, C.: Color image segmentation using adaptive hierarchical-histogram thresholding. PLoS ONE **15**(1), e0226345 (2020)
12. Mújica-Vargas, D., Gallegos-Funes, F.J., Rosales-Silva, A.J., de Jesús Rubio, J.: Robust c-prototypes algorithms for color image segmentation. EURASIP J. Image Video Process. **2013**(1), 63 (2013)

13. Pei, H.X., Zheng, Z.R., Wang, C., Li, C.N., Shao, Y.H.: D-FCM: density based fuzzy c-means clustering algorithm with application in medical image segmentation. Procedia Comput. Sci. **122**, 407–414 (2017)
14. Rockafellar, R.T.: Lagrange multipliers and optimality. SIAM Rev. **35**(2), 183–238 (1993)
15. Sima, H., Guo, P., Zou, Y., Wang, Z., Xu, M.: Bottom-up merging segmentation for color images with complex areas. IEEE Trans. Syst. Man Cybern. Syst. **48**(3), 354–365 (2017)
16. Szeliski, R.: Computer Vision: Algorithms and Applications. Springer, London (2010). https://doi.org/10.1007/978-1-84882-935-0
17. Wang, M., Wan, Y., Gao, X., Ye, Z., Chen, M.: An image segmentation method based on fuzzy c-means clustering and cuckoo search algorithm. In: Ninth International Conference on Graphic and Image Processing (ICGIP 2017), vol. 10615, p. 1061525. International Society for Optics and Photonics (2018)
18. Winn, J., Criminisi, A., Minka, T.: Object categorization by learned universal visual dictionary. In: Tenth IEEE International Conference on Computer Vision (ICCV 2005) vol. 1. vol. 2, pp. 1800–1807. IEEE (2005)
19. Zhou, S., Lu, Y., Li, N., Wang, Y.: Extension of the virtual electric field model using bilateral-like filter for active contours. Signal Image Video Process. **13**(6), 1131–1139 (2019)

Restoration of Range Images by the Gaussian Pyramid Method, Testing Different Interpolation Techniques to Select the Best Performance

Enrique Chavira Calderón◉ and Alejandra Cruz-Bernal$^{(\boxtimes)}$ ◉

Universidad Politécnica de Guanajuato, Cortazar, Gto, Mexico
{echavira,acruz}@upgto.edu.mx

Abstract. The inpainting method implemented in this work was used to estimate the missing information in a range image from a single image, achieved independence of the RGB image of the scene or multiple range images to perform the restoration. The proposal is based on improving the results of restoring range images using the Gaussian Pyramid method. This, finding the best interpolation technique to use in this method to estimate the missing information. Different interpolation techniques were computed and applied in order to know the best option to implement. This is carried out considering the amount of information that can be estimated, processing time and the total of information missing in the image to be restored. The method was tested with five different databases, one of which was created specifically for this work. These databases include different interior scenarios with several objects. A qualitative and quantitative comparative analysis of the obtained results was performed.

Keywords: Range image · Image restoration · Gaussian Pyramid method

1 Introduction

The range image is obtained from a stereo system or a depth sensor, with which a disparity map or a depth image is formed, respectively. These images have attractive characteristics, such as invariance to lighting, rotation or scaling as presented by Creusot [1], allowing to work with data without prior processing. However, the stereo system and depth sensors such as the Kinect present images with areas without information, because infrared light does not find a surface where it is reflected. These areas can be presented as small spaces scattered throughout or as large regions of null information (without intensity levels).

There are different works in the literature focused on the restoration of range images, which we can classify into four groups according to the information they use to perform this task. The first consists of techniques that make use of one or several RGB images of the same scene for restoration, as presented by Pertuz et al. [2] and Torres and Dudek [3]. Wang et al. [4] use multiple range and RGB images. Additionally, the inpainting method is used to estimate depth and color information together. The second group is

© Springer Nature Switzerland AG 2020
K. M. Figueroa Mora et al. (Eds.): MCPR 2020, LNCS 12088, pp. 129–138, 2020.
https://doi.org/10.1007/978-3-030-49076-8_13

conformed of proposals that implement multiple range images obtained by the same sensor. Examples are found in Kolmogorov and Zabih [5] and Lin et al. [6] use a couple of images to carry out the restoration, both use the graphic cutting method for this task. Lin et al. [7] use a sequence of depth images obtained by the Xtion pro live sensor, achieving both spatial and temporal noise reduction in depth images. The third group makes use of several images, but these come from different sensors. The works presented by Zhu et al. [8] and Gudmundsson et al. [9], use images obtained by the ToF sensor, as well as, a stereo system. The authors take advantage of both systems, obtaining higher quality range images. However, prior alignment and calibration of these sensors is required. Finally, the fourth group consists of those works that use only the range image to restore. Sruthy et al. [10] and Chen et al. [11] manage to restore range images without using RGB images or multiple images. Both works detect regions without information, classify or reduce these regions in a preprocessing, and use linear and non-linear filters to restore the image.

This proposal implements an inpainting method that allows restoring the range image from the same information, without using other images (RGB or range). The processing is carried out by the Gaussian Pyramid method proposed by Ogden [12], which is mainly based on processes of reduction, enlargement and interpolation. In addition to implementing the method for range images, the work is based on improving the results of the Gaussian Pyramid by modifying the interpolation technique to be used. Usunariz in [13] uses this method but applying the 4-directions interpolation technique. The proposed work aims to improve the Gaussian Pyramid method in order to carry out the interpolation technique to be used, this to know which can be the most appropriate technique to achieve the best results. The obtained results are analyzed qualitatively and quantitatively, evaluating aspects such as the percentage of estimation achieved and the processing time. The structure of the work presented is described below. Section 2 describes the proposed methodology, as well as the interpolation techniques that were implemented. Section 3 exposes the obtained experimental results and Sect. 4 shows the conclusions based on the results.

2 Methodology

In this section, both the inpainting method for range images and the different interpolation techniques to be evaluated are described. In addition, in Sect. 2.3, it is detailed how the pixel estimation is performed applying an interpolation technique.

2.1 Restoration by Gaussian Pyramid Method

Fig. 1. Block diagram representative of the Gaussian Pyramid method to restored range image.

The proposed method for restoring range images is illustrated in Fig. 1. The first block is made up of the initialization processes, in which different matrices are created to store the corresponding information to be used in the following stages (Fig. 2, Block 1). A counter is also initialized to carry the number of reductions that make up the Gaussian reduction pyramid and a variable called "flag", is declared with a value of one that will serve as the start and end the indicator for the next stage.

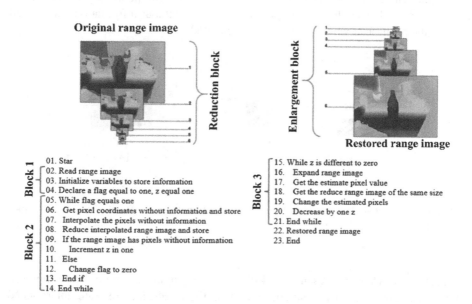

Fig. 2. Visual diagram and pseudocode of the process of restoring a range image. Block 1 corresponding to the initialization of the process; Block 2 refers to compute of the Reduction process and Block 3 aims to realize the Enlargement process.

Second block consists of a cycle for the processes of estimating information and removes areas without information (Fig. 2, Block 2). First process uses a function named "Fill_holes". This function estimates the values of the empty pixels contain in the outline of the regions without information on the image being processed. For this task, it is proposed to implement four different interpolation techniques (see Sect. 2.2), in order to know which technique allows us to obtain the best restoration. Second process involves reducing regions without information present in the original image (Fig. 2, Reduction block). The cycle ends when there are no more zones without information, indicating the last reduction. Finally, third block consists of a cycle to carry out the enlargement of the restored but reduced image; as well as the replacement of the estimated information in each image. Applying the Gaussian Pyramid technique, the enlargement process is realized. By means of several substitution processes (Fig. 2, Block 3), an increasingly restored image is obtained (Fig. 2, Enlargement block). The cycle repeats until an image of the same size as the initial image is reached, indicating that the restored image has been obtained. The result is the restored image, which is the initial image, but with the estimated information inserted in the areas that initially did not contain information.

2.2 Interpolation Techniques

4-directions. This interpolation technique was implemented according to the technique proposed by Usunariz in [13]. Staring from a pixel without information, it is necessary to confirm that, the two consecutive neighboring pixels have information. This can happen to the right, left, up or down. Figure 3a shows a representative diagram of this technique, where the possible information to use in the interpolation process (purple area) is observed. The black box represents the pixel without information and the red point is the position at which its value is interpolated.

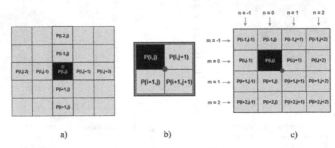

a)   b)   c)

Fig. 3. Representative diagram of a) 4-directions, b) Bilinear and c) Bicubic technique. (Color figure online)

4-directions 2. Here, is presented a 4-directions technique variation. The difference with respect to the original technique consists in the values that are going interpolated and these are not consider for the following interpolations. Therefore, all interpolated values, are stored in a vector, until the interpolation process is finished, these new values are substituted in the corresponding pixels. Figure 4 shows a comparison of the two techniques.

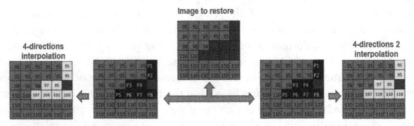

Fig. 4. Representative diagram of the estimation of pixels without information by 4-directions and 4-directions 2 interpolation techniques. The estimated value of the pixels P6, P7 and P8 changes according to the technique implemented.

Bilinear. In digital image processing, Bilinear interpolation makes use of the four pixels closest to the position to be interpolated [14]. A representative diagram of the Bilinear interpolation for pixel estimation without information is shown in Fig. 3b. The purple area encloses the 2×2 neighborhood pixels. The black box represents the pixel without information, which can take any of the four positions within the red area. The point is the position of which the pixel value is interpolated. The estimated value is calculated with (1), which ponders the influence of the neighborhood pixels and their corresponding weights in both directions. The parameters a and b are the distances in the vertical and horizontal direction, respectively, to the point interpolated from the pixel $P(i, j)$. The function $H(x)$ is the core function of the Bilinear interpolation given by (2).

$$P(i, j) = H(-a) * H(b) * P(i, j) + H(-a) * H(-(1 - b)) * P(i, j + 1)$$
$$+ H(1 - a) * H(b) * P(i + 1, j) + H(-(1 - a)) * H(-(1 - b)) * P(i + 1, j + 1)$$
$$\tag{1}$$

$$H(x) = \begin{cases} 1 - |x|, x \in [-1, 1] \\ 0, otherwise \end{cases} \tag{2}$$

Bicubic. This technique considers the pixels within a 4×4 neighborhood to interpolate the desired value [15]. A representative diagram of this interpolation technique for pixel modification without information is shown in Fig. 3c. The purple area encloses 16 pixels within the 4×4 neighborhood; the black box represents the empty pixel, which can take any of the four positions within the red area. The red point is the position at which it interpolates in value of the empty pixel. The variables m and n indicate the rows and columns, respectively. This contains the neighborhood pixels in a 4×4 region for the point to be interpolated. Equation (3) allows us to calculate the value to be estimated; which is the pixel interpolated by a double sum of the product between each pixel, that is contained in the neighborhood and this is multiplied by the value of the core function $H_c(x)$, calculate with (4), in both directions.

$$P(i, j) = \sum_{m=-1}^{m=2} \sum_{n=-1}^{n=2} P(i + m, j) * H_c(m - a) * H_c(n - b) \tag{3}$$

$$H_c(x) \begin{cases} (\alpha + 2) * |x|^3 - (\alpha + 3) * |x|^2 + 1, & x \in [0, 1) \\ \alpha * |x|^3 - 5\alpha * |x|^2 + 8\alpha * |x| - 4\alpha, & x \in [1, 2) \\ 0, & x \geq 2 \end{cases} \tag{4}$$

The process for the estimation of the pixel without information through this interpolation technique considers that, several pixels within the neighborhood will take the value of zero. Therefore, the contribution within the double sum will be null by these pixels. For the above, the processing time is reduced due to redundant calculations must be avoided. That is, if should know what are the pixels that really have information within the neighborhood, then these are the ones that contribute their weight to obtain the estimate. For this, the position of the pixel $P(i, j)$ must be known, since it will act as a pivot in (3), which allows us to know according to the location of the pixel without information, the values that m and n must take.

2.3 Fill_holes Function

All scheduled versions of the "Fill_holes" function follow the same execution sequence. Figure 5 presents a diagram with the steps performed by the "Fill_holes" function in general. The diagram begins with a matrix that represents an image that contains a region without information (the blue pixels make up the region without information while the orange pixels contain information). First step that takes place is an inverse binarization, identifying the regions without information. Second step is carried out is an emptying of all the regions present in the binary image. That is, all the pixels that do not correspond to the contour of each region will take a value of zero. In the third step, the interpolation process is performed to estimate the value of the pixels corresponding to the contour of the region without information. Here the different interpolation techniques described above are implemented, where each uses information from the neighborhood surrounding the pixel to be interpolated.

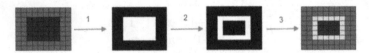

Fig. 5. Representative diagram of the process carried out by the "Fill_holes" function.

2.4 Analysis of the Amount of Missing Information in Range Images

Additionally, an analysis was carried out to know if the amount of missing information in the range images influences with respect to the estimated information rate. For this, all the images of the databases were used, being a total of 159. A statistical analysis of frequency distribution was performed, to know the average value of information estimation at different intervals of missing information. Eight classes were obtained, with a class width of 9. However, classes 5–8 were grouped into one (new class 5), because they had few elements in comparison with to the other classes, making the results insignificant. The five classes, identified by C1, C2, C3, C4 and C5, contain 51, 43, 37, 14 and 14 images, respectively.

3   Results

To validate and know the performance of the proposed method using the different interpolation techniques, it was tested with five image range databases. Database B1 [16] with 43 images of 581 × 421 pixels, B2 generated for this research work, that contains 26 images of 627 × 464 pixels, B3 comprehends 26 images of the generic Middlebury database [17, 18] of 1282 × 1110 pixels, B4 [19, 20], with 24 images of 581 × 421 pixels, and B5 [21] with 40 images of 581 × 421 pixels. Figure 6 shows the qualitative results of applying our proposed method, using different interpolation techniques to restore range images. Two images of each databases are presented. The images in the first column presents the RGB image as reference only of the scene. Column 2 illustrates the range images to be restore. From the third to the sixth columns, the images restored by interpolation techniques are shown, corresponding to the techniques 4-directions, 4-directions 2, Bilinear and Bicubic, respectively. According to the qualitative results, since the implementation of the proposed method with interpolation in 4-directions, an image restoration is obtained (Fig. 6, column 3). However, this technique can add non-existent artifacts (Fig. 6, row 5, column 3) due to the how interpolation is performed. The second technique, 4-directions 2, does not present this problem (Fig. 6, row 5, column 4); this is due to not considering the interpolated pixels for the following interpolations. In the same way, an improvement is qualitatively obtained in several estimated regions, this with respect to the 4-directions (Fig. 6, row 2, column 4). Bilinear and Bicubic techniques offer the best qualitative results; because increasing the number of estimated regions with a major homogeneity with respect to intensity values (Fig. 6, row 1, 3–4, column 5–6).

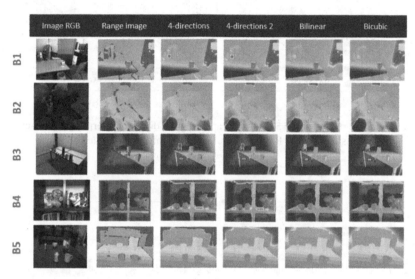

Fig. 6. Qualitative results of the restoration applying our proposed method with different interpolation techniques using several generic and own databases. Range images are presented in the HSV color space, where regions in red represent pixels without information.

To compare and determine which of these techniques is the most appropriate to use in our estimation method, three metrics were calculated to evaluate them: the mean square error (MSE), the estimated information rate and the processing time. Figure 7 presents the obtained results for the estimated information rate (Fig. 7b) and the processing time (Fig. 7a), applying the four interpolation techniques in each database. Considering the individual average of each technique in the different databases, we calculate a global average to compare them with each other and know the overall result of implementing these techniques in range images. First, we present the global results regarding the percentage of estimated information: For the 4-directions technique, 79.33% is presented, for 4-directions 2 with of 79.9%, for Bilinear and Bicubic, 83.76% and 83.57%, respectively. According to the above, the 4-directions, the original technique, is the one that presents the lowest estimated information rate. The technique 4-directions 2, Bilinear and Bicubic, presents 0.71%, 5.58% and 5.34%, respectively, of increase with respect to the 4-directions. Now we present the global results regarding the processing time:

For the 4-directions a 0.84 s, 4-directions 2 an average of 1.04 s, for the Bilinear and Bicubic interpolation, there are 30.60 s and 12.23 s, respectively. Therefore, the original technique is the one that presents the best processing time, followed by the 4-directions 2, then the Bicubic and finally, the Bilinear. For the MSE, all techniques have a value greater than 97%, so it is ensured that the original information is maintained in the depth image, regardless of the interpolation technique implemented.

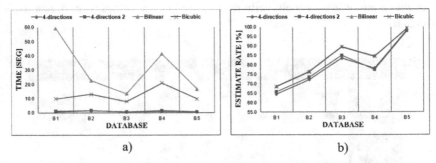

a)   b)

Fig. 7. Quantitative results in the 5 databases, applying the different interpolation techniques. a) Results of the processing time. b) Results of the estimated information rate.

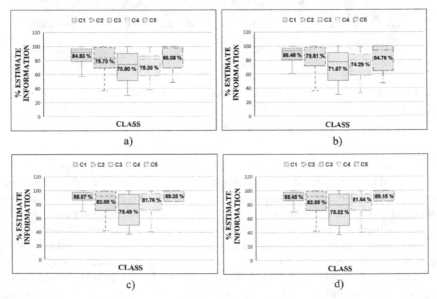

a)   b)

c)   d)

Fig. 8. Estimated information rate by class, applying the different interpolation techniques. a) 4-directions, b) 4-direcctions 2, c) Bilinear and d) Bicubic.

The results of the estimated information rate with respect to the percentage of missing information presented by the range images are presented below. First, for the 159 images, with a maximum missing information of 68.2% and a minimum of 0.5%. The analysis was carried out in all classes, applying several interpellation techniques, the results are shown in Fig. 8. The 4-directions, Bilinear and Bicubic techniques have a maximum percentage of estimated pixels for C5, images with the greatest lack of information. C3 is the one that, regardless of the interpolation technique implemented, presents the minimum amount of estimated information. The 4-directions 2 technique allows obtaining a higher estimation rate for images belonging to class C1. Therefore, the present proposal offers repetitiveness and consistency with respect to the different interpolation techniques here tested.

4 Conclusions

The implementation of the Gaussian Pyramid method allows the restoration of range images from the same image, without making use of multiple range images or RGB image. The interpolation technique used in this method does affect the result of the restoration of the range images. The original interpolation technique, 4-directions, can present non-existent artifacts in the restored image. However, this problem does not occur when applying the other interpolation techniques. According to the amount of information missing in the range images, the interpolation techniques in 4-directions, Bilinear and Bicubic, have a maximum of estimated pixels for the C5. The 4-directions 2 technique has a value maximum estimate for C1. Finally, it is concluded that, if the processing time is not an important point to consider, the Bilinear interpolation technique is the recommended technique to implement. If the processing time is important, it is recommended to implement the 4-directions 2 technique, since, although it has a longer time than the original technique, it allows to increase the amount of estimated pixels and does not show the problem of unwanted artifacts.

Future work implies the restored range images will be used to perform object detection tests, whose results in processing time and detection accuracy will be compared with those obtained from the detection of objects in range images without process.

References

1. Creusot, C.: A machine-learning approach to keypoint detection and landmarking on 3D meshes. Int. J. Comput. Vision **102**, 146–179 (2013)
2. Pertuz, S.: Region-based depth recovery for highly sparse depth maps. In: Proceedings - International Conference on Image Processing, pp. 2074–2078 (2018)
3. Torres, L.: Reconstruction of 3D models from intensity images and partial depth. In: AAAI, pp. 476–481 (2004)
4. Wang, L.: Stereoscopic inpainting: joint color and depth completion from stereo images. In: 26th IEEE Conference on Computer Vision and Pattern Recognition (2008)
5. Kolmogorov, V.: Computing visual correspondence with occlusions using graph cuts. In: Proceedings of the Eighth IEEE International Conference on Computer Vision, vol. 2, pp. 508–515 (2001)
6. Lin, M.: Surfaces with occlusions from layered stereo. In: IEEE Computer Society Conference on Computer Vision and Pattern Recognition (2003)

7. Lin, B.: Temporal and spatial denoising of depth maps. Sensors (Basel, Switzerland) **15**, 18506–18525 (2015)
8. Zhu, J.: Fusion of time-of-flight depth and stereo for high accuracy depth maps. In: 26th IEEE Conference on Computer Vision and Pattern Recognition, pp. 1–8 (2008)
9. Gudmundsson, S.: Fusion of stereo vision and Time-Of-Flight imaging for improved 3D estimation. Int. J. Intell. Syst. Technol. Appl. **5**, 425 (2008)
10. Sruthy, T.: Novel method for depth map pre-processing in depth image based rendering. Int. J. Eng. Sci. Res. Technol. **6**, 185–190 (2017)
11. Chen, W.: Efficient depth image based rendering with edge dependent depth filter and Interpolation. In: IEEE International Conference on Multimedia and Expo, pp. 1314–1317 (2005)
12. Ogden, J.: Pyramid-based computer graphics. RCA Eng. **30**(5), 4–15 (1985)
13. Usunariz, I.: Tesis Restauración de imágenes mediante Pirámide Gaussiana y técnicas de reducción y ampliación. Universidad Publica de Navarra (2014)
14. Han, D.: Comparison of commonly used image interpolation methods. In: Proceedings of the 2nd International Conference on Computer Science and Electronics Engineering, vol. 1, pp. 1556–1559 (2013)
15. Qifang, X.: Super-resolution reconstruction of satellite video images based on interpolation method. Procedia Comput. Sci. **107**, 454–459 (2017)
16. Bernal, A.: Object detection from range imagen using the sparse keypoint detector technique. IEEE Latin Am. Trans. **16**(5), 1532–1538 (2018)
17. Scharstein, D.: High-accuracy stereo depth maps using structured light. In: IEEE Computer Society Conference on Computer Vision and Pattern Recognition, vol. 1, pp. 195–202 (2003)
18. Scharstein, D.: Learning conditional random fields for stereo. In: IEEE Computer Society Conference on Computer Vision and Pattern Recognition (2007)
19. Yaman, M.: Multimodal stereo vision using mutual information with adaptive windowing. In: 13th IAPR Conference on Machine Vision and Applications (2013)
20. Yaman, M.: An iterative adaptive multi-modal stereo-vision method using mutual information. J. Vis. Commun. Image Represent. **26**, 115–131 (2015)
21. Lai, K.: Unsupervised feature learning for 3D scene labeling. In: IEEE International Conference on Robotics and Automation, pp. 3050–3057 (2014)

A Novel Set of Moment Invariants for Pattern Recognition Applications Based on Jacobi Polynomials

Rafael Augusto Rocha Angulo, Juan Martín Carpio⬤,
Alfonso Rojas-Domínguez$^{(\boxtimes)}$ ⬤, Manuel Ornelas-Rodríguez, and Héctor Puga⬤

Tecnológico Nacional de México-Instituto Tecnológico de León, 37290 León, Gto., Mexico
Alfonso.Rojas@gmail.com

Abstract. A novel set of moment invariants for pattern recognition applications, which are based on Jacobi polynomials, are presented. These moment invariants are constructed for digital images by means of a combination with geometric moments, and are invariant in the face of affine geometric transformations such as rotation, translation and scaling, on the image plane. This invariance is tested on a sample of the MPEG-7 CE-Shape-1 dataset. The results presented show that the low-order moment invariants indeed possess low variance between images that are affected by the mentioned geometric transformations.

Keywords: Jacobi polynomials · Orthogonal polynomials · Geometric moment invariants · Jacobi moment invariants · Moments

1 Introduction

The invariant moments are a concept very often used in pattern recognition. Hu [1] presented a set of invariant moments which were obtained through the geometric moments that can be applied. Using Hu's moments, Paschalakis and Lee presented a method in which they classified images using these invariants [2].

Orthogonal moments have been frequently used in image processing. Shu et al. presented a new approach to calculate 2-dimensional moments using Chebyshev orthogonal polynomials in binary and grayscale images [3]. Teague calculated invariant moments of images with Zernike orthogonal polynomials, instead of moments as Hu did before [4]. Benzzoubeir et al., using Legendre orthogonal polynomials and hypergeometric functions, presented a faster and more efficient way to perform 2-dimensional image analysis using Legendre's orthogonal properties in [5].

Orthogonal moments have also been used to measure the quality of an image, i.e. to quantify how distorted or legible an image is. In [6] Abudhahir et al. presented an image quality assessment metric to detect and determine the level of distortion in these by calculating and applying Chebyshev moments. Hosny presented a more efficient way to obtain moments from an image using Gegenbauer polynomials [7]; and more recently Hosny also presented invariants based on Gegenbauer polynomials combined with geometric moments which can be applied to recognition of images [8].

© Springer Nature Switzerland AG 2020
K. M. Figueroa Mora et al. (Eds.): MCPR 2020, LNCS 12088, pp. 139–148, 2020.
https://doi.org/10.1007/978-3-030-49076-8_14

Finally Herrera-Acosta et al. through the use of Gegenbauer polynomials, presented an image descriptor which allows the recognition of visual scenes and compared its performance against the popular SIFT image descriptor [9].

In this paper, a set of orthogonal moment invariants is presented. These moment invariants are obtained by the use of the Jacobi orthogonal moments and can be used in pattern recognition applications. These invariants are expressed as linear combinations of geometric moment invariants, which are presented in image geometric transformations like translation, rotation and scale.

2 Theoretical Background

In this section, basic concepts needed are introduced including regular moment invariants (Subsect. 2.1) and the Jacobi polynomials (Subsect. 2.2).

2.1 Regular Moment Invariants (RMIs)

Regular moment invariants are image characteristics that remain unchanged when a geometric transformation like translation, rotation or scaling is applied on an image [10]. Invariance to translation is achieved by computing the position of the center of mass or centroid (x_c, y_c) of an image [8, 9]:

$$x_c = \mu_{10}/\mu_{00}, \quad y_c = \mu_{01}/\mu_{00} \tag{1}$$

In general, the central geometric moments can be computed as [8, 10]:

$$\mu_{p,q} = \int_{-\infty}^{\infty} \int_{-\infty}^{\infty} (x - x_c)^p (y - y_c)^q f(x, y) \, dxdy \tag{2}$$

Scale invariance can be achieved through scale factor elimination, computed by:

$$\mu'_{p,q} = \frac{\mu_{p,q}}{(\mu_{0,0})^\gamma} \tag{3}$$

where $\gamma = \frac{1}{2}(p + q + 2)$. Similarly, the rotation moment invariants can be defined as:

$$M_{p,q}^{rot} = \int_{-\infty}^{\infty} \int_{-\infty}^{\infty} (x \cos(\theta) + y \sin(\theta))^p (y \cos(\theta) - x \sin(\theta))^q f(x, y) \, dxdy \tag{4}$$

where the rotation angle θ is computed by:

$$\theta = \frac{1}{2} \tan^{-1}\left(\frac{2\mu_{1,1}}{\mu_{2,0} - \mu_{0,2}}\right) \tag{5}$$

Normalized Regular Moment Invariants (RMIs) are defined as:

$$RMI = \frac{RMI_{p,q}}{(M_{0,0})^\gamma} \tag{6}$$

Finally, RMIs to translation, rotation and scale are given by:

$$RMI_{p,q} = \frac{1}{\mu_{0,0}^\gamma} \sum_{k=0}^{p} \sum_{m=0}^{q} \binom{p}{k}\binom{q}{m} (-1)^m (\sin(\theta))^{k+m}$$
$$\times (\cos(\theta))^{p+q-k-m} \mu_{(p-k+m),(q-m+k)} \tag{7}$$

2.2 Orthogonal Jacobi Polynomial

The Jacobi polynomials are the most general of the classic orthogonal polynomials in the domain $[-1, 1]$. All the other classical orthogonal polynomials are special cases of the Jacobi polynomials, and are obtained by setting restrictions on the parameters α and β [11]: for instance, $\alpha = \beta = 0$, defines the Legendre polynomials, and more generally, making $\alpha = \beta$, produces the Gegenbauer or Ultraspherical polynomials. Thus, the work carried out on Jacobi polynomials allows one to work with other classic orthogonal polynomials simply by selecting the values of the parameters α and β.

The Jacobi orthogonal polynomials of order n are defined as follows [12]:

$$P_n^{(\alpha,\beta)}(x) = \frac{1}{2^n} \sum_k^n \binom{n+\alpha}{k}\binom{n+\beta}{n-k}(x-1)^{n-k}(x+1)^k \tag{8}$$

The explicit expansion of $P_n^{(\alpha,\beta)}(x)$ can be rewritten as [12]:

$$P_n^{(\alpha,\beta)}(x) = \sum_{r=0}^n k_{r,n}^{(\alpha,\beta)} x^r \tag{9}$$

with the coefficient matrix $k_{r,n}^{(\alpha,\beta)}$ defined as follows for two different cases:
If $\alpha = \beta$:

$$k_{r,n}^{(\alpha,\beta)} = \frac{(-1)^n(\alpha+1)_n(-n)_r(n+2\alpha+1)_r \Gamma(\alpha+1+r)\Gamma(\frac{1}{2})}{2^r r!(\alpha+1)_r \Gamma(\frac{r-n+1}{2})\Gamma(\frac{r+n}{2+\alpha+1})n!} \tag{10}$$

Otherwise:

$$k_{r,n}^{(\alpha,\beta)} = \frac{(-1)^n(\alpha+1)_n(-n)_r(n+\lambda)_r}{r!(\alpha+1)_r 2^r n!}\ {}_2F_1\left(-n, n+\lambda+r, \alpha+1+r\middle|1/2\right) \tag{11}$$

with two special cases:

$$k_{n,n}^{(\alpha,\beta)} = \frac{(n+\lambda)_n}{2^n n!} \tag{12}$$

and

$$k_{n-1,n}^{(\alpha,\beta)} = \frac{(\alpha-\beta)\Gamma(2n+\lambda-1)}{2^n(n-1)!\Gamma(n+\lambda)} \tag{13}$$

Where $r = 0, 1 \ldots n$, and n is the maximum degree.

The Jacobi polynomials are orthogonal on $[-1, 1]$, and satisfying the relation:

$$\int_{-1}^1 P_n^{(\alpha,\beta)}(x) P_m^{(\alpha,\beta)}(x) w^{(\alpha,\beta)}(x)\, dx = 0 \tag{14}$$

with respect to the weight function defined by:

$$w^{(\alpha,\beta)}(x) = (1-x)^\alpha(1+x)^\beta \tag{15}$$

3 Jacobi Moment Invariants

Following [8], the Jacobi-based 2-D moments of order n, m can be defined as:

$$A_{n,m} = \frac{1}{h_n(\alpha, \beta)h_m(\alpha, \beta)} \int_{-1}^{1} \int_{-1}^{1} f(x, y)k_n^{(\alpha,\beta)}k_m^{(\alpha,\beta)} w^{(\alpha,\beta)}(x)w^{(\alpha,\beta)}(y)\,dxdy \quad (16)$$

where $f(x, y)$ represents a 2-D array (e.g. a digital image) and the Jacobi normalization function is:

$$h_n(\alpha, \beta) = \frac{2^\lambda \Gamma(n + \alpha + 1)\Gamma(n + \beta + 1)}{(2n + \lambda)n!\Gamma(n + \lambda)} \quad (17)$$

and $\lambda \equiv \alpha + \beta + 1$.

Equation (9) can be rewritten in a more computationally efficient manner as:

$$A_{n-m,m} = \frac{1}{h_{n-m}(\alpha, \beta)h_m(\alpha, \beta)} \int_{-1}^{1} \int_{-1}^{1} f(x, y)k_{n-m}^{(\alpha,\beta)}k_m^{(\alpha,\beta)}$$
$$\times w^{(\alpha,\beta)}(x)w^{(\alpha,\beta)}(y)\,dxdy \quad (18)$$

Now, the Jacobi moments invariants (*JMI*) can be defined as:

$$\hat{A}_{n-m,m} = \frac{1}{h_{n-m}(\alpha, \beta)h_m(\alpha, \beta)} \sum_{r=0}^{n-m}\sum_{q=0}^{m} k_{n-m}^{(\alpha,\beta)}k_m^{(\alpha,\beta)}$$
$$\times \int_{-1}^{1} \int_{-1}^{1} T(x, y)x^r y^q\,dxdy \quad (19)$$

where the so-called transformation function $T(x, y)$ is:

$$T(x, y) = (1 - x)^\alpha (1 + x)^\beta (1 - y)^\alpha (1 + y)^\beta f(x, y) \quad (20)$$

The integral in (19) corresponds to the *RMI*s of the intensity function of an image, $f(x, y)$, given in Eq. (7), so that (19) can be rewritten as:

$$\hat{A}_{n-m,m} = \frac{1}{h_{n-m}(\alpha, \beta)h_m(\alpha, \beta)} \sum_{r=0}^{n-m}\sum_{q=0}^{m} k_{n-m}^{(\alpha,\beta)}k_m^{(\alpha,\beta)} RMI_{r,q} \quad (21)$$

4 Methodology

Based on the theory described in the previous section, the Jacobi-based moment invariants were implemented in MATLAB. The pseudocode for the different functions implemented is shown in Algorithms 1 to 4.

Algorithm 1.- Main Routine	
1	$f \leftarrow$ image; $(\alpha, \beta) \leftarrow$ Jacobi parameters
2	Compute image centroids $M_{u,v} \leftarrow$ moments$(f, u, v, x_c, y_c, \alpha, \beta)$
3	Define image centroids using Eq. (1)
4	Define rotation angle through Eq. (5)
5	for $n = 1$ to N:
6	for $m = 1$ to M:
7	$i \leftarrow i + 1$
8	$A_{n,m}[i] = $ JMI$(N, M, \alpha, \beta, x_c, y_c, \theta, f)$
9	end
10	end
11	Return: $A_{n,m}$

Algorithm 2. Jacobi moment invariants (JMI)	
1	**Inputs:** $N, M, \alpha, \beta, x_c, y_c, \theta, f$
2	$\lambda \leftarrow \alpha + \beta + 1$
3	$A_{nm} \leftarrow 0$
4	for $r = 1$ to N:
5	for $q = 1$ to M:
6	Compute $K_{r,N}(r, N, \alpha, \beta)$ and $K_{q,M}(q, M, \alpha, \beta)$ via **Algorithm 3**
7	$RMI = RMI(f, r, q, x_c, y_c, \alpha, \beta, \theta)$
8	$A_{n,m} \leftarrow A_{n,m} + (RMI)(K_{r,N})(K_{q,M})$
9	end
10	end
11	Jacobi normalization through Eq. (17)
12	**Return:** Jacobi moment invariants, JMI

Algorithm 3. Jacobi coefficients calculations	
1	**Inputs:** r, N, α, β
2	$k \leftarrow 0$,
3	$\lambda \leftarrow \alpha + \beta + 1$
4	if $\alpha \neq \beta$
5	$K \leftarrow$ Compute Jacobi coefficient through Eq. (11)
6	if $r = N-1$
7	$K \leftarrow$ Compute Jacobi coefficient through Eq. (13)
8	else
9	$K \leftarrow$ Compute Jacobi coefficient through Eq. (12)
10	end
11	else
12	If mod(N-r, 2) = 0
13	$K \leftarrow$ Compute Jacobi coefficient through Eq. (10)
14	end
15	end
16	**Return:** Jacobi constant K

Algorithm 4. Regular moment invariants (RMI)
1	Inputs: $N, M, \alpha, \beta, x_c, y_c, \theta, f$
2	$RMI \leftarrow 0$
3	for $k = 0$ to p:
4	for $m = 0$ to q:
5	$u \leftarrow p - k + m$
6	$v \leftarrow q - k + m$
7	Compute moments: $M_{u,v} \leftarrow$ moments$(f, u, v, x_c, y_c, \alpha, \beta)$
8	$RMI = $ Eq. (6)$\times M_{u,v}$
9	end
10	end
11	Normalize RMI through Eq. (7)
12	Return: RMI

The Jacobi orthogonal polynomials can be used to obtain moment invariants to geometric transformations in a plane, like translation, rotation and scale. We show this application on a set of images from the MPEG-7 CE-Shape-1 dataset, which is a dataset created to evaluate the performance of 2-D shape descriptors. This dataset includes 1,440 shapes grouped in 70 classes, each containing 20 similar objects [13]. A small sample of these images is shown in Fig. 1. One fourth of the images in the CE-Shape-1 dataset (i.e. 5 images per class) were selected. These images were scaled down to 25% their original size and zero-padded to make all the images 301×301 pixels in size. Afterwards the images were modified through geometric transformations: translation, scaling and rotation with the values in Table 1.

Fig. 1. Subset of images from the MPEG-7 CE-Shape-1

Table 1. Values used for geometric transformations of test images.

Geometric transformation	Applied values
Translation of centroid	(30, 30), (−30, −30)
Scaling	0.75, 1.25
Rotation	−45°, 45°

The result of this procedure is that two extra sets of images for each transformation in Table 1 are produced. Next, the *JMIs* for each of these sets and the original images are computed through Eq. (21), and the differences between the transformed datasets and the original image set are recorded. The parameters used to compute the *JMIs* are $\alpha = \beta = 0.5$, and these were computed from order 0 to 21. Several of these moments are always zero, and these were eliminated from the reported results, so that we finally end up with 14 non-zero moment invariants for each of the geometric transformations. Numerical results are reported in the next section.

5 Experimental Results and Discussion

The differences between the moment invariants of the original image and those of the transformed images were computed in order to observe their variation. The results are shown as boxplots in Figs. 2, 3 and 4. For clarity, the outliers were not plotted. The boxplots presented show the differences between the moment invariants computed on the original images and the moment invariants computed on the modified (translated, rotated or scaled) images. For the sake of a full disclosure, it must be reported that three of the moment invariants computed produce numerical values that are several orders of magnitude larger than the rest of them, and their differences were not plotted because doing so would hinder the appreciation of the rest of the values plotted.

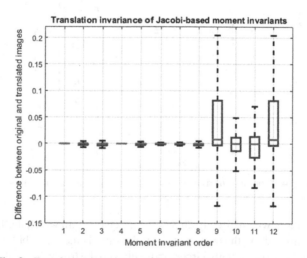

Fig. 2. Translation invariance of Jacobi-based moment invariants.

The boxplots show that for low-order moment invariants the differences are quite small (indicating these are truly invariant to the changes introduced by the geometric transformations); however, as the order increases the differences begin to be more significant. We believe that there are several factors that can explain this behavior. One factor is

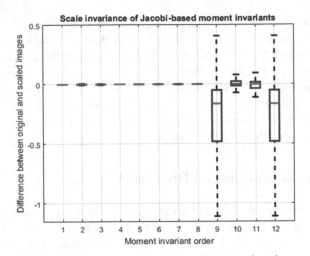

Fig. 3. Scale invariance of Jacobi-based moment invariants.

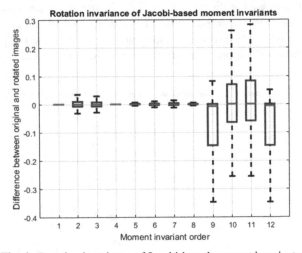

Fig. 4. Rotation invariance of Jacobi-based moment invariants.

the images resolution, which directly affects the precision with which the Jacobi polynomials are approximated. As the degree of the polynomials increases but the image resolution is kept fixed, an increasingly larger error between the true value of the polynomials and their computational approximation is introduced.

A second factor that is also related to the precision with which the polynomials are approximated is how well the orthogonality condition is satisfied by the polynomials as their order increases. For low order polynomials the condition is easily satisfied, but as the order increases orthogonality is no longer guaranteed. This in turn means that image descriptors, such as the moments described, gradually lose their descriptive power and are more prone to be affected by image differences like those introduced by the geometric transformations in our experiments. Finally, a third factor is that, whenever an approximation is employed, the addition of polynomials beyond a certain order is detrimental to the reconstruction ability of this technique.

6 Conclusions

A novel set of moment invariants for pattern recognition application with Jacobi-based orthogonal polynomials was described. Experiments were performed on images from the MPEG-7 CE-Shape-1 dataset. Translation, scaling and rotation were applied to the images and the Jacobi-based image moments were computed. The differences between the image moments of the original and the transformed images were reported to demonstrate the invariance of the proposal. Invariance was confirmed and clearly observed for low-order moments (differences were nearly zero in most cases), while the differences of higher-order moments were more noticeable. We believe that the precision with which the polynomials are computationally approximated is responsible for this behavior. Although low-order moment invariants can be used for pattern-recognition applications, we would like to explore possible solutions to increase the order at which invariance is achieved. In conclusion, the invariants of Jacobi polynomial-based moments work well, but more work is necessary to improve the polynomials approximation and to define the optimal degree to use for each particular image, so that we may obtain more exact descriptors and more uniformly invariant moments.

Acknowledgements. This work was supported by the National Council of Science and Technology of Mexico, through Research Grant CÁTEDRAS-2598 (A. Rojas) and Postgraduate Scholarship 712960 (Rafael A. Rocha).

References

1. Hu, M.K.: Visual pattern recognition by moment invariants. IRE Trans. **8**(2), 179–187 (1962)
2. Paschalakis, S.: Pattern recognition in grey level images using moment based invariant features. In: 7th International Conference on Image Processing and its Applications, Manchester, UK, pp. 245–249, July 1999
3. Shu, H., Zhang, H., Chen, B., Haigron, P., Luo, L.: Fast computation of Tchebichef moments for binary and grayscale images. IEEE Trans. Image Process. **19**(12), 3171–3180 (2010)
4. Teague, M.R.: Image analysis via the general theory of moments. J. Opt. Soc. Am. **70**, 920–930 (1980)
5. Benzzoubeir, S.: Image analysis by hypergeometric function of Legendre moments. In: MELECON 2006 - 2006 IEEE Mediterranean Electrotechnical Conference, pp. 506–509 (2006)
6. Abudhahir, A., Begum, A.H.R Manimegalai, D.: Tchebichef moment based image quality measure. In: 2014 International Conference on Electronics and Communication Systems, ICECS, pp. 1–5 (2014)
7. Hosny, K.M.: Image representation using accurate orthogonal Gegenbauer moments. Pattern Recogn. Lett. **32**(6), 795–804 (2011)
8. Hosny, K.M.: New set of Gegenbauer moment invariants for pattern recognition applications. Arab J Sci Eng. **39**(10), 7097–7107 (2014). https://doi.org/10.1007/s13369-014-1336-8

9. Herrera-Acosta, A., Rojas-Domínguez, A., Carpio, J.M., Ornelas-Rodríguez, M., Puga, H.: Gegenbauer-Based Image Descriptors for Visual Scene Recognition. In: Castillo, O., Melin, P., Kacprzyk, J. (eds.) Intuitionistic and Type-2 Fuzzy Logic Enhancements in Neural and Optimization Algorithms: Theory and Applications. SCI, vol. 862, pp. 629–643. Springer, Cham (2020). https://doi.org/10.1007/978-3-030-35445-9_43
10. Flusser, J., Suk, T., Zitov, B.: Moments and Moment Invariants in Pattern Recognition. Wiley, Chichester (2009)
11. Spencer Doman, B.G.: The Classical Orthogonal Polynomials. World Scientific, New Jersey (2016)
12. Luke, Y.L.: Mathematical Functions and their Applications. Academic Press, New York (1975)
13. Nunes, J.F.: Shape based image retrieval and classification. In: 5th Iberian Conference on Information Systems and Technologies, pp. 1–6 (2010)

Orthogonal Local Image Descriptors
with Convolutional Autoencoders

Edgar Roman-Rangel[1]([⊠]) and Stephane Marchand-Maillet[2]

[1] Instituto Tecnologico Autonomo de Mexico, ITAM, 01080 Mexico City, Mexico
edgar.roman@itam.mx
[2] University of Geneva, 1227 Geneva, Switzerland
stephane.marchand-maillet@unige.ch

Abstract. This work proposes the use of deep learning architectures, and in particular Convolutional Autencoders (CAE's), to incorporate an explicit component of orthogonality to the computation of local image descriptors. For this purpose we present a methodology based on the computation of dot products among the hidden outputs of the center-most layer of a convolutional autoencoder. This is, the dot product between the responses of the different kernels of the central layer (sections of a latent representation). We compare this dot product against an indicator of orthogonality, which in the presence of non-orthogonal hidden representations, back-propagates a gradient through the network, adjusting its parameters to produce new representations which will be closer to have orthogonality among them in future iterations. Our results show that the proposed methodology is suitable for the estimation of local image descriptors that are orthogonal to one another, which is often a desirable feature in many patter recognition tasks.

Keywords: Local image descriptors · Orthogonal bases · Convolutional autoencoders

1 Introduction

The use of orthogonal bases in the estimation of local image descriptors was a widely used paradigm in many computer vision scenarios before the deep learning era [1], specially because this approach allows the definition of over-complete dictionaries for robust image description [1, 2]. However, recent developments of deep architectures seem to disregard the potential of incorporating orthogonal bases in their models, perhaps because of the indisputable success that these deep models, and in particular Convolutional Neural Networks (CNN's), have already shown in solving several computer vision problems [3, 4], even without the explicit consideration of orthogonality.

Since CNN's are often designed for end-to-end processing, the estimation of local image descriptors also seems to be unnecessary lately, i.e., the focus is in solving directly tasks like classification or localization [5, 6]. Therefore, it has

© Springer Nature Switzerland AG 2020
K. M. Figueroa Mora et al. (Eds.): MCPR 2020, LNCS 12088, pp. 149–158, 2020.
https://doi.org/10.1007/978-3-030-49076-8_15

become common to overlook at intermediate representations during the image
description process, as long as they get the task solved. Nonetheless, looking
at intermediate representations of CNN's [9] might still prove beneficial for the
estimation of local image descriptors, which might be desirable in at least two
scenarios. First, when fine local details are highly relevant for a given task, as
global descriptors risk overlooking at them. Second, when dealing with small
datasets that could limit the capacity for properly training a large set of parameters, as is often the case with many deep neural networks architectures [7].

In this work, we propose the re-consideration of orthogonality as a constraint
for the estimation of local image descriptors, which are computed using Convolutional Autoencoders (CAE's) [8]. We develop a methodology that readily
inserts itself as another layer in a deep CAE architecture, and that allows to
impose orthogonality constraints to intermediate representation of the network.
We evaluate the impact of our model in the task of image reconstruction, and
our results show that this approach is suitable for obtaining orthogonal local
descriptors while still being able to reconstruct images at high precision rates.

The rest of this paper is organized as follows. Sect. 2, gives details about
our proposed approach for generation of orthogonal local descriptors. Sect. 3
describes the protocol followed to evaluate our method. Sect. 4 discusses our
results. Finally, Sect. 5, presents our conclusions.

2   Orthogonal Local Descriptors

This section explains the proposed deep learning architecture designed to compute orthogonal local descriptors, which corresponds to a type of convolutional
autoencoder (CAE). This deep convolutional autoencoder simultaneously opti-
mizes two objective functions: the reconstruction error of the autoencoder itself
and an orthogonality constraint.

2.1   Architecture

An overview of our CAE-like architecture is shown in Fig. 1. As it happens with
standard autoencoders, ours is composed of two stages: encoding and decoding,
where the output of the central layer is considered an appropriate representation
of the input image, as long as it allows the model to reconstruct its own input.

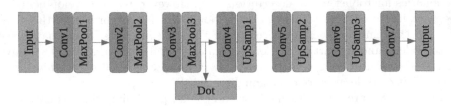

Fig. 1. Model architecture. Orthogonal convolutional autoencoder.

The encoding part of our model starts with a set of convolutional and max-pooling layers packed into blocks, whose tasks is that of applying a cascade of low-level filters that identify or enhance the visual information relevant for local description. There are three such convolutional-pooling blocks, as suggested by previous works [4], in which it has been observed that three blocks suffice for learning to detect edges, corners and contours, and object parts, respectively [9].

Likewise, we also implement three blocks with convolution filters and up-sampling operations for the decoder stage, i.e., the reconstruction section of the model. This decoding section has the only task of recovering the initial visual information from whatever representation had resulted after the initial encoding process. There is an additional final convolutional layer whose purpose is to smooth out the output of the last up-sampling operation, this is, it corrects for the abrupt zero-order hold extrapolation produced by the up-sampling layer.

In this model, all convolutional operations in the encoding and decoding stages are performed by filters of size 5×5, and are followed by $ReLU$ activation functions. Regarding the max-pooling layers, all of them operate over 2×2 pixels neighborhoods. Similarly, the up-sampling steps correspond to zero-order hold interpolation processes performed in localities of 2×2 pixels.

The central layer in our model, indicated by the name "Dot" in Fig. 1, is the one where the orthogonality between convolutional filters is optimized. See Sect. 2.2, for further details about this process.

2.2   Orthogonality

For the purpose of measuring orthogonality, we consider individually, the output of each convolutional filter in the central layer (*latent representation*). This is, we optimize for each convolutional unit to produce outputs that are orthogonal to one another. Concretely, we measure the orthogonality between pairs of outputs of the layer *maxpool3*, and from there, we backpropagate a loss measurement indicating a notion of *lack of orthogonality*.

More formally, the orthogonality between two convolutional outputs corresponds to the dot product computed between their respective vectorized forms v_i and v_j, i.e., the output of the convolutional filter is a matrix, however, vectorizing it has no impact for the optimization process. Namely, the orthogonality score $\hat{o}_{i,j}$ between vectors v_i and v_j is computed as,

$$\hat{o}_{i,j} = \langle v_i, v_j \rangle. \tag{1}$$

Computing this dot product for each pair of the C convolutional outputs from a given layer, results in a matrix $\hat{O}$ of $[C \times C]$ elements, which indicates the degree of correlation between pairs of outputs, and thus some sort of similarity between the convolutional filters that generated them themselves. Moreover, having the off-diagonal elements of $\hat{O}$ all equal to zero, indicates that the operand vectors that originated them are pair-wise orthogonal.

Using this notion of orthogonality, we compute the orthogonality loss $\mathcal{L}^o$ as,

$$\mathcal{L}^o = \frac{1}{M}\|O - I\|_1, \tag{2}$$

where, O is the orthogonal matrix normalized through,

$$o_{i,j} = \frac{\hat{o}_{i,j}}{\max_{i,j} \hat{O}},$$ (3)

and I is the identity matrix of size $[C \times C]$. This is, Eq. (2) computes the element-wise mean absolute error between O and I.

In practice, max-pooling layers contain no parameters that can be optimize via gradient descent. Therefore, the orthogonality loss $\mathcal{L}^o$ is back-propagated directly to the previous convolutional layer (i.e., *conv3*), whose parameters are updated to maximize the orthogonality of future outputs.

2.3   Loss Function

The training of the proposed model consists in minimizing simultaneously a reconstruction loss $\mathcal{L}^r$ and the orthogonality loss $\mathcal{L}^o$ defined in Eq. (2). This is,

$$\mathcal{L} = \mathcal{L}^r + \lambda \mathcal{L}^o,$$ (4)

where, λ is a coefficient that weights the contribution of the orthogonality loss $\mathcal{L}^o$ to the total loss function, and,

$$\mathcal{L}^r = \mathcal{L}^r(X, X; \Omega),$$ (5)

indicates a notion of the error obtained when using X (an image patch) as input to our model, and trying to reconstruct it using the set of parameters Ω. Note that the specific form of $\mathcal{L}^r$ might vary depending on the nature of the data and the problem that is being addressed.

3   Experiments

This section provides information regarding the evaluation of the proposed orthogonal local descriptor. Concretely, it describes the dataset used for evaluation, provides several implementation details, and presents the two types of experiments we performed to validate our methodology.

3.1   Data

We used a dataset of binary images [10] containing arrangements of hieroglyphs from the ancient Maya culture. These arrangements of hieroglyphs are known as glyph-blocks, or simply blocks. Figure 2 shows a few examples of them.

This glyph-blocks dataset is formed by 5000 images, each containing from 1 to 6 individual signs visually located at arbitrary positions. In turn, each individual sign belongs to one of 255 semantic classes (a notion of word)[1]. It is indeed, the

---

[1] Approximately, 1000 different Mayan glyph-signs have been identified thus far by archaeologists, but our dataset only contains instances from 255 of them.

Fig. 2. 16 examples of glyph-blocks in our dataset.

relative small size of this dataset that has motivated the investigation on the use of convolutional autoencoders to generate local image descriptors.

During our experiments, we randomly chose 80 glyph-blocks for training and 20 for validation, leaving 4900 aside for testing. For the generation of the local image descriptors, we input square image patches uniformly sampled from the complete glyph-blocks. The size of these patches is 64 × 64 pixels, sampled at strides of 16 pixels. Since glyph-blocks images are of varying size, this segmentation resulted in 39,125 training and 10,251 validation patches.

3.2 Implementation Details

We implemented our proposed model using python 3.7 and the keras module of the tensorflow 2.0 library.

Conceptually, our model is a branched network as depicted in Fig. 1. Its main branch consists of 15 layers organized in three types of blocks: convolution plus max-pooling, convolution plus up-sampling, and only convolution blocks. Its purpose is to process input images extracting relevant information into a compact latent representation, and then reconstruct the original image starting from such latent representation.

With the exception of its last convolutional layer, which implements the *sigmoid* activation function for recovering pixel values within the interval $[0, 1]$, all other convolutional layers use the *ReLU* activation function.

The three layers in the encoding stage consists of 32, 16, and C convolutional filters, respectively. Note the parameter C (the number of filters in the third convolutional layer is an hyper-parameter, which determines the number of layers that allow appropriate orthogonality rates). Similarly, the last four layers in the decoding stage are formed by 8, 16, 32, and 1 convolutional filters. All convolutional filters in all convolutional layers are of 5 × 5 pixels. Also, all max-pooling and up-sampling layers were fixed to pooling size equals 2×2, thus generating outputs half, or double, the size of their inputs, accordingly.

The second branch of our model corresponds to the "Dot" layer, which is connected after the third max-pooling layer. This layer receives as input a tensor of size $[W, H, C]$, where W and H indicates the *width* and *height* of the image response after the previous convolution-pooling block, and C corresponds to the *number of responses* (channels or filters) resulting from that previous stage. The activation function of this layer is the dot product applied on its input tensor, channel-wise, which produces matrix O as output (as explained in Sect. 2.2). The reference data used to compare the output of this second branch, and therefore to calculate the error function defined in Eq. (2), corresponds to the identity matrix of size $C \times C$, as we are using C filters in the third convolutional layer.

We trained our model during 64 epochs using batches of 32 local patches and the *adam* optimizer with default parameters [11]. Since our data consists of binary images, we optimize the *binary cross entropy* as reconstruction loss $\mathcal{L}^r$.

3.3   Evaluation

We evaluated two aspects that the proposed orthogonality constraint could induce in the estimation of local image descriptors via convolutional autoencoders. First, its impact in the reconstruction loss with respect to its contribution to the whole optimization process, as dictated by the coefficient λ. And second, its impact in the reconstruction loss in relation with the dimensionality of the generated local descriptor, i.e., the impact that the number C of convolutional units used to generate the local image descriptor.

4   Results

This section presents the results obtained during the evaluation of the proposed orthogonal local descriptors. Our evaluation focuses on the impact induced in the reconstruction loss of the CAE, by the addition of the orthogonality constraint and by the length of the resulting local descriptor.

4.1   Orthogonality Impact

Table 1 shows the impact of enforcing the orthogonality constraint into the loss function, evaluated on the validation set. These results correspond to the reconstruction loss $\mathcal{L}^r$ (binary cross entropy, bce), the orthogonality loss $\mathcal{L}^o$ (mean average error, mae), and the total loss $\mathcal{L} = \mathcal{L}^r + \lambda \mathcal{L}^o$, as detailed in Sect. 2.3. Moreover, this evaluation corresponds to the use of 512 elements in the real-valued vectors used to compute orthogonality, which, given the fact that the output of our model is of size 8×8 pixels after the third max-pooling layer, implies that there are $C = 8$ filters in the third convolutional layer.

From Table 1, one can see a clear opposite tendency between the reconstruction and orthogonality losses. In general, all of our experiments showed that the

Table 1. Comparison of different values of λ, used for enforcing the orthogonality constraint into the loss function, evaluated on the validation set.

$\mathcal{L}^o$ contribution (λ)	3.00	0.90	0.60	0.30	0.09	0.06	0.03
$\mathcal{L}^r$ (bce)	0.126	0.115	0.108	0.108	0.102	0.102	0.098
$\mathcal{L}^o$ (mae)	0.071	0.080	0.091	0.104	0.118	0.129	0.138
$\mathcal{L}$	0.169	0.163	**0.163**	0.162	0.173	0.179	0.181

more strict the orthogonality penalty λ, the higher the reconstruction loss (bce). Since their combination attains its minimum when using $\lambda = 0.6$, we kept this value fixed for subsequent evaluations.

To validate that, effectively this approach is able to generate local descriptors that are orthogonal to one another, in Fig. 3 we show the visual representations of the orthogonal matrix O (Eq. 3) for different values of λ. Although all three matrices show a diagonal-like patter, it is clear that $\lambda \geq 0.6$ enforces better orthogonality between pairs of convolutional outputs.

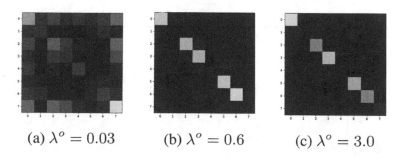

$\quad$ (a) $\lambda^o = 0.03$ $\qquad$ (b) $\lambda^o = 0.6$ $\qquad$ (c) $\lambda^o = 3.0$

Fig. 3. Visual representations of the orthogonal matrix O for different values of λ. The more the off-diagonal elements are close to zero, the more orthogonal are the corresponding vectors, which are nothing but the responses to the convolutional filters.

For better understanding the impact of the orthogonality penalty λ, Fig. 4 shows examples of patches that have been reconstructed using our methodology, with $C = 8$ filters in the third convolutional layer and $\lambda = 0.6$ (as suggested by the previous analysis). Images in the first row are input local patches segmented from the glyph-blocks, while images in the second row correspond to their reconstructed counterparts. All images in Fig. 4 are well defined in visual terms, and highly similar to their original counterparts. Moreover, only a few pixels have changed their real value. This indicates that allowing a reconstruction loss of around 0.1 in terms of binary cross entropy (induced by $\lambda = 0.6$), brings no serious damage to the reconstruction process.

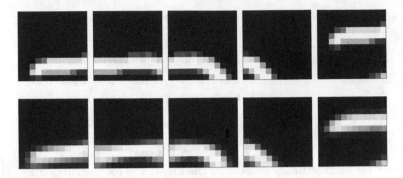

Fig. 4. Examples of local image patches reconstructed by our model, using $C = 8$ filters in the third convolutional layer and $\lambda = 0.6$. First row corresponds to the original image patches. Second row corresponds to the reconstructed patches.

Our results also showed that the proposed approach has good generalization behavior, as the validation error is only slightly higher than the training error for both types of losses, as shown in Fig. 5.

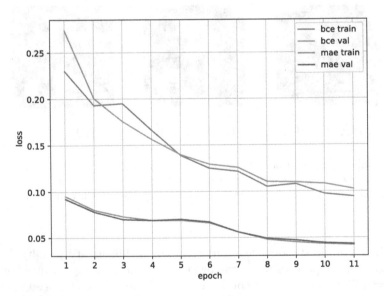

Fig. 5. Training an validation performance for the reconstruction and orthogonal losses.

4.2   Length Impact

The number of elements in the resulting local descriptor is also an important parameter that must be evaluated. On one hand, we would like to obtain descriptors that are large enough to facilitate distributing relevant visual information among their elements, thus favoring orthogonality and sparsity. On the other hand, short descriptors could be desirable for further processing, e.g., indexing or aggregation.

Given the architecture of our model, the output after the third convolution-pooling block is fixed to 8×8 pixels. Therefore, the only varying parameter to modify the total number of elements of this intermediate output is the number C of filters (channels) located in the third convolutional layer. We evaluated the impact on the different losses of our model when varying the number of filters in the set $C = \{1, 2, 4, 8, 16, 32, 64\}$, which respectively correspond to having $64, 128, 256, 512, 1024, 2048, 4096$ elements in the local descriptor.

Table 2 shows evidence of the relation that the length of the local descriptor has with the reconstruction and orthogonality losses, using a fixed $\lambda = 0.6$ as suggested by the results shown in Table 1.

Table 2. Reconstruction and orthogonal losses with respect to the length of the local image descriptor, using fixed $\lambda = 0.6$.

Length	64	128	256	512	1024	2048	4096
$\mathcal{L}^r$ (bce)	0.121	0.109	0.162	0.108	0.112	0.117	0.171
$\mathcal{L}^o$ (mae)	0.148	0.132	0.130	0.091	0.129	0.131	0.162

This evidence shows that local patches are well described using 512 elements, as this length provides the lowest reconstruction loss (bce). This, however, is but a consequence of the design of the model, which we have set to receive inputs of size 64×64 pixels, and process them through three convolution-pooling blocks, which results in responses of 8×8 elements. Different combination of these hyper-parameters might require different numbers of filters in the third convolution, thus resulting in varying lengths for the local image descriptor.

5   Conclusions

We proposed the re-consideration of orthogonality as a constraint for the unsupervised estimation of local image descriptors using Convolutional Autoencoders (CAE). For this purpose we presented a methodology based on the use of a hidden layer that computes the dot product between intermediate outputs, and uses it as a secondary model output, which is subject to a loss estimation, and therefore allows to adjust the network parameters to induce orthogonality.

Our results show that the proposed methodology is suitable for the estimation of local image descriptors that are orthogonal to one another, this without hurting the reconstruction process of the CAE. We also investigated the impact of the length of the resulting local descriptor in the process of reconstructing binary images, and noticed that reconstruction of high visual quality are possible.

Currently we are investigating whether the proposed method might also have an impact in the degree of sparsity of the resulting local descriptors, or serve as a new type of regularizer. Additionally, this approach can be tested in specific tasks like image classification or image retrieval.

Acknowledgments. This research was supported by the Asociación Mexicana de Cultura A.C.

References

1. Aharon, M., Elad, M., Bruckstein, A.: K-SVD: an algorithm for designing overcomplete dictionaries for sparse representation. IEEE Trans. Signal Process. **54**(11), 4311–4322 (2006)
2. Roman-Rangel, E., Odobez, J.-M., Gatica-Perez, D.: Assessing sparse coding methods for contextual shape indexing of Maya hieroglyphs. J. Multimedia **7**, 179–192 (2012)
3. He, K., Zhang, X., Ren, S., Sun, J.: Deep residual learning for image recognition. In: IEEE Conference on Computer Vision and Pattern Recognition, CVPR (2012)
4. Simonyan, K., Zisserman, A.: Very deep convolutional networks for large-scale image recognition. In: International Conference on Learning Representations, ICLR (2014)
5. Szegedy, C., et al.: Going deeper with convolutions. In: IEEE Conference on Computer Vision and Pattern Recognition, CVPR (2015)
6. Redmon, J., Divvala, S., Girshick, R., Farhadi, A.: You only look once: unified, real-time object detection. In: IEEE Conference on Computer Vision and Pattern Recognition, CVPR (2016)
7. Roman-Rangel, E., et al.: Transferring neural representations for low-dimensional indexing of Maya hieroglyphic art. In: Hua, G., Jégou, H. (eds.) ECCV 2016. LNCS, vol. 9913, pp. 842–855. Springer, Cham (2016). https://doi.org/10.1007/978-3-319-46604-0_58
8. Masci, J., Meier, U., Cireşan, D., Schmidhuber, J.: Stacked convolutional autoencoders for hierarchical feature extraction. In: Honkela, T., Duch, W., Girolami, M., Kaski, S. (eds.) ICANN 2011. LNCS, vol. 6791, pp. 52–59. Springer, Heidelberg (2011). https://doi.org/10.1007/978-3-642-21735-7_7
9. Zeiler, M.D., Fergus, R.: Visualizing and understanding convolutional networks. In: Fleet, D., Pajdla, T., Schiele, B., Tuytelaars, T. (eds.) ECCV 2014. LNCS, vol. 8689, pp. 818–833. Springer, Cham (2014). https://doi.org/10.1007/978-3-319-10590-1_53
10. Gatica-Perez, D., et al.: MAAYA: Multimedia Methods to Support Maya Epigraphic Analysis. Arqueologia computacional: Nuevos enfoques para el analisis y la difusion del patrimonio cultural (2017)
11. Kingma, D.P., Ba, J.L.: Adam: a method for stochastic optimization. In: International Conference for Learning Representations, ICLR (2014)

Digital Assisted Image Correlation for Metal Sheet Strain Measurement

García-Alcalá Carlos-Eduardo[1]($\boxtimes$) ⓘ, Padilla-Medina José-Alfredo[1]($\boxtimes$) ⓘ, and Barranco-Gutiérrez Alejandro-Israel[1,2]($\boxtimes$) ⓘ

[1] TecNM en Celaya, 38010 Guanajuato, Mexico
cgalcala92@gmail.com,
{alfredo.padilla,israel.barranco}@itcelaya.edu.mx
[2] Cátedras CONACyT, 03940 Ciudad de México, Mexico

Abstract. Current methods of correlation and point matching between stereo-scopic images produce large errors or are completely inefficient when the surface has a repetitive, non-isotropic, low contrast pattern. In this article a new method of Digital Assisted Image Correlation (DAIC) is presented to match specific points in order to estimate the deformation of the surface in the metal sheets used in the automotive industry. To achieve this, it is necessary to stamp the surface to be measured with a regular pattern of points, then a digital image processing is done to obtain the labels of the circles of the pattern. After this, a semi-automatic search is made in the labels of both images to correlate all of them and perform the triangulation. DIC is used to corroborate the correspondence between points and verify the accuracy and efficiency of the developed method. This allows the 3D reconstruction of the sheet with a minimum of information and provides more efficiency and a great benefit in computational cost. Deformation is calculated by two methods, which show similarity between the values obtained with a digital microscope. It is assumed that quality of marks stamping, lighting, and the initial conditions, also contribute for trustworthy effects.

Keywords: Image matching · Steel industry · Stereo vision · Digital Image Correlation

1 Introduction

The deformation measurement in metal sheets is a very important activity to know the material properties used to manufacture them, to assure the quality and applications design where is used, in this case, the automotive industry [1]. Commonly, multi-camera vision has been used to measure it, especially stereoscopic vision [2]. The surface deformation measurement of the metal sheets depends on the 3D points reconstruction efficiency from a stereoscopic digital camera system and the latter is subject to points matching. One of the most popular methods in mechanics to strain estimation is called Digital Image Correlation (DIC). This is a full-field non-contact optical-numerical technique to measure shape, motion, and deformation, on almost any kind of material, even in extreme experimental settings [3], as long as the region of interest (ROI) on the sample's

© Springer Nature Switzerland AG 2020
K. M. Figueroa Mora et al. (Eds.): MCPR 2020, LNCS 12088, pp. 159–171, 2020.
https://doi.org/10.1007/978-3-030-49076-8_16

surface is provided with a natural or synthetic speckle pattern [4]. This allows finding the best match between corresponding points in the two images by comparing the local grey scale distribution of square pixel subsets on the basis of the normalized cross correlation coefficient. The uniqueness of each signature is only guaranteed if the surface has a non-repetitive, isotropic, high contrast pattern [5, 6] (Fig. 1). An efficient matching operation requires the two images to be similar in terms of speckle pattern appearance. Extracting information from such images is particularly challenging because the success of a DIC matching is guaranteed only when a sufficient similarity exists between the images to be correlated [7–9]. This can be achieved by using a pair of 'twin' cameras (with identical settings) and proper illumination, or by capturing both views simultaneously with one single camera and additional external optical devices [10]. Nonetheless, the use of DIC data to validate models in a quantitative way or to identify with precision several constitutive parameters, remains not easy work [11]. One of the reasons is the complicate compromise between the measuring resolution and the large space for measuring to be done. A second reason is the state of frontiers. A third reason is that measured displacements are not directly compared with simulations.

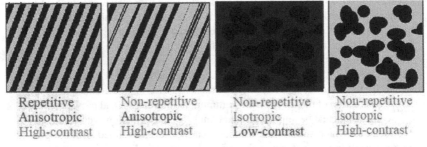

Repetitive	Non-repetitive	Non-repetitive	Non-repetitive
Anisotropic	Anisotropic	Isotropic	Isotropic
High-contrast	High-contrast	Low-contrast	High-contrast

Fig. 1. Image specifications to implement DIC correctly [12].

On the other hand, the grid of circles as references to measure deformation in metal sheets, is widely used [13–16, 29] because the accuracy and precision of the measurements can be analyzed manually with a microscope. Figure 2 shows the deformation phenomenon of the metal sheets and what happens with the stamped marks, as the distance between the centroids changes.

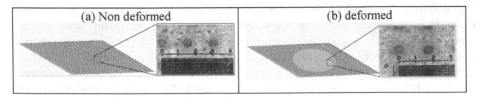

Fig. 2. (a) Circles on metal sheet without deformation; (b) Circles on deformed metal sheet.

There are several efforts presenting promising results like [8, 11, 17–25]. In ref. [18] they propose a deconvolution algorithm that allows to eliminate, over a certain frequency range, the systematic error for DIC and LSA (Localized Spectrum Analysis). The procedure diminishes the value of the spatial resolution (thus improves it). The drawback is that the noise level impairing the measurements increases, but not in the same proportion as the decrease in spatial resolution. Hence the compromise between measurement resolution and spatial resolution is significantly improved, which makes this deconvolution procedure potentially useful in situations where localized strain gradients occur. In Ref. [19] they proved a new method called Simplified Digital Image Correlation Method (SiDIC) in a rubber balloon to verify if the super pression aerostatic balloon could be measured. The SiDIC correctly identified the non-deformed region, although the deformation is not accurate. In Ref. [11] it is proposed the use of an initial condition which consist in doing click on four points of circles grid to accelerate the marks searching and improve the points matching efficiency. It is observed that the errors of measured displacements using DIC are closely related to the quality of the speckle pattern [21, 24–26]. In other words, the measured displacements of different speckle patterns using the DIC technique may be different even though the deformation state of the specimen, the calculation parameters (e.g., the correlation criteria, sub-pixel registration algorithm, subset size, subset shape function, the interpolation scheme, and calculation path) are the same. Nowadays DIC is often used in a qualitative manner rather than as a metrological tool. This is especially due to the time-consuming task related to the post-processing of the images: in Ref. [27] more than 10000 points were exported from the camera measurements.

In this work, we propose a new two-point initialization technique to improve velocity and accurate processing in 3D reconstruction and the calculation of surface deformation in a metallic sheet. This is done by stamping a grid of circular oxide dots on the metal sheet. After obtaining the corresponding labels of each point, a semi-automatic algorithm of coincident points between both images is implemented. The factor correlation is used to verify point matching. Subsequently, the deformation is calculated by the average distance of four neighbors, finally the measurement is compared with that obtained with a digital microscope.

2 Materials and Methods

In order to capture the images a pair of Prosilica GT2750 cameras were used. These are 6.1 megapixels each, with a Gigabit Ethernet port compatible with GigE Vision and a Hirose I/O port. This kind of camera incorporates a high-quality Sony sensor ICX694 EXview HAD CCD that provides extra sensitivity, near IR response, low noise level, anti-blooming effect and excellent image quality. At full resolution, this camera processes 19.8 frames per second. With a smaller region of interest, higher frame rates are possible. It is a robust device designed to operate in extreme environments and fluctuating lighting conditions. It offers precise control of the iris lens that allows users to set the size of the aperture to optimize depth of field, exposure and gain without the need for additional control elements. For the assembly, a metal structure of $40 \times 40 \times 40$ cm was designed, the piece to be measured is approximately at 30 cm from the lens of the cameras. LED lighting was chosen due to the contrast with the circles marked on the sheet: blue LED of 640 nm. The acquired images have a resolution of 2752 × 2200 pixels. To compare the dimensional measurements, a digital microscope (Jiusion 6-06814-24289-8) with a scale of 100 μm was used (Fig. 3).

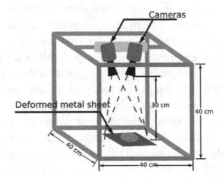

Fig. 3. Configuration of stereo cameras, with lighting and the metal sheet.

The followed methodology has the purpose of measuring the surface deformation in a metal sheet used for car bodies.

1. Calibrations of the cameras.
2. Stamping of known circle grid on the not deformed metallic sheet.
3. Deformation of the metal-sheet by the mechanical stamping process.
4. Illumination of the piece with LED blue light for being measured.
5. Capture of stereo images.
6. Digital image processing to obtain the labels of the points of the metal sheet.
7. Manual selection of the same point in both images to allow the algorithm to matching all the remaining points among them.
8. Triangulation of points to obtain their position in 3D space and reconstruction of the metal sheet.
9. Estimate the deformation by two methods:

   • From the average distances of each point with its neighbors in 3D space.
   • Through the depth value of each point (measurement on Z axis).

For the individual and stereo calibration of the cameras, the defined functions provided by the OpenCV library were used within the Python programming language. The process includes the stamping of the grid of points in the metal sheet without deforming, this involves an electrochemical process in which an electrolyte is applied as reagent on the surface of the sheet to engrave a thin pattern so that when the sheet is painted, the marking is imperceptible. After the sheet is subjected to the inlaying process, the circles are distorted in the form of ellipses and the distances between the centroids of these are modified, which are used in the digital images to determine the deformation states in the testing metal sheet.

2.1 Two Points Labels-Matching Initializations

After obtaining the first six steps of the methodology as detailed in the previous work [11], they have the right and left labeled images as shown in Fig. 4. In these images each label corresponds to one mark of the dot pattern. The noise was eliminated by filtering the labels by areas so that only those corresponding to the dot pattern remained.

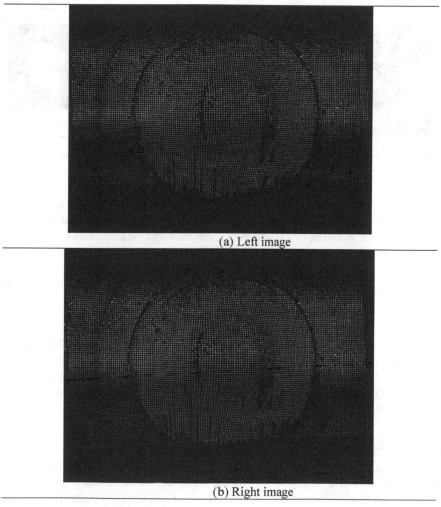

(a) Left image

(b) Right image

Fig. 4. Labeled images from stereo cameras after image processing process

The method's aim is to determine the correspondences between 2D centroid coordinates of both images for each circle of the grid pattern on the metal piece giving only one click on each image (left and right). First a click is given on any circle on the image taken by a left camera, then another click is given at that same circle but on the other image taken by the right camera. With this, the centroid of the labels corresponding to these marks is determined and the first correspondence between both images is obtained manually (red circle in Fig. 5a). Then a search of neighboring labels in areas near the central circle is made, as shown in Fig. 5a, here are observed in yellow boxes the regions where tags are searched in both images. A new correspondence is obtained if both labels are found in the corresponding boxes of both images. The process is iterative, taking as a central point each new matched label correctly.

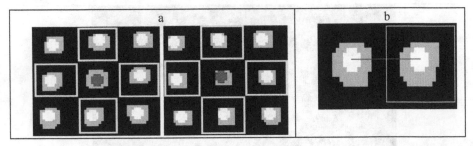

Fig. 5. (a) Semi-automatic matching of labels between both images. (b) Delimiting the area for searches of neighboring labels.

The dimensions of each region of 2D space where each neighboring label is searched and its exact location in space depend on the configuration and size of the dot pattern. One way to do this would be by calculating the distance and the slope between the central point and a neighbor found.

$$d_{a\leftrightarrow b} = \sqrt{(y_a - y_b)^2 + (x_a - x_b)^2} \tag{1}$$

$$m_{a\leftrightarrow b} = \frac{(y_b - y_a)}{(x_b - x_a)} \tag{2}$$

In Eqs. (1) and (2) the coordinates of the centroids of the labels are used. An imaginary square will be constructed to delimit the search area of each neighboring label (Fig. 5b), each side will have a length equal to the segment d(a–b), one side of the square will cut it perpendicularly at its midpoint. With this the remaining square is built, within which it will be verified pixel by pixel if there is a label.

2.2 Verify the Point-Pairing Through DIC

2D-DIC is used to correlate a given set of points in the two stereo views of the reference configuration and match these points along the sequence of images. The Fourier methods can be used to calculate the correlation in a fast way. Equation (3) presents the definition of normalized cross correlation.

$$NCC = \frac{\sum_{(i,j)\varepsilon s}\left[f_{(u,v)} - \bar{f}\right][g(u,v) - \bar{g}]}{\sqrt{\sum_{(i,j)\varepsilon s}\left[f_{(u,v)} - \bar{f}\right]^2 \sum_{(i,j)\varepsilon s}[g(u,v) - \bar{g}]^2}} \tag{3}$$

Here f and g are each the grayscale functions of the windows of the current image at a specific location (x, y). The functions $\bar{f}$ and $\bar{g}$ correspond to the gray scale mean of the reference image and the current subset.

2.3 Triangulation and 3D Reconstruction

In Ref. [22] was described the dimensional estimation using stereoscopic vision systems. They quantitatively concluded that the accuracy and precision depend on the distance between the camera and the object to be measured, as well as the resolution of the cameras used. Stereoscopic vision is a technique frequently used to locate points in three dimensions (3D) based on points in two or more 2D images [10, 11, 27–33]. It is necessary to calibrate both cameras using the PinHole model which is described by Eq. (4).

$$s\tilde{m} = A[R|t]\tilde{M} = \begin{bmatrix} f_x & 0 & u_0 \\ 0 & f_y & v_0 \\ 0 & 0 & 1 \end{bmatrix} \begin{bmatrix} r_{11} & r_{12} & r_{13} | & t_x \\ r_{21} & r_{22} & r_{23} | & t_y \\ r_{31} & r_{32} & r_{33} | & t_z \end{bmatrix} \tilde{M} \tag{4}$$

Since s is the number that defines the scale of the objects with respect to their real size in the image. A is the matrix of intrinsic parameters that describes the position of the center of the image in pixels $(u0, v0)$. $[R|t]$ the matrix of extrinsic parameters of the camera that describe the rigid transformation (rotation and translation) between the coordinate system of the camera and the coordinate system of an object outside the camera. $\tilde{M}$ is a 3D point (x, y, z) of the scene expressed in homogeneous coordinates. Subsequently, to achieve stereoscopic calibration, the translation vector that joins each camera reference system is calculated. The point position in three dimensions can be estimated from the coordinates in two dimensions and the Eq. 5.

$$\begin{bmatrix} um_{31} - m_{11} & um_{32} - m_{12} & um_{33} - m_{13} \\ vm_{31} - m_{21} & vm_{31} - m_{22} & vm_{31} - m_{23} \\ u'm'_{31} - m'_{31} & u'm'_{32} - m'_{32} & u'm'_{31} - m'_{31} \\ v'm'_{31} - m'_{21} & v'm'_{31} - m'_{32} & v'm'_{31} - m'_{33} \end{bmatrix} \begin{bmatrix} \hat{x} \\ \hat{y} \\ \hat{z} \end{bmatrix} = \begin{bmatrix} m_{14} - um_{34} \\ m_{24} - vm_{34} \\ m'_{14} - u'm'_{34} \\ m'_{24} - v'm'_{34} \end{bmatrix} \tag{5}$$

Where (u, v) and (u', v') are the coordinates of the paired points obtained from the left and right cameras that correspond to the 3D point to be reconstructed.

3 Results

In Fig. 6 we present the reconstruction in the three dimensional space of all the points that correspond to the circle grid labels on the metallic sheet that were previously matched.

3.1 Calculation of Superficial Strain Measurement on the Metal Sheet

Punctual deformation was calculated by two methods. The first one consists only in the determination of how much each point was moved from a reference plane (plane in axis towards the cameras, where there is no deformation in the piece) to its current position. This provides a measure of how much each point of the material was stretched from one plane to the cameras. The drawback of this method is that it would not be able to measure the deformation correctly if it were produced in another direction or axis that was not the one that joins the piece to be measured and the reference camera. In Fig. 7,

Triangulation

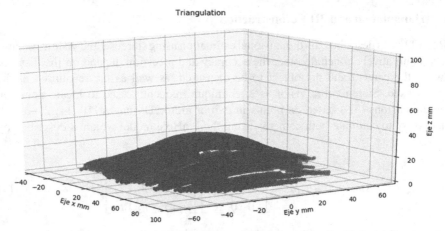

Fig. 6. 3D reconstruction of the metal sheet.

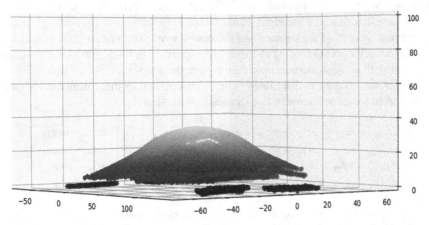

Fig. 7. Superficial strain measurement by the movement of each point on the Z axis.

it is observed in a color scale how the point deformation increases as the material moves away from the reference plane located on the Z axis with $z = 0$ cm.

The other developed method is to calculate the distance in the space between each point and its four neighbors and compare these values with measurements taken in the piece by the digital microscope, as in Fig. 8, where it is observed that there is an average distance of 1.55 mm among each circle of the grid (a), and about 1.7 mm after applying some deformation to the piece (b).

These values will serve as a comparative guide and demonstrate the expansion suffered by the surface when it is deformed. The distance among two points in 3D space is calculated using Eq. 6.

$$d\left(\begin{pmatrix} x_1 \\ y_1 \\ z_1 \end{pmatrix}, \begin{pmatrix} x_2 \\ y_2 \\ z_2 \end{pmatrix}\right) = \sqrt{(x_1 - x_2)^2 + (y_1 - y_2)^2 + (z_1 - z_2)^2} \qquad (6)$$

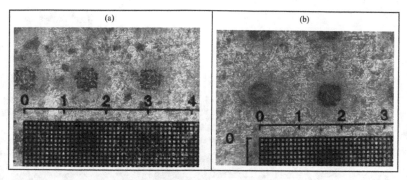

Fig. 8. (a) Measurement of the pattern on the metal sheet without deforming. (b) Measurement of the pattern in a deformed metal sheet.

In the Fig. 9 the deformation of each point is shown in color scale. The green circles have a distance between points less or equal to 1.55 mm, yellows one varies from 1.56 mm to 1.63 mm and reds one are greater than 1.64 mm. It shows a similarity with the previous method, the drawback would be the high computational cost required for the calculation of all points on the surface of the material.

Superficial strain measurement

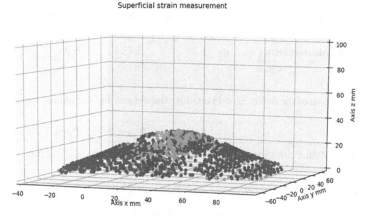

Fig. 9. Strain measurement by calculating the distance between each point and its neighbors.

Figure 10 shows the configurations of two groups of 5 points, one located on an area of the piece without deformation and another in the deformed area. The distance from the central point to each neighbor point in 3D space was calculated, the results are shown in Table 1 and 2 and compared with those obtained by the digital microscope. From these results, the average error in the experiment can be calculated, in this case ε = 1.4451%.

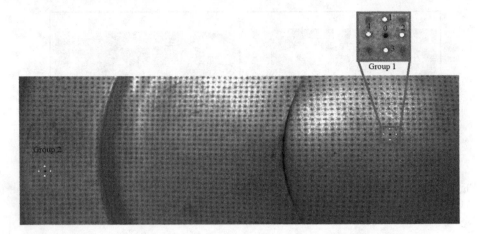

Fig. 10. Configuration of points to measure in planar and deformed regions.

Table 1. Comparison of the distances measured by the system and the microscope in Group 1.

Group 1	Point 1	Point 2	Point 3	Point 4
Distance to the Central Point measured by the algorithm	1.6468 mm	1.6343 mm	1.6436 mm	1.6470 mm
Distance to the Central Point measured by the microscope	1.65 mm	1.65 mm	1.65 mm	1.65 mm
Superficial Strain Measurement (%)	6.24	5.43	6.03	6.25

Table 2. Comparison of the distances measured by the system and the microscope in Group 2.

Group 2	Point 1	Point 2	Point 3	Point 4
Distance to the Central Point measured by the algorithm	1.5276 mm	1.5328 mm	1.5758 mm	1.5692 mm
Distance to the Central Point measured by the microscope	1.55 mm	1.55 mm	1.55 mm	1.55 mm

4   Discussion

A great improvement in the performance of the developed algorithm is observed in Fig. 9 and Tables 1 and 2 compared with the method developed by Barranco (Ref. [11]). This is due to the fact that the area where the neighboring labels are sought is greater, giving possibility to correspond those labels that suffer a great deformation between one step and the next. Also, the search area is not one-dimensional, making it possible to search also for up and down displacements of neighboring labels. The new algorithm also needs less marks in both images matched manually to correspond the others, although it fails when it finds empty areas where labels of the marks stamped were not obtained due to bad image processing or due to presenting the piece oxidation spots. The Table 3 summarizes these comparative aspects.

Table 3. Comparison between methods for properly matched labels.

	(Barranco et al., 2019)	(García et al., 2020)
Initialization points quantity	4	2
Total of founded correct labels	4588	48556

5 Conclusion

A method has been developed that allows correct triangulation and three-dimensional reconstruction of a metal sheet to calculate surface deformation. This method takes into account the problems existing in the matching of points by the Digital Image Correlation (quality of the speckle pattern, compromise between the measuring resolution and the large space for measuring to be done, time-consuming task related to the post-processing of the images, etc.). This is why a known pattern of circles was developed, allowing the 3D reconstruction of the sheet with a minimum of information, this provides more efficiency and a great benefit from the point of view of computational cost. Finally, DIC is used to corroborate the correspondence between points and verify the accuracy and efficiency of the developed method. The innovative part is the development of the semiautomatic matching algorithm, which allows to match all the points among both images using the labels that were obtained in the digital processing of the images. There is great similarity between the deformation values acquired by the algorithm and the digital microscope. The error in deformation measurements can vary according to many factors, including poor lighting conditions in the acquisition of images, incorrect digital processing of images, and even oxidation spots on the metal sheet that do not correspond to the pattern of drawn circles can contaminate and affect the results of point deformation.

References

1. Hilditch, T.B., de Souza, T., Hodgson, P.D.: Properties and automotive applications of advanced high-strength steels (AHSS). In: Shome, M., Tumuluru, M. (eds.) Welding and Joining of Advanced High Strength Steels (AHSS), pp. 9–28. Woodhead Publishing, Cambridge (2015)
2. Malesa, M., et al.: Non-destructive testing of industrial structures with the use of multi-camera digital image Correlation method. Eng. Fail. Anal. **69**, 122–134 (2016)
3. Sutton, M.A., Orteu, J.J., Schreier, H.: Image correlation for shape, motion and deformation measurements: basic concepts, theory and applications. Springer, Boston (2009). https://doi.org/10.1007/978-0-387-78747-3

4. Solav, D., Moerman, K.M., Jaeger, A.M., Genovese, K., Herr, H.M.: MultiDIC: An open-source toolbox for multi-view 3D digital image correlation. IEEE Access **6**, 30520–30535 (2018)
5. Lecompte, D., et al.: Quality assessment of speckle patterns for digital image correlation. Opt. Lasers Eng. **44**, 1132–1145 (2006)
6. Pan, B., Lu, Z., Xie, H.: Mean intensity gradient: an effective global parameter for quality assessment of the speckle patterns used in digital image correlation. Opt. Lasers Eng. **48**, 469–477 (2010)
7. Genovese, K., Sorgente, D.: A morphing-based scheme for large deformation analysis with stereo-DIC. Opt. Lasers Eng. **104**, 159–172 (2018)
8. Schreier, H.W., Sutton, M.A.: Systematic errors in digital image correlation due to under-matched subset shape functions. Exp. Mech. **42**, 303–310 (2002). https://doi.org/10.1007/BF02410987
9. Wang, Y., Sutton, M., Bruck, H., Schreier, H.: Quantitative error assessment in pattern matching: effects of intensity pattern noise, interpolation, strain and image contrast on motion measurements. Strain **45**, 160–178 (2009)
10. Genovese, K., Casaletto, L., Rayas, J., Flores, V., Martinez, A.: Stereo-digital image correlation (DIC) measurements with a single camera using a biprism. Opt. Lasers Eng. **51**, 278–285 (2013)
11. Barranco-Gutiérrez, A.-I., et al.: New four points initialization for digital image correlation in metal-sheet strain measurements. Appl. Sci. **9**, 1691 (2019)
12. C Solutions: Short-course (2014)
13. Grediac, M., Frédéric, S., Benoît, B.: The grid method for in-plane displacement and strain measurement: a review and analysis. Strain **52**(3), 205–243 (2016)
14. Badulescu, C., et al.: Applying the grid method and infrared thermography to investigate plastic deformation in aluminium multicrystal. Mech. Mater. **43**(1), 36–53 (2011)
15. Zhou, M., Xie, H.: An identification method of mechanical properties of materials based on the full-field measurement method based on the fringe pattern. Strain **55**(5), e12326 (2019)
16. Bomarito, G., Hochhalter, J., Ruggles, T., Cannon, A.: Increasing accuracy and precision of digital image correlation through pattern optimization. Opt. Lasers Eng. **91**, 73–85 (2017)
17. Bruck, H., McNeill, S., Sutton, M.A., Peters, W.: Digital image correlation using Newton-Raphson method of partial differential correction. Exp. Mech. **29**, 261–267 (1989). https://doi.org/10.1007/BF02321405
18. Grediac, M., Blaysat, B., Sur, F.: A robust-to-noise deconvolution algorithm to enhance displacement and strain maps obtained with local DIC and LSA. Exp. Mech. **59**, 219–243 (2019). https://doi.org/10.1007/s11340-018-00461-4
19. Koseki, K., Matsuo, T., Arikawa, S.: Measurement of super-pressure balloon deformation with simplified digital image correlation. Appl. Sci. **8**, 2009 (2018)
20. Reu, P.L., et al.: DIC challenge: developing images and guidelines for evaluating accuracy and resolution of 2D analyses. Exp. Mech. **58**, 1067–1099 (2018). https://doi.org/10.1007/s11340-017-0349-0
21. Su, Y., Zhang, Q., Xu, X., Gao, Z.: Quality assessment of speckle patterns for DIC by consideration of both systematic errors and random errors. Opt. Lasers Eng. **86**, 132–142 (2016)
22. Dai, X., et al.: The geometric phase analysis method based on the local high resolution discrete Fourier transform for deformation measurement. Measure. Sci. Technol. **25**, 025402 (2014)
23. Bornert, M., et al.: Assessment of digital image correlation measurement errors: methodology and results. Exp. Mech. **49**, 353–370 (2009). https://doi.org/10.1007/s11340-008-9204-7
24. Haddadi, H., Belhabib, S.: Use of rigid-body motion for the investigation and estimation of the measurement errors related to digital image correlation technique. Opt. Lasers Eng. **46**, 185–196 (2008)

25. Pan, B., Xie, H., Wang, Z., Qian, K., Wang, Z.: Study on subset size selection in digital image correlation for speckle patterns. Opt. Express **16**, 7037–7048 (2008)
26. Yaofeng, S., Pang, J.H.: Study of optimal subset size in digital image correlation of speckle pattern images. Opt. Lasers Eng. **45**, 967–974 (2007)
27. Di Lorenzo, E., Lava, P., Balcaen, R., Manzato, S., Peeters, B.: Full-field modal analysis using high-speed 3D digital image correlation. In: Journal of Physics: Conference Series, p. 012007. IOP Publishing (2018)
28. Tsai, R.: A versatile camera calibration technique for high-accuracy 3D machine vision metrology using off-the-shelf TV cameras and lenses. IEEE J. Robot. Autom. **3**, 323–344 (1987)
29. Grediac, M., Blaysat, B., Sur, F.: Extracting displacement and strain fields from checkerboard images with the localized spectrum analysis. Exp. Mech. **59**, 207–218 (2019). https://doi.org/10.1007/s11340-018-00439-2
30. Shao, X., Dai, X., Chen, Z., He, X.: Real-time 3D digital image correlation method and its application in human pulse monitoring. Appl. optics **55**, 696–704 (2016)
31. Blaber, J., Adair, B., Antoniou, A.: Ncorr: open-source 2D digital image correlation matlab software. Exp. Mech. **55**, 1105–1122 (2015). https://doi.org/10.1007/s11340-015-0009-1
32. Grédiac, M., Blaysat, B., Sur, F.: A critical comparison of some metrological parameters characterizing local digital image correlation and grid method. Exp. Mech. **57**, 871–903 (2017). https://doi.org/10.1007/s11340-017-0279-x
33. Sur, F., Blaysat, B., Grediac, M.: Determining displacement and strain maps immune from aliasing effect with the grid method. Opt. Lasers Eng. **86**, 317–328 (2016)

Structured Pointcloud Segmentation for Individual Mangrove Tree Modeling

José L. Silván-Cárdenas[1]([✉]) [iD], José A. Gallardo-Cruz[2],
and Laura M. Hernández-Huerta[1]

[1] Centro de Investigación en Ciencias de Información Geoespacial, A.C., Contoy 137,
Lomas de Padierna, Tlalpan, 14240 Ciudad de México, Mexico
jsilvan@centrogeo.edu.mx
[2] Universidad Iberoamericana Ciudad de México, Current address: Prol. Paseo de la
Reforma 880, Lomas de Santa Fe, 01219 Ciudad de México, Mexico
jose.gallardo@ibero.mx
https://www.centrogeo.org.mx/areas-profile/jsilvan

Abstract. Tree structure parameters of mangrove forests are hard to measure in the field and therefore inventories of this type of forests are impossible to keep up to date. In this article, we tested a structured point-cloud segmentation method for extracting individual mangrove trees. Structure parameters of individual trees were estimated from the segmented pointcloud and its 3d geometry was generated using revolution surfaces. Estimated parameters were then assessed at both plot and tree levels using field data. It was observed that the number of segments in each test plot agreed well with the number of trees observed in the field. Nonetheless, the estimated parameters exhibited mixed accuracy with top height being the most accurate.

Keywords: LiDAR · Mangrove · Tree crown segmentation · Connected components

1 Introduction

The study and monitoring of fragile ecosystems such as mangrove forests is of vital importance worldwide as they are among the most productive and most Carbon-rich forest in the tropic; they provide habitats to over 1300 species of animals and act as protection of shorelines, hurricanes and tidal surges. It is estimated that between 35–50% of mangrove coverage have been lost in the past 60 years due mainly to human activities and, despite it accounts for only the 0.7% of tropical forest areas, it amounts as much as around 10% of emissions from deforestation globally [3]. Their assessment have been largely carried out through forest inventories that are time consuming, costly and, consequently,

---

This research was funded by "Fondo Institucional de Fomento Regional (FORDECyT)" grant number 273646 and JLS was funded by "Fondo Sectorial CONACyT-INEGI" grant number 268773.

not frequently updated. More recently, efforts have been made to streamline inventorying processes through remote sensing and computational technologies, including pointcloud analysis, which is still limited due to the lack of efficient automation processes.

Among the many alternatives found in the literature, the voxel method is one of the most widely used method for three-dimensional models of trees due to its relative easy structure [14]. Other approaches use simple geometric models such as paraboloids or spheres to approximate the tree crown [7,9,12]. More realistic models have been also investigated, but tend to be computationally costly. For instance, radial basis functions and isosurfaces have been shown to achieve more natural forms of tree crowns [4], while others have focused on the reconstruction of the skeleton [1] or adjust free shapes to pointclouds [2]. From an inventorying viewpoint, the most useful models are those that can encode the most relevant structure parameters with the lowest complexity. One fundamental processing step is the extraction of individual trees pointclouds through a segmentation method. Major pointcloud segmentation strategies have been revised by [13], but all of them can be grouped in one of three types depending on the format of the input: 1) based on unstructured pointclouds, such as unsupervised clustering or primitives fitting [5,15], 2) raster-based methods, which impose a regular spatial structure, either in 2-d (pixels) or in 3-d (voxels) on the pointcloud [6,11], and 3) based on structured pointclouds, where the neighbourhood relationship is imposed using a directed graph. Although the latter approach can be the most accurate, it is also the most difficult to implement and thus the least researched approach. One of the few studies is that of [10] who used graph partition and connected components labelling (CCL) to delineate tree crown over a pine-dominated site. Nonetheless, they used a raster-based segmentation for building a hierarchical structuring prior to graph partitioning.

In order to fill this gap, we propose a novel structured pointcloud-based segmentation method that integrates *a priori* knowledge about the shape of target objects for the neighbourhood definition. The general strategy consists in creating an initial neighborhood connectivity matrix used with the CCL algorithm that is then progressively pruned and re-labelled. In the following sections we present 1) a brief description of the study site and data used, 2) the segmentation method, 3) the 3-d modelling approach, 4) the accuracy assessment and 5) the major conclusions.

2   Study Site and Data Used

The study site is around El Cometa, a small lagoon (67 ha) within the Pantanos de Centla reserve located at the north of the Mexican state of Tabasco (Fig. 1a). This site is mostly covered by the red mangrove (*Rhizophora mangle*), a threatened species (SEMARNAT, 2010) that mixes with medium sub evergreen tropical forest of pucté (*Bucida buceras* L.). There is also a low population of white mangrove (*Laguncularia racemosa*) around the lagoon and channels.

Tree structure data was collected from 10 plots of 50 m by 50 m in 2014 (plots 1–10), 20 plots of 25 m by 50 m in 2016 (plots 1–20) and 7 plots of 25 m by 50 m

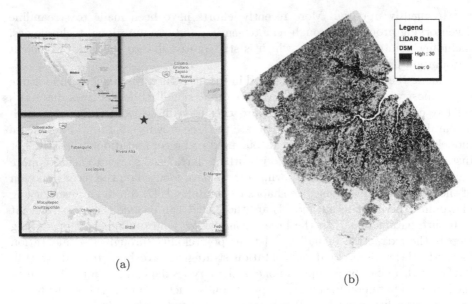

(a)

(b)

Fig. 1. (a) Location of the study area and (b) LiDAR-based DSM and plot locations

in 2017 (plots 21–27). Plot center and orientation were measured with sub-meter precision GPS system. Tree individuals data included species name, xy-location (measured with respect to plot center), total height, diameter at breast height (DBH), diameter above and bellow highest root (mangrove trees only), crown diameters along E-W and S-N orientations, root diameters along E-W and S-N orientations, roots total height, and time and date of measurement. Individuals with lower DBH than 10 cm were not sampled. Only data from 25 plots were used as some were either not fully covered by LiDAR data or repeated in two different years.

The LiDAR sensor was flown in March 26, 2014 over an area of 2.5 km by 3.6 km (Fig. 1b) with an average point density of 20 pts/m^2 and vertical accuracy of ± 0.15 m. Data was delivered with ground points identified, from which a terrain surface was generated. Subsets for each sampling plot with a buffer of 20% where extracted and normalized by subtracting the terrain surface. These data were the main input to the individual tree point extraction method described next.

3   Segmentation Method

Major stages of the proposed pointcloud segmentation method are described in the following subsections, where parameters referred throughout are defined in Table 1.

Table 1. Segmentation parameters used. z_{max} is the maximum z-coordinate of segment.

Symbol	Description	Value
z_{grmax}	Maximum z-coord of ground points	0.15 [m]
r_{max}	Maximum edge horiz. distance	5 [m]
d_{max}	Maximum segment diameter	5 [m]
w_{min}	Minimum points per segment	10 [pts]
E_{min}	Minimum break energy	20 [m*pts]
n_{iter}	Maximum splitting iterations	10
d_{min}	Minimum crown diameter	2 [m]
h_{min}	Minimum tree height	2 [m]
z_{himin}	Minimum z-coord of high points	$0.3z_{max}$ [m]
z_{lomax}	Maximum z-coord of low points	$0.15z_{max}$ [m]

3.1 Point Connectivity and Pruning

Pointcloud neighbourhood is represented through an adjacency or connectivity matrix $C = [C_{i,j}]_{i,j=0,...,n}$, so that a point j is said to be in the neighbourhood of point i if $C_{i,j}$ is one, otherwise it is zero. The connectivity matrix of any order, including the zeroth, shall be denoted by C^*. Recall that the k-th order neighbours are given by the power matrix C^k.

There are several alternatives for defining pointcloud neighbourhoods, such as maximum distance, k-nearest neighbours, and Delaunay tessellation, among others. Here we used the latter option as its computation is efficient yielding a relatively high sparsity, i.e., high fraction of zeroes in C. Hence, the initial connectivity matrix is given by:

$$C_{i,j} = \begin{cases} 1 & \text{if } (i,j) \text{ is a Delaunay edge} \\ 0 & \text{otherwise} \end{cases} \tag{1}$$

The sparsity of the connectivity matrix is further increased through applying the following pruning:

1. All the neighbors must be lower than the point, i.e., $C_{i,j} = 0$, if $z_i \leq z_j$
2. All points must be non-terrain points, i.e., $C_{i,j} = 0$, if $z_i \leq z_{grmax}$
3. Every point is at most in the neighborhood of the nearest option, i.e., $C_{i,j} = 0$, if $d_{i,j} > \min_k\{d_{k,j}\}$
4. Horizontal distance between a pair of neighbors is within a maximum distance, i.e., $C_{i,j} = 0$, if $r_{i,j} > r_{max}$

The first criterion ensure that the graph defined by the connectivity matrix is top-down directed, the second criterion discard terrain points, and the third one ensures no loops are present in the directed graph, thus defining a tree-like structure. The threshold distance r_{max} in the fourth criterion controls the size and number of segments. A large threshold value favors the inclusion of points from distinct nearby trees into a single segment (under segmentation), whereas a small value will tend to separate points from a single tree into several segments (over segmentation). Because of the high density of mangrove forests, no optimal value for r_{max} can be satisfactory and one always needs to undertake further steps to either merge or split segments. The favored option here is to select a relative large threshold value and to apply a progressive splitting strategy. This decision is mainly driven by the difficulty of searching points to reconnect over the option of searching edges to eliminate.

3.2   Segment Splitting

Starting with the segmentation induced by labelling the connected components in C, the segment splitting procedure is applied to wide segments as follows. For each selected segment one of the connection in the connectivity matrix is eliminated and the process repeated until either no more wide segments are available or the maximum number of iterations has been reached.

Segments are considered to be wide if its diameter is greater than a maximum allowed diameter (d_{max}), whereas segment diameter is computed by averaging the ranges of projections $u_i = x_i \cos\theta + y_i \sin\theta$ along four directions: $\theta = 0$, 45, 90 and 135°. Such diameter computation must be based on high points, i.e., the points with z-coordinates greater than threshold (z_{himin}). In addition, segments with lower number of points than a threshold $(2w_{min})$ are not considered candidates for splitting.

The segment splitting consists in eliminating, at most, one edge per connected component, where selected edge fulfill three conditions:

1. Large horizontal distance
2. Similar number of points in generated sub-graphs
3. Low points available in generated sub-graphs

The first condition tends to maintain connected components horizontally compact, the second one reduces the number of required iterations by fast reduction of segments size, and the third one warrants connected components will include points that most likely belong to the aerial roots of mangrove individuals. These conditions are met by maximizing the following edge measure:

$$E_{i,j} = r_{i,j} \min\{w_j, w_j^c\} - \min\{b_j w_j, b_j^c w_j^c\} \tag{2}$$

where $r_{i,j}$ is the horizontal distance of the edge (i, j), w_j is the size of sub-graph at j, w_j^c the size of complement sub-graph at j, so that $w_j + w_j^c$ is the size of original graph, i.e., the total number of points in the segment, and b_j and b_j^c are z-coordinates of lowest point of each sub-graph. Equation (2) can be interpreted through a physical system analogy where points represent particles of unit weight connected trough rigid links, which are defined by the connectivity matrix C. Each link is subject to a pair of forces or weights that excerpt torques with respect to middle point of the link, which is supposed fix. Hence, maximizing of the energy acting on the rigid link while minimizing the tendency to motion yields an expression like Eq. (2). Such energy is required to be over a threshold (E_{min}) to cause the link to break.

At each iteration, Eq. (2) is evaluated for each wide segment and the edge with maximum positive value is eliminated. This can be expressed as:

$$C_{i,j} = 0, \text{ if } E_{i,j} = \max_{(k,l)}\{E_{k,l}\} \text{ and } E_{i,j} \geq E_{min} \tag{3}$$

4   3-D Modelling

4.1   Tree Structure Estimation

Small segments that did not comply with minimum tree height (h_{min}), minimum crown diameter (d_{min}) or samples size ($10w_{min}$) were discarded. Points from remaining segments were then classified into low, mid and high based on thresholds z_{himin} and z_{lomax} defined in Table 1, which had been empirically calibrated. Then, tree location and structure parameters were estimated from segmented pointcloud as described in Table 2.

Table 2. Tree structure parameters as computed from segment points.

Symbol	Name	Computed as[a]
x_{loc}, y_{loc}	tree location	mean of low points
z_{loc}	base tree elevation	median z of terrain points
x_c, y_c, z_c	crown location	mean of high points
h_t	crown top height	maximum z of high points
h_b	crown bottom height	vertical standard deviation of high points ($z_c - \chi\sigma_z$)
h_r	root height	vertical standard deviation of low points ($\chi\sigma_z$)
d_c	crown diameter	radial standard deviation of high points ($2\chi\sigma_r$)
d_t	trunk diameter	empirical relation $d_t = 0.03d_c + 0.05$
d_r	root diameter	radial standard deviation of low points ($2\chi\sigma_r$)
ϕ_t, θ_t	trunk orientation	azimuth and elevation of $(x_c - x_{loc}, y_c - y_{loc}, h_b - h_r)$

[a] $\chi = 2.1459$ for a 90% confidence level.

Assuming a multivariate Gaussian distribution of points belonging to tree crown and to roots, where radial symmetry can be assumed in both cases, and symmetry along z can be further assumed for the roots, one can estimate crown diameter, crown bottom height, root diameter and root height using the ellipse in the rz-plane[1]:

$$\left(\frac{r}{\sigma_r}\right)^2 + \left(\frac{z}{\sigma_z}\right)^2 = \chi^2 \tag{4}$$

---

[1] Root points are in the upper hemisphere of an ellipse.

where the semi-axis of the ellipses are given by the standard deviations times a constant ($\chi = 2.1459$) that is theoretically determined to enclose 90% of points and $\sigma_r^2 = (\sigma_x^2 + \sigma_y^2)/2$.

While high points and low points determined crown and root parameters, trunk diameter had to be computed through an empirical relation between the DBH and crown diameter of red mangrove, which was strongly linear and statistical significant ($R^2 = 0.63$). This was necessary, because trunk points are hard to determine and seldom accessible from airborne LiDAR. Moreover, trunk orientation was defined through the elevation and azimuth angles of a vector joining root top and crown base locations, and where no low points were available, crown location was used, the root height was defined as zero and the root diameter, same as the trunk diameter.

Estimated parameters were represented using a 3-D surface model with three parts (roots, trunk and crown), each of which was represented through a revolution surface of the form:

$$x(u, \theta) = \rho(u) \cos \theta \tag{5}$$

$$y(u, \theta) = \rho(u) \sin \theta \tag{6}$$

$$z(u, \theta) = a + (a - b)(1 - (1 - u^{\alpha_6}))^{\alpha_7} \tag{7}$$

$$\rho(z) = r \left| \alpha_1 \pm \left[\alpha_2 - \alpha_3 \left(\frac{a - z}{a - b} \right) \right]^{\alpha_4} \right|^{1/\alpha_5} \tag{8}$$

for $\theta \in [0, 2\pi)$ and $u \in [0, 1]$, where $\alpha_1, \ldots, \alpha_7$ are shape parameters, a is the top limit, b the bottom limit and r is the radius of the surface. The $\pm$ symbol indicates that there are two types of models: models with the plus sign are of hyperbolic type, whereas the negative are of parabolic type.

Models used for mangrove trees were ellipsoids for crown, with α-values of (1,1,2,2,2,1,1), respectively, cylinders for trunk (2,0,1,0,2,1,1) and flattened parabolid for roots (0,0,1,1,4,1,2). Furthermore, trunk inclination was modeled by shifting the xy-coordinates as function of z-coordinate. In this case, xy-coordinates are given by:

$$x(u, \theta) = \rho(u) \cos \theta + \frac{z - h_r}{\tan \theta_t} \cos \phi_t \tag{9}$$

$$y(u, \theta) = \rho(u) \sin \theta + \frac{z - h_r}{\tan \theta_t} \sin \phi_t \tag{10}$$

5   Accuracy Assesment

The segmentation method was applied on the 25 plots from which tree models were generated. Figure 2 shows the top and lateral views of the segmented pointcloud and the corresponding surface model for a couple of plots. It can be seen that the object level representation captures the coarse shape of the pointcloud, yet whether such a representation match the actual forest structure was subject to a quantitative assessment, both at the plot and individual levels.

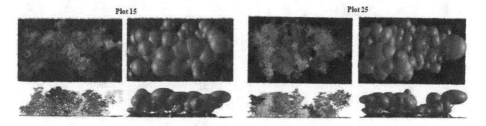

Fig. 2. Top and lateral view of segmented pointcloud (left) and surface model (right) of extracted trees for two plots.

At the plot level, we selected the segments laying within the plot limits based on their location, (x_{loc}, y_{loc}), and compared the averages parameter values. Figure 3-left shows the scatterplot between the number of LiDAR-derived trees within the plots and the groundtruth trees. With exception of plot 8, LiDAR-derived trees seemed to follow a global trend that agrees with respect to those observed in the field, with a median absolute error of 7 trees per plot.

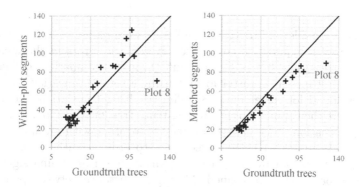

Fig. 3. LiDAR-derived vs. groundtruth trees based on number of trees within plot limits (left) and number of matched trees (right). See text for further details.

Figure 4a shows the scatterplots of per-plot averages and Table 3a provides the comparative analysis in terms of the coefficient of determination (R^2) and of the root mean squared error (RMSE). The scatterplots reveal that the crown diameter, root diameter and root height were generally overestimated, whereas such a bias was not present in the case of top height, which exhibited the largest R^2 value (0.18). Nevertheless, the root height showed the lowest RMSE and the root diameter had the largest value. This can be explained in terms of the dynamical range of these structure parameters and in terms of an overestimation of aerial roots for non-mangrove species.

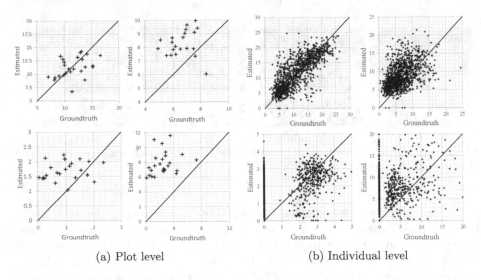

(a) Plot level   (b) Individual level

Fig. 4. Estimated vs. groundtruth scatterplots at the plot- and individual levels for top height (top-left), crown diameter (top-right), root height (bottom-left) and root diameter (bottom right).

At the individual level, LiDAR-derived trees were paired to the ground-truth trees. This process required to correct for systematic errors in the location of ground-truth trees, which was carried out through the spatial correlation of the canopy height models in raster format using a rotation-invariant correlation measure developed for raster data [8]. The resulting translation and rotation parameters were then applied to the ground-truth tree locations to use as ground-truth canopy location. Such canopy locations, together with ground-truth tree height, served to match LiDAR-derived trees to ground-truth trees. A one-to-one pairing was ensured by sequentially pairing the nearest unassigned trees until no more pairs could be formed. Maximum distance between paired trees was limited to 5 m in order to limit the impact from pairing errors over the parameter estimation errors. The number of pairs was generally slightly lower than the actual number of trees in the plot as can be seen in the scatterplot of Fig. 3-right. Figure 4b shows the scatterplot of matched trees and Table 3b, the corresponding R^2 and RMSE measures. In this case, it was possible to segregate mangrove trees using the species information from field data. The overestimation bias that was observed at the plot level was again observed at the individual level for crown diameter and root diameter, but not for root height. Top height was again unbiased and showed the highest R^2 value (0.61), although in this case the pairing process must have had an influence on these. Scatterplots also reveal that non-null root parameters were retrieved for non-mangrove species thus indicating a limitation of the segmentation method, which may have mistaken understorey vegetation as roots.

Table 3. Coefficient of determination (R^2) and root mean square error (RMSE) at the plot and individual levels. (Values in parenthesis were based on mangrove species only).

Parameter	R^2	RMSE [m]
Top height	0.18	2.41
Crown diameter	0.03	2.62
Root height	0.03	0.93
Root diameter	0.07	5.67

(a) Plot level: $n = 25$

Parameter	R^2	RMSE [m]
Top height	0.61(0.42)	3.61(3.81)
Crown diameter	0.22(0.13)	4.15(4.59)
Root height	0.16(0.03)	1.64(1.40)
Root diameter	0.05(0.08)	7.23(5.30)

(b) Individual level: $n = 1100(370)$

6 Conclusions

Most existing tree crown segmentation methods have focused on temperate forests, where intertwined branches and aerial roots do not represent an issue. In contrast, in this study we developed and tested a segmentation method that incorporates information about the structure of objects embedded in the point-cloud, namely, the mangrove trees. The method used a sparse matrix that defines the neighbourhood relation among points, from which the connected-component labelling method is repeatedly applied together with a segment splitting strategy. The accuracy assessment showed a good promise for automated mangrove forest inventories. Nonetheless, methods for parameters estimation must be further improved, specially root structural parameters, specially because they are critical for quantifying blue Carbon storage by mangrove forests.

References

1. Bucksch, A., Lindenbergh, R., Menenti, M., Rahman, M.Z.: Skeleton-based botanic tree diameter estimation from dense lidar data. In: Lidar Remote Sensing for Environmental Monitoring X. vol. 7460, p. 746007. International Society for Optics and Photonics (2009)
2. Côté, J.F., Widlowski, J.L., Fournier, R.A., Verstraete, M.M.: The structural and radiative consistency of three-dimensional tree reconstructions from terrestrial lidar. Remote Sens. Environ. **113**(5), 1067–1081 (2009)
3. Donato, D.C., Kauffman, J.B., Murdiyarso, D., Kurnianto, S., Stidham, M., Kanninen, M.: Mangroves among the most carbon-rich forests in the tropics. Nat. Geosci. **4**(5), 293 (2011)
4. Kato, A., Moskal, L.M., Schiess, P., Swanson, M.E., Calhoun, D., Stuetzle, W.: Capturing tree crown formation through implicit surface reconstruction using airborne lidar data. Remote Sens. Environ. **113**(6), 1148–1162 (2009)
5. Li, W., Guo, Q., Jakubowski, M.K., Kelly, M.: A new method for segmenting individual trees from the lidar point cloud. Photogramm. Eng. Remote Sensing **78**(1), 75–84 (2012)
6. Miliaresis, G., Kokkas, N.: Segmentation and object-based classification for the extraction of the building class from lidar dems. Comput. Geosci. **33**(8), 1076–1087 (2007)

7. Morsdorf, F., Meier, E., Kötz, B., Itten, K.I., Dobbertin, M., Allgöwer, B.: Lidar-based geometric reconstruction of boreal type forest stands at single tree level for forest and wildland fire management. Remote Sens. Environ. **92**(3), 353–362 (2004)

8. Silván-Cárdenas, J.L., Salazar-Garibay, A.: Local geometric deformations in the dht domain with applications. IEEE Trans. Image Process. **28**(4), 1980–1992 (2019)

9. Silván-Cárdenas, J.L.: A segmentation method for tree crown detection and modelling from LiDAR measurements. In: Carrasco-Ochoa, J.A., Martínez-Trinidad, J.F., Olvera López, J.A., Boyer, K.L. (eds.) MCPR 2012. LNCS, vol. 7329, pp. 65–74. Springer, Heidelberg (2012). https://doi.org/10.1007/978-3-642-31149-9_7

10. Strîmbu, V.F., Strîmbu, B.M.: A graph-based segmentation algorithm for tree crown extraction using airborne lidar data. ISPRS J. Photogramm. Remote Sensing **104**, 30–43 (2015)

11. Vo, A.V., Truong-Hong, L., Laefer, D.F., Bertolotto, M.: Octree-based region growing for point cloud segmentation. ISPRS J. Photogramm. Remote Sensing **104**, 88–100 (2015)

12. Vosselman, G.: 3D reconstruction of roads and trees for city modelling. Int. Arch. Photogramm. Remot Sensing Spat. Inf. Sci. **34**, 3 (2003)

13. Vosselman, G., Gorte, B.G., Sithole, G., Rabbani, T.: Recognising structure in laser scanner point clouds. Int. Arch. Photogramm. Remot Sensing Spat. Inf. Sci. **46**(8), 33–38 (2004)

14. Wang, Y., Weinacker, H., Koch, B.: A lidar point cloud based procedure for vertical canopy structure analysis and 3D single tree modelling in forest. Sensors **8**(6), 3938–3951 (2008)

15. Zhang, Z., et al.: A multilevel point-cluster-based discriminative feature for ALS point cloud classification. IEEE Trans. Geosci. Remote Sens. **54**(6), 3309–3321 (2016)

Computer Vision

Vision-Based Blind Spot Warning System by Deep Neural Networks

Víctor R. Virgilio G.[1](✉)(iD), Humberto Sossa[1,2](iD), and Erik Zamora[1](iD)

[1] Instituto Politécnico Nacional - CIC, Av. Juan de Dios Batiz S/N,
Gustavo A. Madero, 07738 Ciudad de Mexico, Mexico
vvirgiliog@gmail.com, hsossa@cic.ipn.mx, ezamorag@ipn.mx
[2] Tecnológico de Monterrey, Unidad Guadalajara, Av. Gral. Ramón Corona 2514,
45201 Zapopan, Jalisco, Mexico

Abstract. Traffic accidents represent one of the most serious problems around the world. Many efforts have been concentrated on implementing Advanced Driver Assistance Systems (ADAS) to increase safety by reducing critical tasks faced by the driver. In this paper, a Blind Spot Warning (BSW) system capable of virtualizing cars around the driver's vehicle is presented. The system is based on deep neural models for car detection and depth estimation using images captured with a camera located on top of the main vehicle, then transformations are applied to the image and to generate the appropriate information format. Finally the cars in the environment are represented in a 3D graphical interface. We present a comparison between car detectors and another one between depth estimators from which we choose the best performance ones to be implemented in the BSW system. In particular, our system offers a more intuitive assistance interface for the driver allowing a better and quicker understanding of the environment from monocular cameras.

Keywords: ADAS (advanced driver-assistance systems) · BSW (blind spots warning) · SIDE (single image depth estimation) · Object detection · Neural networks

1 Introduction

Transport can be involved in daily traffic accidents which are one of the most serious problems currently facing modern societies. According to 2017 figures from the World Health Organization (WHO), each year around 1.3 million people die in road accidents worldwide, and between 20 and 50 million suffer non-fatal injuries that cause disabilities [17]. According to data from the National Institute of Public Health (INSP), Mexico ranks seventh in the world and third in the Latin American region in terms of road deaths, with 22 deaths of young people between 15 and 29 years of age per day [9].

Road specialists and road safety experts report that behind every vehicle accident the human factor is involved in 90% [6]. So for several years, car manufacturers have implemented technologies such as ADAS which assist the driver in

© Springer Nature Switzerland AG 2020
K. M. Figueroa Mora et al. (Eds.): MCPR 2020, LNCS 12088, pp. 185–194, 2020.
https://doi.org/10.1007/978-3-030-49076-8_18

the driving process. ADAS goal is to increase automobile safety and road safety in general using Human-Machine Interfaces (HMI). These systems use multiple sensors (radar, lidar, camera, GPS, etc.) to identify the environment with which the vehicle interacts.

When driving a vehicle the driver depends on rear-view mirrors and body movements to observe other vehicles approaching, however, this practice represents risks due to the generation of areas where vision is partially or completely occluded, these areas are called "blind spots". Due to the large number of accidents caused by this situation, BSW systems have been developed which provide the driver with information about the vehicles around him to avoid possible collisions.

This document is organized as follows. Section 2 describes details of the existing State-of-the-Art (SOTA) of BSW systems and the type of processing they perform. Section 3 presents the different techniques and technologies implemented in the proposed BSW system, such as the neural models, the applied transformations and the visualization platform used. Section 4 shows the results obtained qualitatively and quantitatively from the implemented technologies. Section 5 the conclusions obtained with the development of this work are presented.

2 Related Work

Although the objective is the same (alerting the driver to the presence of vehicles in occlusion areas) BSW systems can be developed from different technologies and implement different sensors such as: ultrasonic, optical, radar, cameras, etc; in addition, they can provide visual (e.g. outside image), audio (e.g. voice prompt) or tactile (e.g. steering wheel vibration) information to indicate that it is not safe to change lanes. Typically there are two basic approaches to obtain and processing information: range-based and vision-based.

Works such as presented in [14,16,22,23] describe range-based systems that implement ultrasonic or radar devices mounted around the vehicle to estimate the distance of approaching objects, subsequently alert the driver by means of indicators on the side mirrors.

Vision-based systems aim to obtain information from the environment using cameras and then perform image analysis for obstacles detection while driving. Most BSW systems employ classic image processing techniques for their development. Such as [3,13,18,19,23] histogram of oriented gradients (HOG), filters for edge detection, entropy, optical flow, Gabor's filter, among others are used to extract useful information and techniques such as clustering and vector support machines [13,18] to classify where vehicles are. In [11] the concept of depth estimation is implemented to determine whether a vehicle is near or far from the driver's vehicle, they make use of features such as texture and blur in the image, and techniques such as principal component analysis (PCA) and discrete cosine transformation.

In recent years, neural models have been implemented for the classification and detection of objects in images due to good performance obtained. In [15,21] fully connected neural networks (FCN) are used for vehicle detection in blind spot areas, in addition to techniques such as HOG, heat mapping and threshold levels for pre-processing of images.

Other types of BSW systems have been developed with more complex neural models; such is the case of [26] where first the objects are located by classic image segmentation, then the candidates are classified with a Convolutional Neural Network (CNN) and the vehicle is tracked using optical flow analysis. On the other hand in [27] blind spot vehicles are treated as a classification problem in which a CNN takes full responsibility for classifying whether or not a vehicle exists in the predetermined area.

Lastly, in [19] a BSW system is developed implementing multi-object tracking (MOT) from a fusion of sensors, including cameras, LIDAR, among others; in addition, techniques such as decision by Markov models and reinforcement learning for information processing are applied.

3   Proposed Method

We propose a BSW system capable of providing a driver assistance interface that virtualizes the cars around him on a 3D platform. The system contains (i) a neuronal model for car detection, (ii) a neuronal model for depth estimation, (iii) a processing module to generate car location and (iv) a graphical interface module to visualize the cars, as illustrated in Fig. 1.

The presented system was implemented using monocular images from the KITTI database [8]. KITTI provides stereoscopic images (1242 × 375) of front view using cameras mounted on top of the vehicle at a rate of 10 frames per second. All scenes are recorded in similar weather conditions during the day.

3.1   Car Detection

For car detection in the images, two very popular neural architectures were tested: YOLOv3 and Detectron2.

YOLOv3 [20] is a neural model for object detection that processes approximately 30 images per second in COCO test-set obtaining an average precision of 33% and consists of 53 convolutional layers (Darknet 53). This model has several advantages over systems based on classifiers and sliding window, for example, it examines the entire image at the time of inference so that predictions have information about the overall context of the image. In addition, it develops the predictions with a single evaluation of the image which makes it a very fast network.

Detectron2 is a neural model developed by Facebook AI Research that implements SOTA object detection algorithms. It is a rewrite of the previous version, Detectron, and originates from the benchmark Mask R-CNN [12]. The average precision of this model is 39.8% obtained in COCO test-set.

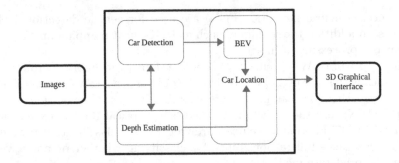

Fig. 1. Proposed system diagram. The images are passed through the detector to infer areas where there are cars, subsequently distance is estimated in the previously detected areas using the neuronal model (depth, Z axis) and the BEV transformation (horizontal, X axis). Later, the information is given to the 3D graphical interface to visualize the cars.

3.2   Depth Estimation

Considering that car detecting in images does not give us clear information about the distance they are, which is fundamental for the understanding of a scene, a single-image depth estimation (SIDE) has been implemented to know the distance in the Z-axis (deep). Different neuronal models were considered.

DenseDepth [2] is a model that consists of a convolutional neural network for computing a high-resolution depth map given a single RGB image. Following a standard encoder-decoder architecture, they leverage features extracted using high performing pre-trained networks when initializing the encoder along with augmentation and training strategies that lead to more accurate results.

MonoDepth2 [10] is a depth estimation network is based on the general U-Net architecture with skip connections, enabling to represent both deep abstract features as well as local information. They use a ResNet18 as encoder, unlike the larger and slower DispNet and ResNet50 models used in existing SOTA.

monoResMatch [24] is a deep architecture designed to infer depth from a single input image by synthesizing features from a different point of view, horizontally aligned with the input image, performing stereo matching between the two cues. In contrast to previous works sharing this rationale, this network is the first trained end-to-end from scratch.

3.3   Car Location

Following the steps described in [25], and using OpenCV, we apply a bird's eye view transformation (BEV) to estimate the distance of the vehicles in the X axis (horizontal). Then we organize and give the detections and estimated distances to virtualization platform.

3.4   3D Graphical Interface

In this module, we generate a 3D graphical interface to achieve a more natural and intuitive interface for the driver. Unlike the typical 2D interface, which BEV is presented, UBER's interface [1] virtualizes the cars in 3D which represents an environment similar to the one humans face daily, so it directly impacts on the speed of assimilation/interpretation of the environment.

4   Results

In this section we present the qualitative and quantitative results obtained by the neuronal models for car detection and depth estimation, as well as ones obtained by the BEV transformation. In addition, the final results of the BSW system are shown through the interface generated by the UBER platform.

Although the BSW system aims to process complete information on the environment around the vehicle, the results presented are the first tests carried out using the KITTI database. However, the system could be evaluated with another database that offers images of the complete environment using cameras located at different points of the vehicle as well as scenes recorded in more challenging weather conditions.

This work aims to demonstrate the feasibility of using deep neural models in BSW systems, the experiments were individually carried out offline using a Tesla P100 (16 GB) GPU.

Car Detection. Following [4], we evaluate car detectors using 3,769 images for validation set at KITTI 2D detection benchmark [8]. Evaluation is done for car class in three regimes: Easy, Moderate and Hard, which contain objects of different box sizes, and different levels of occlusion and truncation. The results in Table 1 show that, in general, car detection is feasible even in high complexity situations such as moderate and hard KITTI levels, with 0.07 s for images with few detected cars (less than 5) and 0.1 s for many cars (more than 10). Figure 2 shows some results of detectors in the validation set.

The main reason why the AP is below 50% is because both models have not been retrained in the KITTI database; instead, these models have been pre-trained in the COCO database with almost 100 classes. In addition, both neural models are the most popular and intuitive to implement but not the best performing in the SOTA. Based on the experimental results we conclude that Detectron2 is a better choice for this type of problem in a BSW system.

Table 1. Performance on KITTI validation set for Car class using the KITTI standar metric, Average Precision Metric (AP).

	AP (%)			Time (s)	
	Easy	Moderate	Hard	min	max
YOLOv3	**47.3**	41.4	30.4	0.07	0.1
Detectron2	46.1	**49.5**	**39.9**	0.07	0.1

Fig. 2. Groundtruth (first row), YOLOv3 detection (second row), Detectron2 detection (third row) are presented. It is possible to observe that Detectron2 adjusts bounding boxes better and detects cars that Yolov3 does not.

Depth Estimation. SOTA single-image depth estimators were compared in KITTI's benchmark [7]. Table 2 shows that neural models compared present a very good and similar performance, which demonstrates that they are a good alternative to the problem of depth estimation; it is worth mentioning that MonoDepth2 processes information in a considerably less amount of time than the other methods, which would be important when testing the system on embedded hardware.

Implementing SOTA depth estimation models allows us to obtain more precise information about the location of previously detected trolleys. Based on the experimental results we conclude that DenseDepth is the best option to depth estimation problem in a BSW. Figure 3 shows some results of depth estimators.

BEV Transformation. Some results of the BEV transform are presented in Fig. 4. Later, the information was organized to be sent to the graphic interface platform.

Table 2. Quantitative evaluation on the test set of KITTI dataset [7] using the standard six metrics used in [5], maximum depth: 80 m.

	Higher is better			Lower is better				
	$\delta 1$	$\delta 2$	$\delta 3$	rel	sq. rel	rms	log10	Time (s)
DenseDepth	0.886	**0.965**	**0.986**	**0.093**	**0.589**	**4.170**	**0.171**	0.08
MonoDepth2	**0.890**	0.961	0.981	0.096	0.673	4.351	0.184	0.007
monoResMatch	0.876	0.958	0.980	0.106	0.806	4.630	0.193	0.66

Fig. 3. The original image (first row), depth estimation by DenseDepth (second row), depth estimation by MonoDepth2 (third row), depth estimation by MonoResMatch (fourth row) are presented. It is possible to observe that, in the case of defined shapes (such as cars and people), DenseDepth has a higher level of detail than the rest.

Blind Spot Warning System. To test the BSW system we use the previously chosen neural models, then we apply the BEV transformation and give the data to the UBER platform to generate the 3D graphical interface.

Figure 5 shows the result of the BSW system, where different 3D views generated by the graphical interface are displayed in addition to the indication (by color) of the closest cars, which offers greater assistance and comfort to the driver in terms of how he or she perceives the environment.

Fig. 4. BEV transformation results. The original image (first row) and Bird's Eye View transformation (second row) are presented.

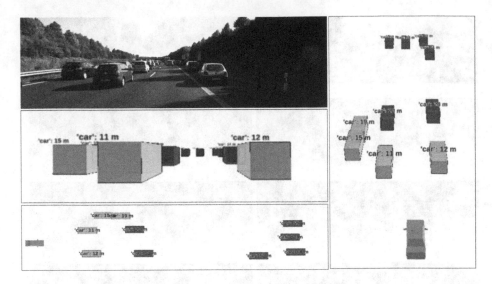

Fig. 5. The original image (top left), driver's view (center left), bird's view (bottom left) and perspective view (right) generated in the graphical interface are presented.

5   Conclusion

A single-image BSW system was developed based on artificial intelligence technologies such as neural models for object detection and depth estimation. In addition, the visualization system development on a 3D graphics platform offers the driver a much more intuitive interface than SOTA BSW systems and presents a much faster way to understand the behavior of the vehicles around.

This work shows a BSW system with complex interfaces through the unique use of vision sensors, which represents a cost reduction compared to range-based systems that employ sensors such as LIDAR or radar. Finally, the presented system contributes to the approach of understanding the scene, since it offers an alternative of car virtualization that works as a reference for the perception of the environment.

Acknowledgments. V. Virgilio acknowledges CONACYT for the scholarship granted towards pursuing his postgraduate studies. H. Sossa and E. Zamora would like to acknowledge the support provided by SIP-IPN (grant numbers 20190166, 20190007, 20200651 and 20200630).

References

1. Chen, X., Lisee, J., Wojtaszek, T., Gupta, A.: Introducing AVS, an open standard for autonomous vehicle visualization from uber. Accessed, February 2020. https://eng.uber.com/avs-autonomous-vehicle-visualization/
2. Alhashim, I., Wonka, P.: High Quality Monocular Depth Estimation via Transfer Learning (2018). http://arxiv.org/abs/1812.11941

3. Chang, S.M., Tsai, C.C., Guo, J.I.: A blind spot detection warning system based on gabor filtering and optical flow for e-mirror applications. In: Proceedings - IEEE International Symposium on Circuits and Systems 2018-May, pp. 1–5 (2018). https://doi.org/10.1109/ISCAS.2018.8350927

4. Chen, X., Kundu, K., Zhu, Y., Ma, H., Fidler, S., Urtasun, R.: 3D object proposals using stereo imagery for accurate object class detection. IEEE Trans. Pattern Anal. Mach. Intell. **40**(5), 1259–1272 (2018). https://doi.org/10.1109/TPAMI.2017.2706685

5. Eigen, D., Puhrsch, C., Fergus, R.: Depth map prediction from a single image using a multi-scale deep network. Adv. Neural Inf. Process. Syst. **3**(January), 2366–2374 (2014)

6. Fundación Carlos Slim: Las causas más comunes en accidentes de tránsito - Seguridad Vial. Accessed, February 2020. http://fundacioncarlosslim.org/12022-2/

7. Geiger, A., Lenz, P., Stiller, C., Urtasun, R.: Vision meets robotics: The KITTI dataset. Int. J. Robot. Res. **32**(11), 1231–1237 (2013). https://doi.org/10.1177/0278364913491297

8. Geiger, A., Lenz, P., Urtasun, R.: Are we ready for autonomous driving? the KITTI vision benchmark suite. In: Proceedings of the IEEE Computer Society Conference on Computer Vision and Pattern Recognition, pp. 3354–3361 (2012). https://doi.org/10.1109/CVPR.2012.6248074

9. Gobierno de México: Accidentes viales, primera causa de muerte en los jóvenes. Accessed, February 2020. https://www.gob.mx/salud/prensa/accidentes-viales-primera-causa-de-muerte-en-los-jovenes

10. Godard, C., Mac Aodha, O., Firman, M., Brostow, G.: Digging into self-supervised monocular depth estimation (1), 3828–3838 (2018). http://arxiv.org/abs/1806.01260

11. Guo, Y., Kumazawa, I., Kaku, C.: Blind spot obstacle detection from monocular camera images with depth cues extracted by CNN. Automot. Innov. **1**(4), 362–373 (2018). https://doi.org/10.1007/s42154-018-0036-6

12. He, K., Gkioxari, G., Dollár, P., Girshick, R.: Mask R-CNN. IEEE Trans. Pattern Anal. Mach. Intell. **42**(2), 386–397 (2020). https://doi.org/10.1109/TPAMI.2018.2844175

13. Jung, K.H., Yi, K.: Vision-based blind spot monitoring using rear-view camera and its real-time implementation in an embedded system. J. Comput. Sci. Eng. **12**(3), 127–138 (2018). https://doi.org/10.5626/JCSE.2018.12.3.127

14. Kedarkar, P., Chaudhari, M., Dasarwar, C., Domakondwar, P.B.: Prevention device for blind spot accident detection and protection. Int. Res. J. Eng. Technol. (IRJET) **6**(1), 624–627 (2019). https://www.irjet.net/archives/V6/i1/IRJET-V6I1112.pdf

15. Kwon, D., Malaiya, R., Yoon, G., Ryu, J.T., Pi, S.Y.: A study on development of the camera-based blind spot detection system using the deep learning methodology. Appl. Sci. **9**(14), 2941 (2019). https://doi.org/10.3390/app9142941. https://www.mdpi.com/2076-3417/9/14/2941

16. Liu, G., Wang, L., Zou, S.: A radar-based blind spot detection and warning system for driver assistance. In: Proceedings of 2017 IEEE 2nd Advanced Information Technology, Electronic and Automation Control Conference, IAEAC 2017, pp. 2204–2208 (2017). https://doi.org/10.1109/IAEAC.2017.8054409

17. Organización Mundial de la Salud: Accidentes de tránsito. Accessed February 2020. https://www.who.int/es/news-room/fact-sheets/detail/road-traffic-injuries

18. Ra, M., Jung, H.G., Suhr, J.K., Kim, W.Y.: Part-based vehicle detection in siderectilinear images for blind-spot detection. Expert Syst. Appl. **101**, 116–128 (2018). https://doi.org/10.1016/j.eswa.2018.02.005

19. Rangesh, A., Trivedi, M.M.: No blind spots: full-surround multi-object tracking for autonomous vehicles using cameras & LiDARs, pp. 1–12 (2018). http://arxiv.org/abs/1802.08755
20. Redmon, J., Farhadi, A.: YOLOv3: an incremental improvement (2018). http://arxiv.org/abs/1804.02767
21. Rusiecki, A., Roma, P.: Framework of blind spot information system using feedforward neural networks, March 2016. https://doi.org/10.13140/RG.2.1.3252.3921/1
22. Sheets, D.: Semi-Truck Blind Spot Detection System Group **32** (2016)
23. Tigadi, P., Gujanatti, P.B., Patil, R.: Survey on blind spot detection and lane departure warning systems. Int. J. Adv. Res. Eng. **2**(5), 2015 (2015). https://pdfs.semanticscholar.org/aae1/85ec8c8caef29389d5b6253c0b2c9bdf4a0c.pdf
24. Tosi, F., Aleotti, F., Poggi, M., Mattoccia, S.: Learning monocular depth estimation infusing traditional stereo knowledge. In: Proceedings of the IEEE Computer Society Conference on Computer Vision and Pattern Recognition 2019-June, pp. 9791–9801 (2019). https://doi.org/10.1109/CVPR.2019.01003
25. Tuohy, S., O'Cualain, D., Jones, E., Glavin, M.: Distance determination for an automobile environment using inverse perspective mapping in OpenCV. In: IET Conference Publications 2010(566 CP), pp. 100–105 (2010). https://doi.org/10.1049/cp.2010.0495
26. Wu, L.T., Lin, H.Y.: Overtaking vehicle detection techniques based on optical flow and convolutional neural network. In: VEHITS 2018 - Proceedings of the 4th International Conference on Vehicle Technology and Intelligent Transport Systems 2018-March(Vehits), pp. 133–140 (2018)
27. Zhao, Y., Bai, L., Lyu, Y., Huang, X.: Camera-based blind spot detection with a general purpose lightweight neural network. Electronics **8**(2), 233 (2019). https://doi.org/10.3390/electronics8020233

Onboard CNN-Based Processing for Target Detection and Autonomous Landing for MAVs

A. A. Cabrera-Ponce[1] and J. Martinez-Carranza[1,2]([⊠])

[1] Instituto Nacional de Astrofísica, Óptica y Electrónica (INAOE), Puebla, Mexico
{aldrichcabrera,carranza}@inaoep.mx
[2] University of Bristol, Bristol, UK

Abstract. In this work, we address the problem of target detection involved in an autonomous landing task for a Micro Aerial Vehicle (MAV). The challenge is to detect a flag located somewhere in the environment. The flag is posed on a pole, and to its right, a landing platform is located. Thus, the MAV has to detect the flag, fly towards it and once it is close enough, locate the landing platform nearby, aiming at centring over it to perform landing; all of this has to be carried out autonomously. In this context, the main problem is the detection of both the flag and the landing platform, whose shapes are known in advanced. Traditional computer vision algorithms could be used; however, the main challenges in this task are the changes in illumination, rotation and scale, and the fact that the flight controller uses the detection to perform the autonomous flight; hence the detection has to be stable and continuous on every camera frame. Motivated by this, we propose to use a Convolutional Neural Network optimised to be run on a small computer with limited computer processing budget. The MAV carries this computer, and it is used to process everything on board. To validate our system, we tested with rotated images, changes in scale and the presence of low illumination. Our method is compared against two conventional computer vision methods, namely, template and feature matching. In addition, we tested our system performance in a wide corridor, executing everything on board the MAV. We achieved a successful detection of the flag with a confidence metric of 0.9386 and 0.9826 for the Landing platform. In total, all the onboard computations ran at an average of 13.01 fps.

Keywords: CNN · SSD · Target detection · Autonomous landing

1 Introduction

Nowadays, target detection is a traditional problem in computer vision, which involves having to identify features describing relevant information about an object or set of objects. In robotics, target detection is a problem for robots that perform some tasks in real scenarios, mostly due to poor illumination.

© Springer Nature Switzerland AG 2020
K. M. Figueroa Mora et al. (Eds.): MCPR 2020, LNCS 12088, pp. 195–208, 2020.
https://doi.org/10.1007/978-3-030-49076-8_19

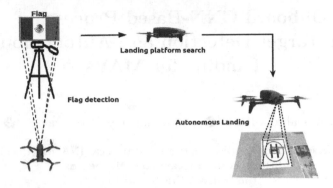

Fig. 1. Target detection for autonomous landing based on a mission of indoors competition in IMAV2019. A video of this work for reviewing purpose is found at https://youtu.be/sYn9mo-2hvA

Although the use of sensors can facilitate target detection, the information can be different in indoor and outdoor environments, thus varying the information around of the target.

Micro Aerial Vehicles (MAVs) have become popular in the research community for easy control and manipulation using the GPS devices and RGB cameras for solving multiple problems like inspection, detection, surveillance, rescue and localisation in indoors and outdoors environments. These tasks have been carried out with vision methods such as optical flow, segmentation, edge detector, morphological operations, feature extractor, feature matching and template matching. Besides, some methods have been combined with two or more techniques for suitable detection, while a MAV performs an autonomous flight in an unknown environment. Also, the combination of different types of cameras such as depth cameras, thermal cameras and stereo cameras enable to capture other types of information useful for detection. Nevertheless, the use of this information can be computationally expensive to perform detection onboard of the MAV in real-time, affect the speed performance. Likewise, it can be affected much for changes of illumination and environments, including oblique views, scale and rotations even that the object is partially occluded.

From the above, several events around the world have proposed competitions of robotics focused on the use of MAVs to solve tasks in real-time. The International Micro Aerial Vehicles and competition (IMAV) is an event focused on aerial robotics, including conference and competition in outdoors and indoors environments. The event consists of the development of new systems and methods to solve problems such as detection, control, pose estimation and autonomous navigation.

Deep learning has become a useful tool for classification, segmentation and detection without having to explicitly design a detector, descriptor and matcher components, typical of traditional computer vision techniques. Convolutional Neural Networks (CNNs) have been used to obtain results by training a dataset, allowing the learning of features to recognise multiple objects in one single pass without importance the views, occlusion and changes of illumination. YOLO, FRCNs and Single Shot Detector (SSD) are CNNs to detect classes of objects in an image, learning their features without using much computationally cost.

Therefore, motivated by the effectiveness of deep learning for the detecting task, in this work, we present a detection system to solve one of the missions included in the indoors competition of the IMAV2019. This mission consisted in detect a given flag, which is used to indicate the position of a landing platform. The goal is to a MAV navigate autonomously detecting the flag to fly towards its location, and then identify the landing platform. Once the landing platform is detected, the MAV has to maintain the detection, while performing autonomous flight to centre its position w.r.t. the platform, seeking to secure the landing on the platform in an autonomous manner, see Fig. 1.

Our detection system is based on Single Shot Detector architecture with seven convolutional layers (SSD7). We have manually generated a training dataset of the flag and platform in several views, environments and changes of illumination to obtain an improved result before realising the autonomous landing. The SSD network was chosen due to its fast performance on micro computer boards with low budget processing powers and without GPU. In average, we have tested and observed that detection tasks can be performed with an average processing speed of 15 fps; this includes the controller responsible for the autonomous flight and landing routines.

In order to present our work, this paper is organised as follows. Section 2 provides related works about object detection and autonomous landing using deep learning and vision methods. Section 3 describes the dataset generation, the hardware used for the training and experiments, and our approach for detection. Section 4 shows the experimental design and the comparison of our approach with other methods for the flag and platform detection. In Sect. 5, we present the results running on board the MAV. Finally, conclusions and future work are outlined in Sect. 6.

2   Related Work

Object detection is a problem that has addressed for a long time in image processing, pattern recognition, and robotics using multiples techniques of recognition. In aerial robotics, recent works have sought out new techniques for target detection using sensors or vision during autonomous flight. However, due to onboard cameras of the MAVs, vision methods have used to perform tasks of detection, search and tracking with visual descriptors being the most widely used due to its fast application. For instance, in [6] detect regions of interest to the runway of wind-fixes UAVs applying sparse coding spatial pyramid matching (ScSPM), others create a keypoints database for feature matching [17] or the improvement of a descriptor using CamShift based on colour information [24]. Others prefer the use patterns or marks to detect a landing platform [2, 3] and template-based matching in an image pyramid scheme for the target detection in multiple scales [5]. Likewise, methods based on RANSAC allow the search and detection of landing sites with multi-scale features using 3D maps for pose estimation of landing sites [21,22].

For one hand, machine learning and Artificial Neural Networks have leveraged the learning to detect and recognise landing targets using several methods in combination. For instance, the use of nearest neighbour with CNN layers to have effective in recognition [7] and category maps using counter propagation networks (CPNs) to identify multiple objects from aerial images [8]. Also, they are suitable for learning the skill of pilots through generated models from datasets [1], even to cooperative detections and tracking onboard [13]. Likewise, deep reinforcement learning can identify the position of the land the UAV on uniform textures using a Deep Q-Networks (DQNs) for vertical descent on a variety of simulated and real-world environments [10] or in several simulated environments with relevant noise [11]. Some works employ different deep reinforcement learning methods for the autonomous landing. Thus, [19] they show an improved deep reinforcement learning (DRL) trained on Gazebo simulation for the autonomous landing. In [12], use Deep Q-Networks (DQNs) to perform autonomous landing on the deck of a USV subject to perturbations induced by sea, and [15] use a Gazebo-based reinforcement learning framework for UAV landing on a moving platform.

On the other hand, the target detection onboard of the MAVs using deep learning has promising results, such as YOLO, FRCN and SSD. The training of CNN models is an alternative for target detection, estimating heading angles to guide the aircraft to runway landing [4] or to obtain high-level commands directly to MAV respect to target [20]. Furthermore, some CNN allows detecting broad zones for autonomous landing using depth estimation networks in real environments from a simulate dataset [16]. However, it is necessary to take into account that some sites are not wides and a precise landing is required, providing a bounding box of the landing target [14]. Hence, the detection of the targets is one of the main tasks in aerial robotics before to do an autonomous landing, in [23] uses YOLO and SqueezeNet to detect marks on the landing zone in synthesised and real-world scenarios. Finally, another work performs deep learning-based reconstruction and marker detection for MAV landing with YOLOv2 [18], and [9] uses lightDenseYOLO in combination with Kalman Filter for detecting markers and estimating the direction to perform the autonomous landing.

Despite detect targets and landing zones with deep learning, these works perform an onboard detection using computers with GPU architecture like Nvidia TX1, Nvidia TX2 and Snapdragon. Therefore, in this paper, we present a detection system using an SSD network for target detection and autonomous landing onboard of a MAV without a computer with GPU architecture.

3   Methodology

Our detection system is based on SSD architecture with seven convolution layers (SSD7). This CNN is an optimised network build to be used in computers with low performs or without GPU architecture, including on micro computer boards. The SSD is a CNN for detect multiples objects through predictions of bounding boxes around them with the capability to learn up to twenty classes of an only image and being faster to train than Yolo, FRCN and tinyYolo. In this paper, we have been trained the SSD7 with two classes: Mexican flag and Landing platform, using images captured with the Drone Bebop 2 through ROS (Robot Operating System) establishing communication between the MAV and the computer. The images were resized to QVGA (320 × 240) resolution to accelerate the training of the network and manually labelled selecting the bounding box around of the interest object. The configuration in Fig. 2 has used to detect the flag, and the platform to then send control commands in Roll, Pitch and Yaw to the aerial vehicle.

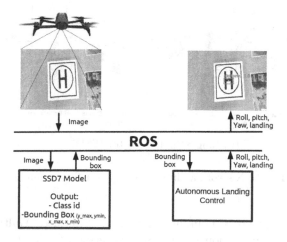

Fig. 2. System of communication used to send control commands in Roll, Pitch and Yaw to the MAV.

3.1 Single Shot Detector (SSD)

The SSD is a detection network composes of 2 parts: extract feature maps, and apply convolution filters to make predictions and detect objects, using a VGG16 network as a feature extractor (Fig. 3). Each convolution filter makes a prediction composes of bounding boxes and scores for each class. In contrast to other detection techniques, learn main features such as the form, colour, aspect, scale, saturation and texture regardless of illumination changes, partial occlusion and changes in the environment that may impair the appearance of the object. Therefore, in this paper, we use SSD7 architecture (Fig. 3) to perform the object detection onboard of the MAV in the Intel Stick Computer without GPU architecture. The input of the network is an RGB image with QVGA (320 × 240) resolution passing for filters in each convolution layer to producing bidimensional maps that generate bounding boxes around of the object.

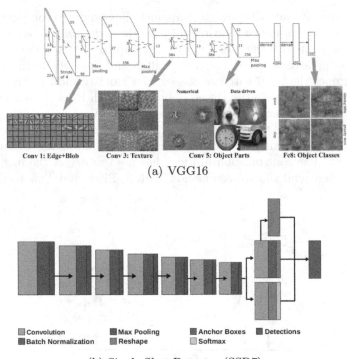

(a) VGG16

(b) Single Shot Detector (SSD7).

Fig. 3. Network architectures. (Color figure online)

To cover more forms of bounding boxes, the SSD uses Multi-scale features maps and data augmentation to improve the accuracy, flipping, cropping and distorting the colour of the image to handle variants in various object sizes and shapes. Our SSD architecture makes 6340 predictions for better coverage of location, scale and aspect ratios, more than many other detection methods. Besides, the predictions are classified as the intersection over the union and are a measure of the ratio between the intersected area over the joined area for two regions. This strategy makes that each prediction have shapes closer to the corresponding ground truth (Fig. 4), where its value is of 0.0 to 1.0, being the value 1.0 the proper detection.

In the last layer, is apply Non-maximum Suppression (NMS) to clear the unnecessary bounding boxes and remove duplicate predictions to the same object. On this way, we keep 200 predictions per image and drawing the bounding box whose confidence value is above 0.8. In Fig. 5, we show an example of the bounding boxes predicted and the final result applying the threshold. Finally, in the output of the network, we obtain a vector whose information have the bounding box coordinates (x_min, x_max, y_min, y_max), class_id and a confidence metric where the object is localised in the image.

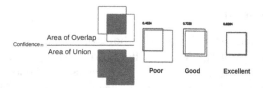

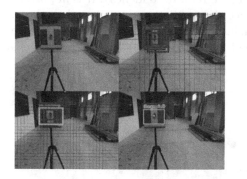

Fig. 4. Confidence metric to object detection. (Color figure online)

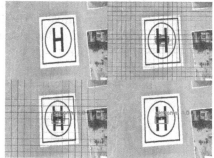

Fig. 5. Top left: original image; Top right: bounding boxes obtain with SDD; Bottom left: bounding box selected applying the confidence threshold; Bottom right: final result. (Color figure online)

3.2 System Overview

Our system has tested with two different computers Fig. 6. The first computer was used to train the SSD network and to validate our system offboard the MAV, whose specifications are: Lenovo Y700 with 16 GB of RAM, Nvidia GTX 960M with 640 CUDA cores, with CUDA 9.0, Keras 2.2.4 and TensorFlow 1.12.0. The second computer was used to validate our system onboard the MAV, whose specifications are: Intel Computer Stick with a processor core M3-Y30 2.20 Ghz, 4 Mb, 64 GB, 4 GB DDR3 without GPU, with Keras 2.1.4 and TensorFlow nightly (optimised version to computers without GPU architecture).

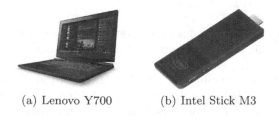

(a) Lenovo Y700   (b) Intel Stick M3

Fig. 6. Computers used by our detection system.

3.3   Dataset Generation

The dataset was generated inside of our laboratory using the Bebop 2 drone and ROS to obtain images of the Mexican flag and landing platform. The dataset consists of 9000 images to the "Mexican flag" class and 5000 to "Landing platform" class in multiple views, rotations, scales and changes of illumination. We labelled whole the images manually using the *LabelImg* tool selecting with a bounding box in the image the object that we require to identify. It is important to carefully label the bounding boxes since the predictions start based on those. In Fig. 7, we show an example of the images captured to train the SSD whose training parameters are: the Batch size of 16, Adam Optimiser and 100 epochs with 1000 steps of training.

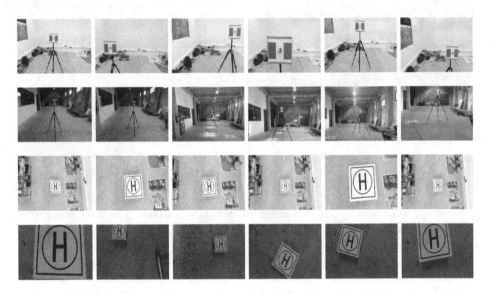

Fig. 7. Training dataset generated for the "Mexican flag" and "Landing platform".

4   Experiments

The carried out experiments focus on the two target detection in different rotations, scales and change of illumination, using our system, and the comparison with Template matching and Feature matching. The tests have performed in a wide corridor with low illumination Fig. 8, adapting to an indoor environment like the one presented in the competition. In addition, we use the same search template with respect to the bounding box labelled for detection Fig. 9, validating the effectiveness of the features extracted and learned by our network and the features of the methods of comparison.

Fig. 8. Wide corridor where we perform the experiments.

Fig. 9. Search templates used for template matching and feature matching.

4.1   Mexican Flag Detection

We evaluated detection performance using 999 images of validation, splitting into 333 images rotated, 333 scaled and 333 with changes of illumination. The results obtained are shown in Table 1, presenting the number of times the flag is detected by each method and the percentage of success. In Fig. 10, we show the results of the detection.

Table 1. Mexican flag detection with different methods.

Method	Rotated	Scaled	With illumination	% successful
Template matching	117	294	33	74.47
Feature matching	85	107	238	43.04
Our system	308	326	331	**96.59**

The results obtained with Feature Matching achieves a 43.04% due to the lack of features in the template, causing the search for the flag to be missed in some cases. Instead, Template Matching obtains a suitable result 74.47% by using the cross-correlation and pyramidal scale, detecting the flag more times than Feature Matching. However, that method has problems of detection with rotated images in different angles. Nonetheless, our system implement with the SSD network finds the majority of images no matter the illumination, scales and rotations.

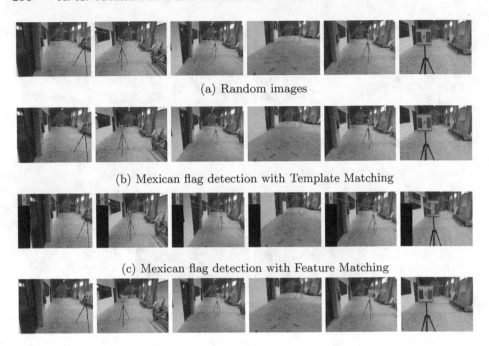

(a) Random images

(b) Mexican flag detection with Template Matching

(c) Mexican flag detection with Feature Matching

(d) Mexican flag detection with our system

Fig. 10. Detection of the Mexican flag with different methods.

4.2   Landing Platform Detection

The landing platform detection was performed in the same way that the flag detection. We evaluated our system using 999 images which 333 are rotated, 333 scales, and 333 in the presence of changes of illumination, presenting the results in Table 2. Also, we show the landing platform detection using our system and the comparison with other methods in Fig. 11.

Table 2. Landing platform detection with different methods.

Method	Rotated	Scaled	With illumination	% successful
Template matching	25	280	184	48.94
Feature matching	10	17	29	5.60
Our system	298	329	333	**96.09**

The second result shows that the feature matching is not suitable for this test due to not finding enough features. The template matching method achieves 48.94% by realises a sweep in all the input image to localise the search template, obtaining a better result that feature matching method. Notwithstanding the

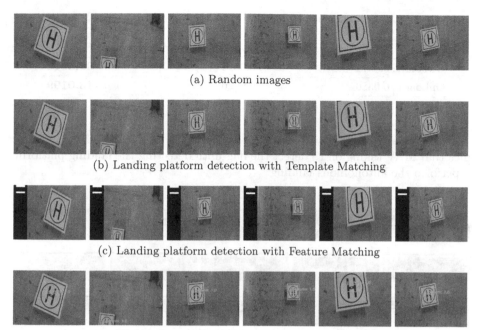

(a) Random images

(b) Landing platform detection with Template Matching

(c) Landing platform detection with Feature Matching

(d) Landing platform detection with our system

Fig. 11. Detection of the landing platform with different methods.

result, the speed performance is slow by performing the sweep in the whole image; therefore, it is not suitable for real-time tasks. For another hand, our system achievement 96.09% finding the landing platform in the different conditions of the image and faster than the other methods.

5   Autonomous Landing Results

The final test consists of the target detection and autonomous landing onboard of the MAV using our system in the Intel Computer Stick, communicating the vehicle with the computer via WIFI to obtain the images in real-time. This test is focused on the problem presented in the mission of the indoors competition in IMAV2019, which consist of autonomous navigation to detect a flag and then perform an autonomous landing. We validate our detection system carry out 40 autonomous flights split into 20 to offboard and 20 onboard of the MAV, taking the average confidence metric when detecting the targets, and the computationally cost of our system in fps. Table 3 shows the data of the autonomous flight offboard and onboard, obtaining a constant velocity of 90 fps offboard and 13 fps onboard. Fps represents the speed performance in frame per second.

Table 3. Autonomous landing results offboard and onboard of MAV.

Flight	Average flag confidence	Average platform confidence	Fps
Offboard	0.8971	0.9843	**90.5913**
Onboard	0.9386	0.9826	**13.0199**

Figure 12 and Fig. 13, we present a set of images that show all the process since that MAV taking off to detect the flag until detecting the landing platform to perform the autonomous landing.

Fig. 12. Images sequence of the flights performed where we show the detection of the Mexican flag and landing platform. A video o this work for reviewing purpose is found at https://youtu.be/sYn9mo-2hvA

Fig. 13. Images sequence that shows all the process since the drone is taking off until detecting the landing platform to perform the autonomous landing. A video o this work for reviewing purpose is found at https://youtu.be/sYn9mo-2hvA

6   Conclusion

We have presented a target detection system using a deep learning implementation based on the SSD network to detect a flag and a Landing platform. This work is motivated by the challenge of having to perform autonomous landing as part of a mission included in the indoors competition of the IMAV 2019. The mission represents an existing problem in aerial robotics which consists of target detection while a MAV performs autonomous navigation, where the place to land has to be located by detecting a flag and then, the landing has to be performed by centring on a landing platform performing a landing routine autonomously. Thus, we have presented a detection system using the SSD7 network running on the Intel Computer Stick without GPU and architecture carried by the MAV, thus enabling it to perform onboard processing. This enabled the MAV to detect a flag and later on the landing platform while performing an autonomous flight. We validated our detection system with image datasets under multiple conditions of illumination even when the object is scaled or rotated, obtaining success of 96.59% for the flag detection and 96.09% for the landing platform detection. We compared our approach against other methods based on traditional computer vision techniques such as template and feature matching. Also, we test our system in real-time with offboard and onboard flights, obtaining metric confidence output of 0.9386 for the flag, and 0.9826 for the Landing platform, everything running on the Intel Stick at an average of 13.01 fps.

Future work involves the use of this framework for more sophisticated tasks such as object tracking during autonomous flight, involving much more targets and in outdoor environments.

References

1. Baomar, H., Bentley, P.J.: Autonomous navigation and landing of airliners using artificial neural networks and learning by imitation. In: 2017 IEEE Symposium Series on Computational Intelligence (SSCI) (2017)
2. Bartak, R., Hraško, A., Obdržálek, D.: A controller for autonomous landing of AR. Drone. In: The 26th Chinese Control and Decision Conference (2014 CCDC), pp. 329–334. IEEE (2014)
3. Barták, R., Hrasko, A., Obdrzalek, D.: On autonomous landing of AR. Drone: hands-on experience. In: The Twenty-Seventh International Flairs Conference (2014)
4. Bicer, Y., Moghadam, M., Sahin, C., Eroglu, B., Üre, N.K.: Vision-based UAV guidance for autonomous landing with deep neural networks. In: AIAA SciTech 2019 Forum, p. 0140 (2019)
5. Cabrera-Ponce, A.A., Martinez-Carranza, J.: A vision-based approach for autonomous landing. In: 2017 Workshop on Research, Education and Development of Unmanned Aerial Systems (RED-UAS), pp. 126–131. IEEE (2017)
6. Fan, Y.M., Ding, M., Cao, Y.F.: Vision algorithms for fixed-wing unmanned aerial vehicle landing system. Sci. China Technol. Sci. **60**(3), 434–443 (2017). https://doi.org/10.1007/s11431-016-0618-3
7. Homma, Y., Moro, S.: Recognition of landing target of UAV by vision using machine learning. J. Signal Process. **23**(4), 193–196 (2019)
8. Madokoro, H., Kainuma, A., Sato, K.: Non-rectangular RoI extraction and machine learning based multiple object recognition used for time-series areal images obtained using MAV. Procedia Comput. Sci. **126**, 462–471 (2018)

9. Nguyen, P.H., Arsalan, M., Koo, J.H., Naqvi, R.A., Truong, N.Q., Park, K.R.: LightDenseYOLO: a fast and accurate marker tracker for autonomous UAV landing by visible light camera sensor on drone. Sensors **18**(6), 1703 (2018)

10. Polvara, R., et al.: Autonomous quadrotor landing using deep reinforcement learning. arXiv preprint arXiv:1709.03339 (2017)

11. Polvara, R., et al.: Toward end-to-end control for UAV autonomous landing via deep reinforcement learning. In: 2018 International Conference on Unmanned Aircraft Systems (ICUAS), pp. 115–123. IEEE (2018)

12. Polvara, R., Sharma, S., Wan, J., Manning, A., Sutton, R.: Autonomous vehicular landings on the deck of an unmanned surface vehicle using deep reinforcement learning. Robotica **37**(11), 1867–1882 (2019)

13. Price, E.: Deep neural network-based cooperative visual tracking through multiple micro aerial vehicles. IEEE Robot. Autom. Lett. **3**(4), 3193–3200 (2018)

14. Recker, S., Gribble, C., Butkiewicz, M.: Autonomous precision landing for the joint tactical aerial resupply vehicle. In: 2018 IEEE Applied Imagery Pattern Recognition Workshop (AIPR), pp. 1–8. IEEE (2018)

15. Rodriguez-Ramos, A., Sampedro, C., Bavle, H., De La Puente, P., Campoy, P.: A deep reinforcement learning strategy for UAV autonomous landing on a moving platform. J. Intell. Robot. Syst. **93**(1–2), 351–366 (2019). https://doi.org/10.1007/s10846-018-0891-8

16. Rojas-Perez, L.O., Munguia-Silva, R., Martinez-Carranza, J.: Real-time landing zone detection for UAVs using single aerial images. In: Watkins, S. (ed.) 10th International Micro Air Vehicle Competition and Conference, Melbourne, Australia, pp. 243–248, November 2018

17. Skoczylas, M.: Vision analysis system for autonomous landing of micro drone. Acta Mechanica et Automatica **8**(4), 199–203 (2014)

18. Truong, N.Q., Nguyen, P.H., Nam, S.H., Park, K.R.: Deep learning-based super-resolution reconstruction and marker detection for drone landing. IEEE Access **7**, 61639–61655 (2019)

19. Xu, Y., Liu, Z., Wang, X.: Monocular vision based autonomous landing of quadrotor through deep reinforcement learning. In: 2018 37th Chinese Control Conference (CCC), pp. 10014–10019. IEEE (2018)

20. Xu, Y., Zhang, Y., Liu, H., Wang, X.: Deep learning for UAV autonomous landing based on self-built image dataset. In: Eleventh International Conference on Machine Vision (ICMV 2018), vol. 11041, p. 110412I. International Society for Optics and Photonics (2019)

21. Yang, S., Scherer, S.A., Schauwecker, K., Zell, A.: Onboard monocular vision for landing of an MAV on a landing site specified by a single reference image. In: 2013 International Conference on Unmanned Aircraft Systems (ICUAS), pp. 318–325. IEEE (2013)

22. Yang, S., Scherer, S.A., Schauwecker, K., Zell, A.: Autonomous landing of MAVs on an arbitrarily textured landing site using onboard monocular vision. J. Intell. Robot. Syst. **74**(1–2), 27–43 (2014). https://doi.org/10.1007/s10846-013-9906-7

23. Yu, L.: Deep learning for vision-based micro aerial vehicle autonomous landing. Int. J. Micro Air Veh. **10**(2), 171–185 (2018)

24. Zhao, Y., Pei, H.: An improved vision-based algorithm for unmanned aerial vehicles autonomous landing. Phys. Procedia **33**, 935–941 (2012)

COUPLED: Calibration of a LiDAR and Camera Rig Using Automatic Plane Detection

Omar Montoya[1], Octavio Icasio[2], and Joaquín Salas[1]([✉])

[1] CICATA Querétaro, Instituto Politécnico Nacional, Cerro Blanco 141, Cimatario, 76030 Querétaro, México
jsalasr@ipn.mx
[2] Centro Nacional de Metrología, Querétaro, México

Abstract. LiDARs and cameras are two widely used sensors in robotics and computer vision, particularly for navigation and recognition in 3D scenarios. Systems combining both may benefit from the precise depth of the former and the high-density information of the latter, but a calibration process is necessary to relate them spatially. In this paper, we introduce COUPLED, a method that finds the extrinsic parameters to relate information between them. The method implies the use of a setup consisting of three planes with charuco patterns to find the planes in both systems. We obtain corresponding points in both systems through geometric relations between the planes. Afterward, we use these points and the Kabsch algorithm to compute the transformation that merges the planes between both systems. Compared to recent single plane algorithms, we obtain more accurate parameters, and only one pose is required. In the process, we develop a method to automatically find the calibration target using a plane detector instead of manually selecting the target in the LiDAR frame.

1 Introduction

In the field of mobile robotics, sensors to understand the world around them are required. Two commonly used sensors are cameras and LiDARs (*Light Detection and Ranging*). Cameras allow proper feature extraction, but it is challenging to obtain depth information from a single camera. In contrast, LiDARs provide precise spatial details but at a much lower density, which makes feature extraction difficult. In our research, we study systems that combine both technologies to take advantage of their strengths. Nonetheless, one of the main challenges is that while each sensor outputs spatial data in its reference frame, typically we process their information in a common one, which requires a calibration process.

To calibrate a camera with a LiDAR, one usually finds corresponding points in both systems, which we use to calculate a transformation that relates them. Often, one uses the corner points of a checkerboard on a rectangular board. The LiDAR can capture the boards pose by finding its edges, and the camera can

© Springer Nature Switzerland AG 2020
K. M. Figueroa Mora et al. (Eds.): MCPR 2020, LNCS 12088, pp. 209–218, 2020.
https://doi.org/10.1007/978-3-030-49076-8_20

estimate the pose of the checkerboard. These methods typically suffer from noise in using edge points to find the corners in the LiDAR [3,15]. Also, even though finding the target in the camera is easy, finding the target in the LiDAR frame is relatively more complicated. LiDARs typically use an array of angled lasers rotating over an axis to generate a point cloud that is denser in the horizontal direction than in the vertical one. This configuration makes it difficult to find the target with conventional plane detection methods. Thus, most calibration methods either manually find the target and isolate it [3,10], which can be time-consuming when making acquisitions to reduce calibration error. Alternatively, other methods physically isolate the target from other objects to facilitate plane detection [15], which is not ideal because we would need to reserve a dedicated area exclusively for calibration.

In this paper, we introduce COUPLED, a method for calibrating a LiDAR-camera rig that uses three planes. In the process, we develop an approach to automatically find the target in the LiDAR reference frame using a plane detector. Combining both, we develop a system for automatic calibration, no longer requiring a dedicated area or manually selecting the target for the LiDAR frame. We divide the rest of the paper into a review of related literature, followed by our methodology, then our experiments, and finally, a conclusion summarizing the relevant findings.

2   Related Literature

We review the literature on two fronts: Methods for the automatic detection of planar surfaces and the calibration of a LiDAR-camera rig.

Plane Detection with LiDAR. Finding planes within 3D point clouds is a fundamental step for complex algorithms. The introduction of LiDAR and other light-based distance sensors has made this activity vital. Usually, when working with dense homogenous point clouds, Hough transform and RANSAC are tried and true approaches [1,16]. However, the mechanical workings of certain LiDAR and MLS (*Mobile Laser Scanning*) sensors do not output point clouds favorable for these techniques, so novel methods are required.

Commonly, LiDARs have an array of angled lasers rotating on an axis from point clouds that are sparse on its vertical axis relative to its horizontal axis. The path traced by any of the lasers forms a cone, and when a plane intersects the cone, we get a conic section. Grant *et al.* [7] segments the LiDAR lines into conic sections and then uses a Hough transform where they accumulate the planes that can be formed by each line, and the planes with enough votes are taken. Another sensor that presents problems with classic plane detection methods is MLS since it usually has its laser head perpendicular to the trajectory of a carrier vehicle. Nguyen *et al.* [13] uses a similar approach segmenting scan points into straight lines, then parallel lines are grouped, and the singular vectors for each group are obtained to determine whether the grouped lines form a plane.

LiDAR-Camera Rig Calibration. In mobile robotics, combining sensors such as multiple cameras or cameras and LiDAR has become common [2,5,8]. Many techniques have been developed to accomplish this task. Single checkerboards are the most usually involved [10,15] but also researchers have developed techniques using different kinds of targets [3,11] or no targets at all [9,12].

Practitioners have created variations using a single checkerboard. For instance, Verma *et al.* [15] detect the centroid of the target, in at least three poses, and its normal, then they use genetic algorithms to obtain the parameters. Kim *et al.* [10] proposed another technique that requires three poses. In their case, they employ the normals and use an energy function to calculate the rotation and the translation that minimizes the distance to the camera and the LiDAR's plane. Kümmerle *et al.* [11] use a spherical target because its center can be more accurately extracted relative to checkerboards. Chai *et al.* [3] use a cube with aruco markers printed on its sides. The LiDAR detects the three sides, and the aruco markers are used to detect the poses of the sides in the camera.

Researchers have developed techniques that require no target at all to allow calibration when no target is available. For instance, Kang *et al.* [9] use edge detection in both the camera and LiDAR to find the transformation between both sets of edges. Similarly, Nagy *et al.* [12] use structure from motion to create a 3D point cloud for the camera reference frame. Then, they detect objects in both systems by grouping near points.

3   Method

Calibrating our LiDAR-camera rig means finding the parameters of a rotation matrix $\boldsymbol{R}_c^L \in SO(3)$ and translation vector $\boldsymbol{t}_c^L \in \mathbb{R}^3$ that transforms a 3D point set $\boldsymbol{P} = \{\boldsymbol{p}_1, \boldsymbol{p}_2, ..., \boldsymbol{p}_m\}$ in the camera reference frame into $\boldsymbol{Q} = \{\boldsymbol{q}_1, \boldsymbol{q}_2, ..., \boldsymbol{q}_m\}$, its corresponding in the LiDAR reference frame, as $\mathbf{R}_c^L \mathbf{p}_i + \mathbf{t}_c^L = \mathbf{q}_i$, $\forall\, i = 1, \ldots, m$. Because of noise in the sensors, a perfect solution normally does not exist, so we instead minimize the sum of squares as

$$(\mathbf{R}_c^L, \mathbf{t}_c^L) \leftarrow \arg\min_{R,t} \sum_{i=1}^m \|\mathbf{R}\boldsymbol{p}_i + \mathbf{t} - \boldsymbol{q}_i\|^2. \tag{1}$$

3.1   Calibration Pattern

First, we need a target for which we can find corresponding points in the LiDAR and the camera. We propose to use a pattern that consists of three planes with charuco boards [6]. We use OpenCV to find the planes by detecting the charucos for the camera, and plane fitting to find the three planes in the LiDAR. However, to find precise point to point correspondences, we use geometric relations such as the vertex common to the three planes, and the lines formed by the intersection of a pair of planes, as there are three pair combinations we obtain three lines. With this, we can obtain four point correspondences and proceed to obtain the parameters minimizing (1).

To compute the pose of our target planes in the camera reference frame, we use charuco markers printed on our pattern. Our design combines aruco markers and checkerboards into charuco [6]. It uses the aruco markers to interpolate the corners of the checkerboards, and since each aruco has a unique ID, each checkerboard corner can also be identified even if part of the checkerboard is occluded. Then, we refine the position of the checkerboard corners with subpixel accuracy. Finally, we compute the pose of the board, as with regular checkerboards, using PnP (Fig. 1).

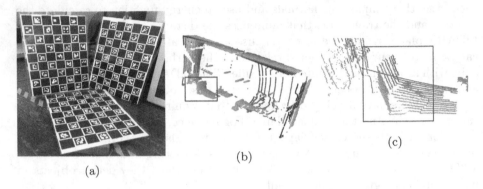

(a)   (b)   (c)

Fig. 1. Calibration pattern. (a) Each plane has a different set of charuco markers for the camera to detect. (b) The full point cloud: The calibration target is enclosed in the green rectangle. (c) Zooming in on the target in the previous point cloud: The calibration pattern is enclosed in the green rectangle.

3.2   Automatic Target Detection for LiDAR

To find the target in the LiDAR reference frame, we developed an algorithm to detect the planes in the point cloud sensed by the LiDAR and segment the three planes belonging to our target. There exist many methods to find planes within a point cloud [1,16], but for some LiDARs, with few lasers, the problem is particularly challenging. Take, for instance, the VLP-16 sensor, which consists of 16 laser range finders spinning along an axis, making the density of points much higher horizontally than vertically. This arrangement causes problems with RANSAC and Hough transform-based plane finders, when the best fits for a plane erroneously end up being horizontal planes that contain all the points of a single beam. Note that rotating laser LiDAR beams form cones as they spin. When a cone is intersected by a plane, a conic section is formed. This observation is the basis of our algorithm, which consists in finding the curves, grouping them into planes and segmenting the target from the planes found.

Curve Finding. The first step for our plane detection is finding the conic sections. Because fitting such a high number of points to a conic section equation is computationally intensive, we use an approximation and instead look for smooth curves. We start by sampling each of the lasers separately.

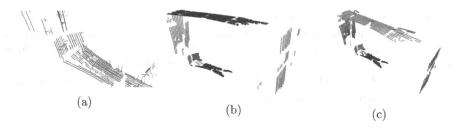

(a)

(b)

(c)

Fig. 2. Illustration of the steps of the plane detection process. (a) The point cloud is segmented into smooth curves with a normal vector assigned to them. (b) We group the lines by similar normals. We end up with groups containing one or more parallel planes. (c) We use RANSAC plane fitting to segment the points to their appropriate planes.

First, we take a single beam and treat its points as a 1D signal ordered by the azimuth given by the LiDAR, which starts at positive Y and runs along the Z axis clockwise. Then, we apply a spatial Gaussian filter with a standard deviation σ to reduce the noise in the point cloud. Now, to segment parts of the 1D signal that have a smooth trajectory, we apply a custom kernel $\mathbf{k}$ that was made empirically to simulate a Laplacian to help detect rapid changes in the signal. We run the kernel through the signal and threshold to highlight where we separate the curves. We also discard segments that have less than a certain number of points p to avoid short curves. Finally, we combine curves by verifying whether their direction is similar, and they are close enough together.

Grouping Plane Proposals. Once we have curves, we need to find a way to group lines belonging to the same plane. To do this, we take a random line, and the nearest line to it. We calculate the principal components for the group of points of the two curves via SVD (*Singular Value Decomposition*). Then, we test whether the ratio between the first and second singular values is below a certain threshold r_{12} to avoid planes formed from very narrow lines, which can be noisy. Next, we test wether the ratio r_{23} between the second and third components is large to determine that the points form a valid flat plane. If both tests are passed, the normal vector of the plane is saved in an accumulator. We repeat this process for the lines within a certain maximum distance $l_{\max}$ from our original line. Finally, we assign the normal vector with the most votes. We do this for each line, so the lines end up with a normal vector assigned. We then group lines by normal vectors in the same direction using DBSCAN [4] (see Fig. 2). After this process, we have groups of lines likely belonging to one or more planes with the same normal as the lines. We can now easily segment applying RANSAC on each group.

Finding the Target. We have now extracted the planes in our point cloud, but for our application, we need the planes that correspond to our target. To isolate these planes, we use OpenCV to calculate the pose of our three target planes in the camera frame. We also calculate the center of the target planes. So now, we can calculate the angles between the normals and the distances between centroids of any two planes of the target. With this, we end up with three angles and three distances that we use as a descriptor for the target. Finally, we use brute force matching to find the combination of three planes found by our detector that best matches the descriptor of our target.

3.3 Camera and LiDAR Calibration

Once we have our target in the LiDAR and the cameras, we get the poses in the camera reference frame using the charucos. OpenCV gives us a translation and rotation from a reference frame with its origin on one of the outer most corners of the board, and its X and Y axis aligned with the sides of the board to the camera frame [6]. We obtain a vector normal to the board in the camera reference frame using $\mathbf{n}_i^c = \mathbf{R}_r^c \mathbf{e}_z$, where $\mathbf{n}_{ci}$ is the vector normal to plane i in the camera frame, $\mathbf{R}_r^c$ is the rotation from the charuco i frame to the camera frame, and $\mathbf{e}_z^T = (0, 0, 1)$. With this rotation, we obtain the normals for the planes containing the targets. For the LiDAR, we get the principal components of the planes obtained in the previous section.

Next, we calculate the vertex between the three planes and the three intersections from two planes. The intersections can be defined as vectors of unitary magnitude. Now, we have four corresponding points to obtain the extrinsic parameters, P points in the camera frame, and Q points in the LiDAR frame. We use Kabsch algorithm [14] to obtain the rotation and translation from the camera to the LiDAR that minimizes the mean square error expressed in (1).

We call COUPLED to our method to calibrate the LiDAR-camera rig using automatic plane detection.

4   Experimental Results

To test our algorithm, we took 40 readings with our system, moving the LiDAR-camera rig to different positions, making sure that the target remains within the fields of view of both sensors. To show the relevance of COUPLED, we compare our results with a method recently introduced.

4.1   Experimental Setup

For our experiments, we used a Velodyne VLP/16 LiDAR. It consists of 16 lasers operating at a wavelength of 903 nm and turning at a programmable rotational speed between 5 and 20 Hz. With a range of 100 m, it has a range accuracy of ±3 cm and a vertical field of view of ±15°. Also, we employed a MicaSense Parrot Sequoia multispectral camera, which weighs about 72 g (the additional sunshine sensor weights 35 g). It produces images with spectral response peaking at 550 nm (green), 660 nm (red), 735 nm (red edge), and 790 nm (near infrared). Each of these images has a spatial resolution of 1,280 (horizontal) × 960 (vertical) pixels.

Fig. 3. Our LiDAR-camera rig, consisting of a VLP-16 LiDAR and a Sequoia Multi-spectral camera. (Color figure online)

Also, the Sequoia includes an RGB color camera with a resolution of 4,068 (h) × 3,456 (v) pixels resolution. We print the charucos targets on 3 mm thick mirror surfaces measuring 0.5 m per side each (Fig. 3).

In our experiments, the Gaussian filter has a spread of $\sigma = 0.08$. We discard segments with fewer than $p = 5$ points. Also, we set the distance between end-points $d = 10$ cm. In addition the angle between them has to be $\alpha < 5°$. To filter out elongated segments, we set $r_{12} = 1/80$ and $r_{23} = 1/200$. Finally, we define the maximum distance between lines at 40 cm.

4.2 LiDAR-Camera Rig Calibration

With the data, we used three procedures to find the calibration target. In the first one, we manually selected the three planes of our target from the LiDAR point cloud. In the second one, we automatically found the target by introducing the entire point cloud to our plane detector and finding the best three planes (the method introduced in this paper). In the third procedure, we limited the point cloud to an azimuth between 230° and 330° and automatically find the planes within the limited point cloud (we call this procedure *restricted*). We know the target is in this azimuth because this direction is required in our rig for the camera to see the target.

We calculated the extrinsic parameters for the 40 views using the three procedures described. Moreover, to verify the effect of using multiple views, we calculate the accumulated extrinsic parameters in which we use the Kabsch algorithm on the points from the concatenation of the current frame points and the previous frames. Although our target detection algorithm finds the correct target for most of the frames, there are still outliers. We eliminated the outliers by using the DBSCAN clustering algorithm on the translation vectors, knowing that the correct translation will form the largest cluster. After the clustering step, 10 out of the 40 frames were discarded in the fully automatic procedure, while only 4 out of 40 were discarded in the restricted procedure.

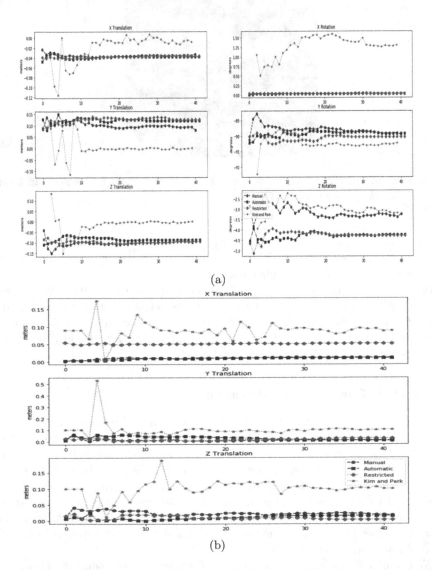

Fig. 4. Results of 40 calibrations (best seen in color). The blue, green, red and yellow lines show when we manually select the LiDAR planes, give the entire point cloud to the target detector, provided the target detector a reduced azimuth point cloud knowing that the target is within that cloud, and for Kim *et al.* [10] method for comparison. (a) Calibration results for accumulated acquisitions to demonstrate convergence. (b) Plotted error from the accumulated calibration.

We compared our method against Kim *et al.* [10] who uses a checkerboard and fits a normal vector to his target, but only uses one plane. In Fig. (4a), we plot the results of accumulated acquisitions. We can see that the estimation of rotation is similar, deviating by a maximum of three degrees. At the same time, the translation differs by as much as 12 cm and does not converge after 40 acquisitions. In Fig. (4b), we plot the error between the calculated translation and the one we measured, we can see that our method allows us to obtain extrinsic parameters with a single acquisition compared with the three acquisitions required by Kim *et al.*'s method and is more accurate. Both methods run in a couple of seconds.

5 Conclusion

In this paper, we present COUPLED, a method to obtain the extrinsic parameters of a LiDAR-camera rig that uses three planes with charuco boards printed on them. We use the charuco boards to find the pose of the planes and a plane detection algorithm to find the planes in the LiDAR frame. Our experimental results show its benefits when compared with the manual selection of the target or the region of interest.

By using multiple frames, we can refine the extrinsic parameter calibration. Here, using the automatic target detector can be very beneficial because it allows us to quickly find our target in multi-capture settings instead of manually selecting it. However, notice that using the automatic detector with a restricted azimuth is an excellent middle ground as it only requires the input of the azimuth, and it has a better performance than the plane detector on the full point cloud. We also presented a new method for plane detection in point clouds generated by LiDARs. Rotational LiDARs have a much higher horizontal density compared to vertical density, which makes it challenging to use traditional methods such as RANSAC and Hough Transform. Our system combines both methods, allowing for automatic calibration by using the plane detector to find the target in the LiDAR frame as opposed to manually selecting it. This permits smooth refinement since we can quickly capture many frames and compute the extrinsic parameters using the points from the different frames.

References

1. Borrmann, D., Elseberg, J., Lingemann, K., Nüchter, A.: The 3D Hough Transform for plane detection in point clouds: a review and a new accumulator design. 3D Res. **2**(2), 3 (2011). https://doi.org/10.1007/3DRes.02(2011)3
2. Caltagirone, L., Bellone, M., Svensson, L., Wahde, M.: LiDAR-camera fusion for road detection using fully convolutional neural networks. Robot. Auton. Syst. **111**, 125–131 (2019)
3. Chai, Z., Sun, Y., Xiong, Z.: A novel method for LiDAR camera calibration by plane fitting. In: International Conference on Advanced Intelligent Mechatronics, pp. 286–291 (2018)

4. Ester, M., Kriegel, H.P., Sander, J., Xu, X.: A density-based algorithm for discovering clusters in large spatial databases with noise. In: KDD, vol. 96, pp. 226–231 (1996)
5. Gao, H., Cheng, B., Wang, J., Li, K., Zhao, J., Li, D.: Object classification using CNN-based fusion of vision and LiDAR in autonomous vehicle environment. IEEE Trans. Ind. Inform. **14**(9), 4224–4231 (2018)
6. Garrido-Jurado, S., Muñoz-Salinas, R., Madrid-Cuevas, F., Marín-Jiménez, M.: Automatic generation and detection of highly reliable fiducial markers under occlusion. Pattern Recogn. **47**(6), 2280–2292 (2014)
7. Grant, S., Voorhies, R., Itti, L.: Finding planes in LiDAR point clouds for real-time registration. In: RSJ International Conference on Intelligent Robots and Systems, pp. 4347–4354 (2013)
8. Hwang, S., Kim, N., Choi, Y., Lee, S., Kweon, I.: Fast multiple objects detection and tracking fusing color camera and 3D LiDAR for intelligent vehicles. In: International Conference on Ubiquitous Robots and Ambient Intelligence, pp. 234–239. IEEE (2016)
9. Kang, J., Doh, N.: Automatic Targetless camera-LiDAR calibration by aligning edge with Gaussian mixture model. J. Field Robot. **37**(1), 158–179 (2020)
10. Kim, E.S., Park, S.Y.: Extrinsic calibration of a camera-LiDAR multi sensor system using a planar chessboard. In: International Conference on Ubiquitous and Future Networks, pp. 89–91 (2019)
11. Kümmerle, J., Kühner, T., Lauer, M.: Automatic calibration of multiple cameras and depth sensors with a spherical target. In: International Conference on Intelligent Robots and Systems, pp. 1–8 (2018)
12. Nagy, B., Kovács, L., Benedek, C.: Online targetless end-to-end camera-LiDAR self-calibration. In: International Conference on Machine Vision Applications, pp. 1–6 (2019)
13. Nguyen, H., Belton, D., Helmholz, P.: Planar surface detection for sparse and heterogeneous mobile laser scanning point clouds. J. Photogramm. Remote Sens. **151**, 141–161 (2019)
14. Sorkine-Hornung, O., Rabinovich, M.: Least-squares rigid motion using SVD. Computing **1**(1), 1–5 (2017)
15. Verma, S., Berrio, J.S., Worrall, S., Nebot, E.: Automatic extrinsic calibration between a camera and a 3D Lidar using 3D point and plane correspondences. In: Intelligent Transportation Systems Conference (ITSC), pp. 3906–3912. IEEE (2019)
16. Zeineldin, R.A., El-Fishawy, N.A.: A survey of RANSAC enhancements for plane detection in 3D point clouds. Menoufia J. Electron. Eng. Res. **26**(2), 519–537 (2017)

ModuleNet: A Convolutional Neural Network for Stereo Vision

O. I. Renteria-Vidales[1,2] , J. C. Cuevas-Tello[1] , A. Reyes-Figueroa[2],
and M. Rivera[2(✉)]

[1] UASLP Universidad Autónoma de San Luis Potosí,
Álvaro Obregón 64 Col. Centro, 78000 San Luis Potosí, México
[2] CIMAT Centro de Investigación en Matemáticas A.C., Jalisco S/N Col. Valenciana,
36023 Guanajuato, México
mrivera@cimat.mx

Abstract. Convolutional Neural Networks (CNN) has gained much
attention for the solution of numerous vision problems including disparities calculation in stereo vision systems. In this paper, we present a
CNN based solution for disparities estimation that builds upon a basic
module (BM) with limited range of disparities that can be extended using
various BM in parallel. Our BM can be understood as a segmentation by
disparity and produces an output channel with the memberships for each
disparity candidate, additionally the BM computes a channel with the
out–of–range disparity regions. This extra channel allows us to parallelize
several BM and dealing with their respective responsibilities. We train
our model with the MPI Sintel dataset. The results show that ModuleNet, our modular CNN model, outperforms the baseline algorithm
Efficient Large-scale Stereo Matching (ELAS) and FlowNetC achieving
about a 80% of improvement.

Keywords: Stereo vision · Convolutional Neural Networks · U-Net ·
Census transform · Deep learning

1 Introduction

The purpose of an stereo system is to estimate the scene depth by computing horizontal disparities between corresponding pixels from an image pair (left
and right) and has been intensively investigated for several decades. There is a
wide variety of algorithms to calculate these disparities that are complicated to
include them all in one methodology or paradigm. Scharstein and Szeliski [13]
propose a block taxonomy to describe this type of algorithms, following steps
such as matching cost calculation, matching cost aggregation, disparity calculation and disparity refinement. One example is ELAS, an algorithm which builds
a disparities map by triangulating a set of support points [8].

We present a CNN based solution for disparities estimation that builds upon
a basic module (BM) with limited range of disparities that can be extended
using various BM in parallel. Our BM can be understood as a segmentation

© Springer Nature Switzerland AG 2020
K. M. Figueroa Mora et al. (Eds.): MCPR 2020, LNCS 12088, pp. 219–228, 2020.
https://doi.org/10.1007/978-3-030-49076-8_21

by disparity and produces an output channel with the memberships for each disparity candidate, additionally the BM computes a channel with the out–of–range disparity regions. This extra channel allows us to parallelize several BM and dealing with their respective responsibilities. We list our main contributions as follows: i) We propose ModuleNet, which is a novel modular model to measure disparities on any range, which is inspired on FlowNet and U-Net. ii) We use a low computational time algorithm to measure cost maps. iii) The architecture of our model is simple, because it does not require another specialized networks for refinement as variants of FlowNet do for this problem. iv) Our model improves the baseline model ELAS and FlowNetC (the correlation version of FlowNet) with about 80% of unbiased error.

The paper is organized as follows: Sect. 2 presents the related work. At Sect. 2 are the algorithms FlowNet, Census transform and ELAS. The proposed model is in Sect. 3. Section 4 describes the dataset used in this research. At the end are our results, conclusions and future work.

2   Related Methods

In recent years, Convolutional Neural Networks (CNN) have made advances in various computer vision tasks, including estimation of disparities in stereo vision. Fischer et al. propose a CNN architecture based on encoder-decoder called FlowNet [6]. This network uses an *ad hoc* layer for calculating the normalized cross-correlation between a patch in the left image and a set of sliding windows (defined by a proposed disparity set) of the right window and uses Full Convolutional Network (kind encoder-decoder architecture) for estimate the regularized disparity [11]. Park and Lee [9] use a siamese CNN to estimate depth for SLAM algorithms. Their proposal is to train a twin network that transforms patches of images and whose objective is to maximize the normalized cross correlation between corresponding transformed patches and minimize it between non-corresponding transformed patches. To make the inference of the disparity in a stereo pair, a left patch and a set of displaced right patches are used, then the normalized cross correlation between the twin networks transformed patches and the disparity is selected using a Winner–Takes–All (WTA) scheme. Other authors use a multi-scale CNN, where the strategy is to estimate the disparity of the central pixel of a patch by processing a pyramid of stereo pairs [4]; and the reported processing time for images in the KITTI database is more than one minute [7]. A state of the art method with really good results is reported by Chen and Jung [3], they use a CNN that is fed with patches of the left image and a set of slipped patches of the right image (3DNet). Then, for a set of proposed disparities, the network estimates the probability that each of the disparities corresponds to the central pixel of the left image patch that requires of evaluate as many patches as pixels, so it is computationally expensive.

In this section, we present FlowNet, an architecture designed for optical flow, and it can be used for stereoscopy. Also, this section introduces the Census Transform.

2.1   FlowNet

FlowNet is composed by two main blocks. The network computes the local vector that measure the dissimilarity between each pixel (x, y) in the left image I_l and its corresponding candidate pixel $(x + \delta, y)$, for a given disparity δ, in the right image I_r; where $\delta \in d$ with $d = [d_1, d_2, \ldots, d_h]$ and d_i is an integer value. This block is deterministic (not trainable) and produces a dissimilarity map (tensor) D of size equal to $(h, nrows, ncolumns)$. FlowNet is based on the U-Net [11]. The network computes the regularized disparities d^*; with dimension equal to $(1, nrows, ncolumns)$. The main disadvantage of this method is the computational cost of the normalized cross-correlation layer and it also produces blurred disparity maps [6], see in Fig. 1 the FlowNetC architecture.

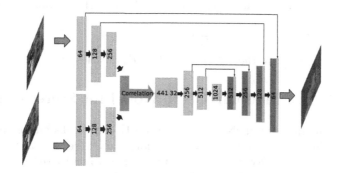

Fig. 1. FlowNet architecture.

2.2   Census Transform

Differently to FlowNet, that uses normalized cross-correlation to measure the cost maps, an alternative is Census Transform [15]. Other algorithms for this task are Sum of Absolute Differences (SAD) [14], Sum of Square Differences (SSD) [14], Normalized Cross-Correlation [5]. Because a low complexity cost function is desirable, we chose the Census Transform [15]. Figure 2 exemplify the Census algorithm, where it transforms the values of the neighbors. The values of the neighbors of a pixel are encoded within a binary chain (it is assigned "1" when they are greater than or equal to the central pixel, or "0" otherwise). This chain is called census signature, the signature retains spatial information of each neighbor given the position within the string where each bit is stored.

For a 3×3 window, the census signature contains eight values and can be saved in one byte, this transformation can be computed with:

$$C_l(x, y) = Bitstring_{(i,j) \in w}(I_l(i, j) \geq I_l(x, y)) \tag{1}$$

for the case of the left image I_l; and in a similar is computer the census transform C_r for the right image I_r. To obtain the level of correspondence, the Hamming

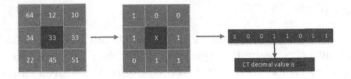

Fig. 2. Census transform

distance (H) is used to count how many bits are different between two census signatures:

$$D_m(x, y; d) = H(C_l(x, y), C_r(x + d_m, y)) \qquad (2)$$

We can denote this stage by the representational function F_c that transforms the information in the images I_l and I_r into the distance tensor $D = [D_1, D_2, \ldots, D_h]$:

$$D = F_c(I_l, I_r; d) \qquad (3)$$

where the parameters are the set of candidate disparities, d.

3   ModuleNet: Modular CNN Model for Stereoscopy

Our proposed model (ModuleNet) builds upon U-Net blocks and is inspired on the FlowNet. First, we describe the general block U-Net (see Fig. 3) that can find disparities in a range d. Second, we introduce the cascade U-Net for refinement, see Fig. 4. Finally, the modular CNN model (ModuleNet) for disparities out of the range d is presented, see Fig. 5.

3.1   General Block: U-Net U-Net Module

Our neural network for stereo disparity estimation is composed with blocks based on the UNet. Indeed, the most basic construction block can be seen as a simplified version of the FlowNet where the Disparity Map D is computed with the Hamming distances between the Census transformed patches (the fixed and the δ-displaced one). Another difference between our basic block and the FlowNet model is that, instead of computing directly a real valued map of disparities, we estimate the probability that a particular candidate disparity δ is the actual one at each pixel. We also compute an additional layer that estimates outliers: the probability that the actual disparity in each pixel is not included in the set of disparities d. As input to the U-Net, we have h channels of distances corresponding to the h candidate disparities and, as output, we have $h+1$ probability maps; see Fig. 3. We can represent this U-Net block by the representational function F_1 that transforms the information in the distance tensor $D = [D_1, D_2, \ldots, D_h]$ into the probabilities tensor $P = [P_1, P_2, \ldots, P_h, P_{h+1}]$:

$$P = F_1(D, \theta_1) \qquad (4)$$

where θ_1 are the network weight set.

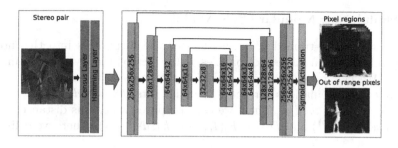

Fig. 3. General block (U-Net)

The representational U-Net F_1 (4) can be seen as a regularizer of the noisy Census-distance maps. We observed that the output of the basic (trained) block can be refined by a second U-Net. This second U-Net (in cascade) is trained using as input the census cost maps, the initial estimation of the disparity probabilities maps and the outliers' probability map and produces as output refined versions of the inputs. We represent this U-Net block by the representational function F_2 that refine probabilities tensor P using also as input the distance tensor D:

$$\hat{Y} = F_2(P, D, \theta_2) \tag{5}$$

where θ_2 are the weight set. We denote our basic module for disparity estimation by

$$D = F_c(I_l, I_r; d) \tag{6}$$

$$\hat{Y} = F(D) \stackrel{def}{=} F_2(F_1(D), D). \tag{7}$$

where we omitted the parameters θ_1 and θ_2 in order to simplify the notation. Once we have trained a basic module (7), it can be used for estimating disparities into the range defined by the disparity set d. The regions with disparities outside such a range are detected in the outliers' layer. Figure 4 depicts our block model based on two cascaded U-Nets (general blocks, see Fig. 3).

Fig. 4. Our Basic Block composed with two U-Net in cascade.

3.2   ModuleNet: Modular CNN Model

Assume, we have a trained basic module for the disparities into the interval $[d_1, d_h]$ and the actual range of disparities, in the stereo pair, lays into the interval $[d_1, 2d_h]$. We can reuse our basic model for processing of such a stereo pair if we split the calculations for the disparities sets $d^{(0)} = [d_1, d_2, \ldots, d_h]$ and $d^{(1)} = [d_{h+1}, d_{h+2}, \ldots, d_{2h}]$. Then, we can compute two census distance tensors $D^{(0)} = F_c(I_r, I_l; d^{(0)})$ and $D^{(1)} = F_c(I_r, S\{I_l, h\}; d^{(1)} - h)$; where we define the shift operator

$$S\{I, d_h\} \overset{def}{=} I(x + d_h, y). \tag{8}$$

Thus, we can estimate the probability that the disparity is in the set $d^{(0)}$ with $\hat{Y}^{(0)} = F(D^{(0)})$ and in the set $d^{(1)}$ with $\hat{Y}^{(1)} = F(D^{(1)})$; where F is our basic module 7.

This idea can be extended for processing stereo pair with a wide range of disparities. First we define the k-th set of disparities as

$$D^{(k)} = F_c(I_r, S\{I_l, kh\}; d^{(k)} - kh) \tag{9}$$

for $k = 1, 2, \ldots, K$. Second, we estimate, in parallel, the K tensor of probability:

$$\hat{Y}^{(k)} = F(D^{(k)}) \tag{10}$$

Note that the network F is reused for processing the K modules. The CNN transforms the representation $D^{(k)}$ into $\hat{Y}^{(k)}$: the probability that disparities $\delta^{(k)}$ of the module k at the pixel (x, y) are the correct displacement. To estimate the tensor $\hat{Y}$ that integrates the individual probability tensors $\hat{Y}^{(k)}$'s, we use the additional layer with the probability that the correct displacement of each pixel is not the k-th interval:

$$\hat{Y}_{(kh+i)} = \hat{Y}_i^{(k)} \odot \left(1 - \hat{Y}_{h+1}^{(k)}\right) \tag{11}$$

for $i = 1, 2, \ldots, h$, $k = 0, 1, \ldots, K - 1$ and $\odot$ denotes the element-wise product. Finally, the disparity estimation, d^* is computed by applying a WTA procedure in the disparities map $\hat{Y}$:

$$d^*(x, y) = \arg\max_l \hat{Y}_l(x, y) \tag{12}$$

for $l = 1, 2, \ldots, Kh$. Figure 5 depicts ModuleNet – our modular model.

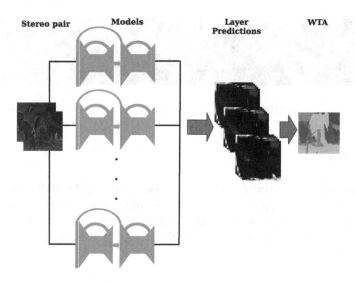

Fig. 5. ModuleNet: Modular CNN Model

4 Dataset and Training Parameters

We used the MPI Sintel dataset for train our model. The MPI Sintel-stereo dataset is a benchmark for stereo, produced from the open animated short film Sintel produced by Ton Roosendaal and the Blender Foundation [1]. This dataset contains disparity maps for the left and right image, occlusion masks for both images. The dataset consist of 2128 stereo pairs divided in clean and final pass images. The left frame is always the reference frame. For our experiments, we use the clean subset pairs that consist of 1064 pairs; 958 for training and 106 for testing. See example in Fig. 6, the disparity map is the ground truth. Our training set consisted on patches (256×256 pixels) randomly sampled from of 958 stereo pairs (1024×460 pixels) and 106 stereo pairs were leave-out for testing.

We change the number of filters distributions across the layers according to Reyes-Figueroa et al. [10]. It has been shown that in order to have more accurate features and to recover fine details, more filters are required in the upper levels of U-Net and less filters in the more encoded levels. Our model's architecture is summarized in Fig. 3. We trained our model during 2000 epochs with mini-batches of size eight.

We used data augmentation by randomly resizing the frames (random scaling factor into the range $[.6, 1]$), adding Gaussian noise (mean zero with standard deviation equal 1% the images' dynamic range). The ADAM optimization algorithm was used with fixed $lr = 1 \times 10^{-4}$ and $\beta = [0.9, 0.999]$. For processing the data set, we used a basic block with sixteen disparities ($h = 16$) and $K = 24$ parallels blocks.

Fig. 6. Example of MPI Sintel data: left and right images and disparity map.

5   Results

In Fig. 7 are shown the results from seven scenes by using the MPI Sintel dataset. We show a single image per scene for illustrating the algorithm's performance. We compare the results from our model versus ELAS and FlowNetC. Visually, one can see that the proposed model is closer to the ground truth than ELAS and FlowNetC.

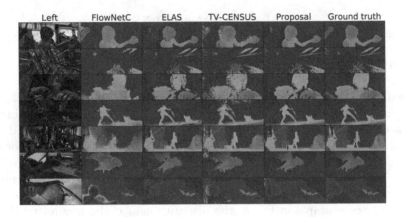

Fig. 7. Results from MPI Sintel dataset on selected scenes

In Table 1 is the comparison of results from applying a Total–Variation potential for edge–preserving filtering to the Distance Tensor D (here named TV–Census) [2], ELAS, FlowNetC and our proposal (ModuleNet); in bold font the best results. We use the metric Mean Absolute Error (MAE) in non-occluded areas to measure the results quantitatively. Our proposed model outperforms the compared methods. The advantage of the MPI Sintel dataset is that the ground truth is provided, so the accuracy (MAE) is unbiased. Show particular results from seven representative stereo pairs and the average over the total of frames. Additionally we tested our method with the Middlebury Stereo Datasets 2014 [12] which consist of 33 image pairs, divided in 10 evaluation test sets with hidden ground truth, 10 evaluation training sets with ground truth and 13 additional sets, the first 20 sets are used in the new Middlebury Stereo Evaluation. Figure 8 shows a visual comparison of the computed results.

Table 1. MAE results from MPI Sintel dataset on selected scenes

Scene	FlowNetC	ELAS	TV–Census	Proposed
alley_1	2.98	2.98	0.92	**0.44**
bamboo_1	2.91	2.39	0.63	**0.51**
bandage_2	14.09	12.77	2.60	**2.14**
cave_2	3.95	3.10	1.85	**0.65**
market_2	1.94	2.07	0.54	**0.43**
temple_2	2.26	2.44	0.60	**0.38**
temple_3	6.09	2.85	0.74	**0.43**
All test images	24.3	14.1	1.7	**1.5**

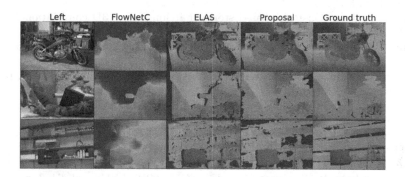

Fig. 8. Results from Middlebury dataset on selected stereo pairs

6   Conclusions and Future Work

We proposed a new model called ModuleNet for disparities estimation that can be applied in stereoscopy vision. Our model is build upon FlowNet, U-Net and Census transform. The modularity of our method allows generating disparity maps of any size simply by adding more blocks. The extra layer, for detecting pixels with disparities out of range, helps us to classify pixels that usually adds noise since these pixels are outside the range of work or are pixels of occluded regions. Our results show that qualitatively and quantitatively our model outperforms Census–Hamming approach (robustly filtered), ELAS and FlowNetC; which are baseline methods for disparities estimation. The unbiased error was improved by about 80%.

Our future work will focus on extend the training set with real stereo pairs, conduct more exhaustive evaluations and implement our model on an embedded system (e.g. NVIDIA® Jetson Nano™ CPU-GPU and Intel®Movidius™ USB stick). We plan to compare the performance of our model with other state-of-the-art methods, regardless the complexity and computational time with GPU hardware. As most of the methods, the texture-less regions are difficult to identify. So an algorithm to detect such textures is desired.

Acknowledges. Part of this work was conducted while O. Renteria was at IPICYT AC, SLP-Mexico. This work was supported in part by CONACYT, Mexico (Grant A1-S-43858).

References

1. Butler, D.J., Wulff, J., Stanley, G.B., Black, M.J.: A naturalistic open source movie for optical flow evaluation. In: Fitzgibbon, A., Lazebnik, S., Perona, P., Sato, Y., Schmid, C. (eds.) ECCV 2012. LNCS, vol. 7577, pp. 611–625. Springer, Heidelberg (2012). https://doi.org/10.1007/978-3-642-33783-3_44
2. Charbonnier, P., Blanc-Féraud, L., Aubert, G., Barlaud, M.: Deterministic edge-preserving regularization in computed imaging. IEEE Trans. Image Process. **6**(2), 298–311 (1997)
3. Chen, B., Jung, C.: Patch-based stereo matching using 3D convolutional neural networks. In: 25th ICIP, pp. 3633–3637 (2018)
4. Chen, J., Yuan, C.: Convolutional neural network using multi-scale information for stereo matching cost computation. In: ICIP, pp. 3424–3428 (2016)
5. Duda, R.O., Hart, P.E.: Pattern Classification and Scene Analysis, XVII, p. 482. Wiley, New York (1973)
6. Fischer, P., et al.: FlowNet: learning optical flow with convolutional networks. In: CoRR, pp. 2758–2766 (2015)
7. Geiger, A., Lenz, P., Urtasun, R.: Are we ready for autonomous driving? The KITTI vision benchmark suite. In: CVPR, pp. 3354–3361 (2012)
8. Geiger, A., Roser, M., Urtasun, R.: Efficient large-scale stereo matching. In: Kimmel, R., Klette, R., Sugimoto, A. (eds.) ACCV 2010. LNCS, vol. 6492, pp. 25–38. Springer, Heidelberg (2011). https://doi.org/10.1007/978-3-642-19315-6_3
9. Park, J., Lee, J.: A cost effective estimation of depth from stereo image pairs using shallow siamese convolutional networks. In: IRIS, pp. 213–217, October 2017
10. Reyes-Figueroa, A., Rivera, M.: Deep neural network for fringe pattern filtering and normalisation (2019). arXiv:1906.06224)
11. Ronneberger, O., Fischer, P., Brox, T.: U-Net: convolutional networks for biomedical image segmentation. In: Navab, N., Hornegger, J., Wells, W.M., Frangi, A.F. (eds.) MICCAI 2015. LNCS, vol. 9351, pp. 234–241. Springer, Cham (2015). https://doi.org/10.1007/978-3-319-24574-4_28
12. Scharstein, D., et al.: High-resolution stereo datasets with subpixel-accurate ground truth. In: Jiang, X., Hornegger, J., Koch, R. (eds.) GCPR 2014. LNCS, vol. 8753, pp. 31–42. Springer, Cham (2014). https://doi.org/10.1007/978-3-319-11752-2_3
13. Scharstein, D., Szeliski, R.: A taxonomy and evaluation of dense two-frame stereo correspondence algorithms. Int. J. Comp. Vision **47**(1), 7–42 (2002). https://doi.org/10.1023/A:1014573219977
14. Tamura, H., Mori, S., Yamawaki, T.: Textural features corresponding to visual perception. IEEE Trans. Sys. Man Cybern. **8**, 460–473 (1978)
15. Zabih, R., Woodfill, J.: Non-parametric local transforms for computing visual correspondence. In: Eklundh, J.-O. (ed.) ECCV 1994. LNCS, vol. 801, pp. 151–158. Springer, Heidelberg (1994). https://doi.org/10.1007/BFb0028345

Industrial and Medical Applications of
Pattern Recognition

A Method for Estimating Driving Factors of Illicit Trade Using Node Embeddings and Clustering

Jorge Ángel González Ordiano[1]($\boxtimes$)(iD), Lisa Finn[2], Anthony Winterlich[2],
Gary Moloney[2], and Steven Simske[1](iD)

[1] Colorado State University, Fort Collins, CO, USA
{jorge.gonzalez_ordiano,steve.simske}@colostate.edu
[2] Micro Focus International, Galway, Ireland
{finn,winterlich,gary.moloney}@microfocus.com

Abstract. The trade on illegal goods and services, also known as illicit trade, is expected to drain 4.2 trillion dollars from the world economy and put 5.4 million jobs at risk by 2022. These estimates reflect the importance of combating illicit trade, as it poses a danger to individuals and undermines governments. To do so, however, we have to first understand the factors that influence this type of trade. Therefore, we present in this article a method that uses node embeddings and clustering to compare a country based illicit supply network to other networks that represent other types of country relationships (e.g., free trade agreements, language). The results offer initial clues on the factors that might be driving the illicit trade between countries.

Keywords: Node embedding · Clustering · Data mining

1 Introduction

Illicit trade, i.e. the trade in illicit goods and services, poses a danger to our communities [12]. For instance, the ICC estimates that by 2022 counterfeit and piracy will put 5.4 million jobs at risk and drain 4.2 trillion dollars of the world economy,[1] while the OECD estimates that in the UK 86,300 jobs were lost due to counterfeiting and piracy in 2016 alone [11]. In addition, the dangers of illicit trade go beyond economic loses. For example, illicit medicines have been recorded to cause malaria and tuberculosis deaths [10], while counterfeits have been shown to finance terrorists organizations [1]. For these reasons, getting a better understanding of the factors that might be driving illicit trade is of major importance, if we are to develop methods that will aid in its disruption.

A possibility for getting a better grasp on these driving factors is to use networks to describe not only the illicit trade between countries (i.e. the illicit supply network), but also other aspects that countries might have in common,

---

[1] iccwbo.org/global-issues-trends/bascap-counterfeiting-piracy/, Accessed: 12/05/19.

© Springer Nature Switzerland AG 2020
K. M. Figueroa Mora et al. (Eds.): MCPR 2020, LNCS 12088, pp. 231–241, 2020.
https://doi.org/10.1007/978-3-030-49076-8_22

such as language, geographic proximity, etc. By comparing communities (i.e. groups of countries that have a strong relationship) within the illicit supply network to those within the others, we can qualitatively estimate the aspects that might be driving illicit trade. However, searching for these communities is not a trivial task, as the different networks may have different properties (directed, undirected, weighted etc.) that influence the community detection algorithms that we can use. Therefore, an algorithm able to deal with all possible network types—without much user involvement—is not immediately clear. To circumvent this issue, we present an approach that combines the creation of node embeddings (i.e. vector representations of the network nodes [9]) with traditional clustering algorithms (such as k-means or affinity propagation).

The remainder of this article is divided as follows: Sect. 2 offers background information on the different concepts and approaches used herein. Section 3 presents this article's method. Section 4 discusses the data used. Section 5 describes the experimental study conducted in this article, while Sect. 6 presents and discusses the results. Finally, Sect. 7 offers the conclusion and the outlook of this article.

2   Preliminaries

2.1   Node Embedding

Many data mining algorithms require feature vectors as input; therefore, if we want to use these approaches to predict, classify, or cluster nodes within a network, we first need to construct vector representations—i.e. embeddings— of them. Currently, methods that automatically construct these representations have become popular in literature [9]. In this article, we specifically use a python implementation [2] of the *node2vec* algorithm [8]; an algorithm that estimates the node embeddings based on a series of random walks.

2.2   Clustering

Finding community structures within a network is useful for finding nodes that have a strong relationship to one another. However, some of the community detection methods are not only computationally expensive, but also have the disadvantage of being dependent on network properties. For instance, only a few of the algorithms used on undirected networks can be extended to directed ones [5]. To overcome this network property dependency, we estimate the network communities using the node embeddings and not the network itself. In other words, we first cluster the embeddings and then we define the clusters as the communities structures we are looking for. This alternative has already proven to be effective [4] and thus is the one used herein. Furthermore, the clustering method that we use is affinity propagation [6], which is implemented within the

---

[2] github.com/eliorc/node2vec; Accessed: 02/05/20.

apcluster R package[3]. We choose this approach, as it does not require a predefined number of clusters to work. Readers are referred to [2] for more information
on the advantages and disadvantages of the affinity propagation algorithm.

3   Method

The method begins with the networks' adjacency matrices, which are given in
the present article as:

$$\mathbf{A}_l = \begin{bmatrix} a_{11} & \cdots & a_{1N_v} \\ \vdots & \ddots & \vdots \\ a_{N_v 1} & \cdots & a_{N_v N_v} \end{bmatrix}_l , \tag{1}$$

where $\mathbf{A}_l$ is the lth network adjacency matrix, N_v is the number of nodes in the
network, and $[a_{ij}]_l$ are the elements of the matrix representing if there is an edge
connecting node i to node j in network l.

By using the *node2vec* algorithm (cf. Sect. 2.1) we obtain a vector representation of the nodes at each network, i.e.:

$$\mathbf{e}_{nl} = [e_{n1}, \cdots , e_{nd_l}]_l^T , \tag{2}$$

where $\mathbf{e}_{nl}$ represents the vector of the nth node at network l and d_l is the vector's
dimension, which can vary depending on the network.

As mentioned previously, we use in this article the affinity propagation clustering algorithm; an algorithm that requires a similarity matrix to work. Therefore, we define for each network the following similarity matrices:

$$\mathbf{S}_l = \begin{bmatrix} s_{11} & \cdots & s_{1N_v} \\ \vdots & \ddots & \vdots \\ s_{N_v 1} & \cdots & s_{N_v N_v} \end{bmatrix}_l , \text{ with } [s_{ij}]_l = -||\mathbf{e}_{il} - \mathbf{e}_{jl}||_2 , \tag{3}$$

with $[s_{ij}]_l$ being the negative Euclidean distance between node i and node j at
network l. Since the similarity matrices do not consider if nodes can reach each
other within the network, nodes that cannot reach each other might end up in
the same cluster. To avoid this issue, we determine at each network if nodes
can reach each other in a walk of length l_r, i.e. the length of the random walks
used to create the embeddings. If that is not the case, we set their similarity
value equal to a threshold t_{diss} that will make those two nodes as dissimilar as
possible.

$$[s_{ij}]_l = \begin{cases} [s_{ij}]_l & \text{, if node } i \text{ can reach node } j \text{ within a random walk of} \\ & \text{length } l_r \text{ in network } l \\ t_{\text{diss}} & \text{, otherwise} \end{cases} . \tag{4}$$

---

[3] cran.r-project.org/web/packages/apcluster/apcluster.pdf; Accessed: 02/05/20.

Note that the creation of the node embeddings and the clustering are not necessarily deterministic. Therefore, it is important to make sure that the obtained results are as representative as possible. To do so, we use the method depicted in Fig. 1.

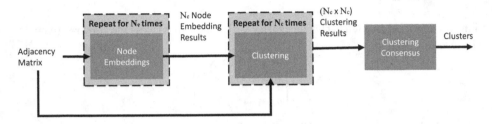

Fig. 1. Clustering method

As Fig. 1 shows, the method repeats for each network the embedding step $N_e \in \mathbb{N}_{>0}$ times and the clustering step an additional $N_c \in \mathbb{N}_{>0}$ times, thus resulting in a total of $N_e \cdot N_c$ clustering results. These results are used as input in a final consensus step for the clustering.

In this final step, we create a new network in which two nodes are connected if they cluster at least a certain number of times. To be more specific, we define a new adjacency matrix A_l^{opt} whose elements $[a_{ij}]_l^{\mathrm{opt}}$ are defined as:

$$[a_{ij}]_l^{\mathrm{opt}} = [a_{ji}]_l^{\mathrm{opt}} = \begin{cases} 1 & \text{, if node } i \text{ and node } j \text{ cluster } N_{\mathrm{th}} \text{ times or more} \\ 0 & \text{, otherwise} \end{cases}, \quad (5)$$

with N_{th} being a threshold defining the number of times that two nodes have to be grouped together for them to be connected in this new network. Afterwards, we define the subcomponents of this new network as the clusters of the lth network.

4   Data

The data we use to represent different types of country-country relationships (such as, licit and illicit trade, amount of traded goods, etc.) are described in the following paragraphs:

- **Licit and Illicit Trade:** The dataset from which we estimate the licit and illicit trade by country comes from the Global Product Authentication Service (GPAS) of MicroFocus International.[4] This dataset contains the authentication results of 55,999 unique serial codes (31,989 authenticated as true and

---

[4] microfocus.com/en-us/services/product-authentication-anti-counterfeit-services; Accessed: 02/03/20.

24,010 authenticated as false), as well as the country and time in which the codes were authenticated. These authentications are all from 2011 to 2015. Readers are referred to [7] for more information on the dataset.

- **Amount of traded Goods:** The amount of traded goods between countries (i.e. exports and imports in US dollars) is modeled using the data reported on the UN Comtrade database.[5] In this article, we only use data from the years 2011 to 2015, to make it consistent with the GPAS data we have available.
- **Free Trade Agreements:** Information about the countries free trade agreements is obtained from the Regional Trade Agreements Database of the World Trade Organization (WTO).[6] Note that in this article we only make use of free trade agreements that came into force before 2016, in order to make the data compatible with the GPAS dataset.
- **Language:** The data used to determine the language of each individual country is taken from the CIA's website.[7] Note that we only consider languages that are listed as an official language, as an official minority language, as a lingua franca, or as a language spoken by at least 10% of the population. If a country we need is missing on the list or if we cannot determine what language we should consider, we use the languages listed as official in the country's Wikipedia page.
- **Geography:** The geographic relationship between countries is modeled in this article as the inverse distance between the countries centroids. To calculate the inverse distances, the necessary centroid coordinates are obtained using the *countrycode* R-package. If the functions within the R-package are unable to provide the coordinates of a given country, we instead take them from a file found on the Periscope Data website.[8]

5   Experimental Study

The goal of this experiment is to gain insight into which factors might be driving the illicit trade between countries. The first step in achieving this goal is to create networks that describe different types of country relationships. To be more specific, the networks used herein model the following aspects: licit and illicit trade estimated using GPAS data; amount of traded goods (i.e. reported exports and imports in US dollars); trade discrepancies (i.e. differences in reported exports and imports); the existence of free trade agreements; the use of a common language; and geographic proximity.

In other words, we create seven distinct networks with different properties. However, before we create the networks, we need to make sure that the countries (i.e. the nodes) we consider appear in all of the datasets we are using, so that they also appear in all of the networks. After some preprocessing we end up with the 146 countries shown in Table 1.

---

[5] comtrade.un.org; Accessed: 11/26/19.

[6] rtais.wto.org/UI/PublicMaintainRTAHome.aspx; Accessed: 12/12/19.

[7] cia.gov/library/publications/the-world-factbook/fields/402.html; Accessed: 12/14/19.

[8] community.periscopedata.com/t/63fy7m/country-centroids; Accessed: 08/26/19.

Table 1. List of countries that are used as nodes within the networks

Countries
Afghanistan; Albania; Algeria; Angola; Argentina; Armenia; Australia; Austria; Azerbaijan; Bahamas; Bahrain; Bangladesh; Barbados; Belarus; Belgium; Benin; Bhutan; Bolivia; Bosnia & Herzegovina; Botswana; Brazil; British Virgin Islands; Brunei; Bulgaria; Burkina Faso; Burundi; Cambodia; Cameroon; Canada; Chile; China; Colombia; Congo-Kinshasa; Costa Rica; Côte d'Ivoire; Croatia; Cyprus; Czech Republic; Denmark; Djibouti; Dominican Republic; Ecuador; Egypt; El Salvador; Ethiopia; Fiji; France; Georgia; Germany; Ghana; Greece; Guatemala; Guinea; Guyana; Haiti; Honduras; Hong Kong (SAR China); Hungary; Iceland; India; Indonesia; Iran; Iraq; Ireland; Israel; Italy; Jamaica; Japan; Jordan; Kazakhstan; Kenya; Kuwait; Laos; Latvia; Lebanon; Liberia; Lithuania; Luxembourg; Macau (SAR China); Macedonia; Madagascar; Malawi; Malaysia; Maldives; Mauritania; Mauritius; Mexico; Moldova; Montenegro; Morocco; Mozambique; Myanmar (Burma); Namibia; Nepal; Netherlands; New Zealand; Nicaragua; Niger; Nigeria; Norway; Oman; Pakistan; Palestinian territories; Panama; Papua New Guinea; Paraguay; Peru; Philippines; Poland; Portugal; Qatar; Romania; Russia; Rwanda; Saudi Arabia; Senegal; Serbia; Singapore; Slovakia; Slovenia; South Africa; South Korea; South Sudan; Spain; Sri Lanka; Sudan; Sweden; Switzerland; Syria; Tanzania; Thailand; Togo; Trinidad & Tobago; Tunisia; Turkey; Uganda; Ukraine; United Arab Emirates; United Kingdom; United States; Uzbekistan; Venezuela; Vietnam; Yemen; Zambia; Zimbabwe

Furthermore, the creation of each one of the networks is described below:

- **Licit and Illicit Trade**: The two networks that describe licit and illicit trade between countries are directed networks with weighted edges created using the GPAS serial codes that were authenticated as true or false, respectively. The weights of an edge joining country i to country j represents the number of times that a serial code is authenticated first in i and then in j.

- **Amount of traded Goods**: This network is created as a directed network with weighted edges. The weight from country i to country j represents the trade value (US dollars) in goods that goes from i to j. Due to reporting discrepancies, the weights are calculated as the arithmetic mean between the exports reported by country i and the imports reported by country j.

- **Trade Discrepancy**: This network is modeled as an undirected network with weighted edges. These weights represent the arithmetic mean between the differences in imports and exports reported by country i and country j.

- **Free Trade Agreements**: This network consists of an undirected and unweighted network, whose adjacency matrix elements are 1 if there is a free trade agreement between two countries and 0 otherwise.

- **Language**: The language network is also an undirected and unweighted network with an adjacency matrix that has elements equal to one if two countries share a language and zero otherwise.

- **Geography**: This network consists of an undirected network with weighted edges, whose weights are the inverse of the distance between the centroids of country i and country j.

After creating the networks, we can start obtaining their necessary embeddings. However, there are parameters of the *node2vec* algorithm that we still need to define: the length of the random walks, the number of random walks that we calculate per node, the search bias parameters that influence the creation of the random walks, the number of random walk elements that define a nodes' context, and the dimension of the embedding vectors.

Considering that we are interested in knowing which aspects might be driving illicit trade, we set the length of the random walks equal to the number of locations we assume an illicit item might visit. That is the mean number of authentications of an illicit serial code, which in our dataset is three (i.e. $l_r = 3$). Note that we set the *node2vec* search bias parameters—which are used to create the random walks—equal to one (i.e. their default value in the implementation we are using). Furthermore, to make sure that the collection of random walks is as representative as possible, we create for each node 1000 of them. In addition, the whole random walk is used as context for estimating the node embeddings.

In contrast to the other parameters, we define the dimension of the embedding vectors of each network by testing the clustering results of several possible dimensions, i.e. $d_e = \{2, 3, 4, 5, 10, 20, 30, 40, 50, 60, 70, 80, 90, 100\}$. In other words, we choose for each network the dimension that delivers the best clustering results according to an objective function.

Before we describe the objective function, it is important to define some parameters that are necessary for the method described in Sect. 3. For instance, the value of t_{diss} (cf. Eq. (4)) is set equal to -Inf. This value is used to indicate countries that have no similarity within the implementation of the affinity propagation algorithm we are using. At the same time, N_e and N_c (cf. Fig. 1) are set equal to 100 and 10, respectively. In other words, we create for each network 100 embedding results that we then cluster 10 different times. Moreover, N_{th} (cf. Eq. (5)) is set equal to 900, i.e. 90% of all clustering results. These values are used to obtain results that are as representative as possible. Finally, it is important to mention that we standardize all embedding vectors within a single embedding result, before any of the clustering steps described in Sect. 3. The standardization is used to prevent variables with large scales from dominating the clustering procedure.

The objective function we use is based on the pseudo F-statistic [3] and is given by the following equation:

$$
c_{ld_e} = \left(1 - \frac{N_{\text{cl},ld_e}}{N_v}\right) \cdot \text{SNR}\{F_{l1d_e}, F_{l2d_e}, \ldots, F_{lN_e d_e}\}, \tag{6}
$$

where N_v is the number of network nodes, N_{cl,ld_e} is the number of clusters found on the lth network using d_e-dimensional embeddings, c_{ld_e} is the objective function value obtained with those clusters, and $\text{SNR}\{\cdot\}$ is an operator that calculates the signal to noise ratio of its input values—i.e. the inverse of the coefficient of variation or more specifically the ratio of the values' mean and standard deviation. Furthermore, F_{lid_e} represents the lth network's pseudo F-statistic obtained with the ith d_e-dimensional embedding result. Note that even though we calculate the F_{lid_e} values on an embedding result basis, we still use for their calculation the clusters of network l that are found using all of the embedding results. Also, the first factor in Eq. (6) is used to penalize a large number of clusters; the larger N_{cl,ld_e} is, the smaller the value of the objective function becomes.

Using Eq. (6), we define the optimal dimension for the lth network, $d_{e,l}^{\mathrm{opt}}$, as:

$$d_{e,l}^{\mathrm{opt}} = \underset{d_e}{\mathrm{argmax}}(c_{ld_e}) . \tag{7}$$

Once the optimal dimension at each network has been found, we use their clustering results to determine which countries cluster not only in the illicit trade network but also in the other ones.

6   Results and Discussion

The objective function values (cf. Eq. (6)) obtained on the different networks using the different embedding dimensions are shown in Table 2. Many node embeddings result in the clustering algorithm not converging. The licit and illicit networks are the most extreme cases of this type of behavior, as only one dimension results in vectors for which the clustering works. This might be caused by the sparsity of the licit and illicit networks. Furthermore, the results also show that in some cases the highest dimensions, i.e. 50, 70, and 100, are the ones with the best results according to Eq. (6).

Table 2. Objective function values obtained using embedding vectors of different dimensions; the missing values represent cases in which the affinity propagation did not converge; the best values for each network are shown in bold.

d_e	Illicit trade	Licit trade	Amount of traded Goods	Trade Discrepancy	Language	FTA	Geography
2	**1.78E−01**	—	6.72E−01	7.63E−01	—	2.35E+00	1.02E+00
3	—	—	1.99E+00	3.81E+00	3.80E+00	2.87E+00	5.35E+00
4	—	—	4.20E+00	2.56E+00	—	6.92E+00	9.79E+00
5	—	—	5.64E+00	3.82E+00	1.18E+01	**8.43E+00**	1.14E+01
10	—	—	1.53E+01	7.77E+00	1.09E+01	—	9.97E+00
20	—	—	—	—	—	—	1.26E+01
30	—	—	2.19E+01	2.57E+01	1.73E+01	—	1.49E+01
40	—	—	3.36E+01	—	—	—	1.55E+01
50	—	—	3.50E+01	3.52E+01	1.85E+01	—	**1.87E+01**
60	—	—	3.30E+01	3.42E+01	—	—	1.60E+01
70	—	—	3.43E+01	—	**2.23E+01**	—	1.51E+01
80	—	—	3.76E+01	—	2.21E+01	—	1.85E+01
90	—	—	3.77E+01	—	2.17E+01	—	1.80E+01
100	—	**3.67E+01**	4.30E+01	3.54E+01	—	—	1.85E+01

The clusters obtained on the illicit trade network with the best embedding dimension (i.e. two) are contained in Table 3. As we can observe, only 20 of the 146 countries listed in Table 1 are contained in Table 3. The ones missing are the ones that did not cluster with any other country within the illicit trade network. In other words, the 20 countries shown are those that have—according to the GPAS data used, cf. Sect. 4—a strong illicit trade relationship.

Table 3. Illicit trade clusters; the countries listed in Table 1 that are missing in Table 3 are those that did not cluster with any other country on the illicit trade network

Cluster 1	Denmark; Greece; Macedonia; Ukraine
Cluster 2	Belarus; Israel; Japan; Moldova
Cluster 3	Chile; Czech Republic
Cluster 4	Benin; Bosnia & Herzegovina
Cluster 5	Djibouti; Georgia
Cluster 6	Haiti; Macau (SAR China)
Cluster 7	Barbados; Portugal
Cluster 8	Bahamas; El Salvador

After finding the illicit trade clusters, we compare them to those of other networks. Table 4 shows the countries that cluster based on illicit trade and on at least one other aspect tested herein.

Table 4. Countries that cluster not only in the illicit trade network, but also on at least one of the other networks.

	Illicit trade
Licit trade	{Greece, Macedonia}; {Denmark, Ukraine}
Amount of traded Goods	{Belarus, Moldova}
Trade discrepancy	—
Language	—
FTA	{Denmark, Greece}
Geography	{Greece, Macedonia}

Table 4 shows that six countries appear to be related by illicit trade and by at least one of the other aspects considered. From these six, Greece is the one that appears the most in Table 4. The results show, that Greece's illicit trade with Macedonia appears to be driven by licit trade and geography, while its illicit trade with Denmark could be explained by the presence of an FTA. Denmark appears again in Table 4, but now together with Ukraine. From what we can observe, it seems that the strong licit trade relationship between these countries could be a possible factor behind their illicit trade. Another pair of countries that group together are Belarus and Moldova. These two countries are shown to have a strong trade relationship (as they cluster based on their amount of traded goods), a relationship that could be facilitating illicit trade between them. The results also show, that countries that group based on trade discrepancy and/or language do not seem to cluster based on illicit trade (at least not in our data).

As exemplified by the previous results, the algorithm described herein enables us to identify possible factors that might be driving illicit trade between countries and that might play an important role when combating this type of trade. However, we must acknowledge that this analysis is limited to the GPAS data used to represent the illicit trade. Henceforth, a future analysis with a larger and/or more diverse dataset still needs to be conducted. Additionally, a comparison of the method described herein and some other network analysis approaches should also be conducted in the future.

7   Conclusion and Outlook

We present a method that is able to find clusters in different types of networks (e.g., directed, undirected) by combining the creation of node embeddings and traditional clustering. With this method we can identify countries that may not only have a strong relationship in terms of illicit trade, but also in terms of some other aspect, such as trade data discrepancy, geographic proximity, etc. In other words, the method allows us to estimate factors that might be driving to some degree the illicit trade between countries. In this article, we apply the new method on data stemming from various real-world datasets. The obtained results enable us to estimate factors that could be playing an important role in the illicit trade between six different countries.

Even though our method shows potential for understanding different aspects of illicit trade, currently its results are only qualitative. Therefore, future works should try to modify the method in such a way that it will allow for more quantitative conclusions, for instance the percentage that a certain aspect (such as geography) influences illicit trade. Furthermore, we also need to compare our method to other network analysis approaches. In addition, the research of country-country relationships that we might not have considered here could be investigated in future related works. Finally, something that could also be interesting for the future is looking at cities instead of countries, as it could give us a better understanding of not only international, but also national illicit trade.

Acknowledgments. Jorge Ángel González Ordiano and Steven Simske acknowledge the support given by the NSF EAGER grant with the abstract number 1842577, "Advanced Analytics, Intelligence and Processes for Disrupting Operations of Illicit Supply Networks".

References

1. Bindner, L.: Illicit trade and terrorism financing. Centre d'Analyse du Terrorisme (CAT) (2016)
2. Brusco, M.J., Steinley, D., Stevens, J., Cradit, J.D.: Affinity propagation: an exemplar-based tool for clustering in psychological research. Br. J. Math. Stat. Psychol. **72**(1), 155–182 (2019)
3. Caliński, T., Harabasz, J.: A dendrite method for cluster analysis. Commun. Stat. Theory Meth. **3**(1), 1–27 (1974)
4. Cui, P., Wang, X., Pei, J., Zhu, W.: A survey on network embedding. IEEE Trans. Knowl. Data Eng. **31**(5), 833–852 (2018)

5. Fortunato, S.: Community detection in graphs. Phys. Rep. **486**(3–5), 75–174 (2010)
6. Frey, B.J., Dueck, D.: Clustering by passing messages between data points. Science **315**(5814), 972–976 (2007)
7. González Ordiano, J.A., Finn, L., Winterlich, A., Moloney, G., Simske, S.: On the analysis of illicit supply networks using variable state resolution-markov chains. In: Proceedings of the 18th International Conference on Information Processing and Management of Uncertainty in Knowledge-Based Systems (Accepted)
8. Grover, A., Leskovec, J.: node2vec: scalable feature learning for networks. In: Proceedings of the 22nd ACM SIGKDD International Conference on Knowledge Discovery and Data Mining, pp. 855–864. ACM (2016)
9. Hamilton, W.L., Ying, R., Leskovec, J.: Representation learning on graphs: methods and applications. arXiv preprint arXiv:1709.05584 (2017)
10. Mackey, T.K., Liang, B.A.: The global counterfeit drug trade: patient safety and public health risks. J. Pharm. Sci. **100**(11), 4571–4579 (2011)
11. OECD: Trade in Counterfeit Goods Costs UK Economy Billions of Euros - 2019 Update (2019)
12. Shelley, L.I.: Dark Commerce: How a New Illicit Economy is Threatening our Future. YBP Print DDA. Princeton University Press, Princeton (2018)

Accurate Identification of Tomograms of Lung Nodules Using CNN: Influence of the Optimizer, Preprocessing and Segmentation

Cecilia Irene Loeza Mejía[1]⬤, R. R. Biswal[2](✉)⬤, Eduardo Rodriguez-Tello[2]⬤, and Gilberto Ochoa-Ruiz[2]⬤

[1] Departamento de Posgrado, Instituto Tecnológico Superior de Misantla, Misantla, Veracruz, Mexico
[2] Tecnologico de Monterrey, Escuela de Ingenieria y Ciencias, Zapopan, Jalisco, Mexico
rroshanb@tec.mx

Abstract. The diagnosis of pulmonary nodules plays an important role in the treatment of lung cancer, thus improving the diagnosis is the primary concern. This article shows a comparison of the results in the identification of computed tomography scans with pulmonary nodules, through the use of different optimizers (Adam and Nadam); the effect of the use of pre-processing and segmentation techniques using CNNs is also thoroughly explored. The dataset employed was Lung TIME which is publicly available. When no preprocessing or segmentation was applied, training accuracy above 90.24% and test accuracy above 86.8% were obtained. In contrast, when segmentation was applied without preprocessing, a training accuracy above 97.19% and test accuracy above 95.07% were reached. On the other hand, when preprocessing and segmentation was applied, a training accuracy above 96.41% and test accuracy above 94.71% were achieved. On average, the Adam optimizer scored a training accuracy of 96.17% and a test accuracy of 95.23%. Whereas, the Nadam optimizer obtained 96.25% and 95.2%, respectively. It is concluded that CNN has a good performance even when working with images with noise. The performance of the network was similar when working with preprocessing and segmentation than when using only segmentation. Also, it can be inferred that, the application of preprocessing and segmentation is an excellent option when it is required to improve accuracy in CNNs.

Keywords: Lung nodule · CNN · Lung TIME · Tomograms · Adam optimizer · Nadam optimizer

1 Introduction

At present, there has been an incredible growth in the use of machine learning techniques in medical research, mainly applied to genetics [1], disease detection,

K. M. Figueroa Mora et al. (Eds.): MCPR 2020, LNCS 12088, pp. 242–250, 2020.
https://doi.org/10.1007/978-3-030-49076-8_23

biomedical image segmentation [2,3] and classification, thus showing the efficacy of machine learning in clinical decisions and monitoring systems [4]. The use of convolutional neural networks (CNN) in deep learning has helped in the automatic detection of various diseases particularly through the processing of biomedical images and clinical data. Recently, CNN research related to lung cancer, has focused on the automatic diagnosis of cancer [5,6], lung segmentation [7–9], segmentation of pulmonary nodules [10–13], lung nodules detection [14,15], cancer classification [16], nodule categorization [17] and nodule malignancy assessment [18–26]. Various investigations, related to lung nodules, report the influence of the data augmentation [14,24,26], number of input channels [20] and the use of dropout [8,14,18,20,21,24,26], in order to improve the accuracy of the network and to avoid overfitting. Likewise, some other researchers report the influence of the number of parameters [20,23] and training time [20]. Nonetheless, the use of preprocessing and segmentation has been little explored; the same applies to the effect of various available optimizers. The main goal of this investigation is to evaluate the influence of the optimizer (Adam [27] and Nadam [28]), preprocessing and segmentation in CNN for the precise identification of tomograms with pulmonary nodules. The evaluation was carried out considering both in precision and training time. The experiments were carried out on the Lung TIME [29] dataset, which is publicly available. In continuation, the paper is organized as follows: Sect. 2 deals with the materials and methods used while in Sect. 3 the results obtained are discussed and finally in the Sect. 4, the conclusions and future work are presented.

2   Materials and Methods

Three scenarios (see Fig. 1, the yellow color indicates the first case analyzed, while the blue color illustrates the second and the green color denotes the third) were considered to carry out the identification of tomograms with lung nodules applying a convolutional neural network: (i) to rescale the tomograms to 96×96 pixels and pass them as an input to CNN. (ii) to segment the tomograms to obtain the pulmonary regions and rescale them, then pass them as input to CNN. (iii) to preprocess the tomograms by applying filters (median and Gaussian), then the preprocessed image was binarized, subsequently the tomograms were scaled, which were taken as input to CNN. The motivation to perform the downsampling of the tomograms was to decrease the training time.

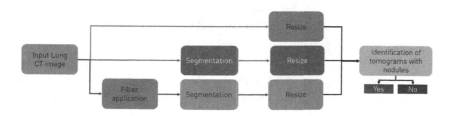

Fig. 1. Pipeline of Methodology (Color figure online)

2.1 Dataset Used in the Study

In this study, CT thorax scans in DICOM format with annotations of the pulmonary nodules in XML format of Lung TIME [29] was used. 62 CT thorax scans were chosen, which had 2003 tomograms with nodules and 12934 without nodules. To validate the results, 70% of the tomograms was randomly selected and utilized for training and the rest for testing.

2.2 Preprocessing

To improve the quality of the tomograms, the median filter and afterwards the Gaussian filter were applied, as discussed in [31] to eliminate salt-and-pepper noise, and the mottled noise from the image. The applied median filter mask was 5×5 pixels. On the other hand, standard deviation for Gaussian kernel was equal to 2.

2.3 Segmentation

To perform the segmentation, the thresholding technique was chosen. Thresholding is a simple and efficient technique for partitioning an image into a foreground and background [30]. According to Alakwaa et al. [16] it produces the best lung segmentation compared to clustering techniques (K-means and Mean Shift) and Watershed. Binarization was performed with a threshold of -350 HU as suggested by Pulagam et al. [32] to separate the pulmonary region tomography. Finally, the components connected to the edge of the binarized image were removed.

2.4 CNN

The description of the layers of the CNN architecture is indicated in Table 1, which consists of multiple convolutional layers with ReLU activation, maxpooling, flatten, dense and a final fully connected softmax layer to carry out the classification between tomograms with nodules and tomograms without nodules. Table 2 shows the CNN architecture using the Dropout layer, which helps

Table 1. CNN architecture

Layers
Conv2D
MaxPooling2D
Conv2D
Conv2D
MaxPooling2D
Flatten
Dense
Softmax

Table 2. CNN architecture with Dropout

Layers
Conv2D
MaxPooling2D
Conv2D
Conv2D
MaxPooling2D
Flatten
Dense
Dropout 0.0002
Softmax

selectively ignore neurons during training [33]. Both architectures were tested with Adam [27] and Nadam [28] optimizers. A batch size of 32, 5 epochs and a sparse categorical crossentropy loss function [34] was applied.

2.5   Computer Equipment

To implement CNN, Tensor Flow 2.0 was utilized in Python 3.7. The imageio [35] library was employed to read the DICOM images. For the preprocessing SciPy [36] library was used, while for segmentation of tomograms the scikit-image [37] library was used. The equipment on which the tests were performed has the following characteristics:

– Operating System: Windows 10 Home 64-bit (Build 18362)
– Processor: Intel(R) Core(TM) i3-5015U CPU @ 2.10 GHz
– Memory: 6 GB

3   Experimental Results and Analysis

Figure 2 shows an example of the application of filters (first the median filter and then the Gaussian) to the tomograms. The use of preprocessing significantly

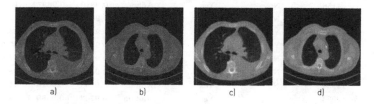

Fig. 2. (a, b) original images of slices, and (c, d) images obtained after application of filters

increases image quality, thus helping to reduce both salt and pepper and the mottled noises from the images.

Figure 3 shows examples of binarization in the tomograms. By means of the segmentation, the pulmonary region could be obtained, which allowed to improve the performance of the CNN.

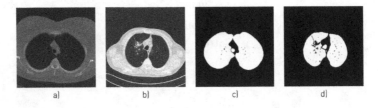

a)   b)   c)   d)

Fig. 3. (a, b) original images of slices, and (c, d) binarized slices

Table 3 gives a summary of the experiments performed without using Dropout while Table 4 reports the experiments carried out with a 0.0002 Dropout rate. Also tests were performed with/without preprocessing, with/without segmentation and with different number of tomograms. Performance was compared between Adam and Nadam optimizers. When carrying out the segmentation, better results were obtained, however, the execution time increased. In most tests (both using the Dropout layer and without using it), in which preprocessing was not carried out, better results were observed using the Nadam optimizer

Table 3. Results obtained from the comparison experiments without using Dropout

# tomograms with nodules	# tomograms without nodules	Pre-processing	Segmentation	Optimizer	Training ACC	Test ACC	Runtime in minutes
2003	2003	No	No	Adam	0.9472	0.9567	10.13
2003	2003	No	No	Nadam	0.9704	0.9642	9.98
2003	2003	No	Yes	Adam	0.9843	0.9734	13.19
2003	2003	No	Yes	Nadam	0.9847	0.9676	12.18
2003	2003	Yes	Yes	Adam	0.9800	0.9617	24.43
2003	2003	Yes	Yes	Nadam	0.9861	0.9709	24.40
2003	4158	No	No	Adam	0.9024	0.8680	14.53
2003	4158	No	No	Nadam	0.9685	0.9676	12.53
2003	4158	No	Yes	Adam	0.9819	0.9697	18.85
2003	4158	No	Yes	Nadam	0.9863	0.9659	22.17
2003	4158	Yes	Yes	Adam	0.9826	0.9708	33.05
2003	4158	Yes	Yes	Nadam	0.9814	0.9762	35.68
2003	12934	No	No	Adam	0.9269	0.9346	37.60
2003	12934	No	No	Nadam	0.9415	0.9449	38.60
2003	12934	No	Yes	Adam	0.9753	0.9610	45.78
2003	12934	No	Yes	Nadam	0.9763	0.9589	44.12
2003	12934	Yes	Yes	Adam	0.9652	0.9525	77.24
2003	12934	Yes	Yes	Nadam	0.9682	0.9485	78.49

Table 4. Results obtained from the comparison experiments using Dropout

# tomograms with nodules	# tomograms without nodules	Pre-processing	Segmentation	Optimizer	Training ACC	Test ACC	Runtime in minutes
2003	2003	No	No	Adam	0.9419	0.9434	13.93
2003	2003	No	No	Nadam	0.9693	0.9676	9.48
2003	2003	No	Yes	Adam	0.9832	0.9667	11.86
2003	2003	No	Yes	Nadam	0.9850	0.9692	12.25
2003	2003	Yes	Yes	Adam	0.9807	0.9676	24.74
2003	2003	Yes	Yes	Nadam	0.9843	0.9709	23.77
2003	4158	No	No	Adam	0.9522	0.9562	17.35
2003	4158	No	No	Nadam	0.9817	0.9605	14.35
2003	4158	No	Yes	Adam	0.9840	0.9719	19.80
2003	4158	No	Yes	Nadam	0.9835	0.9735	18.92
2003	4158	Yes	Yes	Adam	0.9789	0.9713	37.40
2003	4158	Yes	Yes	Nadam	0.9824	0.9703	35.04
2003	12934	No	No	Adam	0.9079	0.9141	45.74
2003	12934	No	No	Nadam	0.9473	0.9460	44.44
2003	12934	No	Yes	Adam	0.9719	0.9507	42.50
2003	12934	No	Yes	Nadam	0.9747	0.9589	46.27
2003	12934	Yes	Yes	Adam	0.9641	0.9520	87.01
2003	12934	Yes	Yes	Nadam	0.9688	0.9471	86.14

and a shorter runtime. When Dropout was not applied, preprocessing was performed and the Nadam optimizer was used, in some cases the runtime increased, compared to the Adam optimizer. So when the Dropout layer is not used, it is recommended to use the Nadam optimizer on images that have not been preprocessed, instead the Adam optimizer is suggested for images that were preprocessed.

Figure 4 shows the average accuracy of training and testing in the experiments performed. On average, the Adam optimizer obtained a training accuracy

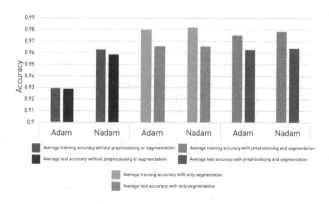

Fig. 4. Influence of the optimizer, preprocessing and segmentation in the accurate identification of tomograms of lung nodules

of 96.17%, test accuracy of 95.23% and training time of 31.95 min in 96 × 96 pixel images. In contrast, the Nadam optimizer obtained 96.25%, 95.2% and 33.23 min respectively. It was observed that when using the Nadam optimizer slightly better results are obtained than when those furnished by Adam. In addition, accuracy using only segmentation is better than when it is combined with preprocessing.

4   Conclusions

An experimental analysis was performed through the preprocessing, segmentation and optimizer on images of Lung TIME dataset resized to 96 × 96 pixels. It is concluded that convolutional neural networks have excellent performance in the identification of tomograms with nodules, obtaining training accuracy above 90.24% and test accuracy above 86.8%, even when working with images with noise. It is suggested that when working with CT thorax scans, no preprocessing be applied and only segmentation can be performed, since better results were observed in this case (a training accuracy above 97.19% and test accuracy above 95.07% were obtained), compared to applying preprocessing and segmentation (a training accuracy above 96.41% and test accuracy above 94.71% were obtained). In addition, the use of preprocessing significantly increases runtime. On average, the Adam optimizer obtained a training accuracy of 96.17%, test accuracy of 95.23% and training time of 31.95 min. In contrast, the Nadam optimizer obtained 96.25%, 95.2% and 33.23 min, respectively. When Dropout is not applied and preprocessing is performed, it is recommended to use the Adam optimizer. On the contrary, the Nadam optimizer is recommended when no preprocessing on the tomogram is performed. Applying segmentation is an excellent option when accurate results are required. We would like to remark that the model obtained can be used as part of a computer-assisted diagnostic system on lung cancer research. As future work, the location of the nodules in the tomograms identified is proposed. In addition, it would be interesting to compare the performance of different preprocessing techniques.

References

1. Holder, L.B., Haque, M.M., Skinner, M.K.: Machine learning for epigenetics and future medical applications. Epigenetics 12(7), 505–514 (2017)
2. Lenchik, L., et al.: Automated segmentation of tissues using CT and MRI: a systematic review. Acad. Radiol. 26(12), 1695–706 (2019)
3. Rizwan-i-Haque, I., Neubert, J.: Deep learning approaches to biomedical image segmentation. Inf. Med. Unlocked 18, 100297 (2020)
4. Zhang, Z., Sejdić, E.: Radiological images and machine learning: trends, perspectives, and prospects. Comput. Biol. Med. 108, 354–370 (2019)
5. Polat, H., Mehr, H.: Classification of pulmonary CT images by using hybrid 3D-Deep convolutional neural network architecture. Appl. Sci. 9(5), 940 (2019)
6. Simie, E., Kaur, M.: Lung cancer detection using convolutional neural network (CNN). Int. J. Adv. Res. Ideas Innov. Technol. 5(4), 284–292 (2019)

7. Zhu, J., Zhang, J., Qiu, B., Liu, Y., Liu, X., Chen, L.: Comparison of the automatic segmentation of multiple organs at risk in CT images of lung cancer between deep convolutional neural network based and atlas-based techniques. Acta Oncol. **58**(2), 257–264 (2019)
8. Abdullah-Al-Zubaer, I., Hatamizadeh, A., Ananth, S.P., Ding, X., Tajbakhsh, N., Terzopoulos, D.: Fast and automatic segmentation of pulmonary lobes from chest CT using a progressive dense V-network. Comput. Methods Biomech. Biomed. Eng. Imaging Vis., 1–10 (2019)
9. Geng, L., Zhang, S., Tong, J., Xiao, Z.: Lung segmentation method with dilated convolution based on VGG-16 network. Comput. Assist. Surg. **24**(S2), 27–33 (2019)
10. Hamidian, S., Sahiner, B., Petrick, N., Pezeshk, A.: 3D convolutional neural network for automatic detection of lung nodules in chest CT. In: Proceedings SPIE International Society for Optical Engineering (2017)
11. Dey, R., Lu, Z., Hong, Y.: Diagnostic classification of lung nodules using 3D neural networks. In: IEEE International Symposium on Biomedical Imaging (2018)
12. Tong, G., Li, Y., Chen, H., Zhang, Q., Jiang, H.: Improved U-NET network for pulmonary nodules segmentation. Optik - Int. J. Light Electron Opt. **174**, 460–469 (2018)
13. Huang, X., Sun, W., Tseng, T., Li, C., Qian, W.: Fast and fully-automated detection and segmentation of pulmonary nodules in thoracic CT scans using deep convolutional neural networks. Comput. Med. Imaging Graph. **74**, 25–36 (2019)
14. Setio, A., et al.: Pulmonary nodule detection in CT images: false positive reduction using multi-view convolutional networks. IEEE Trans. Med. Imaging **35**(5), 1160–1169 (2016)
15. Xie, H., Yang, D., Sun, N., Chen, Z., Zhang, Y.: Automated pulmonary nodule detection in CT images using deep convolutional neural networks. Pattern Recogn. **85**, 109–119 (2019)
16. Alakwaa, W., Nassef, M., Badr, A.: Lung cancer detection and classification with 3D convolutional neural network (3D-CNN). Int. J. Adv. Comput. Sci. Appl. (IJACSA) **8**(8), 99–110 (2017)
17. Tu, X., et al.: Automatic categorization and scoring of solid, part-solid and non-solid pulmonary nodules in CT images with convolutional neural network. Nature **7**(1–10), 8533 (2017)
18. Tajbakhsh, N., Suzuki, K.: Comparing two classes of end-to-end machine-learning models in lung nodule detection and classification: MTANNs vs CNNs. Pattern Recogn. **63**(2017), 476–486 (2017)
19. Yan, X., et al.: Classification of lung nodule malignancy risk on computed tomography images using convolutional neural network: a comparison between 2D and 3D strategies. In: ACCV 2016. LNCS, vol. 10118, pp. 91–101. Springer, Heidelberg (2017). https://doi.org/10.1007/978-3-319-54526-47
20. Kang, G., Liu, K., Hou, B., Zhang, N.: 3D multi-view convolutional neural networks for lung nodule classification. PLoS ONE **12**(11), e0188290 (2017)
21. Zhao, X., Liu, L., Qi, S., Teng, Y., Li, J., Qian, W.: Agile convolutional neural network for pulmonary nodule classification using CT images. Int. J. Comput. Assist. Radiol. Surg. **13**(4), 585–595 (2018). https://doi.org/10.1007/s11548-017-1696-0
22. Causey, J., et al.: Highly accurate model for prediction of lung nodule malignancy with CT scans. Nature **8**(1–12), 9286 (2018)
23. Liu, Y., Hao, P., Zhang, P., Xu, X., Wu, J., Chen, W.: Dense convolutional binary-tree networks for lung nodule classification. IEEE Access **30**(6), 49080–49088 (2018)

24. Gruetzemacher, R., Gupta, A., Paradice, D.: 3D deep learning for detecting pulmonary nodules in CT scans. J. Am. Med. Inf. Assoc. **25**(10), 1301–1310 (2018)
25. Zia, M.B., Juan, Z.J., Rehman, Z.U., Javed, K., Rauf, S.A., Khan, A.: The utilization of consignable multi-model in detection and classification of pulmonary nodules. Int. J. Comput. Appl. **177**(27), 0975–8887 (2019)
26. Onishi, Y., et al.: Automated pulmonary nodule classification in computed tomography images using a deep convolutional neural network trained by generative adversarial networks. J. **2**(5), 99–110 (2019)
27. Kingma, D., Lei, J.: Adam: A method for stochastic optimization. In: 3rd International Conference for Learning Representations, San Diego (2015)
28. Dozat, T.: Incorporating nesterov momentum into Adam. In: International Conference on Learning Representations (2016)
29. Dolejsi, M., Kybic, J., Polovincak, M., Tuma, S.: The Lung TIME: annotated lung nodule dataset and nodule detection framework. In: Proceedings SPIE 7260, Medical Imaging 2009: Computer-Aided Diagnosis, vol. 7260 (2009)
30. Khan, S., Hussain, S., Yang, S., Iqbal, K.: Efective and reliable framework for lung nodules detection from CT scan images. Nature **9**, 1–4 (2019)
31. Makaju, S., Prasad, P., Alsadoon, A., Singh, A., Elchouemi, A.: Lung cancer detection using CT scan images. Proc. Comput. Sci. **125**(2018), 107–114 (2018)
32. Pulagam, A., Rao, V., Inampudi, R.: Automated pulmonary lung nodule detection using an optimal manifold statistical based feature descriptor and SVM classifier. Biomedical & Pharmacology Journal **10**(3), 1311–1324 (2017)
33. Srivastava, N., et al.: Dropout: a simple way to prevent neural networks from overfitting. Journal of Machine Learning Research **15**(2014), 1929–1958 (2014)
34. Sparse categorical crossentropy. https://www.tensorflow.org/api_docs/python/tf/keras/losses/sparse_categorical_crossentropy. Accessed 21 Feb 2019
35. Imageio. https://imageio.readthedocs.io/en/stable/. Accessed 21 Feb 2019
36. Virtanen, P., et al.: SciPy 1.0: fundamental algorithms for scientific computing in Python. Nat. Methods **17**(3), 261–272 (2020)
37. Van der Walt, S., et al.: scikit-image: image processing in Python. PeerJ **2**, e453 (2014)

What the Appearance Channel from Two-Stream Architectures for Activity Recognition Is Learning?

Reinier Oves García[⊠] and L. Enrique Sucar

Computer Science Department, Instituto Nacional de Astrofísica
Óptica y Electrónica, Sta. María Tonantzintla, 72840 Puebla, CP, Mexico
{ovesreinier,esucar}@inaoep.mx

Abstract. The automatic recognition of human activities from video data is being led by spatio-temporal Convolutional Neural Networks (3D CNNs), in particular two-stream architectures such as I3D that reports the best accuracy so far. Despite the high performance in accuracy of this kind of architectures, very little is known about what they are really learning from data, resulting therefore in a lack of robustness and explainability. In this work we select the appearance channel from the I3D architecture and create a set of experiments aimed at explaining what this model is learning. Throughout the proposed experiments we provide evidence that this particular model is learning the texture of the largest area (which can be the activity or the background, depending on the distance from the camera to the action performed). In addition, we state several considerations to take into account when selecting the training data to achieve a better generalization of the model for human activity recognition.

1 Introduction

Automatic decision making based on machine learning models has become in a tendency today, with applications in real-world scenarios such as medicine, robotics, and video surveillance among others. Sometimes, models based on deep learning cannot be well explained [13], resulting in that way in a lack of reliability, and therefore, they are rejected, especially in such areas where a mistake has severe implications (e.g. medical diagnosis and terrorism detection) [14]. Apart from ethical reasons, knowing what these models are learning can be crucial for areas where it is essential to prevent that recognition systems being deceived (e.g. security environments and autonomous navigation) [11].

Nowadays two-stream CNNs with three-dimensional convolutions [3] constitute the strongest tool to tackle video classification problems. These particular architectures can be seen as a combination of two independent models that learn independent features from two different representations: appearance, and motion. The appearance model learns from pure RGB frames while the motion model learns from the optical flow [19].

© Springer Nature Switzerland AG 2020
K. M. Figueroa Mora et al. (Eds.): MCPR 2020, LNCS 12088, pp. 251–260, 2020.
https://doi.org/10.1007/978-3-030-49076-8_24

Leading the state-of-the-art we can situate the I3D architecture [1] which is a two-stream CNN inflated from a 2D model pre-trained over the ImageNet dataset with spatio-temporal convolutions and pooling layers. Despite the high performance, this particular architecture constitutes a black box and little is know about what it is learning from the input data. Towards a better understanding and explainability of 3D CNNs for action recognition, we selected the appearance channel from the I3D architecture and the UCF101 dataset [17] in the conducted experiments. The motion channel will be omitted from the experiments, since the images produced by the optical flow, considerably lack texture.

This work, far from being a criticism, is presented to clarify some points that remain unclear when using two-stream architectures, especially the appearance model. Besides, it is intended to establish new guidelines for making a suitable selection of datasets that guarantee that the appearance model learns the appearance of the body language and nor the background steadiness. Additionally, we investigate the sensitivity of the appearance channel from the I3D architecture to various factors presented in the training data that could dramatically affect a posterior evaluation of the model: the texture of the background and the area covered by the action. To determine how sensitive the 3D CNNs can be to all these factors, we guide the conducted experiments towards answering the following questions:

- How good the performance of the appearance channel can be if the activity is always associated with the context (e.g. brushing your teeth is always done in a bathroom or boxing is always performed in a ring)?
- What happens if the context where the activity is performed changes abruptly?
- What is the impact of training only considering the region that occupies the activity (background-independent activities)?
- How much the camera target distance affects the generalization of the model?

Finally, a set of evidence that leads that 3D CNNs are learning the largest region in the video (the texture of the background or the texture of the activity) is presented. Furthermore, we provide a set of considerations that are useful for the suitable selection of training data to build models hard to beat.

The rest of the paper is organized as follows: Sect. 2 relates the main advances in the computer vision area for action recognition as well as the main drawbacks discovered so far. The experimental configurations and results are given in Sect. 3. In Sect. 4 we relate some guidelines and considerations useful for selecting a suitable dataset that guarantees the generalization of the models. Finally, in Sect. 5 the conclusions and future work are given.

2   Related Work

Human Action Recognition has presented a significant improvement in accuracy during the last years by applying CNNs [11] and transfer learning. The clever transformation of 2D models pre-trained over ImageNet [1,8] into models with spatio-temporal convolutions has resulted in the more powerful tool to tackle this challenging task.

One of the most revolutionary approaches for action recognition are two-stream CNNs with 2D convolutional kernels. In [16] Simonyan et al. showed that the combination of the appearance and motion has the ability to improve action recognition accuracy. The new era of two-stream CNNs is marked by 3D convolutional kernels, which have outperformed 2D CNNs through the use of large-scale video datasets [1]. Currently, a two-stream model, with spatio-temporal convolutions over appearance and motion, joined at the fully connected layer, shows the most promise [1,8]. There is evidence that combining two-stream CNNs with a third representation can improve the accuracy results [2].

Two-stream architectures, despite being powerful tools for video classification, are considered black boxes due to the little information that they provide about the learning process, aggravated by the amount of parameters to be trained [22]. At the same time that CNNs evolve, several authors have questioned the strength of the models while others try to explain what is happening inside those black boxes. The work presented in [9] introduces an approach that deciphers which portions of the face are more concerned with model predictions. [12] demonstrates that adversaries can easily craft adversarial examples without any internal knowledge of the target network. In [14], the authors found that the question "Husky or Wolf?" does not depend on the animal but the snow in the background. Several works have focused in models unboxing via decision trees [21] and gradient-based visualization techniques [20]. In [4,5] are presented several clues about what are learning patio-temporal CNNs by visualizing the internal excitation of the models but they do not provide any lead about where the excitation occurs: within the background or over the actors.

Until recently, it was believed that 2D CNNs were able to recognize objects through the learning of non-handcrafted features [10]. In [7] is shown that CNNs trained over ImageNet are strongly biased towards recognizing textures rather than shapes. This is the main reason why these models are very susceptible to adversarial attacks [6]. The fact that these models are biased towards texture also makes difficult the training process over small datasets and far from favoring the learning, it causes significant harm to the performance of the model [15].

Given the success of deep learning architectures, there is recent interest to have a deeper understanding of how and what they learn. Until now, some works have been directed to explain or criticize deep architectures used in image classification, but it does not happen in the same way for video processing (3D CNNs).

3 Experiments and Results

To investigate what are learning 3D CNNs we focused on the appearance channel from the I3D architecture. For that, we implement a training procedure for the model [1] published on github[1]. Given that all the models used in our experiments

---

[1] https://github.com/deepmind/kinetics-i3d.

were trained using our code we conducted the first experiment (Sect. 3.1) to validate the quality of our training procedure. The second experiment (Sect. 3.2) is mainly focused on demonstrating that the appearance channel is learning the largest part of the scene: the area covered by the action or the background, depending on the camera target distance. In the third experiment (Sect. 3.3) are presented several considerations that inform us the appearance channel is more prone to learn the background than to learn the activity and we show that the model is considerably affected by the suppression of the background.

To visualize the outcomes we present histograms for each experiment, in which each bar relates to one class of the 101 classes in the UCF101 dataset. For data representation, we adopted the following convention over the bar chart visualization technique: cyan (light) bars represent how many videos were tested for each class while magenta (dark) bars represent the number of missclassified videos. The 101 classes in the dataset were sorted alphabetically in order to maintain the correspondence between the visualization of different experiments.

3.1   Towards the Reproduction of the Results Presented in [1]

In Table 1.a are presented the results achieved by our implementation after combining both channels, appearance and motion. The variation presented in the reported results is given by the introduction of random parameters in the model, data augmentation and random crop during training. Despite this, our implementation achieves similar results than those reported by the authors and hence can be used as a baseline for further experimentations.

Since we are focused on exposing what part of the scene the appearance channel is learning, we report the results of the RGB model for each partition of the dataset in Table 1.b. In Fig. 1 is shown that the model has, in general, a decent performance over the appearance channel. Classes with higher accuracy are those in which the activity is performed in a specific scenario and the objects involved in the activity are presented in both phases train and test (e.g. $BoxingPunchingBag_{18}$, $PlayingGuitar_{63}$, etc.). On the other hand, classes with

Table 1. In these tables, we report the accuracy achieved by our implementation over the three partitions of the UCF101 dataset; compared with the original publication of Carreira et al. [1]. **a)** presents the accuracy obtained by combining the appearance and motion channels and **b)** presents the accuracy of the appearance and motion channels.

UCF101	Carreira et al. [1]	Ours
Split-1	-	97.60
Split-2	-	97.99
Split-3	-	97.72
Average	98.0	97.77

a)

UCF101	RGB channel	Motion channel
Split-1	94.55	96.40
Split-2	95.66	96.97
Split-3	94.34	96.42
Average	94.85	96.59

b)

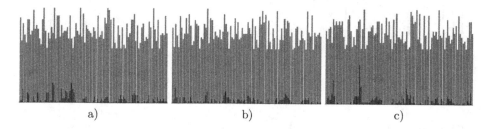

Fig. 1. These pictures depict the performance of the appearance channel from the I3D. **a)**, **b)** and **c)** reflect the results achieved by the model for each partitions on the UCF101 dataset, respectively. The cyan color represents how many instances were evaluated per class and the magenta color denotes the amount of misclassified instances. Horizontal axis refers to the index of each class ordered alphabetically while the vertical axis represents the amount of instances per class (Best seen in color). (Color figure online)

a worse performance are those in which the activities are performed in different scenarios (e.g $CricketBowling_{23}$, $Hammering_{36}$, $CricketShot_{24}$, etc.). The subindex refers to the index of the corresponding bar in the visualization.

Until now, we only have clues that point to the fact that the appearance channel is learning from the background texture. For this reason, we put this hypothesis to a quantitative test where the quality of the appearance channel is evaluated.

3.2 Background Inclusion and Exclusion During the Evaluation Phase

This experiment is focused on demonstrating that the appearance channel is learning the texture of the largest region of the image, say the activity (very close to the camera) or the background (when the activity is performed away from the camera). To accomplish the aim of this experiment we employ a mask

Table 2. These tables report the accuracy achieved by the model trained eliminating the background or the activity. **a)** presents the accuracy of the model when the background are replaced by a black mask and **b)** presents the opposite case, when the activities are replaced by a black mask.

UCF101	RGB channel
Split-1	19.16
Split-2	18.31
Split-3	23.53
Average	20.33

a)

UCF101	RGB channel
Split-1	58.92
Split-2	54.28
Split-3	56.54
Average	56.58

b)

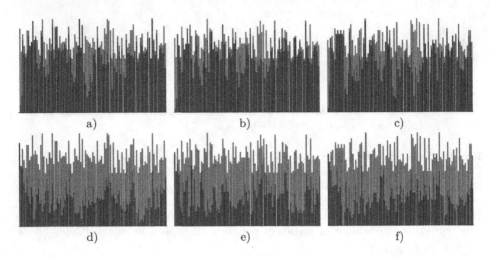

Fig. 2. These images show the performance of the appearance channel from I3D. Figures **a)**, **b)** and **c)** visualize the results achieved by the model when the background is replaced by a black mask (only the activity is taking into consideration). Figures **d)**, **e)** and **f)** visualize the results achieved by the model when the activity is replaced by a black mask (only the background). The cyan color represents how many instances were evaluated per class and the magenta color denotes the amount of misclassified instances. Notice how the images have a complementary behavior (when the results in the first are good in the second are bad). Horizontal axis refers to the index of each class ordered alphabetically while the vertical axis represents the amount of instances per class (Best seen in color). (Color figure online)

r-CNN[2] [18] for human body segmentation. Since the quality of the extracted human masks is not always the best, a morphological operation of dilation is used to reduce this problem and ensure that people involved in the activity are always included in the analysis. However, we manually check the 13320 videos within the dataset for corroborating the quality of such masks. For those cases where the person performing the activity was undetected by the mask, we used the original RGB video.

To assess how sensitive the model can be concerning the area occupied by the activity, the training generated in Sect. 3.1 is selected and the test is performed over the three partitions of the dataset. The first test is carried out taking into account only the area occupied by the activity and the background is replaced by a black mask. Quantitative results are presented in Table 2.a. For the second test, the activity is replaced by the black mask and the results are presented in Table 2.b.

Contrary to the results presented in Sect. 3.1, the results achieved when the background is removed are catastrophic (See Table 2.a). The classes that report better accuracy are those that are performed near to the camera with static background (e.g $ApplyEyeMakeup_1$, $ApplyLipstick_2$, $JumpRope_{47}$,

---

[2] https://github.com/facebookresearch/detectron2

Jumping Jack$_{48}$ etc.). Note how the performance decreases while the area covered by the activity decreases or the background changes for instances of the same class. This means that a reduction in texture strongly affects the final decision of the appearance channel (e.g *Basketball*$_8$, *Drumming*$_{27}$, *SkyDiving*$_{83}$, etc.). See Fig. 2.

After analyzing Table 2.b , we can arrive at the conclusion that the obtained results are not as good as those in Table 1.b but it do show a better performance than those achieved when the background is removed (See Table 2.a). This experiment provides us evidence about how important is the background for the model. For this particular dataset, the background results more important than the activity itself as the results are almost 3 times better than those reported in Table 2.a (See Fig. 2).

From this experiment, we can conclude the premise that the appearance channel is favoring the largest regions in the videos. When this area corresponds to the execution of the activity, the model ends up learning what is expected (spatio-temporal features of the activity). Unlike this, in cases where the background predominates, the model ends up learning the invariability of the background texture. The reason why the activities carried out near the camera now provide the worst results is because the background lacked texture and that is why the model is learning the activity (See Fig. 3).

3.3 Model Performance Evaluation When the Activity and Background Are Isolated

This experiment tries to answer two fundamental questions of the learning process: (i) how much does the overall performance of the model is affected if the background is the same for all classes during training and testing? and (ii) which is more discriminating for the model the appearance of the activity or the background? To answer the first question, we replace the background of every video in the dataset with a black mask in both phases, training and testing. The results achieved in this experiment are presented in Table 3.a. To answer the second question, the opposite strategy is followed. This time, the action is replaced by a black mask during both phases, training, and testing. Additionally, videos were resized to 224×224 without preserving the aspect ratio to guarantee that action

Table 3. These tables report the accuracy achieved by the model when the activity and background are isolated. **a)** presents the accuracy of the model when background is replaced by a black mask and **b)** presents the opposite case, when the activities are replaced by a black mask. The mask is applied in both phases, training and testing.

UCF101	RGB channel
Split-1	78.27
Split-2	78.68
Split-3	77.13
Average	78.02

a)

UCF101	RGB channel
Split-1	90.69
Split-2	93.10
Split-3	92.90
Average	92.23

b)

performers were fully included in the video. Results of this experiment can be seen in Table 3.b.

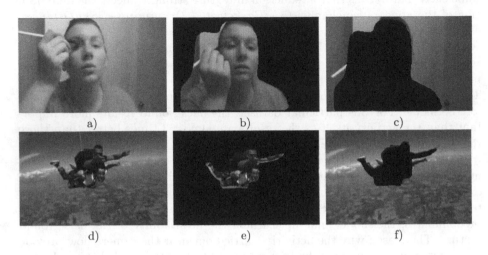

Fig. 3. The first row (subimages a), b) and c)) displays an instance where the model learned the activity and not the background ($ApplyEyeMakeup_1$). In the second row (subimages d), e) and f)), an instance in which the model learned the background instead of the activity is presented ($SkyDiving_{83}$).

Note how the performance of the model is improved when the background is included during the training process. This is due to models pre-trained on ImageNet are biased to learn texture instead of shapes [7]. When the background is removed from training videos, the texture is diminished drastically and hence the performance of the model also decreases. This arises by the fact the I3D model was initialized with weights learned from ImageNet and a lack of texture during the fine tuning process significantly harm the global performance of the model. Finally, it can be concluded that the appearance channel from the I3D model learns in most of the classes the background. This is because most of the activities in this dataset are tied to the context and the largest area in the scenes correspond to the background texture.

4   Discussion and General Considerations

In Fig. 3 are depicted, in three different ways, two instances from two different classes: (i) a) and d) are the original RGB frames, (ii) b) and e) show the human mask over a black background and finally, (iii) c) and f) show the background without the activity. For images within the first row, the background lacks texture and for this reason, the model learns the texture of the activity. For cases, where the background is very similar for different activities, training data produces the desired effect over the model; the appearance of the activity is learned. The second row of Fig. 3 shows the opposite case. Here, the background is highly textured and is very similar within the same class (videos are recorder from aerial views). For this specific class, the model learns the background.

Another important factor to consider during training is the random cropping of the videos. There is nothing that guarantees the people involved in the activity remain within the selected region (partially or totally) each time the video is included in a batch. Note how, in Table 3.b the performance is similar to produced by the original model in Table 1.b. Finally, we propose two foremost considerations that have to be taken into account when selecting datasets and training the appearance channel from the I3D architecture for human activity recognition. The first one establishes that the strength of the model will be given by the diversity of backgrounds in each activity class. The second aspect to take into consideration is that using data augmentation far from improving the performance of the model creates an irreparable situation since it introduces more of the same texture and this biases the model.

5 Conclusions

In this paper, we provided evidence that clarifies some points that remain unclear when using two-stream CNNs, especially the appearance channel. From the experimentation, we can conclude that the appearance channel from the I3D architecture is learning the texture of the largest region of the video. In other words, if the activity is closer to the camera, the model learns the human texture and becomes in a stronger classifier invariant to scale and background changes. In the opposite case, when the area covered by the background is larger than the area of the performed activity, the model learns the background texture, resulting in a weak classifier, easy to deceive and susceptible to changes in the scale as well as in the background. Besides, this particular model does not work well when different activities are performed over the same background. For these cases, we should pay special attention when using this model in real scenarios where the background can change such as surveillance, autonomous navigation, etc. So we can conclude with the following statement: similar to 2D CNNs, it seems that 3D CNNs are learning the texture of the background and its steadiness. A possible solution is to mask the videos in the training phase keeping only the humans performing the activities; and base the recognition more in the appearance of the activity than in the appearance of the scene.

References

1. Carreira, J., Zisserman, A.: Quo vadis, action recognition? a new model and the kinetics dataset. In: CVPR, pp. 6299–6308 (2017)
2. Choutas, V., Weinzaepfel, P., Revaud, J., Schmid, C.: Potion: pose motion representation for action recognition. In: CVPR, pp. 7024–7033 (2018)
3. Diba, A., Pazandeh, A.M., Van Gool, L.: Efficient two-stream motion and appearance 3D CNNs for video classification. arXiv preprint arXiv:1608.08851 (2016)

4. Feichtenhofer, C., Pinz, A., Wildes, R.P., Zisserman, A.: What have we learned from deep representations for action recognition? In: CVPR, pp. 7844–7853 (2018)

5. Feichtenhofer, C., Pinz, A., Wildes, R.P., Zisserman, A.: Deep insights into convolutional networks for video recognition. In: IJCV, pp. 1–18 (2019)

6. Ford, N., Gilmer, J., Carlini, N., Cubuk, D.: Adversarial examples are a natural consequence of test error in noise. arXiv preprint arXiv:1901.10513 (2019)

7. Geirhos, R., Rubisch, P., Michaelis, C., Bethge, M., Wichmann, F.A., Brendel, W.: Imagenet-trained cnns are biased towards texture; increasing shape bias improves accuracy and robustness. arXiv preprint arXiv:1811.12231 (2018)

8. Hara, K., Kataoka, H., Satoh, Y.: Can spatiotemporal 3D CNNs retrace the history of 2D CNNs and ImageNet? In: CVPR, pp. 6546–6555 (2018)

9. Khorrami, P., Paine, T., Huang, T.: Do deep neural networks learn facial action units when doing expression recognition? In: CVPR, pp. 19–27 (2015)

10. Krizhevsky, A., Sutskever, I., Hinton, G.E.: ImageNet classification with deep convolutional neural networks. In: Advances in Neural Information Processing Systems, pp. 1097–1105 (2012)

11. Kumar, A.D., Chebrolu, K.N.R., Soman, K.P., et al.: A brief survey on autonomous vehicle possible attacks, exploits and vulnerabilities. arXiv preprint arXiv:1810.04144 (2018)

12. Narodytska, N., Kasiviswanathan, S.: Simple black-box adversarial attacks on deep neural networks. In: CVPRW, pp. 1310–1318. IEEE (2017)

13. Papernot, N., McDaniel, P., Goodfellow, I., Jha, S., Berkay Celik, Z., Swami A.: Practical black-box attacks against machine learning. In: Proceedings of the 2017 ACM on Asia Conference on Computer and Communications Security, pp. 506–519. ACM (2017)

14. Ribeiro, M.T., Singh, S., Guestrin, C.: Why should i trust you?: explaining the predictions of any classifier. In: Proceedings of the 22nd ACM SIGKDD, pp. 1135–1144. ACM (2016)

15. Ringer, S., Williams, W., Ash, T., Francis, R., MacLeod, D.: Texture bias of CNNs limits few-shot classification performance. arXiv preprint arXiv:1910.08519 (2019)

16. Simonyan, K., Zisserman, A.: Two-stream convolutional networks for action recognition in videos. In: Advances in Neural Information Processing Systems, pp. 568–576 (2014)

17. Soomro, K., Zamir, A.R., Shah, M.: Ucf101: a dataset of 101 human actions classes from videos in the wild. arXiv preprint arXiv:1212.0402 (2012)

18. Wu, Y., Kirillov, A., Massa, F., Lo, W.-Y., Girshick, R.: Detectron2. https://github.com/facebookresearch/detectron2 (2019)

19. Zach, C., Pock, T., Bischof, H.: A duality based approach for realtime TV-L^1 optical flow. In: Hamprecht, F.A., Schnörr, C., Jähne, B. (eds.) DAGM 2007. LNCS, vol. 4713, pp. 214–223. Springer, Heidelberg (2007). https://doi.org/10.1007/978-3-540-74936-3_22

20. Zeiler, M.D., Fergus, R.: Visualizing and understanding convolutional networks. In: Fleet, D., Pajdla, T., Schiele, B., Tuytelaars, T. (eds.) ECCV 2014. LNCS, vol. 8689, pp. 818–833. Springer, Cham (2014). https://doi.org/10.1007/978-3-319-10590-1_53

21. Zhang, Q., Yang, Y., Ma, H., Wu, Y.N.: Interpreting CNNs via decision trees. In: CVPR, pp. 6261–6270 (2019)

22. Zhou, H., Alvarez, J.M., Porikli, F.: Less is more: towards compact CNNs. In: Leibe, B., Matas, J., Sebe, N., Welling, M. (eds.) ECCV 2016. LNCS, vol. 9908, pp. 662–677. Springer, Cham (2016). https://doi.org/10.1007/978-3-319-46493-0_40

Automatic Estrus Cycle Identification System on Female Dogs Based on Deep Learning

Gustavo Calderón[1] , Cesar Carrillo[1] , Mariko Nakano[1(✉)] , Jeanine Acevedo[2] ,
and José Ernesto Hernández[2]

[1] Graduate Section, ESIME-Culhuacan, Instituto Politecnico Nacional, Av. Santa Ana No.
1000, Col. San Francisco Culhuacan, Coyoacán, 04420 Mexico City, Mexico
gus_auza@hotmail.com, mnakano@ipn.mx
[2] Reproduction Management Laboratory, Universidad Autónoma Metropolitana-Xochimilco,
Calzada del Hueso 1100, Colonia Villa Quietud, Coyoacán, 04960 Mexico City, Mexico
ehernan@correo.xoc.uam.mx

Abstract. Vaginal cytology is a complementary economic method and of simple realization, an indicative to determine in which stage of the estrous cycle the dog is, to achieve a higher fertility and fertility rate. This method is based on determining the type and quantity of cells of the different stages of the estrous cycle, since the hormonal changes that the vaginal mucosa undergoes during the estrous cycle are shown in the morphology of its epithelial cells. The canine female in her reproductive life goes through different phases of activity and hormonal rest that are repeated cyclically. This is called the estrous cycle and consists of 4 stages: proestrus, estrus, diestrus and anestrus. The interpretation of vaginal cytology's, is a process to which a considerable amount of time is dedicated by its observation in the microscope and the same interpretation by the doctor which can become subjective and poorly performed, causing economic losses for the owners. Therefore, this work proposes an automatic system that will identify six types of cells and the quantity of them in the glass slide, based on a Faster R-CNN to determine in which stage of the estrous cycle the dog is. Our results show an accuracy of 91.6%. The proposed system will improve the efficiency and speed of cytology's to decreased from 1 h approximately to just a few seconds.

Keywords: Vaginal cytology · Estrous cycle · Faster R-CNN · Deep learning · Cells

1 Introduction

Dogs have always been a fundamental pillar in the different facets of people's lives. Hence the importance of dogs in society, not only to go for a walk with them but for other beneficial activities, such as: search and rescue, medical pets, emotional support, hunting, grazing and protection. The goal of every living being is the perpetuation of its species. To achieve this, they must fulfill the function of reproducing, which consists in the ability of every living being to produce another similar individual. This function

K. M. Figueroa Mora et al. (Eds.): MCPR 2020, LNCS 12088, pp. 261–268, 2020.
https://doi.org/10.1007/978-3-030-49076-8_25

becomes a transcendent biological fact of great importance for the survival of the species, since it perpetuates life beyond the individual [1].

The canine female in her reproductive life goes through different phases of activity and hormonal rest that are repeated cyclically. This is called the estrous cycle which consists of 4 stages: proestrus, estrus, diestrus and anestrus [2]. The first estrus appears in female dogs between the first 6 and 10 months of their life and then they experience a new ovarian cycle approximately every 6 months. Canine infertility can derive from multiple etiologies, but statistically the rejection of the mating or the bad synchronization ovulation-mount, represent approximately 80% of the failures of reproduction in this species. Although artificial insemination resolves the rejections of the mating, it will not be successful, if it is not done at the right time, being currently the vaginal cytology as the best way to determine that moment [3].

Vaginal cytology is the most applied procedure to verify the status of the female reproductive system. Despite this method being old, it is preferred due to its remarkable scope, it is practical, fast and economical, and it can be done by any specialized veterinary professional. The study consists of introducing a clean swab - preferably sterilized - in the vagina of the female. Subsequently, epithelial cells should be analyzed under a microscope to find out the status of the female dog's reproductive system. However, this analysis can be very time-consuming and tedious, since the doctor will count and classify the cells seen in the microscope manually, consuming approximately 1 h for each study performed.

Under these conditions, we have been interested in detecting the dog's estrous cycle using an automatic system based on convolutional neural networks, mainly in the Faster Region-based CNN (R-CNN) [4]. The objective of this work is to detect, classify and count the 6 different types of cells that will be seen in the microscope in a faster and more efficient way, and thus get to know the state of the estrous cycle where the female dog is. Unlike another estrous cycle identification proposal [5], in which the system classifies the estrous cycle directly from the input image, our proposed system provides the number of different types of cells, which indicates the female dog's estrous cycle. In this sense, our proposal provides reasons about the final classification decision to expert.

This paper is organized as follows: Sect. 2 a brief review of deep learning in veterinary medicine. Section 3 shows the methodology of the proposed system and the creation of the database. In Sect. 4, we provide some experimental results. Finally, Sect. 5 concludes this paper.

2   Deep Learning in Veterinary Medicine

In some aspects, veterinary medicine can be compared with the human medicine. Many basic laboratory tests are still too expensive for pet owners or simply not feasible due to the lack of automated methods and the large number of different species.

An example would be the white blood cell count (WBC). In human medicine, this is one of the most basic blood tests and is performed almost every time blood is drawn. On the other hand, in birds and reptiles, this laboratory test must be done manually (unlike humans, the red blood cells in birds and reptiles have a nucleus that interferes with most automated counting methods). However, due to the large number of different species and the morphological differences in their white blood cells, this test can only be performed by specialists in this field and, therefore, is rarely used in practice [6].

This emerging technology could provide a solution to this and other similar problems in veterinary medicine. In recent years, deep learning applications have been used to solve several problems in medical imaging, resulting in an improvement over previous generation results [7]. So far, to name just a few, this technique has been used in tumor detection, blood flow quantification, brain image analysis and pathology images [8]. In some cases, these deep learning techniques even surpassed humans in these tasks [6].

Unfortunately, despite its successful use in human medicine, deep learning applications are still lacking in veterinary imaging. It is argued that this should change, because not only deep learning can allow more accurate, faster and less expensive diagnoses in veterinary medicine and it can even be used easily by any veterinarian [8].

Currently there are studies conducted by the Faculty of Veterinary Medicine of Zagreb in Croatia, which decided to implement deep learning in a real-world task in veterinary medicine that is usually done manually, in this scope they counted the percentage of reticulocytes in cats [6] and also in [5] authors classify the estrus cycle in rats by using features of whole image and transfer learning.

3   Methodology

3.1   Dataset

In this work we create a dataset consisting of vaginal cytology samples in female dogs collected by the reproduction management laboratory of the Universidad Autónoma Metropolitana - Xochimilco. The vaginal samples are smeared into a glass slide and stained with pap smears [9]. The images were taken with an inverted microscope (see Fig. 1a) with an integrated camera with 40X magnification objective lens, without zoom, with the shutter open at 2.6. We obtained a total of 250 images of size 1600 × 1200 pixels in an RGB color space with jpg format. (see Fig. 1b). The next step was to manually label the cell types (see Fig. 2) in each of the images in the database, which was performed by an expert in the reproduction laboratory. Finally, the dataset was divided into two parts: 70% for training and 30% for test.

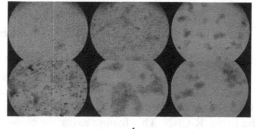

a.   b.

Fig. 1.   a) Inverted microscope with integrated camera and b) Example of images obtained

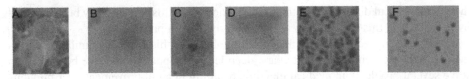

Fig. 2. Epithelial cell types to recognize during a vaginal cytology; A. Parabasal cells, B. Superficial cells with a pyknotic nucleus, C. Intermediate cells, D. Anucleate (squamous) cells, E. Neutrophils, F. Red blood cells.

3.2 Faster R-CNN Method for Identification of Cells

The Faster R-CNN is a method that allows the classification and localization of objects in an image, this is an improvement of its predecessors R-CNN [10] and Fast R-CNN [11] where execution time is decreased. The architecture of a Fast R-CNN (see Fig. 3) is composed by a Region Proposal Network (RPN) with a backbone CNN that extracts the features from the image. The RPN works on top of the feature map of the CNN and creates its own region proposals inside the network, then a Region Of Interest (ROI) Pooling layer warps the region proposal and takes the feature maps to fed them into fully connected layers that aim to predict the class probability and the bounding boxes. Finally, a regression is used to correct the offset of the proposed bounding boxes. Because this is a complete network that combines the extraction of features and the proposal of regions, its computational time is low.

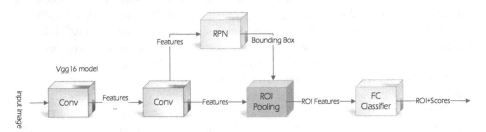

Fig. 3. Faster R-CNN architecture

3.3 Estrus Identification Automatic System on Female Dogs

There are several architectures for feature extraction widely used for classification tasks such as Resnet-101, Resnet-50, Inception V2, Vgg16, Vgg19 and so on. The aim of this scope is to achieve a high performance by using low computational resources in the shortest amount of time, therefore the Vgg16 architecture is chosen as the backbone for the Faster R-CNN. This feature extractor consists in 13 convolutional layers which have proven to be enough. For the training, 70% of the images were fed into the network along with their bounding boxes previously segmented by the experts.

The method for determining the estrous cycle consists in taking 6 photographs from the glass slide to acquire the most information from it. Then, from each photograph the different cells are counted and grouped among all images. According to the specialist, to indicate the stage of the estrous cycle the presence of different cells is close to the percentages in the following Table 1, the percentages may vary but the relation between cells is close, the ± sign indicates that the cells may appear but they are not relevant to the cycle, the + sign indicates that the cells will be present but the number of them is not relevant, and finally the − sign indicates the absence of the cell, although it is irrelevant to the cycle. This tells us that if we can find cells and count them, we can know in which stage of the estrous cycle the canine is.

Table 1. Approximate cell percentages for each stage of the canine estrous cycle [12].

Cells	Proestrus %	Estrus %	Diestrus %	Anestrus %
Anucleated	10	90	30	10
Superficial	30	8	20	10
Intermediate	50	2	20	20
Parabasal	10	0	30	60
Neutrophil	±	+	+	+
Erythrocytes	+	−	−	−

The proposed method (see Fig. 4) consists in use of the Faster R-CNN to detect the cells in the acquired images (6 images). Then, just by counting the number of bounding boxes and polling them given their label, we can compute the percentages of cells and determine the stage of the estrous cycle. This can be done easily and much faster than manual counting.

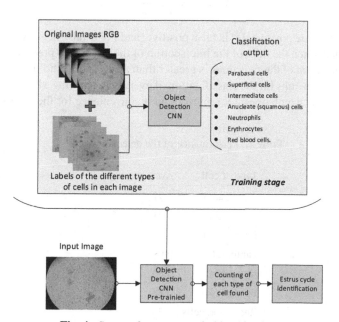

Fig. 4. System for estrus cycle identification

4 Results

For the detection the Faster R-CNN was used with the Vgg16 feature extractor as previously discussed, for the training parameters we used the stochastic gradient descent with momentum optimizer with a L2 regularization of 0.0005 and a momentum of 0.900, the model was trained in two stages for a total of 300 epochs, with an initial learning rate of 0.001 during 200 epochs and then with a learning rate of 5e−8 for 100 epochs, the mini-batch size was set to 1. These parameters depend on the feature extractor chosen, for our scope these showed the best performance.

The system is capable of recognizing parabasal, superficial, intermediate, neutrophil, erythrocytes and anucleate cells, plus it is also capable of recognizing red blood cells which provide some extra information; however, it does not belong to the estrous cycle. The system was tested on the 30% remaining information and its performance was evaluated by using the Average Precision (AP) metric given by (1).

$$AP = \int_0^1 p(r)dr \tag{1}$$

The definition of AP represents the area under the precision-recall curve, the precision (2) tells us how accurate the predictions are and recall (3) tells how good it can find all the correct regions.

$$Precision = \frac{TP}{TP + FP} \tag{2}$$

$$Recall = \frac{TP}{TP + FN} \tag{3}$$

Where TP is true positive, FP is false positive, and FN is false negative, respectively. A TP is defined when the ratio of the intersection of the two areas (predicted and ground truth) over the union of the two areas is greater than a certain threshold in this case 0.75. Table 2 shows the results for the classification of every cell, showing a lower performance for red blood cells which does not represent an inconvenience for the estrus cycle.

Table 2. Performance of the detection of cells

Type of cell	Average precision
Anucleated	0.91
Superficial	0.91
Intermediate	0.97
Parabasal	0.94
Neutrophil	0.86
Erythrocytes	0.88
Red blood cells	0.23

Then the counting of the cells is done by counting the bounding boxes with a higher score of 90%, an example is show in Table 3 where the Anestrus and Estrus cycles are identified.

Table 3. Demonstration of cell count for a previously diagnosed cytology.

Images belonging to a smear	Diagnosis of the proposed system	Diagnosis by manual cell count (veterinarian)
	The total cells detected in the image are: Anucleated = 3 ->>>3.49% Superficial = 6 ->>>6.98% Intermediate = 74 ->>>86.05% Parabasal = 3 ->>>3.49% Neutrophil = 3 Erythrocytes = 9 Red blood cells = 0 This citology belongs to Proestrus	Proestrus
	The total cells detected in the image are: Anucleated = 26 ->>>92.86% Superficial = 2 ->>>7.14% Intermediate = 0 ->>>0.00% Parabasal = 0 ->>>0.00% Neutrophil = 32 Erythrocytes = 0 Red blood cells = 0 This citology belongs to Estrus	Estrus
Diagnostic time	5 sec	1 hour

Finally, we evaluated our proposed system with 12 new tests, which had already been classified by an expert (see Table 4), of which we were right at 11, having a percentage of identification of the estrous cycle of 91.6%.

Table 4. Number of new samples for evaluation by an expert and our proposed system

Estrus cycle	Veterinarian	System proposed	Detection rate %
Anestrus	3	3	100
Proestrus	3	3	100
Estrus	3	3	100
Diestrus	3	2	66.6
Total	12	11	91.6

5 Conclusion

In this paper a new system to identify the estrus cycle of a female dog is proposed, it is based on a Faster R-CNN detection model with the Vgg16 as feature extractor. In general, it achieved an accurate prediction of the different types of cells, except in red blood cells, which although it is not necessary to decide the classification of the estrus cycle, it might be of great importance to detect any anomaly different from our objective. On the other hand, in the test of the complete system the experts are still better to classify, the difference with our system lies in the time to classify the estrus cycle, being 5 s, which is much faster compared to approximately 1 h that the expert takes. The results have shown that our proposed approach in this classification task is effective and accurate. However, we still need to improve the robustness of our method by increasing the size of the database. It is worth noting that our proposed system provides the number of different types of cells to determine the estrus cycle, which is the same procedure performed by experts, and then the proposed system can be expanded easily for any other purposes, such as determine some specific diseases of dogs.

References

1. Galina, C., Valencia, J.: Reproducción de animales domésticos, 3ª. edn. Ed. Limusa, México D.F. (2008)
2. Stornelli, M.A., Savignone, C.A., Tittareli, C.M., Stornelli, M.C.: Citología vaginal en caninos: metodología y aplicaciones clínicas. Revista Veterinaria Cuyana 1(1), 15–21 (2006). (Spanish)
3. Monachesi, M.: El ciclo sexual de la perra y la llegada a la pubertad. Mascotas Foyel, Facultad de Veterinaria de la Universidad de Buenos Aires (2010). Disponible en. http://www.foyel.com/paginas/2010/02/1252/el_ciclo_sexual_de_la_perra_y_la_llegada_a_la_pubertad/
4. Shaoqing, R., Kaiming, He., Girshick, R., Sun, J.: Faster R-CNN: towards real-time object detection with region proposal networks. In: Advances in Neural Information Processing Systems, vol. 28 (2015)
5. Hernández, G., et al.: Estrous cycle classification through automatic feature extraction. Computación y Sistemas 23(4), 1249–1259 (2019)
6. Vinicki, K., Ferrari, P., Belic, M., Turk, R.: Using Convolutional Neural Networks for Determining Reticulocyte Percentage in Cats, Croatia (2018)
7. Arsomngern, P., Numcharoenpinij, N., Piriyataravet, J., Teerapan, W., Hinthong, W., Phunchongharn, P.: Computer-aided diagnosis for lung lesion in companion animals from x-ray images using deep learning techniques. In: 2019 IEEE 10th International Conference on Awareness Science and Technology (iCAST), Morioka, Japan, pp. 1–6 (2019)
8. Nguyen, A., Pierre Jr., Y., Snapp-Childs, W., Birch, S.: Visualizing veterinary medical data sets with Jetstream. IUScholarWorks (2019)
9. Papanicolau, G.N.: A new procedure for staining vaginal smears. Science 95(2469), 438–439 (1942)
10. Girshick, R., Donahue, J., Darrell, T., Malik, J.: Rich feature hierarchies for accurate object detection and semantic segmentation. In: CVPR 2014 Proceedings of the 2014 IEEE Conference on Computer Vision and Pattern Recognition, pp. 580–587 (2014)
11. Girshick, R.: Fast R-CNN. In: Proceedings of the IEEE International Conference on Computer Vision (2015)
12. Hernández, P.J.E., Fernández, R.F., Cortés, S.: Fundamento Teórico Prácticos De La Citología Exfoliativa En Medicina Veterinaria. Manual # 5, CBS. 5, UAM Xochimilco (2008)

Natural Language Processing and Recognition

Machine Learning Techniques for Identity Document Verification in Uncontrolled Environments: A Case Study

Alejandra Castelblanco$^{(\boxtimes)}$, Jesus Solano, Christian Lopez, Esteban Rivera, Lizzy Tengana, and Martín Ochoa

AppGate Inc., Bogotá, Colombia
{alejandra.castelblanco,jesus.solano,christian.lopez,esteban.rivera,
lizzy.tengana,martin.ochoa}@appgate.com

Abstract. Distributed (i.e. mobile) enrollment to services such as banking is gaining popularity. In such processes, users are often asked to provide proof of identity by taking a picture of an ID. For this to work securely, it is critical to automatically check basic document features, perform text recognition, among others. Furthermore, challenging contexts might arise, such as various backgrounds, diverse light quality, angles, perspectives, etc. In this paper we present a machine-learning based pipeline to process pictures of documents in such scenarios, that relies on various analysis modules and visual features for verification of document type and legitimacy. We evaluate our approach using identity documents from the Republic of Colombia. As a result, our machine learning background detection method achieved an accuracy of 98.4%, and our authenticity classifier an accuracy of 97.7% and an F1-score of 0.974.

Keywords: Machine learning · Identity document verification

1 Introduction

Due to the popularity of mobile devices and internet connectivity, interest in distributed enrollment or onboarding processes is raising. Such services typically require pictures of identity documents (ID) as part of the identity verification procedure [1]. In some businesses the proof of identity is crucial and, therefore, it is important to have security mechanisms to prevent identity theft in remote ID verification systems. In fact, several challenges should be addressed in order to accept a document as genuine in scalable onboarding systems [2]. First, the system should localize the document and extract relevant information from pictures taken by the users in uncontrolled environments, such as variable backgrounds, angles, and mobile camera qualities. Second, the system should ensure that the input corresponds to the expected document type. Finally, perceptible document forgery should be detected before accepting the document as genuine.

© Springer Nature Switzerland AG 2020
K. M. Figueroa Mora et al. (Eds.): MCPR 2020, LNCS 12088, pp. 271–281, 2020.
https://doi.org/10.1007/978-3-030-49076-8_26

In the literature, multiple approaches tackle some of these issues individually, for instance, methods for document localization [6,7], text recognition [3,5] and visual similarity comparison [8] have been proposed. However, few papers have addressed complete pipelines for identity document verification using machine learning algorithms [3]. Therefore, more evidence of reliable pipelines and features evaluated in a wide range of datasets is required.

In this paper we propose a practical pipeline for identity document acquisition and verification. Our goal is to design a complete pipeline that takes into account the challenges of real-life acquisition and that could be easily extrapolated to many identity document types (i.e. driving licenses, IDs from various countries). Our contributions are twofold: the first one is related to document localization, where we share gained insights of implementing deep learning techniques for background removal. Also, we propose a set of methods that are necessary for pre-processing images from real-life scenarios. The second contribution is an accurate classifier for document verification based on visual pattern features. For this we rely on novel and already published techniques, which we evaluate on a case study. We also review and evaluate the impact of feature combinations in the performance of classification algorithms.

2   Related Work

Identity document verification aims to determine if an input image belongs to an authentic document class and if the document is legitimate. As described by [8], verification can be performed at the level of content consistency, layout resemblance and visual similarity.

Before performing document verification, the document should be localized and processed from the input image. This step, guarantees a standard input for the authenticity verification system. Most previous studies rely on text recognition or image processing to find the document. For instance, in [6] line segmentation and three-based representations were used to detect quadrilateral shapes. Also, the use of Viola-Jones algorithm complemented with a classifier was proposed by [5]. An accuracy of 68.57% was reported for ID vertices detection in the wild in [2]. Text recognition was used by [3] for document localization. Our work stands out from the literature because it combines a deep learning model to remove complex backgrounds, facilitating the document crop and perspective alignment.

Document verification can be performed by analyzing visual similarity. The pixel-wise information of the document image can be synthesized via features. These descriptors contain unique information from different image components (i.e. Luminance, texture, and structure). Methods such as histogram analysis [20], and color coherence [12] complement the information by comparing intensities and spatial regions. Moreover, analysis of local information has been proposed, with methods such as edge-histograms [11], and structural similarity [19].

Furthermore, studies that perform document type classification and feature extraction were found. Simon et al. [16] classified 74 different ID types through

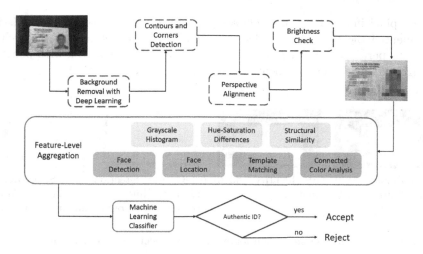

Fig. 1. Pipeline to analyze documents in uncontrolled environments. Blue dashed line boxes depict localization (Module 1). Steps in purple solid line boxes depict authenticity classification (Module 2). (Color figure online)

an SVM. They used a combination of HOG and Color features to gather spatial information achieving a mean class-wise accuracy of 97.7%. Ghanmi et al. [8] performed ID classification with a descriptor based on spatial color distribution, achieving an accuracy of 94.5%. Additional studies that rely heavily on text recognition and deep learning for document classification were found [10,16,18]. Although text extraction is a valuable approach that could complement our proposed pipeline, there is a trade-off, since in-the-wild environment conditions can dramatically impact the performance of the OCR Engines [16] and high resolution images would be required from the end users.

Few papers have addressed complete pipelines for identity document verification in uncontrolled environments. To the best of our knowledge ours is the first work that relies only on visual features to perform all processes (ID localization, classification and verification) in a comprehensive manner.

3   Approach

The proposed pipeline for document analysis is divided in two modules, see Fig. 1. The first module addresses the pre-processing requirements of a smartphone document capture in the wild. The second module extracts local and global descriptors of the input image to perform: a) image matching with expected identity document class and b) a basic evaluation of the document authenticity.

3.1   Module 1 - Document Acquisition

Deep Learning Model for Background Removal: We used semantic segmentation to detect the document in the image. This method, consists in the classification of each pixel into two possible classes, identity document or background. We implemented the UNETS deep learning architecture developed by researchers in [15] to perform pixel classification and build an image with a high contrast background where the document is clearly highlighted.

(a) Original document photo taken by the user.
(b) Identity document mask
(c) Corner detection based on linear regression of contours.
(d) Straightened document after alignment process

Fig. 2. Semantic segmentation followed by perspective alignment and crop.

Crop and Align Perspective: Once the background has been removed, we perform a corner detection analysis, as shown in Fig. 2. First, we find the contour along the document border [17]. Then, the contour is used to perform a linear regression on each side of the document, the four line intersections are defined as the corners of the document. From the selected corners, a geometric transformation matrix is found. The calculated matrix is used to transform the original image into a well oriented document, we used the `warp-perspective` tool from [4]. The sequence of steps is depicted in Fig. 2. We calculated the highest score of template matching, see Sect. 3.2, to detect if the document is upside down.

Brightness Analysis: A brightness analysis is then performed in order to reject images with unsuitable lightning conditions (i.e. flashes). Initially, we separated the image into hue, saturation and value channels (hsv). The third channel, value (v), is used as our measure of brightness. Later, the image is divided into a $n \times m$ bins grid. The brightness value of each bin corresponds to the mean brightness of all pixels which make up that bin. The average brightness (Br_μ) and its standard deviation (Br_σ) are calculated for all bins. A maximum intensity threshold is then computed with Eq. 1, where α controls our *brightness threshold*.

$$Br_{max} = Br_\mu + \alpha \cdot Br_\sigma \qquad (1)$$

Following the process, a Gaussian blur filter is applied to reduce noise. Then, each pixel above our given threshold Br_{max} is modified to 255 (white) and below Br_{max} to 0 (black). Afterwards, we group sets of white pixels using a connected component labelling process. These pixel groups are classified as bright zone candidates. Finally, we define a bright spot if the number of pixels in the label is above 2% of the image size.

3.2   Module 2 - Document Verification

The document verification pipeline classifies a set of features that best describe the visual and layout information of the input image. These features should distinguish the original document class from others, and check basic characteristics about the document authenticity. We refer to *global* features as the features that describe the whole image. We call *local* features, the descriptors from a specific region or a particular characteristic in the document which can be adjusted between document types. For this module, we assume that the document is correctly cropped and aligned, and images are resized to (459×297) pixels, this resolution was selected to include some of the lowest picture resolutions available in the smartphone camera market (640×480), keeping document proportions.

Global Features: The first global feature compares the grayscale histograms of the input image against an authentic document image, defined as the ground truth. To handle the variability from the light conditions, the histograms are normalized using a min-max feature scaling. Histogram similarity was measured using the Wasserstein distance (WD). The WD metric proposed by [14], is based on the theory of optimal transport between distributions. WD provided better discrimination between classes, compared to other goodness of fit metrics such as Pearson's chi-squared distance and histogram bin to bin intersection.

The second global feature is generated with a sum of the *hue* and *saturation* differences (HSD) between the input document image X and the ground truth G. For this feature, channels were converted to the HSV space and the document area was split in N rectangular bins, inspired by the bin to bin comparison proposed by [8]. For each bin i, the differences between the average hue $\overline{h}$ and average saturation $\overline{s}$, for X and G were summed. The overall *hue* and *saturation* differences were normalized dividing by the maximum possible differences. The final feature HSD was calculated as seen in Eq. 2, with $N = 50$, that is 5 and 10 sections along the height and width respectively.

$$HSD = \frac{\sum_{i=0}^{N} \overline{h}(i)_X - \overline{h}(i)_G}{179 \cdot N} \cdot \frac{\sum_{i=0}^{N} \overline{s}(i)_X - \overline{s}(i)_G}{255 \cdot N} \tag{2}$$

The third global feature, structural similarity score (SS), extracts information from the spatial dependencies of the pixel value distributions. For this method, images are compared evaluating functions dependent on the luminance, contrast and value correlations of the pixel arrays, as defined by [19]. This metric compares the structural composition of the background between the input document and the ground truth.

Local Features: Local features are useful to verify the existence of individual elements that are specific to the type of ID document, for instance, pictures, patterns in the background, symbols, bar-codes or headers.

A face within a specific region of the document is represented with two different features. First, a simple 5 point landmark detection was calculated, based on the Histogram of Oriented Gradients and a sliding window. The *Dlib* python library was used [9]. The output features were: an integer with the number of faces found (NF) on the input image (if all landmarks were found), and a boolean indicating if the face location (FL) matched a predefined valid region.

We used template matching to verify the existence of a specific visual patterns. For this analysis, the input image is analyzed in grayscale, together with an example of the template region from an authentic document. The method consists in sliding a window of the original template over the input image and calculating a correlation measurement. Afterwards, the algorithm returns the coordinates on the input image that has highest correlation with the template. We used *OpenCV* library for the implementation [4].

Fig. 3. Color coherence analysis. From left to right: 1) Region analyzed. 2–4) Masks of connected pixels with similar hue values. 5) Mask of connected pixels with similar saturation.

For the Colombian ID case, we chose the document header as template. The correlation measurement that provided better results for discrimination of the authentic document class was the metric *TM-COEFF-NORMED*. The template matching score (TMS) and coordinates of the template location (TML) are exported as features for the classification model.

A variation of the color coherence analysis methods proposed by [8] and [12] was implemented. The proposed method identifies continuous regions with connected color and saturation values and compares these regions between two images. First, the input image is transformed to the HSV space, the hue and saturation channels are discretized in β number of bins. Then, a structural window, that acts as a filter, slides through the discretized image to identify connected color regions, using the tool *label*, from the ndimage-scipy python library. Afterwards, connected regions, larger than a certain threshold size, are selected to create binary masks. After applying the described procedure to the hue channel and the saturation channel, a number of N_h hue binary masks and N_s saturation binary masks are created, for both the ground truth image G and an input document image X. To calculate the output features, each mask in G is compared with the closest mask from the image X. For instance, if we are comparing the ith hue mask $M_{huei(G)}$ from image G, the selected mask $M_{huei(X)}$ of image X is the mask with the closest hue value and with the closest euclidean distance to the 2D center of mass from $M_{huei(G)}$. Finally, the Jaccard similarity coefficient between the masks $M_{huei(G)}$ and $M_{huei(X)}$ is the output feature.

In this case study, a section in the front of the Colombian ID cover, that represents a complex pattern with multiple colors was selected, see Fig. 3. For our use case example $\beta = 6$, image G had three binary masks with different hues $N_h = 3$ and one binary mask for saturation $N_s = 1$. The Jaccard similarity coefficients comparing masks in G and X were calculated, thus, the number of color coherence features was four (CC_1, CC_2, CC_3, CS). The binary masks for a Colombian ID document are shown in Fig. 3.

4 Evaluation

4.1 Data Set

The evaluation dataset comprised a total of 101 Colombian identity documents, obtained with the voluntary participants consent. Pictures of the documents were taken by the participants with their own smartphones, without any restrictions on the camera, light conditions or scenario. Image resolutions ranged from (580×370) to (4200×3120) pixels and 40 documents from the collected dataset presented backgrounds with low contrast. For the document verification model (module 2), the machine-learning classifier was tested and trained with features from a subset of 81 identity documents from the collected dataset (positive class). Negative class samples consisted of 40 IDs of other countries and 40 images with multiple environments and patterns. All of them aligned and cropped.

The background removal model (module 1) was built with an augmented dataset. This dataset was generated by applying geometric transformations over different backgrounds. For that purpose, 40 documents were cropped, aligned and placed over 50 different backgrounds. The process was automated through a script, which produced artificial perspectives with specific up-down, right-left tilts in the range of $-15°$ to $15°$ around each axes, and rotations in the range of $[0°, 359°]$. The final result was an augmented dataset consisting of 33382 images. For each document, a ground-truth binary mask was created, representing the desired output. The final images were resized to 128×128 pixels.

4.2 Module 1 - Document Acquisition

Background Removal: We trained a deep neural network using synthetic data augmented from the dataset described in Sect. 4.1.

This dataset was also augmented with empty backgrounds without ID Documents for training, a total of 2254 negative examples, composed of random images and 0-filled masks, were added to the dataset.

For the training, parameters were adjusted to obtain the best performance. The input was tested with both color images and grayscale images; also, a smaller, and more balanced dataset, with only 4766 images was tested. Binary cross entropy (BCE) was used as loss function as it is the default option for binary classification problems, nevertheless, a Jaccard-based loss was also tested.

The best results were obtained after 32 epochs: 98.49% accuracy for the training, 98.41% accuracy for the test, and 0.98 for the Jaccard index for the test as well. For this model, grayscale images worked better than color images as input. Additionally, the variability of the dataset proved to be more important than the size, since the smaller dataset, generated better results on pictures of ID's over real backgrounds. Finally, BCE showed better results than the Jaccard-based loss. Examples of the outputs from the final neural network configuration in a real world environment can be observed on Fig. 4.

Crop and Align Perspective: The steps of contour and corner detection were evaluated on 96 documents from the real world environment dataset, where the background was removed. In this case, we defined that a crop was successful, with two criteria. First, checking that the score of the template matching analysis was higher than 0.65, which is a good indicator of a correct perspective transformation, and second, by performing visual confirmation of the final result. With those evaluation criteria, we found an accuracy of 88.54%.

Fig. 4. Document localization process by using image semantic segmentation. Upper images are original pictures and lower images are the deep learning generated masks.

Brightness Analysis: In order to test the brightness analysis, we used a subset of 80 documents, already cropped and aligned, from the original 101 Colombian IDs dataset. We labeled samples with two classes, documents with bright spots (12) and documents without bright spots (68). $\alpha = 2$ was selected to reduce false positives. The proposed method to detect flashes yielded an accuracy of 87.5%.

4.3   Module 2 - Document Verification

Two classification models: Support Vector Machine (SVM) and Random Forest (RF) were tested for document classification, using 11 visual features explained in Sect. 3.2. Features were rescaled to a standard score. The classification tested the features of 81 colombian ID documents, against 80 negative class examples.

Table 1. Document authenticity classification with SVM and random forest.

Features	Accuracy		F1-score	
	SVM	RF	SVM	RF
All (11)	97.5%	97.7%	0.972	0.974
Global (3)	93.0%	90.7%	0.923	0.900
Local (8)	96.7%	97.3%	0.966	0.972

A two-class SVM classifier [13] with RBF kernel was trained. 5-fold cross-validation was used for train-test splits. Using all of the features available, and repeating the train test validation 10 times, an average accuracy of 97.5% with an F1-score of 0.972 was obtained. Classification results with only local or global features can be found on Table 1. In addition, a two-class random forest classifier [13], with gini index as information gain parameter was used. Training with all the features, yielded an average accuracy of 97.77% with an F1-score of 0.974.

Feature contributions for RF are shown on Fig. 5. The results from Table 1 indicate that the visual features selected for document classification are adequate for a production environment. These features can be complemented with content consistency methods or bar-code reading to perform confirmation with official sources.

As depicted Fig. 5, TMS, TML, SS, HSD, and CCS features contributed the most to document verification. We also observed that for the model trained with all the features, three of them explained 90% of the classifier decision.

Additionally, even though the prediction accuracy found when using only global features is 4.5% lower than the SVM model trained with all features, such accuracy is still practical for the proposed verification pipeline. This result encourages to explore the adaptation of global features to other documents, since they do not rely on individual document characteristics.

Threats to Validity: Our results indicate that our approach could be a practical and scalable automatic pipeline for remote onboarding processes. The average processing time to execute the document acquisition module was 0.44 s for image sizes of

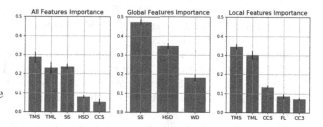

Fig. 5. Feature importance for document classification.

approximately (1200 × 850) pixels. Document verification takes in average 0.61 s. Additionally, the effort required to adapt the pipeline to other types of documents is expected to be relatively small. However, it would still require a collection of at least 80 authentic documents to train the model, which could be an impediment in many cases due to privacy concerns. For future work it would be interesting to evaluate the performance of the model with fewer training samples. A thorough exploration of the scalability of the approach to different document types is currently missing.

Further explorations on the types of forgery attacks and the degree of the pattern alterations detectable by the classification algorithm are required and could be investigated in future work.

5 Conclusion

A pipeline for identity document analysis was proposed. A module for document acquisition that integrates deep learning for background removal in complex scenarios was formulated and tested. A set of visual features designed for verification of the document type and authenticity were evaluated using machine learning classifiers. Results of this case study show the potential of the methods for complete enrollment processes. In the future we plan to verify if the proposed pipeline can be easily adapted to other document types and larger datasets.

References

1. Arlazarov, V.V., Bulatov, K., Chernov, T., Arlazarov, V.L.: MIDV-500: a dataset for identity documents analysis and recognition on mobile devices in video stream. Comput. Opt. **43**(5), 818–824 (2019)
2. Attivissimo, F., Giaquinto, N., Scarpetta, M., Spadavecchia, M.: An automatic reader of identity documents. In: Conference Proceedings - IEEE International Conference on Systems, Man and Cybernetics, vol. 2019–10, pp. 3525–3530 (2019)
3. Awal, A.M., Ghanmi, N., Sicre, R., Furon, T.: Complex document classification and localization application on identity document images. In: 2017 14th IAPR ICDAR, pp. 426–431 (2017)
4. Bradski, G.: The OpenCV Library. Dr. Dobb's Journal of Software Tools (2000)
5. Bulatov, K., Arlazarov, V.V., Chernov, T., Slavin, O., Nikolaev, D.: Smart IDReader: document recognition in video stream. In: 2017 14th IAPR (ICDAR), vol. 6, pp. 39–44. IEEE (2017)
6. Burie, J.C., et al.: ICDAR 2015 competition on smartphone document capture and OCR (SmartDoc). In: 2015 13th (ICDAR), pp. 1161–1165. IEEE (2015)
7. Chazalon, J., et al.: SmartDoc 2017 video capture: mobile document acquisition in video mode. In: 2017 14th IAPR (ICDAR), pp. 11–16. IEEE (2017)
8. Ghanmi, N., Awal, A.M.: A new descriptor for pattern matching: application to identity document verification. In: 2018 13th IAPR International Workshop on Document Analysis Systems, pp. 375–380. IEEE (2018)
9. King, D.E.: Dlib-ml: a machine learning toolkit. J. Mach. Learn. Res. **10**, 1755–1758 (2009)
10. Kopeykina, L., Savchenko, A.V.: Automatic privacy detection in scanned document images based on deep neural networks. In: Proceedings RusAutoCon 2019, pp. 1–6 (2019)
11. Park, D., Jeon, Y., Won, C.: Efficient use of local edge histogram descriptor, vol. 2, pp. 51–54 (2000)
12. Pass, G., Zabih, R., Miller, J.: Comparing images using color coherence vectors. In: Proceedings of the Fourth ACM International Conference on Multimedia. ACM (1996)
13. Pedregosa, F., et al.: Scikit-learn: machine learning in Python. J. Mach. Learn. Res. **12**, 2825–2830 (2011)

14. Ramdas, A., Garcia, N., Cuturi, M.: On Wasserstein two sample testing and related families of nonparametric tests. arXiv:1509.02237 [math, stat] (2015)
15. Ronneberger, O., Fischer, P., Brox, T.: U-Net: convolutional networks for biomedical image segmentation. arXiv:1505.04597 [cs] (2015)
16. Simon, M., Rodner, E., Denzler, J.: Fine-grained classification of identity document types with only one example. In: Proceedings of the 14th IAPR, MVA 2015, pp. 126–129 (2015)
17. Suzuki, S., et al.: Topological structural analysis of digitized binary images by border following. Comput. Vis. Graph. Image Process. **30**(1), 32–46 (1985)
18. Wang, J.: Identity authentication on mobile devices using face verification and ID image recognition. Procedia Comput. Sci. **162**, 932–939 (2020)
19. Wang, Z., Bovik, A., Sheikh, H., Simoncelli, E.: Image quality assessment: from error visibility to structural similarity. IEEE Trans. Image Process. **13**(4), 600–612 (2004)
20. Van der Weken, D., Nachtegael, M., Kerre, E.: Using similarity measures for histogram comparison. In: Bilgiç, T., De Baets, B., Kaynak, O. (eds.) IFSA 2003. LNCS, vol. 2715, pp. 396–403. Springer, Heidelberg (2003). https://doi.org/10.1007/3-540-44967-1_47

Not All Swear Words Are Used Equal: Attention over Word n-grams for Abusive Language Identification

Horacio Jesús Jarquín-Vásquez[✉], Manuel Montes-y-Gómez,
and Luis Villaseñor-Pineda

Instituto Nacional de Astrofísica, Óptica y Electrónica (INAOE), Puebla, Mexico
{horacio.jarquin,mmontesg,villasen}@inaoep.mx

Abstract. The increasing propagation of abusive language in social media is a major concern for supplier companies and governments because of its negative social impact. A large number of methods have been developed for its automatic identification, ranging from dictionary-based methods to sophisticated deep learning approaches. A common problem in all these methods is to distinguish the offensive use of swear words from their everyday and humorous usage. To tackle this particular issue we propose an attention-based neural network architecture that captures the word n-grams importance according to their context. The obtained results in four standard collections from Twitter and Facebook are encouraging, they outperform the F_1 scores from state-of-the-art methods and allow identifying a set of inherently offensive swear words, and others in which its interpretation depends on its context.

Keywords: Abusive language · Text classification · Attention mechanism · Social media

1 Introduction

The exponential growth of user interactions through social media has revolutionized the way we communicate and share information. Unfortunately, not all these interactions are constructive; it is common to see that users make use of abusive language to criticize others, disqualify their opinions, or win an argument. As a consequence, affected users may present some psychological damage, and even, in extreme cases, commit suicide [9]. This situation has stimulate the interest of social media companies and governments in the automatic identification of abusive language.

Abusive language is characterized by the presence of insults, teasing, criticism and intimidation. Mainly, it includes epithets directed at an individual's characteristic, which are personally offensive, degrading and insulting. Its identification in social media is not an easy task, the use of word filters and moderators is far from being a good and sustainable solution to the problem.

© Springer Nature Switzerland AG 2020
K. M. Figueroa Mora et al. (Eds.): MCPR 2020, LNCS 12088, pp. 282–292, 2020.
https://doi.org/10.1007/978-3-030-49076-8_27

One of the most important issues in the abusive language identification task is to distinguish between the use of swear words and vulgarities in offensive and non-offensive contexts. As an example consider the following two tweets using the word "fucking"[1]: "@USER You're a fucking idiot" and "@USER I'm so fucking ready". They clearly show that the importance and interpretation of a word is highly context dependent, and accordingly they evidence one of the reasons why traditional bag-of-words methods and deep learning models tend to generate many false positives in their predictions.

Only few works related to abusive language identification have explored the importance of words in accordance to their context; particularly, the use of attention mechanisms has been the most used approach to handle this issue [5,14]. The idea behind attention is to provide the classification model with the ability to focus on a subset of inputs (or features), handling in this way the importance of words in their context. However, this importance has been only observed at a single word level. We hypothesize that not only the interpretation of swear words is highly context dependent, but also the meaning of certain word sequences, and, therefore, that extending the use of attention to word sequences will allow capturing distinctive patterns for the abusive language identification task. As shown in the previous examples, word n-grams such as "fucking idiot", "fucking ready", and even "You're" and "I'm", are very important in discriminating offensive from non-offensive posts.

The main contribution of this work is the extraction of two groups of swear word expressions relevant for the task of abusive language identification, one consisting of inherently offensive word sequences, and another consisting of word sequences with context-dependent offensive interpretation. To extract these word patterns, we propose an attention-based deep neural network architecture that allows capturing the importance of word n-grams, and an approach to extract and visualize inherently and context-dependent offensive word sequences, through the attention weights of our proposed architecture.

2   Related Work

Several works have proposed different models and datasets for the task of automatic abusive language identification [6,9,16,18]. Among them, a great variety of features have been used to tackle this problem. Initial works used bag-of-words representations, considering word n-grams as well as character n-grams as features [4,13,16]. Aiming to improve the generalization of the classifiers, other works have also considered word embeddings as features [13,19]. More recently, some works have used sophisticated text representations by applying pre-trained ELMO and BERT models, and fine-tune their parameters to the abusive language identification task [10,12].

Regarding the classification stage, different approaches and techniques have also been proposed. These approaches could be divided in two categories; the first category relies on traditional classification algorithms such as Support Vector

---

[1] Taken from the Offensive Language Identification Dataset [18].

Machines, Naive Bayes, Logistic Regression and Random Forest [4,6,8,15,16], on the other hand, the second category includes deep learning based methods, which employ Convolutional Neural Networks (CNN) for word and character based feature extraction [2,7], Recurrent Neural Networks (RNN) for word and character dependency learning [2,5], and the combination of both for creating powerful structures that capture order information between the extracted features [19].

Finally, it is important to mention that some recent works in abusive language identification have considered deep learning methods with attention mechanisms. One of the first works introducing the attention into the task employed self-attention models to detect abuse in portal news and Wikipedia [14]. Subsequently, [5] showed that contextual attention improved the results of self-attention in this task. Contextual attention was first introduced by [17] with the use of a hierarchical contextual attention neural network, based on a Gated Recurrent Unit (GRU) architecture, and used for document classification. Motivated by the results from [5,17], in this paper we extend the use of contextual attention by proposing an attention-based deep neural network architecture that attempt to capture the word n-grams importance, and also by presenting an approach that measures and plots the relevance of word sequences in accordance to their context.

3   Proposed Method for Abusive Language Identification

Figure 1 shows the general architecture of the proposed attention-based deep neural network for abusive language identification. This architecture consists of the following four major stages.

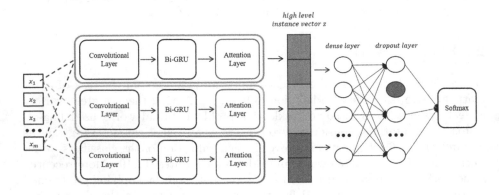

Fig. 1. Attention-based deep neural network architecture.

First stage: it corresponds to the input layer, which receives a sequence of m d-dimensional word vectors x_i; in other words, an input matrix of size $d \times m$.

Second stage: it is conformed by the convolutional layers, the bidirectional GRU layers, and the attention layers. We use an arrangement of them for each one of the considered channels, with the purpose of independently computing the weights of n-grams of different lengths. In the figure, the yellow, green, and blue rectangles correspond to the unigrams, bigrams and trigrams channels respectively.

In particular, the convolutional layer is used to extract different features of word n-grams from the input sequence X. The output of the convolutional layer passes to the bidirectional GRU layer to accomplish the sequence encoding. This layer captures word n-grams annotations by summarizing information from both directions. To get a word n-gram annotation h_i (Eq. 1), the forward and backward hidden states of the bidirectional GRU are concatenated, this summarizes the information of the whole sequence centered around the word n-gram annotation.

$$h_i = [\overrightarrow{h_i}, \overleftarrow{h_i}] \tag{1}$$

Since not all word n-grams contributes equally for the meaning and representation of an instance, we used the attention layer to extract the importance of each word n-gram, and combine them with its corresponding word n-gram annotation h_i, forming a new instance vector v. Below are listed the attention mechanism equations.

$$u_i = tanh(W_h.h_i + b_h) \tag{2}$$

$$\alpha_i = exp(u_i^T u_h)/\sum_j exp(u_j^T u_h) \tag{3}$$

$$v = \sum_j \alpha_j h_j \tag{4}$$

To obtained the instance vector v (refer to Formula 4), we first feed each word n-gram annotation h_i to a one Multi-Layer Perceptron (MLP) layer, getting this way a hidden representation u_i (Formula 2) of h_i. Later, we measure the word n-gram importance as the similarity of u_i with the word n-gram level context vector u_h and get a normalized importance weight α_i (Formula 3) through a softmax function. After that, the instance vector v (Formula 4) is computed as a weighted sum of the word n-gram annotation h_i and its importance α_i; the word n-gram context vector u_h is randomly initialized and jointly learned during the training process.

Third stage: it performs the concatenation of the output vector of each channel (instance vector v), forming a new vector z that contains a high level representation of the different word n-grams; this vector is used as input for the instance classification.

Fourth stage: it includes the classification layers; three layers handle the final classification, a dense layer, followed by a dropout layer and a fully-connected softmax layer to obtain the class probabilities and get the final classification.

4   Experimental Settings

This section presets the experimental settings. First, it introduces the four used datasets, which correspond to Twitter and Facebook collections. Then, with the purpose of facilitating the replicability of our results, it shows the implementation details of the proposed attention-based deep neural network.

4.1   Datasets for Abusive Language Identification

Abusive language can be of different types, depending to the target and severity of the insults. Accordingly, different collections have used for its study. Below we present a brief description of the four datasets we used in our experiments. From now on we will refer to them as DS1, DS2, DS3, and DS4.

DS1 [16] and DS2 [6] were some of the first large-scale datasets for abusive tweet detection; DS1 focuses on the identification of racist and sexist tweets, whereas DS2 focuses on identifying tweets with abusive language and hate speech. On the other hand, DS3 [18] and DS4 [9] were used in the SemEval-2019 Task 6, and in the First Workshop on Trolling, Aggression and Cyberbullying respectively. DS3 focuses on identifying offensive tweets, whereas DS4 focuses on identifying Overtly Aggressive (OAG) and Covertly Aggressive (CAG) Facebook posts and comments.

Table 1 resumes information about the classes distribution of the four collections. It is important to notice their high imbalance, which indeed correspond to their real-life occurrence.

Table 1. The classes distribution of the four used datasets.

Dataset	Classes distribution			Total
DS1	Racist	Sexist	Neither	16,914
	1,972	3,383	11,559	
DS2	Offensive	Hate	None	25,112
	19,326	1,428	4,288	
DS3	Offensive	Non-offensive		13,240
	4,400	8,840		
DS4	OAG	CAG	NAG	12,000
	2,708	4,240	5,052	

4.2   Implementation Details

Different text preprocessing operations were applied: user mentions and links were replaced by default words; hashtags were segmented by words in order to enrich vocabulary (e.g. #BuildTheWall - build the wall); all emojis were converted into words; stop words were removed, except personal pronouns, which have been recognized as useful for this task; all text were lowercased and non-alphabetical characters were removed. On the other hand, for word representation we used pre-trained fastText embeddings [3], trained with subword information on Common Crawl.

Table 2. Proposed attention-based deep neural network hyperparameters.

Layer	Settings				
Input	Sequence length		75		
Embedding	Word dimensions		300		
Convolutional	Kernel sizes	{1, 2, 3}	Filters	{256, 256, 256}	
Bi-GRU	Units	{75, 74, 73}	Dropout rate	20%	
Attention	Neurons		{75, 74, 73}		
Concatenation	Vector size		222		
Dense	Neurons	128	Activation function	relu	
Dropout	Rate		20%		
Dense	Neurons	# Classes	Activation function	softmax	

Table 2 presents the hyperparameter settings of our proposed NN architecture. The network was trained with a learning rate of 0.001, using Adam optimizer, and a total of 10 epochs. In order to compare the robustness of our proposal, we consider two baseline architectures: a simple GRU network, which receives words as input but does not use word n-grams nor attention, and a second architecture that employs the same GRU network but including one attention layer. These two baselines architectures and our proposed architecture are referred in the experiments as GRU, GRU+ATT, and CNN-GRU+ATT respectively. It is important to mention that both baseline architectures used the same hyperparameter settings, skipping the attention, concatenation, and convolutional layers, respectively.

5   Results

This section is organized in two subsections. Section 5.1 presents the quantitative results of the experiment; it compares the proposed architecture and baseline approaches with state-of-the-art results. Section 5.2 describes the analysis of the results using the attention word sequences visualization, and presents as qualitative results a list of inherently and context-dependent offensive word sequences.

5.1   Effectiveness of the Proposed Architecture

Table 3 shows the results of the proposed NN architecture (CNN-GRU+ATT) as well as two baselines results obtained by the GRU and GRU+ATT simplified architectures. For sake of comparison, we used two different evaluation measures commonly used in the abusive language identification task; for DS1, DS2, and DS3 the macro-average F_1 score, and for DS4 the weighted macro-average F_1 score. The results indicate that the use of the *contextual attention* outperformed the base GRU network (column 3 vs column 2) by at least a margin of 3%. In addition, the use of *attention over word n-grams* outperformed the use of word attention (columns 4 vs columns 3) by at least a margin of 2%. We compared GRU+ATT vs GRU and CNN-GRU+ATT vs GRU+ATT with McNemar's statistical test and Student's t-test, obtaining statistically significant values with $p \leq 0.05$ and $p \leq 0.01$ respectively.

Table 3 also compares the results from our proposed architecture (CNN-GRU+ATT) and state-of-the-art. It shows that the CNN-GRU+ATT neural network obtained better results in 3 out of 4 datasets, and, therefore, it allows concluding that the use of attention over word n-grams is useful for discriminating between offensive and non-offensive contexts. It is important to note that the result from [1] in DS4 only improved our results by margin of 1%. That work explores techniques of data augmentation and proposes a deep neural network trained on pseudo labeled examples. Despite of its better results, it lacks of interpretability, a key aspect of the current proposal.

Table 3. Comparison results from GRU, GRU+ATT, CNN-GRU+ATT and state-of-the-art methods in four datasets for abusive language identification (*for DS1, DS2 and DS3 the macro-average F_1 was used, and for DS4 the weighted macro-average F_1*)

Dataset	GRU	GRU+ATT	CNN-GRU+ATT	State-of-the-art
DS1	0.76 ± 0.0078	0.81 ± 0.0067	**0.83 ± 00.0066**	0.82 [19]
DS2	0.74 ± 0.0081	0.77 ± 0.0086	**0.79 ± 00.0072**	0.77 [11]
DS3	0.75 ± 0.0062	0.79 ± 0.0059	**0.84 ± 00.0083**	0.83 [10]
DS4	0.58 ± 0.0078	0.61 ± 0.0081	0.63 ± 0.0078	**0.64** [1]

5.2 Inherently and Context-Dependent Offensive Word Sequences

One of the major advantages of attention mechanisms is the interpretability of decisions. As part of this interpretability, we present the extraction and visualization of inherently and context-dependent offensive word sequences.

To extract the importance of the word sequences in accordance to their context, we limit their analysis to an instance level; to that end, the input text is evaluated by the model, and the normalized importance weights for all word n-grams (α_i) are computed. At this step, we process each channel (unigrams, bigrams and trigrams) separately. Then, for visualization, we associate a color intensity to each weight value, the greater the weight (α_i) of a word n-gram, the greater its color intensity. In the case of n-grams greater than one, some words may be contained in several sequences, causing a problem of visualization, to solve it we decide only displaying the word sequences with the greatest weights.

Offensive
user user the fascist are anti american communist scum like yourself now go fuck yourself you piece of human garbage usa maga antifa are terrorist
user radical islam is pile of manure that destroys human freedom human life human expression and creates endless divisiveness
Non-Offensive
user fuck didn realize it until got on and finally played it again
user user user would rather not be involved in christianity islam debate

Fig. 2. Attention visualization for offensive and non-offensive texts from DS1 and DS2.

Figure 2 presents some examples of posts, containing words such as `fuck` and `islam`, which correspond to offensive and non-offensive posts. The produced visualization is able to show that the interpretation of words is context dependent, therefore, the presence of swear words such as fuck, or words commonly used in racist speech such as islam, not necessary indicates an aggression; it is the presence of word sequences like `radical islam` and `go fuck yourself` that provide a better way to explain offensive instances.

Table 4. Examples of inherently and context-dependent offensive word sequences.

	Unigrams	Bigrams	Trigrams
DS1 inherently offensive	dick, bitch, nigga, dumb, idiot	fuck you, woman cant, fuck off, you idiot, stupid woman	radical islam on, sexist but fuck, fuck off my, sluts and cunt, fuck her like
DS1 context dependent	islam, cooking, fuck, black, sucks	they deserved, like islam, woman prefer, islam is, even woman	user islam is, a woman wants, the jews that, say about woman, the muslim immigrants
DS3 inherently offensive	asshole, idiot, nigga, nigger, bitch	evil nazi, fuck you, the nigga, doggie girlfriend, stupid black	go fuck yourself, an ugly black, shut the fuck, buying pussy bitch, she is shit
DS3 context dependent	white, fool, black, fuck, fucking	immigrant children, user fuck, who fucked, this shit, all woman	what the fuck, user oh shit, people like you, blaming woman not, person of color

With the intention of moving one step further in the understanding of aggressive speech, we extracted a set of inherently and context-dependent offensive expressions based on their computed weights. Basically, we define a word n-gram as inherently offensive if it shows high attention values with a small standard deviation, that is, if its presence was always important for the network to discriminate offensive from non-offensive messages. In contrast, context-dependent offensive n-grams are those with the greatest standard deviations, suggesting that their occurrences not always were important for the network decisions. Considering these criteria, we extracted 20 word sequences for each channel and dataset. Table 4 presents five examples of each type from the DS1 (racism and sexism) and DS3 (general offenses) collections. In spite of their clear differences due to the type of abusive language, they show interesting coincidences. For example, swear words related to low intelligence or sex tend to be inherently offensive (e.g., `idiot`, `dump`, `bitch` and `dick`), and, on the other hand, colloquially words and expressions such as `fucking`, `black`, `what the fuck`, and `this shit` can be used in both contexts.

6   Conclusions and Future Work

One of the main problems in abusive language identification is to distinguish between the use of swear words and vulgarities in offensive and non-offensive contexts. To tackle this issue we proposed an attention-based neural network architecture that captures the importance of word n-grams according to their context. Through the use of this architecture, we were able to extract and visualize inherently and context-dependent offensive word sequences. The results obtained in four collections, considering different kinds of aggressive speech, were encouraging, they improved state-of-the-art results in 3 out of 4 datasets, and, therefore, allowed concluding that the use of attention over word n-grams is useful for discriminating between offensive and non-offensive contexts.

As future work we plan to explore the combination of general and specific domain word vectors, with the intention of obtaining a higher quality input text representation. In addition, we consider the use of the inherently and context-dependent offensive word sequences as search keywords, to bootstrap a new abusive language dataset. Finally, we consider the application of the proposed architecture in other tasks where the interpretation of word sequences is highly context dependent such as the detection of deception or the detection of depressed social media users.

Acknowledgements. We thank CONACyT-Mexico for partially supporting this work under project grant CB-2015-01-257383 and scholarship 925996.

References

1. Aroyehun, T., Gelbukh, A.: Aggression detection in social media: using deep neural networks, data augmentation, and pseudo labeling. In: Proceedings of the First Workshop on Trolling, Aggression and Cyberbullying TRAC - 1 (2018)

2. Badjatiya, P., Gupta, S., Gupta, M., Varma, V.: Deep learning for hate speech detection in tweets. In: Proceedings of the 26th International Conference on World Wide Web Companion, pp. 759–760 (2017)
3. Bojanowski, P., Grave, E., Joulin, A., Mikolov, T.: Enriching word vectors with subword information. Trans. Assoc. Comput. Linguist. **5**, 135–146 (2017)
4. Burnap, P., Williams, M.L.: Us and them: identifying cyber hate on Twitter across multiple protected characteristics. EPJ Data Sci.EPJ Data Sci. **5**(1), 11 (2016). https://doi.org/10.1140/epjds/s13688-016-0072-6
5. Chakrabarty, T., Gupta, K., Muresan, S.: Pay "Attention" to your context when classifying abusive language. In: Proceedings of the Third Workshop on Abusive Language Online, pp. 70–79 (2019)
6. Davidson, T., Warmsley, D., Macy, M., Weber, I.: Automated hate speech detection and the problem of offensive language. In: Eleventh International AAAI Conference on Web and Social Media (2017)
7. Gambäck, B., Sikdar, U.: Using convolutional neural networks to classify hate-speech. In: Proceedings of the First Workshop on Abusive Language Online, pp. 85–90. Association for Computational Linguistics (2017)
8. Gaydhani, A., Doma, V., Kendre, S., Bhagwat, L.: Detecting hate speech and offensive language on Twitter using machine learning: an N-gram and TFIDF based approach. In: IEEE International Advance Computing Conference (2018)
9. Kumar, R., Reganti, A.N., Bhatia, A., Maheshwari, T.: Aggression-annotated corpus of Hindi-English code-mixed data. In: Nicoletta Calzolari Proceedings of the Eleventh International Conference on Language Resources and Evaluation (LREC 2018). European Language Resources Association ELRA (2018)
10. Liu, P., Li, W., Zou, L.: NULI at SemEval-2019 Task 6: transfer learning for offensive language detection using bidirectional transformers. In: Proceedings of the 13th International Workshop on Semantic Evaluation SemEval (2019)
11. MacAvaney, S., Yao, H., Yang, E., Russell, K., Goharian, N., Frieder, O.: Hate speech detection: challenges and solutions. PLoS One **14**, e0221152 (2019). https://doi.org/10.1371/0221152
12. Nikolov, A., Radivchev, V.: Nikolov-Radivchev at SemEval-2019 task 6: offensive tweet classification with BERT and ensembles. In: Proceedings of the 13th International Workshop on Semantic Evaluation SemEval (2019)
13. Nobata, C., Tetreault, J., Thomas, A., Mehdad, Y., Chang, Y.: Abusive language detection in online user content. In: Proceedings of the 25th International Conference on World Wide Web, pp. 145–153 (2016)
14. Pavlopoulos J., Malakasiotis, P., Androutsopoulos, I.: Deeper attention to abusive user content moderation. In: Proceedings of the 2017 Conference on Empirical Methods in Natural Language Processing (2017)
15. Schmidt, A., Wiegand, M.: A survey on hate speech detection using natural language processing. In: International Workshop on Natural Language Processing for Social Media, pp. 1–10 (2017)
16. Waseem, Z., Hovy, D.: Hateful symbols or hateful people? Predictive features for hate speech detection on Twitter. In: Proceedings of the NAACL Student Research Workshop, pp. 88–93 (2016)
17. Yang, Z., Yang, D., Dyer, C., He, X., Smola, A., Hovy, E.: Hierarchical attention networks for document classification. In Proceedings of the 2016 Conference of the North American Chapter of the Association for Computational Linguistics: Human Language Technologies, pp. 1480–1489 (2016)

18. Zampieri, M., Malmasi, S., Nakov, P., Rosenthal, S., Farra, N., Kumar, R.: SemEval-2019 task 6: identifying and categorizing offensive language in social media (OffensEval). In: Proceedings of the International Workshop on Semantic Evaluation SemEval (2019)
19. Gangemi, A., Navigli, R., Vidal, M.-E., Hitzler, P., Troncy, R., Hollink, L., Tordai, A., Alam, M. (eds.): ESWC 2018. LNCS, vol. 10843. Springer, Cham (2018). https://doi.org/10.1007/978-3-319-93417-4

Gender Identification in Social Media Using Transfer Learning

Aquilino Francisco Sotelo[1] , Helena Gómez-Adorno[2]([✉]) ,
Oscar Esquivel-Flores[2] , and Gemma Bel-Enguix[3]

[1] Posgrado en Ciencia e Ingeniería de la Computación, UNAM, Mexico City, Mexico
aquilino@comunidad.unam.mx
[2] Instituto de Investigación en Matemáticas Aplicadas y en Sistemas, UNAM,
Mexico City, Mexico
{helena.gomez,oscar.esquievls}@iimas.unam.mx
[3] Instituto de Ingeniería, UNAM, Mexico City, Mexico
gbele@iingen.unam.mx

Abstract. Social networks have modified the way we communicate. It is now possible to talk to a large number of people we have never met. Knowing the traits of a person from what he/she writes has become a new area of computational linguistics called Author Profiling. In this paper, we introduce a method for applying transfer learning to address the gender identification problem, which is a subtask of Author Profiling. Systems that use transfer learning are trained in a large number of tasks and then tested in their ability to learn new tasks. An example is to classify a new image into different possible classes, giving an example of each class. This differs from the traditional approach of standard machine learning techniques, which are trained in a single task and are evaluated in new examples of that task. The aim is to train a gender identification model on Twitter users using only their text samples in Spanish. The difference with other related works consists in the evaluation of different preprocessing techniques so that the transfer learning-based fine-tuning is more efficient.

Keywords: Author profiling · Natural Language Processing · Transfer learning · Classification

1 Introduction

Author profiling (PA) is a Natural Language Processing (NLP) task that aims to determine the characteristics of the author(s) of a given text, such as their gender, age, emotional state, personality, among others. AP can be performed on formal and informal textual sources. Formal texts have a certain structure and

This paper has been partially supported by the PAPIIT-UNAM projects 401219, TA100520, IA-104720, and CONACyT project A1-S-27780.

K. M. Figueroa Mora et al. (Eds.): MCPR 2020, LNCS 12088, pp. 293–303, 2020.
https://doi.org/10.1007/978-3-030-49076-8_28

follow rules while informal texts do not follow rules and are not standardized. A good example of the latter are social networks.

The writing style on social media has special features [10] that make NLP tasks extremely complex processes: the abbreviation rules are not always followed, different use of punctuation marks, new characters are included such as # (*hashtag*), use of the sign @ to mention users, etc.

Given the importance and the enormous amount of information that is produced daily in social media, it is necessary to have computational methods that allow us to automatically analyze the information generated in these networks.

With the information that people publish and consume in their social media, companies can profile their clients and governments can improve security procedures, for example, identifying potential cases of pedophilia, virtual kidnappings, among others. In fact, the providers of these services already profile users, for example Twitter aims to know the patterns of use and personalization of content. For these reasons, the aim of this work is to develop an automatic gender identification model of Twitter users using transfer learning techniques. We also measure and evaluate the impact of text preprocessing on the accuracy of the author profiling model.

The work is presented in 5 sections, including this introduction. Section 2 describes the methods to carry out feature extraction and the machine learning algorithms typically used in AP, in Sect. 3 we introduce the concepts of transfer learning and explain the architecture used in this work, in Sect. 4, the methodology for author profiling and experimental results is presented. The conclusions of this paper are enunciated in the Sect. 5.

2   Related Work

Several supervised learning techniques were used to model author profiles in different text sources. Supervised learning classifiers employ a set of input-output pairs, through which a decision function is learned that associates a class label with a new data within the established classes. Author profiling (AP) consists in identifying the demographic features of the author of a text [6]. These features are those that describe the author in terms of gender, age, level of study, nationality, socio-economic level, among others. So it can be concluded that AP is a multiclass classification problem.

The use of supervised learning algorithms for AP is shown in [15]. *Decision Functions* are a technique to perform a binary classification, whose training consists of finding decision functions from input-output pairs. *Logistic Regression* is used for multiclass classification problems to predict the probability that the data belong to one or another class. *Support Vector Machines* is a technique used in the context of the AP for binary classification; data are linearly separable by several planes. *Neural Networks* are another resource for AP; the goal of the method is to approximate a function $g()$, represented by the neural network, to a function $f()$ as much as possible. This approximate function is the one used classify. *Convolutional Networks* represent an important tool for AP, since they are trained with large sets of information, in addition to setting a feature extractor.

2.1 Features Extraction

Analyzing in detail the large amount of information currently generated in the form of written texts is very complicated. Therefore, it is of interest to create representations of these documents, that is, to obtain their representative characteristics. The features obtained from a text are specific terms that allow analyzing and extracting useful patterns or knowledge from analyzed documents. In the past, this task was performed by linguists, limited to a little thorough manual processing. However, with the advance of science and technology, the methods for the extraction of characteristics changed. Some text representation schemes are:

1. **Bag of words.** In order to deal with complete documents it is necessary to use a computationally viable structure. To fulfil this, we see the documents as strings [7]. Let $S = s_1, s_2, ..., s_k$ be a string, where a word is a substring of S of length 1, which can refer to: an item in the text, an item in lowercase or uppercase, the word with its part of speech label (POS), word lemma, any other variant of the word.
2. **N-grams:** Let $S = s_1, s_2, ..., s_k$ be a string. The N-grams are defined as substrings of S of length N. The 1-gramas are called unigrams, the 2-gramas are called bigrams, and so on. There are two types of N-grams, those of words and those of characters. Word N-grams refer to continuous N-words in the document. Instead, character N-grams refer to the N-characters within the word limit without spaces.
3. **Syntactic N-grams:** Syntactic N-grams try to capture the linguistic structure of a text by organizing the words into nested components in order to show through arrows which words depend on others.

2.2 Weighting Schemes

To obtain a representation of a document, a preprocessing is carried out to see it as a vector. Each dimension of the vector stands for a feature of the document. Each feature is represented by assigning some weight according to its relevance, this process is called *weighing scheme*. The most relevant are described below:

1. **Boolean model and Term Frequency (TF):** There are some very intuitive ways to assign weight, such as identifying whether a term appears or not, counting how many times a term appears in a text and assigning a weight to each term depending on the number of occurrences it has.
2. **Inverse Document Frequency:** To treat high frequencies of certain words (due to the context they are constantly repeated), the weight of the Term Frequency (TF) is reduced by means of the Inverse Document Frequency (IDF). This compensates the weight depending on the appearance of the word in many documents or not. The Inverse Document Frequency of a term t is defined with total frequency in the collection with the expression:

$$idf_t = log(N/df_f).$$

3. **TF-IDF:** It is the product of the Term Frequency (TF) by the Inverse Document Frequency (IDF). Its purpose is to provide a measure that expresses the relevance of words in such a way that it is possible to distinguish between those that describe the document and those that do not. To assign a weight to the words in a document, the frequency of the words is calculated and, in the total of documents, the weight is calculated with the following expression

$$tf - idf_{t,d} = tf_{t,d} \times idf_t$$

4. **Word embeddings:** A different method for weighting schemes are word vectors (*word embeddings*), that use two main approaches: discrete and distributional. The idea of *discrete approach* is to represent a word in a vector of dimension n with 1's and the others with 0's; these are also known as *one-hot vectors*, where n is the number of words in the vocabulary. The *distributional approach* takes into account the similarity between the vectors themselves, when a word appears in a text its context is the set of words that appear near it (a fixed size window). This builds a dense vector for each word, making it similar to the word vectors. The most used methods with this technique are *Word2vec* [13] and *GloVe* [14].

3   Transfer Learning

Transfer learning is a subfield within machine learning that has been studied for more than three decades [2]. It tackles the ability to take advantage of pre-existing data sets when you want to learn from new data. One method that has proven to be effective for obtaining knowledge is the pre-training technique with large amounts of previously available data and the subsequent fine tuning of the pre-trained model based on data from new tasks [5]. This pre-training is also known as *few-shot learning*. In transfer learning, first it is trained a neural network on a given data set and a specific task, then the features learned by the network are reused, transferred to a second network to be trained in another task and a different data set.

The transfer learning technique consists in taking advantage of the weights of an already trained neural network and adjust them to solve other tasks with only few examples [16,17]. The types of strategy to perform transfer learning with a new data set are:

- **Fixed feature extractor**: A pre-trained neural network is taken and the last fully connected layers are removed, then the features are extracted with a fixed extractor for a new dataset. Finally, a linear classifier (for example SVM) is trained for the new dataset.
- **Fine tuning**. In addition to replacing and re-training the classifier, the weights of the pre-trained network are adjusted by continuing back propagation.
- **Pre-trained models**. It consists of taking advantage of the final control points of the neural network already trained to make adjustments.

To know the type of transfer learning that is more suitable to be carried out, the following criteria are taken into account:

- The new dataset is small and similar to the original dataset so it can lead to overfitting the model, fine tuning does not work here. Therefore it is best to train a linear classifier.
- The new dataset is large and similar to the original dataset. As there is more information, the risk of overfitting is low, therefore fine tuning can be applied.
- The dataset is small but very different from the original dataset. Because there is little data, it is best to train a linear classifier. As it is different from the original dataset, it may be very different from its specific characteristics.
- The new dataset is large and very different from the original. As there is enough data and they are different from the original it is best to apply the strategy of pre-trained models.

According to [4] there are two strategies for transfer learning for text:

- **Feature based:** it consists on pre-training vectors that capture the additional context through other tasks. New vectors are obtained for each layer that are then used as characteristics, concatenated with the word vectors or with the intermediate layers, an example of this is *ELMo* [12].
- **Fine tuning:** It consists on pre-training some architecture in an objective language model before refining it for a supervised subsequent task, introducing a minimum number of specific parameters of the task, and training in subsequent tasks simply by refining the pre-trained parameters [8].

In our case, we have a relatively small corpus to perform author profiling, so our strategy is to use the *Fixed feature extractor* technique. Bellow we describe the algorithm for extracting features.

3.1 Universal Sentence Encoder

Here we describe the transfer learning based algorithm we used to extract features for performing author profiling, which is called *Universal Sentence Encoder* (USE) [3]. Although this method is not designed specifically to perform author profiling, it has certain characteristics that can be used for this task. The *Universal Sentence Encoder* encodes text in high-dimensional vectors so that it can be used for text classification, semantic similarity, clustering, and other natural language tasks. The model is trained in a variety of text data sources and a variety of tasks in order to dynamically accommodate a wide variety of natural language comprehension tasks. Specifically, USE has two models to encode documents in word vectors, one makes use of the architecture based on averages called *Deep Averaging Network* (DAN) [9], while the other is based on a convolutional neural network for document classification [11]. These architectures are detailed below for a better understanding:

1. **Deep Averaging Network:** This architecture works in three steps:

– Average the vectors associated to a token sequence
– Pass the average through one or more layers of a Feed Forward
– Make the linear classification in the last layer

2. **Convolutional Neural Network:** This type of network, receives a a document as a sequence of vectors in the input layer. It applies the average sampling (*average pooling*) to convert the word vectors into a document vector representation of fixed length. Document vectors are obtained after averaging the word vectors through one or more feed forward layers with fully connected layers.

For this work we used a USE model trained in multiple tasks across 16 languages, including Spanish. USE receives as input a text of variable length in any of the languages in which it was trained and the output is a vector of 512 dimensions. The USE model we use is available from the *TensorFlowHub*[1] page and can be freely downloaded. In addition to this model, there are several versions of trained USE models with different objectives, including multilingual, size/performance and question-answer systems.

So, in our approach USE receives a 100 tweets samples for each user. In this way the convolutional network will transform them into a vector of 512 dimensions, using the language model that we had already learned and updating with the new textual samples from *Twitter*.

4   Experimental Settings and Results

In this section, we describe the experiments carried out in order to obtain the author profile of Twitter users. First, we describe the evaluation corpus, then *baseline* results are presented, and finally results are shown using our proposed methodology. This baseline results are obtained by the combination of the different types of features (bag or words and N-grams), trained on two classification algorithms and several preprocessing variants (without emojis, without slangs, etc.). For all baseline experiments, the TF-IDF (mentioned above) weighting scheme is used.

4.1   Corpus Description

For training and evaluating our AP approach we used the corpus of PAN2017 competition [15], which was compiled from Twitter in Spanish. Gender and age information has been provided by the users themselves based on an online questionnaire. The corpus consists of 600 users of various nationalities: Mexican, Colombian, Peruvian, Argentine, Chilean, Venezuelan. 50% are male and the other 50% female.

---

[1] https://tfhub.dev/google/universal-sentence-encoder-multilingual/1.

Gender	Authors	Tweets
Male	2100	21000
Female	2100	21000
Total	4200	42000

4.2 Experimental Settings and Results

We performed several experiments considering bag of words and character N-grams as features. For each feature set we evaluated the impact of specific preprocessing strategies. The author profiling models obtained with the different settings were evaluated in terms of *F-1*, *precision*, *recall* and *accuracy*. Table 1 shows the results obtained with the logistic regression classification algorithm. The *Characteristics* column indicates whether the word bag (BoW) or character N-gram (N-char) is used, the *Dim* column indicates the amount of features extracted and therefore features vector dimensionality. Accuracy assessment measures (STD, the standard deviation of accuracy) are computed. The *Preprocessing* column indicates which strategy was followed in each experiment; in this case *NONE* indicates that no preprocessing was performed in that experiment, *without Emojis* indicates that the emojis were removed, as well as URL's, Hashtags, etc. It can be seen that the preprocessing strategy with which the best results are obtained is when user mentions are removed, which allows to infer that these are the ones that provide less information regarding the gender of the person who wrote the tweet.

Table 1. Results of experiments performed to predict gender using bag of words and logistic regression classifier.

Characteristics	Dim.	Accuracy	STD	F-1	Precision	Recall	Preprocessing
BoW	199114	0.6923	0.0287	0.6927	0.6947	0.6923	NONE
BoW	199114	0.6926	0.0289	0.6930	0.6951	0.6926	Without emoticons
BoW	186798	0.6909	0.0318	0.6913	0.6934	0.6909	Without hashtags
BoW	**166070**	**0.6976**	**0.0299**	**0.6979**	**0.6994**	**0.6976**	**Without mentions**
BoW	43089	0.6090	0.0680	0.6409	0.7273	0.6090	Without slangs
BoW	136731	0.6926	0.0289	0.6930	0.6951	0.6926	Without URLs
BoW	199226	0.6925	0.0288	0.6929	0.6950	0.6925	Without emojis
BoW	27137	0.6497	0.0533	0.6830	0.7836	0.6497	ALL

Table 2 presents results of the gender identification using character 3-gram as feature set and logistic regression classification algorithms. It is observed that the best results are also found when removing the mentions of users, however when slangs are removed the algorithm performance drops considerably.

Table 2. Results of experiments performed to predict gender using character N-grams and the logistic regression classifier.

Characteristics	Dim.	Accuracy	STD	F-1	Precision	Recall	Preprocessing
N-char	2550956	0.6833	0.0248	0.6837	0.6858	0.6833	NONE
N-char	2545770	0.6836	0.0243	0.6841	0.6862	0.6836	Without emoticons
N-char	**2309400**	**0.6874**	**0.0279**	**0.6878**	**0.6896**	**0.6874**	**Without mentions**
N-char	2470050	0.6811	0.0289	0.6815	0.6839	0.6811	Without hashtags
N-char	613817	0.5677	0.0537	0.6284	0.7685	0.5677	Without slangs
N-char	2324031	0.6817	0.0251	0.6821	0.6842	0.6817	Without emojis
N-char	1461457	0.6836	0.0243	0.6841	0.6862	0.6836	Without URLs
N-char	276872	0.6240	0.0454	0.6717	0.7990	0.6240	ALL

Table 3 presents the evaluation measures of accuracy, recall, precision and F-1 score obtained by the Support Vector Machine when trained on the BOW feature set. It can be seen that the best results are obtained by removing the mentions of users and the worst when the *slangs* are removed with a difference between them of approximately 10%.

Table 3. Results of the experiments performed to predict gender using bag of words and support vector machine classifier.

Characteristics	Dim.	Accuracy	STD	F-1	Precision	Recall	Preprocessing
BoW	199114	0.6926	0.0294	0.6933	0.6964	0.6926	NONE
BoW	199226	0.6925	0.0293	0.6931	0.6963	0.6925	Without emojis
BoW	186798	0.6933	0.0290	0.6939	0.6971	0.6933	Without hashtags
BoW	**166070**	**0.6981**	**0.0294**	**0.6986**	**0.7009**	**0.6981**	**Without mentions**
BoW	199114	0.6925	0.0296	0.6932	0.6963	0.6925	Without emoticons
BoW	43089	0.5939	0.0595	0.6292	0.7236	0.5939	Without slangs
BoW	136731	0.6925	0.0296	0.6932	0.6963	0.6925	Without URLs
BoW	276872	0.6219	0.0391	0.6753	0.8157	0.6219	ALL

Table 4 presents the results of the gender identification using character 3-grams and as a classification algorithm the Support Vector Machines. Likewise, it is observed that the best results are obtained by removing the mentions of users and the worst results when the *slangs* are removed. However, in the case of characters 3-gram, accuracy difference between the two is approximately 15%.

4.3 Experimental Settings and Results Using Transfer Learning

Table 5 presents results of gender identification using *Universal Sentence Encoder* (USE) to obtain 512-dimensional feature vectors for each user, that is, the 100 tweets are reduced to one 512-dimensional vector. The logistic regression is used as classification algorithm. Table structure is the same as the previous ones and in this case dimensionality of the feature vector is always 512. We present the measures of accuracy, recall, precision and F-1 score. It is observed that the best results in terms of accuracy are obtained by removing the mentions and the worst by replacing the *slangs*.

Table 4. Results of the experiments performed to predict gender using character N-gram and the support vector machine classifier.

Characteristics	Dim.	Accuracy	STD	F-1	Precision	Recall	Preprocessing
N-char	2550956	0.6817	0.0269	0.6824	0.6858	0.6817	None
N-char	2545770	0.6822	0.0270	0.6830	0.6863	0.6822	Without emoticons
N-char	**2309400**	**0.6930**	**0.0296**	**0.6938**	**0.6975**	**0.6930**	**Without mentions**
N-char	2470050	0.6814	0.0261	0.6821	0.6856	0.6814	Without hashtags
N-char	2324031	0.6822	0.0270	0.6830	0.6863	0.6822	Without emojis
N-char	613817	0.5417	0.0314	0.6354	0.8286	0.5417	Without slangs
N-char	1461457	0.6822	0.0270	0.6830	0.6863	0.6822	Without URLs
N-char	27137	0.6517	0.0547	0.6812	0.7723	0.6517	ALL

Table 5. Results of experiments using transfer learning features with the logistic regression classifier to identify gender

Characteristics	Dim.	Accuracy	STD	F-1	Precision	Recall	Preprocessing
USE	512	0.6986	0.0222	0.6989	0.6854	0.6998	NONE
USE	512	0.6977	0.0263	0.6981	0.6808	0.7002	Without emojis
USE	512	0.6989	0.0213	0.6991	0.6854	0.7001	Without emoticons
USE	512	0.7041	0.0241	0.7042	0.6946	0.7036	Without hashtags
USE	512	**0.7156**	**0.0255**	**0.7158**	**0.6972**	**0.7198**	**Without mentions**
USE	512	0.6794	0.0459	0.6856	0.7745	0.6864	Without slangs
USE	512	0.7001	0.0265	0.7004	0.6895	0.7005	Without URLs
USE	512	0.6864	0.0489	0.6900	0.7598	0.7029	ALL

Table 6 presents results of gender identification using *Universal Sentence Encoder* (USE) to obtain 512-dimensional word vectors and support vector machine as classification algorithm. Evaluation measures of accuracy, recall, precision and F-1 score are presented. As with the previous classifier, it is observed that the best results in terms of accuracy are obtained by removing the mentions and the worst by replacing the *slangs*. Although the results are in accordance with those obtained with traditional characteristics in terms of better and worse preprocessing, we can observe that with Universal Sentence Encoder the difference between them does not exceed 3%.

Table 6. Results of experiments using transfer learning with the support vector machine classifier to identify gender

Characteristic	Dim.	Accuracy	STD	F-1	Precision	Recall	Preprocessing
USE	512	0.7068	0.0218	0.7072	0.6838	0.7124	NONE
USE	512	0.7037	0.0281	0.7043	0.6705	0.7137	Without emojis
USE	512	0.7061	0.0213	0.7064	0.6833	0.7115	Without emoticons
USE	512	0.7080	0.0211	0.7084	0.6856	0.7134	Without hashtags
USE	512	**0.7198**	**0.0267**	**0.7201**	**0.6951**	**0.7270**	**Without mentions**
USE	512	0.6955	0.0408	0.6974	0.7340	0.7207	Without slangs
USE	512	0.7009	0.0277	0.7010	0.6987	0.6974	Without URLs
USE	512	0.6992	0.0485	0.7020	0.7563	0.7201	ALL

5 Conclusions

In this paper, we introduced an approach to perform the gender identification of Twitter users using transfer learning. The transfer learning technique is useful when there is no much data for properly training machine learning algorithms. In this case, we had available a corpus of 4200 Twitter users, which is relatively low for training from scratch a deep learning model.

Our approach is based on the *Universal Sentence Encoder* model to obtain low dimensional vectors of documents (Users' tweets) and use them as features to perform author profiling. To evaluate the quality of the vectors (representing all the *tweets* of a user) obtained by USE, we used them as features for training two machine learning algorithm that generally obtain good results in author profiling [1]. With these experiments, we show that these vectors allow us to identify the author's gender with an accuracy of 71.98%, when the mentions to users are removed, with an SVM classifier for the PAN 2017 corpus. We can observe that this result is better than the obtained with the traditional approach for gender classification.

We consider that a possible extension of this work is to evaluate other transfer learning techniques, such as the *Universal Language Model Fine-tuning (ULM-Fit)* [8], which has achieved very good results in text classification problems.

References

1. Aragón, M.E., López-Monroy, A.P.: Author profiling and aggressiveness detection in Spanish tweets: Mex-a3t 2018. In: IberEval@ SEPLN, pp. 134–139 (2018)
2. Caruana, R.: Multitask learning: a knowledge-based source of inductive bias. In: Proceedings of the Tenth International Conference on Machine Learning, pp. 41–48 (1993)
3. Cer, D., Yang, Y., et al.: Universal sentence encoder. arXiv preprint arXiv:1803.11175 (2018)
4. Devlin, J., Chang, M., Lee, K., Toutanova, K.: Bert: Pre-training of deep bidirectional transformers for language understanding. arXiv preprint arXiv:1810.04805 (2018)

5. Finn, C.: Learning to Lear with gradients. Ph.D. thesis, University of California, Berkeley (2018)
6. Gómez-Adorno, H.M.: Extracción de características de texto basada en grafos sintácticos integrados. Ph.D. thesis, Instituto Politécnico Nacional (2008)
7. Gusfield, D.: Algorithms on strings, trees and sequences: computer science and computational biology. Cambridge University Press (1997)
8. Howard, J., Ruder, S.: Universal language model fine-tuning for text classification. arXiv preprint arXiv:1801.06146 (2018)
9. Iyyer, M., Manjunatha, V., Boyd-Graber, J., Daumé III, H.: Deep unordered composition rivals syntactic methods for text classification. In: Proceedings of the 53rd Annual Meeting of the Association for Computational Linguistics and the 7th International Joint Conference on Natural Language Processing, vol. 1, pp. 1681–1691 (2015)
10. Jurida, S.H., Džanić, M., Pavlović, T., Jahić, A., Hanić, J.: Netspeak: linguistic properties and aspects of online communication in postponed time. J. Foreign Lang. Teach. Appl. Linguist. 3(1), 1–19 (2016)
11. Kim, Y.: Convolutional neural networks for sentence classification. arXiv preprint arXiv:1408.5882 (2014)
12. Peters, M.E., Neumann, M., Iyyer, M., Gardner, M., Clark, C., Lee, K., Zettlemoyer, L.: Deep contextualized word representations. arXiv preprint arXiv:1802.05365 (2018)
13. Mikolov, T., Sutskever, I., Chen, K., Corrado, G., Dean, J.: Distributed representations of words and phrases and their compositionality. Advances in Neural Information Processing Systems, pp. 3111–3119 (2013)
14. Pennington, J., Socher, R., Manning, C.: Glove: global vectors for word representation. In: Proceedings of the 2014 Conference on Empirical Methods in Natural Language Processing (EMNLP), pp. 1532–1443 (2014)
15. Rangel, F., Rosso, P., Verhoeven, B., Daelemans, W., Potthast, M., Stein, B.: Overview of the 4th author profiling task at PAN 2016: cross-genre evaluations. In: Working Notes Papers of the CLEF 2016 Evaluation Labs. CEUR Workshop Proceedings, pp. 750–784 (2016)
16. Schmidhuber, J.: Evolutionary principles in self-referential learning, or on learning how to learn: the meta-meta-... hook. Ph.D. thesis, Technische Universität München (1987)
17. Thrun, S.: Is learning the n-th thing any easier than learning the first? In: Advances in Neural Information Processing Systems, pp. 640–646 (1996)

Artificial Intelligence Techniques and Recognition

Experimental Study on Transfer Learning in Denoising Autoencoders for Speech Enhancement

Marvin Coto-Jiménez(✉)

University of Costa Rica, San José 11501-2060, Costa Rica
marvin.coto@ucr.ac.cr
https://eie.ucr.ac.cr/

Abstract. The quality of speech signals is affected by a combination of background noise, reverberation, and other distortions in real-life environments. The processing of such signals presents important challenges for tasks such as voice or speaker recognition. To enhance signals in such challenging conditions several deep learning-based methods have been proposed. Those new methods have proven to be effective, in comparison to classical algorithms based on statistical analysis and signal processing. In particular, recurrent neural networks, especially those with long short-term memory (LSTM and BLSTM), have presented surprising results in tasks related to enhancing speech. One of the most challenging aspects of artificial neural networks is to reduce the high computational cost of the training procedure. In this work, we present a comparative study on transfer learning to accelerate and improve traditional training based on random initialization of the internal weights of the networks. The results show the advantage of the proposal in terms of less training time and better results for the task of denoising speech signals at several signal-to-noise ratio levels of white noise.

Keywords: BLSTM · Deep learning · Transfer learning · Speech processing

1 Introduction

In real-life environments, audio signals are affected by various conditions, such as additive or convolutional noise due to elements that produce sounds simultaneously, obstacles in the signal path of the microphone or room size and materials. Communication devices and applications of speech technologies, such as speech recognition, may be affected in their performance [1–3] by the presence of any of these conditions.

To overcome this problem, many algorithms have been developed over the past few decades to enhance noisy speech. These algorithms try to reduce distortions, as well as improve the quality of the perceived signal. Several successful algorithms have been based on deep neural networks (DNN) [4].

Supported by University of Costa Rica. Project 322-B9-105.

K. M. Figueroa Mora et al. (Eds.): MCPR 2020, LNCS 12088, pp. 307–317, 2020.
https://doi.org/10.1007/978-3-030-49076-8_29

The benefits of achieving this type of speech signal enhancement can be applied to signal processing in mobile phone applications, robotics, voice over Internet protocol, speech recognition systems, and devices for people with diminished hearing ability [5,6].

Models of neural networks that have been successfully applied in denoising speech signals include recurrent neural networks (RNNs); e.g., the Long Short-term Memory (LSTM) neural networks and their bidirectional counterparts (BLSTM). In previous efforts to enhance speech, spectrum-derived characteristics, such as Mel-frequency cepstrum coefficients (MFCC), have been mapped successfully between noisy speech to clean speech [7–9].

The benefits of using LSTM and BLSTM arose from their superior modeling of the dependent nature of speech signals. In particular, LSTM has been applied for denoising speech signals, for applications such as speaker recognition [10]. A comparative study using several types of DNN has been presented in [11], concluding that the best benefits are obtained with LSTM, compared to classical DNN or convolutional networks. In spite of their advantages, one of the drawbacks often reported about LSTM and BLSTM is the high computational cost of their training procedures.

The concept of transfer learning for speech processing has been reported in applications such as speech synthesis [12], music genre classification [13] and robust speech recognition [14]. The results have shown improvement in signal quality, classification, and word error rate in these applications.

For the particular task of denoising speech, the transfer learning process has been tested with other kinds of networks; e.g., general adversarial networks [15]. In this work, the concept of transfer learning between neural networks is applied as a way to increase the effectiveness of BLSTM networks and reduce training time in the task of denoising signals at different signal-to-noise ratio (SNR) levels. To assess the improvements made, a comparative study on transfer learning from a single BLSTM network trained on a particular SNR level, as well as some other networks, is performed.

1.1   Problem Statement

A speech signal y degraded with additive noise from the environment, can be modeled as the sum of a clean speech signal, x, and noise d, given by:

$$y(t) = x(t) + d(t) \tag{1}$$

In classical methods, $x(t)$ is considered uncorrelated to $d(t)$. Many speech enhancement algorithms estimate the spectrum of $x(t)$ from the spectral domain of $y(t)$ and $d(t)$.

In deep learning approaches, $x(t)$ (or the spectrum $X_k(n)$) can be estimated using algorithms that learn an approximated function $f(\cdot)$ between the noisy and clean data of the form:

$$\hat{x}(t) = f\left(y(t)\right). \tag{2}$$

The precision of the approximation $f(\cdot)$ usually depends on the amount of training data and the algorithm selected.

In the approach presented in this work, the information for the training of the artificial neural network for a particular noise level is transferred from another network, so the approximation $f(\cdot)$ can be obtained with better precision and fewer training epochs, which means a significant increase in the efficiency.

For this purpose, several objective measures were used to verify the results, which comparatively show the benefits of the transfer learning for the denoising BLSTM neural networks. The rest of this document is organized as follows. Section 2 provides the background of BLSTM neural networks. Section 3 briefly describes the main definitions of Transfer Learning. Section 4 presents the experimental setup. In Sect. 5, the results and discussion are presented, and finally, Sect. 6 presents the conclusions.

2   BLSTM Neural Networks

Since the appearance of RNNs, new alternatives to model the character dependent on the sequential information have been presented. For example, the neural networks capable of storing information through feedback connections between neurons in their hidden layers or other neurons that are in the same layer [16, 17].

One of the most important models are the LSTM networks shown in [18]. Here, a set of gates is introduced into internal units, making a system capable of controlling access, storage, and propagation of values across the network. The results obtained when using LSTM networks in areas that depend on previous states of information, as is the case with voice recognition, musical composition, and handwriting synthesis, were encouraging [19, 20].

Specifically, each unit in the LSTM networks has additional gates for storing values: one for input, one for memory clearing, one for output, and one for activating memory. With the proper combination of the gates, it is possible to store values for many steps or have them available at any time [18].

The gates are implemented using the following equations:

$$i_t = \sigma\left(\mathbf{W}_{xi}x_t + \mathbf{W}_{hi}h_{t-1} + \mathbf{W}_{ci}c_{t-1} + b_i\right) \tag{3}$$

$$f_t = \sigma\left(\mathbf{W}_{xf}x_t + \mathbf{W}_{hf}h_{t-1} + \mathbf{W}_{cf}c_{t-1} + b_f\right) \tag{4}$$

$$c_t = f_t c_{t-1} + i_t \tanh\left(\mathbf{W}_{xc}x_t + \mathbf{W}_{hc}h_{t-1} + b_c\right) \tag{5}$$

$$o_t = \sigma\left(\mathbf{W}_{xo}x_t + \mathbf{W}_{ho}h_{t-1} + \mathbf{W}_{co}c_t + b_o\right) \tag{6}$$

$$h_t = o_t \tanh\left(c_t\right) \tag{7}$$

where σ is the sigmoid activation function, i is the input gate, f is the memory erase gate, o_t is the exit gate and h is the output of the LSTM memory unit. c is the activation of memory. $\mathbf{W}_{mn}$ is the matrix that contains the values of the connections between each unit and the gates. Additional details about the training process and the implications of this implementation can be found at [21].

An extension of LSTM networks that have had a greater advantage in tasks related to temporal parameter dependence is the Bidirectional LSTM (BLSTM). Here, the configuration of the network allows the updating of parameters in both directions during training.

LSTM networks can handle information over long periods; however, using BLSTM with two hidden layers connected to the same output layer gives them access to information in both directions. This allows bidirectional networks to take advantage of not just the past but also the future context [22].

One of the main architectures applied for speech enhancement is autoencoders. An autoencoder is a particular kind of neural network, which consists of an encoder that transforms an input vector s into a representation in the hidden layers h through a f mapping. It also has a decoder that takes the hidden representation and transforms it back into a vector in the input space. In implementations, the number of units at the inputs correspond to the number of units at the outputs of the network.

3   Transfer Learning

In the context of machine learning with artificial neural networks, transfer learning has been used to improve a model in one domain by transferring information from a model in a related domain. For example, given a source domain D_S with a corresponding task T_S, and a target domain D_T with a corresponding task T_T, transfer learning is the process of improving the target predictive function $f_T(\cdot)$ by using the related information from D_S and T_S [23].

Among the several types that have been developed, homogeneous transfer learning is the most suitable for the approach presented in this work. The homogeneous transfer is properly applied where there is available data that is drawn from a domain related to, but not an exact match for, a target domain of interest.

This process of transfer learning is commonly applied in human learning, where experiences in one task (e.g., playing a musical instrument) can mean a significant improvement in learning a new task (e.g., playing a different musical instrument), relative to learning a new task with no antecedent [24].

In this work, D_S and T_S represent several possibilities: the approximation of the identity function with speech data, the same task with noisy data, or the task of denoising speech with additive noise at SNR0, while D_T and T_T the task of denoising at every other SNR level.

4   Experimental Setup

This section describes in some detail the experimental setup that was followed in the paper. The whole process can be summarized in the following steps:

1. Noisy database generation: Files containing artificially generated white noise were generated and added to each audio file in the database for a given signal-to-noise ratio (SNR). Five noise levels were added, to cover a range from light to heavy noise levels.

2. Feature extraction and input-output correspondence: A set of parameters was extracted from the noisy and the clean audio files, using the Ahocoder system. Those from the noisy files were used as inputs to the networks, while the corresponding clean features were the outputs.

3. Training and validation: During training and validation, using forward pass and backpropagation through time algorithm to train the BLSTM networks, the internal weights of the connections were adjusted as the noisy and clean utterances were presented at the inputs and the outputs. A total of 900 utterances (about 80% of the total database) were used for training and 180 utterances (about 15% of the total database) were used for validation. Details and equations of the algorithm followed can be found in [25].

4. Test: A subset of 50 randomly selected utterances (about 5% of the total amount of utterances of the database) was chosen for the test set. These utterances were not part of the training process, to provide independence between the training and testing.

4.1   Database

In our work, we chose the SLT voice from the CMU ARCTIC databases [26], designed for speech research purposes at the Carnegie Mellon University, in the United States of America. The whole set of 1132 sentences were used to randomly define the training, validation and test sets. In our work, we chose the female SLT voice.

4.2   Initialization and Transfer Learning

To test the proposal, different proposals to initialize the networks, or perform the transfer learning from other networks are compared:

- Base system (random initialization): The set of internal weights of the BLSTM network were initialized randomly, as the common practice in training autoencoders.
- Transfer (AA-clean): In this approach, an auto-associative network (which approximate the identity function between the inputs and the outputs) is trained using the MFCC from the clean speech. The result of this previous training procedure is applied as the initialization weights of the denoising autoencoders for each SRN.
- Transfer (AA-noisy): Similar to the previous case, an auto-associative network is previously trained, but using parameters from the noisy speech for each SNR level. The result of this training procedure is applied as the initialization weights of the denoising autoencoders for each SRN.
- Transfer (TN): A denoising autoencoder was first randomly initialized, and then trained to denoise the parameters of the speech at SNR 0. The resulting weights of this network are then used as the initialization weights of the networks for every other SNR level.

The comparative study aims to find the best option to reduce training time and achieve better results in the denoising task, using the evaluation measures presented in the following section.

4.3   Evaluation

To assess the different to evaluate the results given by the different enhancement methods:

- PESQ: This measure uses a model to predict the perceived quality of speech. As defined in the ITU-T recommendation P.862.ITU, the results are given in interval $[0.5, 4.5]$, where 4.5 corresponds to a perfect reconstruction of the signal [27].
- SSE (Sum of squared errors): This is a common measure to evaluate the lowest validation error during training. SSE is defined as:

$$\mathrm{SSE}(\theta) = \sum_{n=1}^{T} (\mathbf{c_x} - \hat{\mathbf{c}}_{\mathbf{x}})^2 \tag{8}$$

where $\mathbf{c_x}$ is the desired output of the network, $\hat{\mathbf{c}}_{\mathbf{x}}$ is the obtained output, and T the number of frames.
- Number of epochs: During training the BLSTM networks, each epoch consists of a feedforward and backforward step to adjust the weights of the internal connections. The time taken to train the BLSTM is directly associated with the number of epochs in training.

5   Results and Discussion

In Table 1, the results of the training process for each of the initializations and transfer learning are presented. As stated in Sect. 3, the information from the BLSTM autoencoder trained with SNR 0 was transferred to the rest of the autoencoders. This is the reason for the missing values in the corresponding line of the SNR 0 measures.

Due to the random initialization of the networks in the base system, these training procedures were performed three times. Thus, the values reported in Table 1 correspond to the mean values for the base system.

Regarding the efficiency of the training procedure, transfer learning represents a significant advantage over most of the other approaches compared in this study. For example, for SNR −10 (the heavier level of white noise), the training time is reduced by more than 55% in comparison to the base system.

For SNR 10, the training time is reduced 20%, while the reductions for SNR 5 and SNR −5 are 50% and 52% respectively. This represents a significant improvement in efficiency in all cases. The benefits of using transfer learning from a particular SNR level is also clear when compared with the other approaches for the initialization of the BLSTM network. Considering that each epoch requires

Table 1. Average number of epochs for training, SSE and PESQ for training the BLSTM denoise autoencoder with white noise at several SNR. * is the best result for each type of noise and each measure.

SNR 10			
Training model	Avg. epochs	SSE	PESQ
Base system	526	244.49	2.58
Transfer (TN)	417	245.95	2.57
Transfer (AA-clean)	655	243.79*	2.59*
Transfer (AA-noisy)	381*	248.14	2.57

SNR 5			
Training model	Avg. epochs	SSE	PESQ
Base system	318	288.36	2.26
Transfer (TN)	157*	289.39	2.28*
Transfer (AA-clean)	394	283.22	2.27
Transfer (AA-noisy)	508	279.09*	2.27

SNR 0			
Training model	Avg. epochs	SSE	PESQ
Base system	165*	335.13	1.75
Transfer (TN)	–	–	–
Transfer (AA-clean)	374	328.28	1.77*
Transfer (AA-noisy)	328	325.7*	1.76

SNR −5			
Training model	Avg. epochs	SSE	PESQ
Base system	284	387.58	0.96*
Transfer (TN)	136*	342.3*	0.96*
Transfer (AA-clean)	270	392.07	0.96*
Transfer (AA-noisy)	246	387.12	0.96*

SNR −10			
Training model	Avg. epochs	SSE	PESQ
Base system	224	462.04	0.47
Transfer (TN)	96*	447.94*	0.55
Transfer (AA-clean)	196	463.06	0.56*
Transfer (AA-noisy)	206	457.22	0.52

about 60 s in a desktop computer accelerated with an NVIDIA GPU, several hours can be saved for the whole set of experiments.

In terms of SSE, the reduction in the number of epochs is also reflected in better values in two of the four cases compared. For SNR 10 and SNR 5 (the lightest levels of noise), the best SSE value was obtained with the auto-associative initialization with clean and noisy MFCC values. The values obtained with the training performed after the transfer learning do not differ significantly from those of the best case.

Finally, in terms of the PESQ, transfer learning reaches the best case in two of the four cases applied. At all levels, except for SNR 10, there is an increase in the PESQ measure in comparison to the base system.

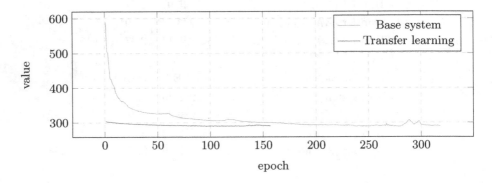

Fig. 1. Evolution of the SSE during training, for SNR5

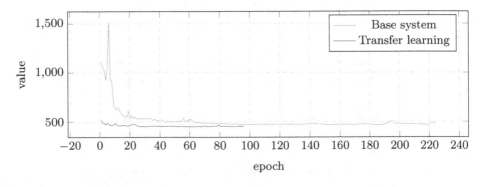

Fig. 2. Evolution of the SSE during training, for SNR-10

With all this information, the benefits of transfer learning in denoising applications, using BLSTM autoencoders, are clear. The training time drops significantly and the objective measures of quality also increase, or do not differ significantly from the best case.

In Fig. 1 and 2 the evolution of the validation error during training is presented. It is remarkable how much less time it takes for the training procedure to reach the lower SEE value. With this reduction in training time and the similar or best results in the other measures, a greater number of experiments or cases can be analyzed using this type of artificial neural network.

6   Conclusions

In this work, a comparative study of four approaches to initialize BLSTM autoencoders was presented. In particular, the main focus was on the transfer learning approach, which brings a set of weights adjusted after a training procedure for a particular level of white noise to other levels of noise.

Transfer learning presents benefits in terms of efficiency during training, in comparison to two other supervised initializations (in the form of auto-associative memories) and the more traditional random initialization approach.

The reduction of training time for this kind of network, with a large number of connections, can be measured in terms of hours or even days in a large set of experiments, such as the one performed in this study.

For future work, more extensive research about the source of the transfer learning (such as the SNR used) can be performed. Statistical validation of the improvements achieved could be also relevant. Finally, additional benefits about transfer learning for different kinds of noise can be of great interest to speech enhancement applications.

References

1. Weninger, F., et al.: Deep recurrent de-noising auto-encoder and blind de-reverberation for reverberated speech recognition. In: 2014 IEEE International Conference on Acoustics, Speech and Signal Processing (ICASSP). IEEE (2014)
2. Donahue, C., Bo, L., Prabhavalkar, R.: Exploring speech enhancement with generative adversarial networks for robust speech recognition. In: 2018 IEEE International Conference on Acoustics, Speech and Signal Processing (ICASSP). IEEE (2018)
3. Coto-Jiménez, M., Goddard-Close, J., Martínez-Licona, F.: Improving automatic speech recognition containing additive noise using deep denoising autoencoders of LSTM networks. In: Ronzhin, A., Potapova, R., Németh, G. (eds.) SPECOM 2016. LNCS (LNAI), vol. 9811, pp. 354–361. Springer, Cham (2016). https://doi.org/10.1007/978-3-319-43958-7_42
4. Abouzid, H., Chakkor, O., Reyes, O.G., Ventura, S.: Signal speech reconstruction and noise removal using convolutional denoising audioencoders with neural deep learning. Analog Integr. Circ. Sig. Process **100**(3), 501–512 (2019). https://doi.org/10.1007/s10470-019-01446-6
5. Lai, Y.-H., et al.: A deep denoising autoencoder approach to improving the intelligibility of vocoded speech in Cochlear implant simulation. IEEE Trans. Biomed. Eng. **64**(7), 1568–1578 (2016)
6. Coto-Jimenez, M., Goddard-Close, J., Di Persia, L., Rufiner, H.L.: Hybrid speech enhancement with wiener filters and deep LSTM denoising autoencoders. In: Proceedings of the 2018 IEEE International Work Conference on Bioinspired Intelligence (IWOBI), San Carlos, CA, USA, 18–20 July 2018, pp. 1–8 (2018)
7. Gutiérrez-Muñoz, M., González-Salazar, A., Coto-Jiménez, M.: Evaluation of mixed deep neural networks for reverberant speech enhancement. Biomimetics **5**(1), 1 (2020)

8. Chakraborty, R., et al.: Front-end feature compensation and denoising for noise robust speech emotion recognition. In: Proceedings of Interspeech 2019, pp. 3257–3261 (2019)
9. Coto-Jiménez, M.: Robustness of LSTM neural networks for the enhancement of spectral parameters in noisy speech signals. In: Batyrshin, I., Martínez-Villaseñor, M.L., Ponce Espinosa, H.E. (eds.) MICAI 2018. LNCS (LNAI), vol. 11289, pp. 227–238. Springer, Cham (2018). https://doi.org/10.1007/978-3-030-04497-8_19
10. Tkachenko, M., Yamshinin, A., Lyubimov, N., Kotov, M., Nastasenko, M.: Speech enhancement for speaker recognition using deep recurrent neural networks. In: Karpov, A., Potapova, R., Mporas, I. (eds.) SPECOM 2017. LNCS (LNAI), vol. 10458, pp. 690–699. Springer, Cham (2017). https://doi.org/10.1007/978-3-319-66429-3_69
11. Liu, M., et al.: Speech enhancement method based on LSTM neural network for speech recognition. In: 2018 14th IEEE International Conference on Signal Processing (ICSP). IEEE (2018)
12. Jia, Y., et al.: Transfer learning from speaker verification to multi speaker text-to-speech synthesis. In: Advances in Neural Information Processing Systems (2018)
13. Song, G., Wang, Z., Han, F., Ding, S.: Transfer learning for music genre classification. In: Shi, Z., Goertzel, B., Feng, J. (eds.) ICIS 2017. IAICT, vol. 510, pp. 183–190. Springer, Cham (2017). https://doi.org/10.1007/978-3-319-68121-4_19
14. Jiangyan, Y.I., et al.: Transfer learning for acoustic modeling of noise robust speech recognition. J. Tsinghua Univ. (Sci. Technol.) **58**(1), 55–60 (2018)
15. Pascual, S., et al.: Language and noise transfer in speech enhancement generative adversarial network. In: 2018 IEEE International Conference on Acoustics, Speech and Signal Processing (ICASSP). IEEE (2018)
16. Fan, Y., Qian, Y., Xie, F.L., Soong, F.K.: TTS synthesis with bidirectional LSTM based recurrent neural networks. In: Proceedings of the Fifteenth Annual Conference of the International Speech Communication Association, Singapore, 14–18 September (2014)
17. Zen, H., Sak, H.: Unidirectional long short-term memory recurrent neural network with recurrent output layer for low-latency speech synthesis. In: Proceedings of the 2015 IEEE International Conference on Acoustics, Speech and Signal Processing (ICASSP), South Brisbane, Australia, 19–24 April 2015, pp. 4470–4474 (2015)
18. Hochreiter, S., Schmidhuber, J.: Long short-term memory. Neural Comput. **9**, 1735–1780 (1997)
19. Graves, A., Jaitly, N., Mohamed, A.R.: Hybrid speech recognition with deep bidirectional LSTM. In: Proceedings of the 2013 IEEE Workshop on Automatic Speech Recognition and Understanding (ASRU), Olomouc, Czech Republic, 8–13 December 2013, pp. 273–278 (2013)
20. Graves, A., Fernández, S., Schmidhuber, J.: Bidirectional LSTM networks for improved phoneme classification and recognition. In: Duch, W., Kacprzyk, J., Oja, E., Zadrożny, S. (eds.) ICANN 2005. LNCS, vol. 3697, pp. 799–804. Springer, Heidelberg (2005). https://doi.org/10.1007/11550907_126
21. Gers, F.A., Schraudolph, N.N., Schmidhuber, J.: Learning precise timing with LSTM recurrent networks. J. Mach. Learn. Res. **3**, 115–143 (2002)
22. Wöllmer, M., Eyben, F., Schuler, B., Rigoll, G.: A multi-stream ASR framework for BLSTM modeling of conversational speech. In: Proceedings of the 2011 IEEE International Conference on Acoustics, Speech and Signal Processing (ICASSP), Prague, Czech Republic, 22–27 May 2011, p. 4861 (2011)
23. Weiss, K., Khoshgoftaar, T.M., Wang, D.D.: A survey of transfer learning. J. Big Data **3**(1), 1–40 (2016). https://doi.org/10.1186/s40537-016-0043-6

24. Pan, S.J., Yang, Q.: A survey on transfer learning. IEEE Trans. Knowl. Data Eng. **22**(10), 1345–1359 (2009)
25. Greff, K., et al.: LSTM: a search space odyssey. IEEE Trans. Neural Netw. Learn. Syst. **28**(10), 2222–2232 (2016)
26. Kominek, J., Black, A.W.: The CMU Arctic speech databases. In: Fifth ISCA Workshop on Speech Synthesis (2004)
27. Rix, A.W., et al.: Perceptual evaluation of speech quality (PESQ) the new ITU standard for end-to-end speech quality assessment Part I-time-delay compensation. J. Audio Eng. Soc. **50**(10), 755–764 (2002)

A Preliminary Study on Score-Based Hyper-heuristics for Solving the Bin Packing Problem

A. Silva-Gálvez[ID], E. Lara-Cárdenas[ID], I. Amaya[ID], J. M. Cruz-Duarte[ID], and J. C. Ortiz-Bayliss[✉][ID]

School of Engineering and Sciences, Tecnologico de Monterrey,
Av. Eugenio Garza Sada 2501, 64849 Monterrey, NL, Mexico
artsg130994@gmail.com, a00398510@itesm.mx,
{iamaya2,jorge.cruz,jcobayliss}@tec.mx

Abstract. The bin packing problem is a widespread combinatorial problem. It aims at packing a set of items by using as few bins as possible. Among the many available solving methods, approximation ones such as heuristics have become popular due to their reduced cost and generally acceptable solutions. A further step in this regard is given by hyper-heuristics, which literature usually defines as "high-level heuristics to choose heuristics". Hyper-heuristics choose one suitable heuristic from a set of available ones, to solve a particular portion of an instance. As the search progresses, heuristics can be exchanged, adapting the solution process to the current problem state under exploration. In this work, we describe how to generate and use hyper-heuristics that keep a record of the scores achieved by individual heuristics on previously solved bin packing problem instances in the form of rules. Then, hyper-heuristics manage those scores to estimate the performance of such heuristics on unseen instances. In this way, the previous actions of the hyper-heuristics determine which heuristic to use on future unseen cases. The experiments conducted under different scenarios yield promising results where some of the hyper-heuristics produced outperform isolated heuristics.

Keywords: Bin packing problem · Heuristic · Hyper-heuristic

1 Introduction

The bin packing problem (BPP) [8,14], in its general formulation, consists of packing a set of items (with their corresponding properties) by minimizing the number of bins used. In general, BPP is an exciting problem since many other optimization problems such as the cutting stock problem [7] and the knapsack problem [10] can be modeled as BPPs [15]. Although there are many variants of this problem, in this investigation, we have focused on the one-dimensional online BPP (1D-BPP). Then, we assume that the only relevant property of the items

© Springer Nature Switzerland AG 2020
K. M. Figueroa Mora et al. (Eds.): MCPR 2020, LNCS 12088, pp. 318–327, 2020.
https://doi.org/10.1007/978-3-030-49076-8_30

is their length and that it is not possible to sort the items as a preprocessing step. An example of such a scenario is given by a production line with a fixed robot arm that packages items into the boxes. Here, items must be packed as they arrived, even if the whole production schedule can be known.

The current literature is vast in methods for solving the BPP [1, 3, 23]. Unfortunately, most of the methods that guarantee to find the optimal solution (also known as exact ones) are limited in the size of the instances they can handle. Conversely, approximation methods, such as heuristics, are fast to implement and execute but cannot guarantee the optimality of the solutions. More importantly, since these heuristics are usually generic methods, their performance may drastically change from one instance to the other, even within the same problem domain. A more robust way to tackle the BPP consists in combining the strengths of single heuristics, employing a hyper-heuristic (HH). A HH is a high-level method that decides when to use the individual heuristics throughout the solving process [4].

This idea of combining solvers dates back to the mid 70s [21]. From that moment onward, different solving strategies have emerged: algorithm portfolios [11], instance-specific algorithm configuration [17], and hyper-heuristics [20, 23], just to mention some. In general, these methods manage a set of solvers and apply the most suitable one for the problem instance. Aiming at unifying terms, from this point on, we will use the term "hyper-heuristic" to refer to the methods proposed in this paper.

In this work, we focus on developing score-based hyper-heuristics through a process that updates the scores of different heuristics according to their performance on a historical basis. Although a few studies have explored similar ideas in the past, the solution model proposed in this work is, to the best of the authors' knowledge, a novel approach. In the literature, we found no previous work that deals with the idea of training hyper-heuristics for the 1D-BPP by using such a straightforward reward-based strategy as the one described in this work.

We have organized the remainder of the document as follows. Section 2 presents the most relevant concepts and works related to this investigation. Section 3 details the hyper-heuristic model proposed in this work. In Sect. 4, we present the experiments conducted, their analysis, and discuss the most relevant findings. Finally, we present the conclusions and future work in Sect. 5.

2   Background

The 1-Dimensional Bin Packing Problem (1D-BPP) is defined by a set of n items and m bins, where w_j and c_j represent the length of item j and the capacity of each bin, respectively. To solve this BPP, it requires assigning each item to one bin such that the total weight of the items in each bin does not exceed c, and the number of bins is minimum.

The current literature contains significant examples of recent advances in solving the 1D-BPP. On the one hand, there are approaches based on metaheuristics. Abdel-Basset et al. [1] enhanced the Whale Optimization Algorithm (WOA) by adjusting positions inside the search space boundaries and implementing a Lévy distribution to draw samples. Similarly, Zhang et al. [24] reported a buffered version of the next fit heuristic. The objective of the buffer is to store some items temporarily so that items with specific characteristics can be packed in the same bin. This allows controlling the wasted space of the bins on a similar range, and even filling the remaining open bins to its full capacity (whenever possible). In a more recent study, Gherboudj [18] adapted the African Buffalo Optimization (ABO) algorithm to solve the 1D-BPP. Their work combined four heuristics with the ABO algorithm to improve its behavior. This combination showed effective results in various test scenarios.

On the other hand, researchers have explored hyper-heuristics (HHs) to solve 1D-BPPs indirectly, because they work on the heuristic space rather than the solution one. When working with hyper-heuristics, they map the problem state through a set of features, so the most suitable heuristic can be applied. In the past, researchers have relied on metaheuristics, such as Genetic Algorithms (GAs) [19], Simulated Annealing (SA) [13], and Ant Colony Optimization (ACO) [6,9] to produce hyper-heuristics. Other authors have preferred machine learning techniques devoting considerable efforts to exploring supervised learning methods [5,16].

2.1 Heuristics

For this preliminary investigation, we have focused on two popular heuristics for solving the BPP: First Fit (FF) and Best Fit (BF). FF, as the name suggests, packs the next item in the first open bin, as long as it fits. One by one, all the bins are revised until it finds one where the item can be packed. If there is not such a bin, it opens a new one to pack the item there. Subsequently, BF looks for the bin with the minimum space to pack the item (*i.e.*, it minimizes the waste). As in FF, if no bin has enough space for the item, a new one is opened.

Forthwith, we describe how these heuristics work by using the instance depicted in Fig. 1. In this example, the next item to pack has a length of four units. Since two of those bins are full, they are considered to be closed. FF will try to pack this item as soon as possible. So, it packs it in the fourth bin since it has five units available. This action leads to a waste of one unit in such a bin. Conversely, BF will try to minimize the waste, looking for the bin where the item fits best. So, BF skips the fourth bin and packs the item into the fifth one, where it fits perfectly.

We are aware that there are many other popular heuristics available for solving the BPP, such as Djang and Finch and their multiple variants [22]. However, analyzing their effect went beyond the scope of this work.

2.2 Instances

In this work, we considered synthetic instances since they allow us to test the methods under specific and controlled scenarios. We now briefly describe them:

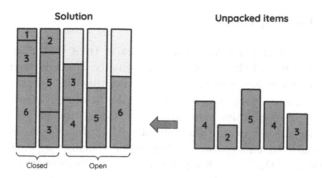

Fig. 1. Example of the solving process of a 1D-BPP instance of 15 items with lengths between one and six units and bins with a capacity of ten units. At the moment, ten items have been packed by using five bins (two closed and three open), and five items remain unpacked.

Training Set. It contains 100 small instances of 20 items with lengths between 1 and 32 units. The bins in these instances accept up to 64 units. This set has a mixture of instances so that no single heuristic performs the best in every instance. Such a fact forces the hyper-heuristic to switch between heuristics as the search takes place. It is noteworthy to mention that this situation might not hold for other sets of instances. To generate the Training Set, we used the evolutionary-based BPP generator introduced by Amaya et al. [2].

Test Set A. It consists of instances similar to the ones used for training. It contains 200 small instances of 20 items whose length varies between 1 and 32 units. The bin capacity is also defined at 64 units. To generate this set, we used the same generator from the previous experiment.

Test Set B. It incorporates the 160 instances proposed by Falkenauer [12]. These instances are classified into two different groups. The first one contains items with lengths uniformly distributed between 20 and 100 units and bins with a capacity of 150 units. The second group has items with sizes between 25 and 50 and bins of 100 units.

To characterize these instances, we used two dynamic features (they change throughout the solving process). These features are the proportion of open items concerning the total number of bins used (OBINS) and the average waste among all the open bins (AVGW). To exemplify how these features work, let us again take a look at the instance depicted in Fig. 1. Under these conditions, we calculate the value of OBINS as the number of open bins divided by the total number of bins. In other words, OBINS equals 3/5 for this example. Regarding the average waste, only open bins waste space. So, it sums 14 (3 + 5 + 6) units. This way, the AVGW value for this instance is 14/5.

3   Model Description

Our hyper-heuristic (HH) model relies on a set of rules that works on two different levels: as a record the historical performance of single heuristics and as an estimation of their future performance. A rule has the purpose of finding a region on the problem space in which one specific heuristic behaves better than the others. Each rule contains two parts: a condition and an action. They are related to the instance state and the heuristic to apply, respectively.

Our HHs need to undergo a training process before we can use them in practical situations. During such a process, the HH iteratively updates the set of rules, one rule at a time. Then, when the hyper-heuristic deals with a new instance, the information within the rules determines which heuristic to use. The rules are different from the ones considered in other HH models, where the rule directly states the actions. In our approach, given a rule, we require an additional calculation to decide which heuristic to apply. The task of the training process is to find a set of rules that best discriminates the instance space. Figure 2 depicts an example of how a rule looks inside the HH.

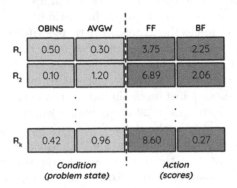

Fig. 2. An example of a hyper-heuristic produced by our solution model. Left: Condition contains the instance space description expressed in terms of the features OBINS and AVGW. Right: Action has the scores of the heuristics (*i.e.,* the larger, the better).

The model randomly initializes k rules by using a set of features that characterize the instance space as the condition and the available heuristics as the action of such rules. The scores of the heuristics in the rules are randomly initialized with values between 0 and 10. When the model deals with a new instance, it iteratively packs the items, one at a time. For each item, the hyper-heuristic decides which heuristic to apply. Let r be the rule with the condition closest to the instance state (via the Euclidean distance). Then, the heuristic with the largest score in the action of r is returned to pack the item. For example, given the rules depicted in Fig. 2 and an instance with values for OBINS and AVGW of 0.08 and 1.12, respectively, the rule with the closest condition to the current problem state is R_2. Now that we know that R_2 will be selected, the scores for

FF and BF are 6.89 and 2.06, respectively. Based on these values, the rule will recommend using FF, since it has the highest score among all the heuristics in R_2.

It is important to remark that the aforementioned rules are updated *iff* the hyper-heuristic is on training mode. Such an update is performed in two different moments, as described:

- Every time the HH makes a decision, it is "rewarded" based on the quality of its decision. This process changes the scores of the selected rule (increases the scores related to the right decisions and decreases the ones related to the bad ones). To decide the value to add or subtract to the scores, we calculate the reward as $0.01/(OBINS \times AVGW)$.
- After the HH has packed all the items in the instance, the system replaces the less used rule. The system generates a new rule according to one out of three initialization functions: RANDOM (a random choice for the conditions), MEAN (the average values of the points visited during the search of the last instance), and LAST (the values of the features of the last visited point in the instance space). In all cases, the scores for the heuristics are randomly initialized by using a uniform distribution function between 0 and 10.

4   Experiments and Results

In this investigation, we conducted two experiments. The first one explored the generation of hyper-heuristics by using three strategies to initialize the rules. For each strategy, we generated 11 hyper-heuristics by using the approach described in Sect. 3. Subsequently, the second experiment compared the performance of the best hyper-heuristics produced from the first experiment on a set of instances with features different from the ones used for training. In other words, the second experiment analyzed the behavior of the most competent hyper-heuristics produced by our solution model on a more realistic and challenging scenario.

4.1   Exploratory Experiment

The objective of this experiment was to evaluate three different methods for initializing rules and their decisions. In all cases, hyper-heuristics contained 20 rules. This value was decided based on our previous experience with this problem. The training process to produce one hyper-heuristic ran for 100 epochs in each case—an epoch occurs when all the instances in the Training Set have been analyzed. We obtained 11 hyper-heuristics by using each initialization function (*i.e.*, RANDOM, MEAN, and LAST). Then, the two heuristics and the 33 hyper-heuristics were applied on the Test Set A. In all cases, the average waste across all the items (AVGW) was used to estimate the quality of the solutions.

Figure 3 presents the resulting data. Among the hyper-heuristics produced, there are two worth analyzing in more detail. Let us call these hyper-heuristics HHA and HHB. The former represents the hyper-heuristic that performed best when initializing them with the MEAN approach. Conversely, HHB represents the best performing hyper-heuristic. It is worth remarking that HHB corresponds to the LAST initialization. While FF and BF produced an average waste of 8.32 and 5.07 units in Test Set A, HHA and HHB reduced the average waste to 4.62 and 3.87 units, respectively. Despite these savings, both of them are still far from the Oracle, which produced an average waste of only 2.76 units for the same set.

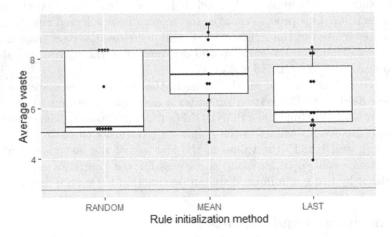

Fig. 3. Average waste on the Test Set A produced by 11 hyper-heuristics generated with each rule initialization method. The red, blue, and green horizontal lines represent the average waste of First Fit (FF), Best Fit (BF), and the Oracle (the best performer for each instance), respectively. (Color figure online)

We now consider the proportion of instances where the solving strategies behave as competent as the Oracle. Let us refer to such a proportion as the success rate. Then, the better the solving strategy, the closer to 100% the success rate becomes. The reason: this would mean that the strategy performed as the Oracle on every instance within the set. The success rate of FF and BF on the Test Set A was 50% and 77.5%, respectively. Conversely, the success rate of HHA and HHB on the same set increased to 82% and 89.5%, respectively.

4.2   Confirmatory Experiment

We are now interested in observing the behavior of the best hyper-heuristics, HHA and HHB, on instances whose features differ from those of the ones used for training. So, we use them to solve the Test Set B. Such a set contains the instances generated by Falkenauer [12], as mentioned before. Once again, performance data are compared against that of the Oracle. Based on the results obtained, we observed many instances where both FF and BF behave in the same way (88.13% of the instances). Nonetheless, both hyper-heuristics (HHA and HHB) proved to be reliable and competent. HHA obtained a success rate of

95%, while HHB obtained 97.5%. These values mean that these hyper-heuristics were unable to replicate the Oracle in only 8 and 4 out of the 160 instances, respectively.

4.3 Discussion

The analysis conducted on three different initialization methods (*i.e.,* RANDOM, MEAN, and LAST) suggests that a simple random function is not powerful enough to outperform individual heuristics. On a closer look, we found that RANDOM tends to replicate the behavior of the single heuristics. Thus, it seems that it reduces the capability of the hyper-heuristic to discriminate between heuristics and alternate their use throughout the solving process. MEAN and LAST methods demonstrate that it is indeed possible to improve the results of the heuristics throughout the proposed approach. Among the three initialization methods, on average, LAST performed best. However, better techniques can likely be found by deepening the study on this matter.

When testing the two best HHs on the Falkenauer dataset [12], we observed that these hyper-heuristics remain competitive, although they were not trained for such instances. The two hyper-heuristics that we analyzed in more detail (HHA and HHB, produced with MEAN and LAST, respectively) were close to fully replicating the behavior of the Oracle, proving its contribution. The difference between Oracle and these hyper-heuristics lies in the way decisions are made. While the Oracle solves an instance with the same heuristic from start to end, HHA and HHB use different heuristics depending on their decision rules. This result means that there may be many different paths that lead to similar and high-quality solutions.

5   Conclusion and Future Work

Throughout this study, we proposed a score-based hyper-heuristic (HH) model for tackling the 1-Dimensional Bin Packing Problem (1D-BPP). This model iteratively updates its internal structure to capture the patterns in the instance space, which suggests when one heuristic performs better than the others. Therefore, the proposed model generates a set of rules that segments the 1D-BPP instance space. This segmentation allows the system to discriminate between heuristics throughout the search, as a means to improve the quality of the solutions. Our findings suggest that the initialization method is crucial for this model to work. By merely using arbitrary rules, the model does not reach a competitive solution against a single heuristic. Moreover, from the three methods we tested, LAST behaved best.

It is imperative to remark that this document describes the first study towards a score-based HHs—at least in the way we propose it. Unfortunately, due to space restrictions, we could only consider two heuristics and two features to characterize the instance space. Moreover, for this preliminary investigation, we wanted to keep a basic set of heuristics to estimate the contribution of the proposed approach. Naturally, we expect to extend this idea and cover more heuristics as part of future work. When new heuristics and features are introduced, the model might behave differently. However, it is noticeable that our proposed model requires no changes to incorporate more heuristics or features, so it can quickly scale to more complex situations.

As part of the future work, we would like to explore how this model behaves on a different problem domain, such as the knapsack problem or the graph coloring problem, which are some exciting and challenging combinatorial optimization problems we would like to address through hyper-heuristics. Also, all the instances considered for this work were synthetic, but other kinds are required to validate the contributions of our approach thoroughly. We also plan on incorporating them as a future step of this work.

Acknowledgments. This research was partially supported by CONACyT Basic Science Project under grant 287479 and ITESM Research Group with Strategic Focus on Intelligent Systems.

References

1. Abdel-Basset, M., Manogaran, G., Abdel-Fatah, L., Mirjalili, S.: An improved nature inspired meta-heuristic algorithm for 1-D bin packing problems. Pers. Ubiquit. Comput. **22**(5–6), 1117–1132 (2018). https://doi.org/10.1007/s00779-018-1132-7
2. Amaya, I., Ortiz-Bayliss, J.C., Conant-Pablos, S.E., Terashima-Marín, H., Coello Coello, C.A.: Tailoring instances of the 1D bin packing problem for assessing strengths and weaknesses of its solvers. In: Auger, A., Fonseca, C.M., Lourenço, N., Machado, P., Paquete, L., Whitley, D. (eds.) PPSN 2018. LNCS, vol. 11102, pp. 373–384. Springer, Cham (2018). https://doi.org/10.1007/978-3-319-99259-4_30
3. Asta, S., Özcan, E., Parkes, A.J.: CHAMP: creating heuristics via many parameters for online bin packing. Expert Syst. Appl. **63**, 208–221 (2016)
4. Burke, E.K., et al.: Hyper-heuristics: a survey of the state of the art. J. Oper. Res. Soc. **64**, 1695–1724 (2013)
5. Choong, S.S., Wong, L.P., Lim, C.P.: Automatic design of hyper-heuristic based on reinforcement learning. Inf. Sci. **436**, 89–107 (2018)
6. Cuesta-Cañada, A., Garrido, L., Terashima-Marín, H.: Building hyper-heuristics through ant colony optimization for the 2D bin packing problem. In: Khosla, R., Howlett, R.J., Jain, L.C. (eds.) KES 2005. LNCS (LNAI), vol. 3684, pp. 654–660. Springer, Heidelberg (2005). https://doi.org/10.1007/11554028_91
7. Delorme, M., Iori, M., Martello, S.: Bin packing and cutting stock problems: mathematical models and exact algorithms. Eur. J. Oper. Res. **255**(1), 1–20 (2016)
8. Drake, J.H., Swan, J., Neumann, G., Özcan, E.: Sparse, continuous policy representations for uniform online bin packing via regression of interpolants. In: Hu, B., López-Ibáñez, M. (eds.) EvoCOP 2017. LNCS, vol. 10197, pp. 189–200. Springer, Cham (2017). https://doi.org/10.1007/978-3-319-55453-2_13
9. Duhart, B., Camarena, F., Ortiz-Bayliss, J.C., Amaya, I., Terashima-Marín, H.: An experimental study on ant colony optimization hyper-heuristics for solving the Knapsack problem. In: Martínez-Trinidad, J.F., Carrasco-Ochoa, J.A., Olvera-López, J.A., Sarkar, S. (eds.) MCPR 2018. LNCS, vol. 10880, pp. 62–71. Springer, Cham (2018). https://doi.org/10.1007/978-3-319-92198-3_7

10. Eliiyi, U., Eliiyi, D.T.: Applications of bin packing models through the supply chain. Int. J. Bus. Manag. **1**(1), 11–19 (2009)
11. Epstein, S.L., Freuder, E.C., Wallace, R., Morozov, A., Samuels, B.: The adaptive constraint engine. In: Van Hentenryck, P. (ed.) CP 2002. LNCS, vol. 2470, pp. 525–540. Springer, Heidelberg (2002). https://doi.org/10.1007/3-540-46135-3_35
12. Falkenauer, E.: A hybrid grouping genetic algorithm for bin packing. J. Heuristics **2**(1), 5–30 (1996)
13. Garza-Santisteban, F., et al.: A simulated annealing hyper-heuristic for job shop scheduling problems. In: 2019 IEEE Congress on Evolutionary Computation (CEC), pp. 57–64, June 2019
14. Hu, H., Zhang, X., Yan, X., Wang, L., Xu, Y.: Solving a new 3D bin packing problem with deep reinforcement learning method. arXiv preprint, August 2017
15. Koch, T., et al.: MIPLIB 2010. Math. Programm. Comput. **3**(2), 103–163 (2011)
16. Lara-Cárdenas, E., Sánchez-Díaz, X., Amaya, I., Ortiz-Bayliss, J.C.: Improving hyper-heuristic performance for job shop scheduling problems using neural networks. In: Martínez-Villaseñor, L., Batyrshin, I., Marín-Hernández, A. (eds.) MICAI 2019. LNCS (LNAI), vol. 11835, pp. 150–161. Springer, Cham (2019). https://doi.org/10.1007/978-3-030-33749-0_13
17. Malitsky, Y.: Evolving instance-specific algorithm configuration. In: Malitsky, Y. (ed.) Instance-Specific Algorithm Configuration, pp. 93–105. Springer, Cham (2014). https://doi.org/10.1007/978-3-319-11230-5_9
18. Odili, J.B., Kahar, M.N.M., Anwar, S.: African buffalo optimization: a swarm-intelligence technique. Procedia Comput. Sci. **76**, 443–448 (2015)
19. Ozcan, S.O., Dokeroglu, T., Cosar, A., Yazici, A.: A novel grouping genetic algorithm for the one-dimensional bin packing problem on gpu. In: Czachórski, T., Gelenbe, E., Grochla, K., Lent, R. (eds.) ISCIS 2016. CCIS, vol. 659, pp. 52–60. Springer, Cham (2016). https://doi.org/10.1007/978-3-319-47217-1_6
20. Pillay, N., Qu, R.: Hyper-Heuristics: Theory and Applications. NCS. Springer, Cham (2018). https://doi.org/10.1007/978-3-319-96514-7_13
21. Rice, J.R.: The algorithm selection problem. Adv. Comput. **15**, 65–118 (1976)
22. Sim, K., Hart, E., Paechter, B.: A hyper-heuristic classifier for one dimensional bin packing problems: improving classification accuracy by attribute evolution. In: Coello, C.A.C., Cutello, V., Deb, K., Forrest, S., Nicosia, G., Pavone, M. (eds.) PPSN 2012. LNCS, vol. 7492, pp. 348–357. Springer, Heidelberg (2012). https://doi.org/10.1007/978-3-642-32964-7_35
23. Sim, K., Hart, E., Paechter, B.: A lifelong learning hyper-heuristic method for bin packing. Evol. Comput. **23**(1), 37–67 (2015)
24. Zhang, M., Lan, Y., Li, H.: A new bin packing algorithm with buffer. In: 2018 International Conference on Intelligent Transportation, Big Data & Smart City (ICITBS), pp. 625–628. IEEE, January 2018

Learning Clasiffier Systems with Hebbian Learning for Autonomus Behaviors

Marco Ramos[1]([✉]) [iD], Vianney Muñoz-Jiménez[1] [iD], and Félix F. Ramos[2] [iD]

[1] Universidad del Estado de México, Toluca, Mexico
{maramosc,vmunozj}@uaemex.mx
[2] CINVESTAV del IPN, Guadalajara, Jalisco, Mexico
framos@gdl.cinvestav.mx

Abstract. One of the main characteristics of multi-agent systems is the ability to solve problems achieving objectives. This is possible because of the learning mechanisms that are embedded in the systems and go from neural networks up to vector support machines. Agent-based systems stand out for their autonomy and adaptation of dynamic conditions of the environment. This article presents the Hebbian theory, which is one of the learning methods from the neuroscience field. A particularity presented by the Hebbian theory from the computer since field perspective is the primary mechanism of synaptic plasticity where the value of a synaptic connection increases if neurons on both sides of a said synapse are activated repeatedly, creating a new one simultaneously. This mechanism is integrated into the Learning Classifier Systems (LCS) to validate its effectiveness in the solution task, and can be used in multi-agent systems.

Keywords: Hebbian theory · Learning · LCS · Multi-agents

1 Introduction

One of the main tasks of artificial intelligence is to be able to create artefacts that show a very similar conscience to that of their creators [11]. It talks about the human being per se. In this sense, it is currently looking for the autonomous generation behavior rather than the optimization of systems. Multi-agent systems allow solving problems using different approaches of artificial intelligence, such as neural networks, fast learning, machine learning, and others. Autonomy and adaptation to the environment presented by the multi-agent systems is possible because of the architecture that makes them up, through the generation mechanism of new knowledge and negotiation protocols that lead them to solve problems and achieve objectives [15].

An important feature of these agents is the way they react immediately to environment changes due to the sensors that are constantly monitoring. This activity is possible because of the learning system that is embedded in the system and because of the way it processes information from the environment [10,15]. Current techniques solve problems for which they were created but do not respond efficiently to behaviors or changes in beliefs to help in human beings' tasks.

© Springer Nature Switzerland AG 2020
K. M. Figueroa Mora et al. (Eds.): MCPR 2020, LNCS 12088, pp. 328–339, 2020.
https://doi.org/10.1007/978-3-030-49076-8_31

This article deals basically with Learning Classifier Systems (*LCS*) [7] because of their features. This means, *LCS* learn and adapt from the environment. These qualities make them highly reactive, and in the event the systems are not able to find an answer within the environment, they do not get blocked, allowing more information to converge towards the best solution.

The most advanced *LCS* have a genetic algorithm that allows them to be evolutionary and a learning algorithm that adds new knowledge to the database. The modularity *LCS* allow modifying the type of learning, and it is in this sense that the Hebbian learning was implemented in *LCS* [5]. This learning comes from the neuroscience and is based on the plasticity of the connections of neurons [6, 13].

2   Learning Classifier Systems (*LCS*)

John H. Holland [7], describes the *LCS* as the framework that uses a genetic algorithm to study learning-based systems in rules and the "condition/action" pair.

The set of *rules* of action is built using the following notation: # Symbol of *"don't care"* or *"doesn't matter"*, ? is the symbol *"fits all"*, 0 = false, 1 = true. The symbols # and ?, are used interchangeably for purposes of the implementation in the *LCS*, because in both cases, they act as wild cards that accept any allowed value in the environment [7, 8].

In Fig. 1, the general architecture of *LCS* can be observed. Considering this architecture as the base, various adjustments and improvements have been made, and authors such as Martin Butz, Wilson, Stolzmann, and Goldberg, focus on the learning reward processes or the error prediction [8].

This article presents an adaptation of the *LCS* architecture that incorporates the Hebbian learning.

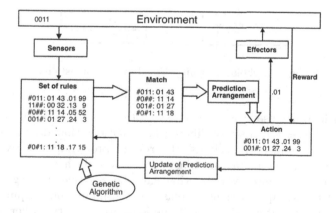

Fig. 1. General architecture of *LCS*

3   Hebbian Learning

Hebbian learning comes from the Donald O. Hebb' postulate [3] studying the neuronal function of the human brain and cognition. Currently, Hebbian learning is applied to neuronal networks and other areas of technology.

Hebb's postulate states: "When an axon of a cell A is close enough to excite a cell B and persistently takes part in its activation, some growth process takes place in one or both cells, so that the efficiency of A, as one of the cells activating B, is increased" [3].

Hebb postulated that the weight of the synaptic connections adjusts by the correlation between the activation values of the two connected neurons. Neurons are activated by thoughts, decisions and experiences from external stimulation, and the brain checks if there has already been a similar or not stimulus and takes the characteristics of the input data generating an association between the inputs and outputs of the system.

The connection of neurons generates a synaptic weight. If a weight contributes to the activation of a neuron, then the weight increases but if the weight is inhibited, then it decreases. This way, the strength of the synapse in the brain changes proportionally according to the firing of the input and output of neurons. This process remodels the old Hebbian networks (those that are not active) or creates new networks generating neuroplasticity. The input neuron is known as pre-synaptic and the output as post-synaptic [5]. The scheme of the neuroplasticity generation is described in Fig. 2.

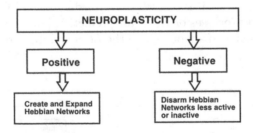

Fig. 2. Hebbian learning, based on neuroplasticity

Hebbian learning uses the rules of synaptic plasticity. A rule of synaptic plasticity can be seen as a set of differential equations that describes the average of tests of the synaptic weights, the role of pre-synaptic activities, post-synaptic, and other factors. In some plasticity models, the activity of each neuron is described as a continuous variable that can take positive and negative values. The value of the synaptic weight increases if the input and output values are positive or negative but will decrease if one is positive and the other negative. A variable activity that takes both values, the positive as well as the negative one, can be interpreted as the difference between the average of tests and a modified background rate, or that they are among the firing rates of two neurons that are treated as a unit [3,13].

There are several models of the Hebbian learning, though, for this research, we only considered those that are somehow normalized and can be implemented. For example, the multiplicative rule, also known as the *Oja* rule, was created for unsupervised learning. The *Oja* rule introduces the restriction dynamically, where the square of the synaptic weights is added. The use of normalization has the effect of introducing competition between neuron synapses over limited resources, which is essential for stabilization from a mathematical point of view. The Eq. (1) describes a convenient form of normalization [12].

$$w_{ij}(q) = w_{ij}(q-1) + \alpha.y_i(q).[x_j(q) - y_i(q).w_{ij}(q-1)] \tag{1}$$

where:
q is the input/output pair that is given a weight
x contains the input values
y contains the output values
α is the learning rate with values between [0,1]
y_i is the output of the neuron i
x_j is the input of the neuron j
w_{ij} is the connection weight of neuron j to neuron i

If the value of α approximates 1, the network will have a small weight but will remember little of what it learned in previous cycles. The term $\alpha y(n)x_i(n)$ represents the Hebbian modifications to the synaptic weight w_i and n the discrete-time. The equation $-y_i(q)w_{ij}(q-1)$ is responsible for the stabilization and is related to the forgetting factor or degradation rate that is generally used in learning rules. In this case, the degradation rate takes a higher value in response to a stronger response. The choice of a degradation rate has a great effect on the rapidity of convergence of the algorithm; particularly, it cannot be too large. Otherwise, the algorithm would become unstable. In practice, a good strategy is to use a relatively large value of α at the beginning to ensure an initial convergence, and gradually make α decrease until the desired precision is achieved [12]. The magnitude of the weights restricted to 0, which corresponds to having no weight, and 1, which corresponds to the input neuron with any weight; this done so that the weight vector is 1 [9].

The ***instar*** rule is an improvement to the Hebb rule with degradation [4] that prevents weights from degrading when a stimulus is not found. *Instar* is considered a neuron with a vector of inputs, and it is the simplest network capable of having pattern recognition. *Instar* is active as long as the internal product of the vector of weights and the input is greater than or equal to $-b$, where b is considered as the "trend" and must have a value between 0 and 1. This rule belongs to unsupervised learning and works locally. Unlike Hebb's rule with degradation, it only allows the degradation of weight when the neuron *instar* is active. That is, when $a \neq 0$. To achieve this, a term that avoids forgetting is added, which is proportional to $y_i(q)$ [14]. This is seen in the following Eq. (2).

$$w_{ij}(q) = w_{ij}(q-1) + \alpha.y_i(q).(x(q) - w_{ij}(q-1)) \tag{2}$$

Where:

$x(q)$ contains all the values of the output vector. α takes values between 0 and 1 to ensure that weights values increase, if α reaches 0 it becomes unstable and, on the contrary, if it gets close to 1, the network begins to forget the old entries quickly and will only remember the most recent patterns allowing to have a limited growth of the weight matrix. The maximum value in weight w_{ij}^{max} is determined by α, which happens when y_i and x_j have values $= 1$ for all q, which maximizes learning.

Another rule that literature classifies as stable is the **outstar**, which has a scalar input and a vector output. This can improve the call pattern by associating a stimulus with the response vector. The *outstar* rule, unlike to the *instar*, makes the degradation of the weight proportional to the x_j network entry. The Eq. (3) shows the rule of *outstar* [4]:

$$w_{ij}(q) = w_{ij}(q-1) + \alpha.(y(q) - w_{ij}(q-1)).x_j(q) \tag{3}$$

Where: $y(q)$ contains all the values of the output vector.

The rule *outstar* belongs to the supervised learning. In it, learning occurs whenever $x_j \neq 0$. If the rule has learned something, the column w_{ij} approaches the output vector, that is, when some weights are equal to those of the desired output [2].

In this first research work, standardized Hebbian learning is used to evaluate the feasibility of implementation in a LCS, and the tests are carried out in environments that the classifiers community uses.

4   Hebbian Learning Implementation in a LCS

The base architecture used is the GXCS classifier [10]. The modules that were added for the incorporation of the Hebbian learning are shown (shaded) in Fig. 3. These specific modules allow the classifier to calculate a vector of weights, composed of environmental conditions, as well as to evaluate each of these conditions to learn about the dynamics of the environment, contrary to the array of predictions used in traditional learning [10]. A module for the values of x and y has also been integrated, which is directly assigned to the conditions of the environment that are embedded in each of the competing rules to perform a specific action. The values that x and y receive, can be scalar or vector according to a Hebbian condition such as *Oja*, *instar* and *outstar*, which are stable rules. That is, they do not generate undesirable states in the [1] environment. A degradation rate is used to evaluate the permanence or erasure of the rules that are within the set of actions by controlling the number of rules produced by the interaction of the environment, thus avoiding over-exploitation of rules that could slow down the system.

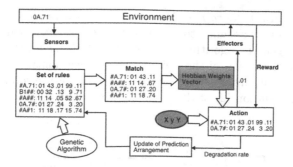

Fig. 3. GXCS-H architecture

The initialization of the synaptic weights vector, as well as the introduction of the Hebbian learning equation represented with $H(e, a)$. The degradation rate is the parameter of deletion or preservation of any specific rule.

The assigned value for the degradation rate is 0.5 [1]. If values outside the range of $(0, 1)$ are used in the area of neural networks, the stability of the Hebbian weights gets broken. To avoid this, Hebbian rules that have these parameters are used, so that they stabilize the equation of the basic rule of Hebb [1,5] and help convergence within the classifiers. These parameters allow the values to be in the range between 0 and 1, values that can be manipulated in the equations, and above all, can be used and read to generate an expected output. The stable rules are: *Multiplicative normalization rule or **Oja**, **Instar** rule and **Outstar** rule.*

The ***instar*, *outstar* and multiplicative (*Oja*)** rules contain a decay parameter that controls the degradation of weights. This parameter prevents the elimination of rules that are useful in future environmental conditions and allows the elimination of those that have not participated or that have an aptitude with a value close to zero, thus avoiding saturation of memory.

4.1 Multiplicative Normalization Rule

This rule takes the information from the synapse that is being modified, preventing Hebbian weights from growing indefinitely. The product of the value of the output, associated with the rule and the Hebbian weight of each rule, is responsible for the stabilization of the weights. This product is known as a forgetting factor or degradation rate and it allows eliminating only the rules that have not been used or have low values, close to zero or even zero [5].

A fragment of the GXCS architecture is shown in Fig. 4 with the integration of the Hebbian learning where the vector of weights that have been assigned to the rules, can be observed. The vector will be in the set of actions and are taken for recalculating the values of inputs and outputs of each of them. The value associated with the entering environment rule is stored in a x scalar. The same applies to the output y that takes its value randomly. Both values fluctuate between 0 and

1. The degradation rate *decay* is also calculated with random values that are between 0 and 1 and is assigned to an element of the set **A** of rules and actions. If necessary, the genetic algorithm used by the *LCS*, included in this version, is invoked. Once the values of the weights **w** (the degradation rate *decay*, the inputs **x** and the outputs **y**) are obtained, the value of the following weight is calculated using equation (2) of the multiplicative normalization (or of *Oja*).

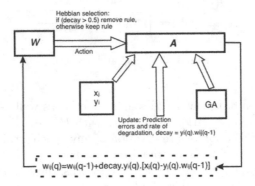

Fig. 4. Standardization of architecture

4.2   Rule of *Instar*

This rule prevents weights from degrading when there is not enough stimulus when calculating the values of inputs and outputs. It allows degradation only if the rule is active; that is, that the output has a value higher than 0.5. The weight values are learned at the same time that the old values of the inputs and outputs are degraded, as well as the Hebbian weight. All of them are assigned to each set of rules and actions within the classifier. The vector of weights has similar values to those of the vector of entries when the rule has an associated value to the aptitude greater than the average. In this case, if the degradation rate is equal to 0, the current weight is equal to the new weight assigned to the rule. If the degradation rate gets a value of 1, then the new Hebbian weight has its maximum value; if the degradation rate has a value of 0.5, then the value of the vector of entries is added to the Hebbian weight. The process is very similar to that of the *Oja* rule. The main difference is that the value of y of the outputs, associated with the actions taken from a set of values that belong to an output vector, takes the most suitable one. The second difference concerning the *Oja* rule is that the *decay* degradation rate is not taken directly from the equation, but is calculated pseudo-randomly with values that fluctuate between 0 and 1.

4.3   Rule of *Outstar*

In this case, the input is a scalar value and the output a vector. The value of the Hebbian weight gets close to the values found in the output vector when the ruler has learned something, acquiring the same value as the output. The weight changes when the ruler has a greater or equal aptitude than the average. The difference concerning the *instar* rule is that the value of x of the entries associated with the rules are taken from a set of values belonging to a vector of entries, from where it takes the fittest. The calculation of the degradation rate *decay* is done in the same way as in the *instar* rule.

5   Experimentation

The tests performed at the GXCS, are based on the environments proposed by the *LCS* community. These are **multiplexer** and **woods** since both allow obtaining an easy to interpret solution. The multiplexer environment is known as static and woods as dynamic. The woods environment is used to test the *Oja* rule with supervised learning and *outstar*. In the multiplexer environment, the multiplicative normalization rule (*Oja*) was tested for unsupervised learning and *instar*. The **woods** environment can be seen as a maze where there are obstacles, and an agent that runs through it to reach a goal and the goal itself. Figure 5 illustrates an example of how a maze can be developed. The agent is shown as a person who will travel through the maze to reach the final goal, which, in this case, is exemplified with a gift. The person has to go through the shortest path avoiding all the obstacles in it.

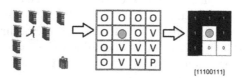

Fig. 5. Woods environment

This environment, computationally speaking, can be seen as an array with values, where each obstacle is assigned with a value of 1 and the cell that has no obstacle with the value of 0. A chain of zeros and ones is arranged by position. Each position in the chain indicates if there is an obstacle or if the way is free. For example, the first position of the chain can indicate the position above the agent, where a number one indicates that there is an obstacle. In the example, the cell that is just above the agent was taken as the first to be added to the rule. From there on, values are taken clockwise. As a result of this example, the generated rule is 11100111, and it can be observed that there are obstacles just above the agent, in the upper right corner and on the right side of it. Then two zeros can be seen, which indicates that there are no obstacles in the lower right corner and precisely below it, and after, there are more obstacles in the next three positions that are at its left side.

The **multiplexer** environment can be illustrated using logic gates where there are several inputs, in this case six, and only one output. It can be observed in Fig. 6, that the entries are associated with the variables x_i where $i = 0, 1, 2, ..., 5$. These inputs enter a circuit with accommodated logic gates similar to the Boolean multiplexer, and the values get mixed with logical operators of AND and OR, achieving a single output F_6.

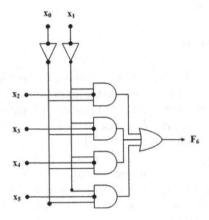

Fig. 6. Multiplexer environment

For a LCS, the multiplexer inputs are part of the rule to be evaluated, where each input represents a particular parameter of that rule, and the output is the action associated with the entire rule. This data is entered into the multiplexer, which evaluates as if it had logic gates and allows the values to be assigned to the corresponding rule/action pair.

Within the first tests, comparisons were made between a GXCS and a GXSC-H. The latter is the one that incorporates the Hebbian learning. The first environment was the multiplexer. After 20,000 rules with the three Hebbian slopes, as seen in Figs. 7, 8 and 9, we analyzed, the performance in the first instance. This one was calculated from the values obtained from the weight vector, the reward, and the aptitude of each rule. The degradation or decay rate allowed us to eliminate the rules that had a lower weight and therefore were not candidates to be taken into account for future calculations. At the implementation level, we generated an output file to store the test results: performance, the number of tests performed, a margin of error in the prediction, and the number of elements for each iteration. It was observed, as shown in the graphs in Figs. 7, 8, and 9 that there is a higher performance. However, a more significant number of tests is necessary to validate these results.

The first tests were done with an initial weight very close to zero, with pseudo-random values between 0.5 and 0.6. Still, it is remarkable that better results were obtained with a wider range, then it was decided to use the range from 0.1 to 0.6, improving the performance. This calculation was used for the three tested Hebbian slopes since better values were found in the weights and the performance of the classifier.

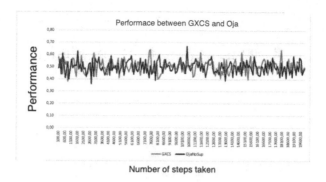

Fig. 7. Comparison between GXCS and GXCS-H with *Oja*

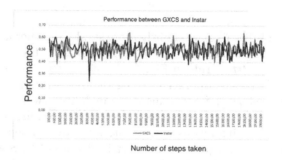

Fig. 8. Comparison between GXCS and GXCS-H with *Instar*

The variable that was used for the degradation rate started with values close to zero. The used range was between 0.1 and 0.7, and then it was applied to erase the rules. Initially, the rules that had a degradation rate greater than 0.5 were deleted. However, this caused the system not to erase enough rules, since there were very few with a rate with those characteristics, and therefore saturated the population as a whole. It was decided to delete rules with degradation values of 0.25. This was applied to the three Hebbian rules that we tested in the system.

The observed behaviors between GXCS and GXCS-H with the rule of *Oja* (Fig. 7), are perceived similarly, especially at the beginning of the iterations. But gradually, GXCS-H begins to stabilize better than the GXCS, increasing the number of steps. More rules are added through the genetic algorithm, and those with a degradation rate greater than 0.5, are eliminated. This indicates that the capability and the Hebbian weights increase and stabilize, which means that more rules are apt to solve a problem through the actions assigned to it.

Figure 8 points out that the *instar* rule has slightly smaller behaviors than GXCS. In this example, it can be seen that the *instar* rule presents a fall in performance in step 3500. This is because a new rule was created that had not been tested and, therefore, it was given Hebbian weights and minimal rewards at the beginning. Later it can be observed that the GXCS-H with the *instar*

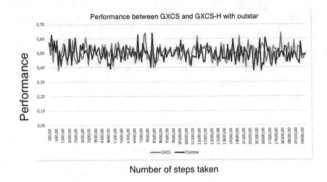

Fig. 9. Comparison between GXCS and GXCS-H with *outstar*

rule is retrieved and the rules are slightly more stable. In general, the *instar* rule generates slightly higher returns than those generated by the GXCS. The same can be seen for the *outstart* rule in Fig. 9.

The results from the incorporation of the Hebbian learning compared to the results of the GXCS show an improvement in capability, reward, and punishment for each condition-action pair. The integration of this learning of the *LCS* gives us the possibility of having an easier adaptation to environmental conditions.

On the other hand, the quantitative part in the use of LCS with traditional learning or with Hebbian learning is a subject of study in future implementations. Where we can carry out simulations with agents, for the moment, we are comparing the convergence and stability of the classifier so that it does not overflow with the generation of rules or their sub-generalization.

6   Conclusion and Future Work

One of the difficulties found within some aspects of the Hebbian learning is that the variation in the number of uncontrolled rules quickly causes instability in the values of the weights when there are too many rules or weights with negative or substantial values. The rules of multiplicative normalization (also called *Oja*, *instar* and *outstar*) are used to solve the problem of instability allowing more stable rules. The integration of the Hebbian learning in a *LCS* is possible, and allows a much better learning of the conditions of the surroundings without losing the re-activity of the system in terms of uncertainty. The use of a degradation variable allows the *LCS* to have only rules that are apt for giving a solution, and the sub-generalization of rules is reduced. The results, in the suggested environments by the community, are satisfactory. However, it is necessary to test other types of environments that have a greater complexity to corroborate results.

References

1. Brodeur, S., Rouat, J.: Regulation toward self-organized criticality in a recurrent spiking neural reservoir. In: Villa, A.E.P., Duch, W., Érdi, P., Masulli, F., Palm, G. (eds.) ICANN 2012. LNCS, vol. 7552, pp. 547–554. Springer, Heidelberg (2012). https://doi.org/10.1007/978-3-642-33269-2_69
2. Carpenter, G.A.: A distributed outstar network for spatial pattern learning. Neural Networks **7**(1), 159–168 (1994)
3. Dayan, P., Abbott, L.: Theoretical neuroscience: computational and mathematical modeling of neural systems. J. Cogn. Neurosci. **15**(1), 154–155 (2003)
4. Demuth, H.B., Beale, M.H., De Jess, O., Hagan, M.T.: Neural Network Design. Martin Hagan, Stillwater (2014)
5. Grabner, C.A.L.: Neuroplasticidad y redes hebbianas: las bases del aprendizaje. Asociación Educar, Buenos Aires (Argentina) (2011)
6. Hebb, D.O.: The Organization of Behavior: A Neuropsychological Theory. Psychology Press, Hove (2005)
7. Holland, J.H., et al.: What is a learning classifier system? In: Lanzi, P.L., Stolzmann, W., Wilson, S.W. (eds.) IWLCS 1999. LNCS (LNAI), vol. 1813, pp. 3–32. Springer, Heidelberg (2000). https://doi.org/10.1007/3-540-45027-0_1
8. Lanzi, P.L., Stolzmann, W., Wilson, S.W. (eds.): IWLCS 1999. LNCS (LNAI), vol. 1813. Springer, Heidelberg (2000). https://doi.org/10.1007/3-540-45027-0
9. Oja, E.: Simplified neuron model as a principal component analyzer. J. Math. Biol. **15**(3), 267–273 (1982). https://doi.org/10.1007/BF00275687
10. Ramos Corchado, M.A.: Etude et proposition d'un système comportemental autonome anticipatif. Thèse de doctorat, Université de Toulouse, Toulouse, France, (décembre 2007)
11. Rennard, J.P.: Vie artificielle. Où la biologie rencontre l'informatique. Vuibert informatique (2002)
12. Rodríguez-Piñero, P.T.: Redes neuronales artificiales para el análisis de componentes principales. la red de oja. Vniversitat de Valéncia (2000)
13. Trappenberg, T.P.: Fundamentals of Computational Neuroscience. Oxford Press, Oxford (2010)
14. Wilamowski, B.: Neural networks and fuzzy systems. In: The Microelectronic Handbook (2002)
15. Wooldridge, M.: An Introduction to Multi-agent Systems. Wiley, Hoboken (2002)

Author Index

Printed in the United States
By Bookmasters